NEW MEXICO

NEW MEXICO
A History

JOSEPH P. SÁNCHEZ, ROBERT L. SPUDE,
AND ART GÓMEZ

University of Oklahoma Press : Norman

This book is published with the generous assistance of
The Kerr Foundation, Inc.

LIBRARY OF CONGRESS CATALOGING-IN-PUBLICATION DATA

Sánchez, Joseph P.
    New Mexico : a history / Joseph P. Sánchez, Robert L. Spude, and Art Gómez.
    pages cm
    Includes bibliographical references and index.
    ISBN 978-0-8061-4256-2 (cloth) 1. New Mexico—History.
    ISBN 978-0-8061-4663-8 (paper)
    I. Spude, Robert L. II. Gómez, Art, 1946– III. Title.
    F796.S26 2013
    978.9—dc23

                            2013012017

The paper in this book meets the guidelines for permanence and durability of the Committee on Production Guidelines for Book Longevity of the Council on Library Resources, Inc. ∞

2   3   4   5   6   7   8   9   10

For Loretta Sánchez
JPS

For Catherine Holder Spude
RLS

For Paul, and to the memory of his brother, Chris
AG

Contents

Illustrations

Maps

Table

Preface

WHY WRITE AN ACCESSIBLE HISTORY of New Mexico? Beginning with Hubert Howe Bancroft, who published *Arizona and New Mexico* in 1889, and Francisco de Thoma, who wrote his Spanish-language *Historia Popular de Nuevo México* in 1896, several authors have followed suit in writing regional or state histories. During New Mexico's territorial period (1850–1912), L. Bradford Prince, who served as chief justice of the Territorial Supreme Court (1879–88) and as governor of New Mexico Territory (1889–93), wrote about New Mexico as local history. His writings include *The Student's History of New Mexico*. Similarly, in 1911 lawyer Ralph Emerson Twitchell began publishing his multivolume *The Leading Facts of New Mexico History*, considered a standard source about New Mexico prior to statehood. That year, former territorial Speaker of the House Benjamin M. Read published *Historia ilustrada de Nuevo México*, a local history with a focus on Santa Fe. While these early writers contributed to the historiography of New Mexico, some of them, like Read and Twitchell, did so to promote New Mexico's quest for statehood.

Since statehood, other textbooklike popular histories about New Mexico have appeared. In the late 1930s, the great historian France V. Scholes published the first serious studies about seventeenth-century New Mexico. His works *The First Decades of the Inquisition in New Mexico* (1935) and *Troublous Times in New Mexico, 1659–1670* (1938) introduced readers to New Mexico's history before the Pueblo Revolt of 1680. Based on documents from Spain and Mexico, his books narrated the conflict between missionaries and civil authorities in New Mexico. By setting a high standard for historical narration, Scholes opened the door for serious scholarly studies by researchers interested in New Mexico's rich history.

Our purpose is to offer a book that differs in important ways from the scholarly monographs just mentioned. First of all, the present work is intended as a sourcebook: not only an introduction to the chronology of events in New Mexico history but also a narrative source that presents up-to-date information and accepted interpretations of related events. In 1962 the University of Oklahoma Press published such a resource: Warren Beck's *New Mexico: A History of Four Centuries.* For decades Beck's book was popularly read and widely used as a textbook in college courses. Over time, though, it has become outdated and has given way to other, more widely available books. We hope to emulate Beck's work, bringing the New Mexico story into the twenty-first century. Since Beck's time, scholarly journals, in particular, have contributed a plethora of specialized studies about New Mexico. Those studies have contributed new information and interpretations about New Mexico's history, some of which we adopt in this volume.

Unlike previous approaches to the history of New Mexico, this book has a broader ambition: to portray New Mexico as part of a global context. The broader history has always been there. The peopling of the Americas in prehistoric times occurred through migration from other parts of the world. Native peoples of North America, particularly those in the American Southwest, probably had their origins in Mongolia, whence they likely migrated across the Bering Strait. The Spaniards, too, arrived in New Mexico from other places in order to explore, settle, develop, and people the land in accordance with western European values. The Camino Real de Tierra Adentro, the Royal Road of the Interior, which ran from Mexico City to Santa Fe, served as the historic conduit that tied European institutions of law, governance, religion, technology, and language to the worlds of the Indian, Hispanic, and Anglo-American. Today, El Camino Real de Tierra Adentro National Historic Trail ties New Mexico's history to our national story.

Similarly, in the Mexican independence period, New Mexico was transformed politically through more enlightened policies, especially in areas of governance and Indian policies, which continued to evolve even after the United States annexed New Mexico and the Greater Southwest. From this perspective, each successive cycle of occupation added another layer to the influence of the greater world on New Mexico's development in terms of science, technology, political and economic institutions, and culture.

Colonialism and imperialism played major roles in the transplantation of diverse cultures to New Mexico. Perhaps the broadest effect of European colonialism in the New World is the transmission of Western civilization, particularly four major common languages: English, Spanish, French, and Portuguese. Aside from Native languages spoken in New Mexico since prehistoric times, one other language made its way into New Mexico with Spanish settlers: Nahua, the language of the Aztecs and other peoples in central and southern Mexico. Today, many Nahua words, among them *coyote, tomate,* and *guajolote* (turkey), are part of the vocabulary of New Mexican Spanish. Cultural changes in each era were tied to the language of the culture in power. The dominant language served as a lingua franca, acting both as a stabilizing force and as a unifier of populations that lived under common sovereign controls. At the same time, however, the preservation of minority languages is important for the survival of ethnic cultures.

The intrusion of colonial and imperialistic forms and social boundaries occurred at the expense of Native groups. In the end, colonialism, even in its vestigial form, had to be adapted to fit the American contexts. It is a truism that America is different from Europe because of the Indian. So too is New Mexico. The adage is true throughout the world wherever indigenous groups have struggled to survive the imposition of the cultural values of the last invading power in their homelands. Theirs has been a long and difficult struggle for equality. In the nineteenth century, the Indian wars waged by the United States spilled into New Mexico, culminating in the near-annihilation of the Apaches and removal of the Diné (Navajos) via the tragic Long Walk to Bosque Redondo near Fort Sumner.

Within the United States, Indian peoples have been historically subjected to governmental policies designed to radically transform their ways of life through acculturation processes. Nineteenth-century Indian policies included forced removal onto reservations, akin to the apartheid practiced in other parts of the world. Other policies of acculturation and dispossession involved boarding schools and land allotments; with the latter, Native American holdings plunged from 138 million acres in 1887 to 48 million by 1934. In the mid-twentieth century, the U.S. government moved to terminate tribal sovereignty, which provoked bitterness among the Indian nations. Finally, in 1975, the U.S. Congress rejected the sovereignty termination policy by passing the Indian Self-Determination and Education Assistance Act, which increased tribal control over local issues. Thus, the history of Indian wars, removal, and alienation demands that the perspectives of Native peoples be taken into account.

"Indigenization" has become a watchword for native groups in Africa, Australia, Canada, the United States, and other places around the world. Today, native peoples have new, sophisticated ways to reclaim their cultures by peaceful means. In New Mexico, as in other places in the United States, the effects of indigenization appear in the reversion of place-names to their Native labels. Many tribes insist on calling their villages or lands by their Native names. Today, Indian peoples demand and deserve recognition as participants in our national story as well as in various state histories.

Similarly, Hispanics in the Greater Southwest have struggled to preserve their culture and language. Their story differs from that of Native Americans but has similar subthemes that call for recognition of their participation in the historical evolution of our national story. In New Mexico, the Hispanic struggle for political and cultural survival has continued over the past four hundred years under Spain, Mexico, and the United States.

New Mexico's motto, "We grow as we go," also has global implications, exemplified by the fact that the atomic age was born in New Mexico. By the end of the twentieth century, New Mexico had been transformed into an important player in both national and international arenas. That transformation began in the late nineteenth century as New Mexico slowly shed its territorial status to become, in 1912, the forty-seventh state of the Union. In all wars since the American Civil War, New Mexico has also participated in the development of the United States as a world power. Indeed, the Spanish American War of 1898 began in faraway Cuba but eventually pulled New Mexico into the limelight of U.S. history. A few years later, New Mexico again participated in one of America's broad-based, politically charged historical movements, the Progressive Era.

Among the events in New Mexico's past, scholars have customarily assigned the greatest historical importance to the European arrival in the sixteenth century, which fueled the Pueblo Revolt a century later, when the Native inhabitants evicted the Spaniards for twelve years; the coming of the railroad in the late nineteenth century; and the sixty-two-year-old territory's admission to the Union in 1912. Collectively, historians recognize statehood as the benchmark for New Mexico's subsequent modernization.

As we clearly document, however, the transformation of New Mexico from provincial frontier into fully modern state did not truly occur until World War II and the decades that followed. The technological advancements of the atomic era, spawned during wartime, rapidly merged into the frenzied space race that characterized the Cold War. In the process, New Mexico found itself at the edge of a new frontier as national centers and installations utilizing new technologies for warfare and peaceful purposes located there, among them Los Alamos National Laboratory and Sandia National Laboratories, not to mention the Very Large Array of radio antennae. Meantime, the state's population nearly tripled between 1950 and 1970. In a futuristic scenario, Spaceport America, located in southern New Mexico, is envisioned as one day complementing (or competing with) Russia's Cosmodrome (космодром) as a port of entry from outer space. Thus, New Mexico has played and continues to play an important role in world history, as we hope this book shows.

 NEW MEXICO

CHAPTER 1

The Earliest People, Pre-1539

> More impressive than the massive ruins themselves is the evident
> force of the human spirit that was responsible for their erection.
> That generating current of incalculable strength, a coalescence of
> drive, adaptability, and muscle power, supercharged a cultural efflo-
> rescence in Chaco Canyon and adjacent areas of the Four Corners
> unique in Prehispanic North America.
>
> ROBERT H. AND FLORENCE C. LISTER, *CHACO CANYON* (1981)

THE PREHISTORY OF NEW MEXICO, the period before written
records, begins with the migration of *Homo sapiens sapiens* out of Asia.
Most Native peoples in New Mexico today believe that the first people originated in the Southwest. But scientific evidence suggests that
between 50,000 and 10,000 years ago a land bridge, Beringia, connected the Asian landmass with North America. Nomadic human
bands crossed Beringia, following migrating game, until the Bering
Sea reclaimed the land, isolating the ancestors of the American Indians
from their Asian roots. Geneticists estimate that nearly all American
Indians descend from six common female ancestors who arrived during this period. Genetic evolution, responses to different environ-
ments, and natural adaptations caused the rise of different cultural
and distinctive linguistic groups as they dispersed throughout North
and South America.

These hunter-gatherers followed the migratory game of the late
Paleozoic epoch at the end of the last ice age. In the eastern plains
of New Mexico, hunters stalked mammoths and the great bison. At
one freshwater pond, for example, mammoths edged into the muck
and were watering themselves when hunters armed with atlatls, darts,
and spears attacked. More than 11,000 years later, scientists uncovered
evidence of this kill and butchering spot, now known as Blackwater

Draw, near Clovis, New Mexico. They found "a retouched flake dressing tool," one scientist wrote, "and cylindrical tapered bone fore-shafts from darts or spears using fluted blades either in a toggle device or lashed directly on the end of the shaft. There were the fluted blades to complete the evidence." These fluted blades, called Clovis points, along with the nearby find of similar points at Folsom, New Mexico, have defined the earliest residents of New Mexico as well as most of the United States. Over many millennia, Archaic hunters depended on wild game and foraged for plant foods across New Mexico, while the ice age receded and the land's ancient moist climate evolved to its present, predominately arid state.

The greatest single change for these peoples came with the slow transition that some groups made to an agricultural or farming way of life (other nomadic groups never made the shift). The genetic mutation of corn to a crop occurred in central Mexico and spread to New Mexico by an estimated 3,500 years ago. In the remains of a prehistoric camp in Bat Cave, at the base of a great rock overhang overlooking the vast Plains of San Augustin, 6,000 years of layered cultural material show this evolution from hunting and gathering to the cultivation of small corncobs, probably the harvest of female gatherers. A supplement at first to the hunter-gatherers' diet, corn became a staple. Over millennia, these early farmers increased the size of corn ears and introduced beans and squash. The growing of these crops coincided with a move to a more settled way of life.

Basketmakers, as archaeologists call these early agricultural people, lived across New Mexico from well before the Christian Era in the Old World to around A.D. 750. Their namesake skill in weaving produced some baskets woven so tightly they could hold water and be used for cooking (when heated stones were dropped into water-filled baskets). They used stone tools for grinding corn into a meal and made various wood and stone tools for planting and hunting. With knives and scrapers they made clothing from furs and wove sandals from yucca fibers. The Basketmakers developed the first permanent dwellings, called pit-houses, some with attached storage spaces or pits. Building a pit-house began with digging a circular space several feet deep and ten to twenty feet wide. Timbers formed the framework over the pit, over which the builders then interwove reeds and grass for sidewalls and roof, all covered with a layer of earth. A small hole in the roof allowed smoke to escape and served as an entrance via a ladder. These residences housed a family or small kin group. The Basketmakers developed the basics of communal society by building a dozen or more pit-houses in village-like clusters in order to share the fruits of their combined labors and defend themselves from intruders. This society was foundational to later Puebloan culture. Through trade connections and exchange these late Basketmakers acquired the bow and arrow and ornamented themselves with beads and shells probably brought via trade routes from the Gulf of California or the Texas coast.

By the end of the Archaic period, these late Basketmakers had further enhanced their diets. Late in the period, Basketmakers in southwestern New Mexico—the early Mogollon culture—domesticated turkey for food (eating the eggs, but only rarely the flesh) and feathers for weaving into thermal clothing. The Mogollons supplemented or replaced baskets with pottery, a technology introduced from Mexico. The advent of pottery revolutionized cooking, from boiling water to more easily blending and cooking corn, beans, and other ingredients into stews, porridge, and broths (the ingredients usually including wild game). The Mogollons built their pit-house villages in ponderosa-fringed upland meadows. They, and especially the later Mimbres subgroup, became known for their distinctive pottery, which they exchanged for other goods in trade and remains of which have been found across the U.S. Southwest and into Mexico. In part because of outside influences, by A.D. 1000 the expanding Mogollon culture had begun moving away from pit-houses to earthen aboveground homes similar to adobe pueblo houses. During this period, which archaeologists call Early Pueblo, these Ancestral Puebloan peoples lived along the headwaters of the Gila and Mimbres Rivers in pueblo communities near their farmsteads and maintained an active trade network.

By the end of the first millennium A.D., the shift to agriculture, the development of trade, and the rise of more populous communities led to the rise of Chaco culture in northwestern New Mexico. The Chaco region had also passed from the Basketmaker to the Pueblo stage. During the eleventh and twelfth centuries, Chaco culture spread across and dominated 40,000 square miles of canyon country and the broad, dramatic landscape of the Colorado Plateau. Often compared to controlling a land area equal to modern Portugal or Scotland, Chaco influence did not rely on the rule of a single ruler or government. Instead, the culture wove the region together economically and spiritually to achieve remarkable buildings, systems of farming, and, at least for elite members of society, a materially rich everyday life.

The Chaco cultural region consisted of 10,000 to 20,000 farming hamlets, from small congregations of pit-houses to earthen protopueblos, and nearly one hundred spectacular district towns, called great houses by archaeologists. The Chaco system included a network of twenty- to thirty-foot-wide roads that tied the cultural world together. At the geographic and spiritual center of this culture was Chaco Canyon. Strong trade connections emanating from this center brought valuable items from central Mexico, such as copper bells and bright-feathered tropical parrots, in exchange for turquoise or decorative pottery. Astronomical observatories and large religious centers known as kivas (the Hopi word for these ceremonial chambers) at the largest great houses suggest that Chaco Canyon served more as a religious than a commercial or agricultural hub. Extant Chaco sites have gained World Heritage Site recognition, while Chaco Canyon is the core of Chaco Culture National Historical Park.

Farming supported the Chacoan system. Farmers captured and diverted water to irrigate their fields and developed dry-farming techniques to improve harvests. The resulting surplus supported a hierarchal society; power and wealth were concentrated in the hands, possibly, of religious leaders who knew how to ensure continued bounty. They studied the seasons and measured and interpreted the movements of stars and the sun, all of which guided the calendar of planting, watering, weeding, and harvesting. According to modern Pueblo oral tradition, the Chacoans followed rituals that involved a sun priest to bless and announce the right time to plant sacred seeds, to sow, and to reap. Solemn rituals and feast days punctuated the annual cycle of farmwork. Chacoans built numerous kivas in the front of the room blocks. Many of these circular, subterranean stone structures still exist, including the Great Kiva of Aztec, fifty feet in diameter.

The Chaco Phenomenon, as described by archeologists, includes more than improved farms and five-story stone great houses. The true genius of Chaco culture lay in the integration of these and many other parts into one powerful operating culture based on ritual, sharing, and trade. Culturally based group actions included management of a large labor force that brought great timbers a hundred miles for house construction, graded arrow-straight road tangents that formed a four-hundred-mile road network, and harvested and shared food surpluses from an expansive but scattered and fragile farmscape. Today, the best places for discerning the ruins of Chacoan great house architecture are Chaco Canyon and Salmon Ruin, north of the San Juan River. In Chaco Canyon the ruins of other worldly places still stand: the vast four-story, semicircular stone structure of Pueblo Bonito encompasses 106,800 square feet and contains five hundred rooms and forty kivas. Nearby, Chetro Ketl had five hundred rooms and a colonnaded façade on its plaza.

These great houses at Chaco Canyon probably attracted many people who spoke different languages. Traders from distant lands may have sold their goods in the plazas. Some speculate that merchants from as far away as central Mexico traded in the canyon. The modern Keresan-, Tewa-, and Zuni-speaking Pueblos relate oral traditions from ancestors descended from Chacoan sites. Nomadic peoples, including the ancestors of the Navajos and Apaches, mingled with the settlements' residents for trade, exchange, and intermarriage.

Chaco's cultural system thrived for two hundred years during the classic period, and then collapsed in a mere forty. Oral traditions and numerous studies have tried to explain Chaco's abandonment. Changing weather patterns (including increasingly erratic rainfall), the stresses of failed agriculture, out-migrations, violence, internal disintegration of religious or governmental power, and nomadic raiders all may have contributed to the decline of Chaco culture by the 1200s. The tragic period that followed the collapse is considered by some the most violent two hundred years in the prehistoric Southwest. The society appears to have been reasonably orderly and safe prior to the droughts of the 1090s, but thereafter declining harvests coincided with increased population to create a period of want and dislocation.

This period of violence and turmoil also coincided with the rise of dwellings built along and under the cliffs of mesas—most notably at Mesa Verde, Colorado, to the north and the Gila cliff dwellings in southern New Mexico. With the Chaco collapse, ancient differences devolved into ethnic and tribal hatreds that led to violence during the following century. By 1300 even the cliff dwellings had been abandoned. In the San Juan Basin, the last of the Ancestral Puebloans permanently vacated the landscape of the Chaco–Mesa Verde complex. The Chaco Phenomenon had passed.

Nonetheless, agricultural society regrouped. During the 1200s these farmers moved onto the tops of mesas along the northern Rio Grande and into the deep canyons in between. Around 1290, farmers settled Tyuonyi, in the Frijoles Canyon, and built a great circular ruin that may be seen today at Bandelier National Monument. Ancestral Puebloans permanently settled upland sites in the best-watered east-facing canyons above the Rio Grande and constructed villages, many with protective palisades. These sites paled in comparison to the Chacoan cultural system and monuments. Although these Puebloan farmers had to husband their meager sources of water, they adapted a host of Chaco cultural characteristics, including the construction of multistory structures and communal living. They retained the kiva and produced and traded pottery both functional and decorative.

During the fourteenth and fifteenth centuries, drier seasons and a decline in water supplies available for irrigation brought about another period of dislocation. As mountain streams dried up, farmers moved out of the uplands and into the valleys of the few permanent rivers. As more people abandoned the compact hilltop forts, unfortified Pueblo villages near good farmland grew dramatically in size. Clusters of multistoried adobe structures housing hundreds of Puebloans formed new centers of farming, trade, and religion. Puebloan blockhouses were entered through an opening in the roof, accessed by ladders—indicating the inhabitants' continued need to protect themselves from intruders, whether unfriendly neighbors or nomadic raiders. In each pueblo, a kiva served as a place to commune, relate stories, and conduct rituals. Pueblo peoples retained centuries of traditions, knowledge, skill, and rituals even as they created a new kind of society, one as complex as the Chacoans' but better adapted to the dry, unpredictable climate.

By the 1400s, Puebloans had built a number of large settlements in open settings near reliable rivers (including the Rio Grande, Pecos, Jemez, San Jose, Puerco, and Chama) and creeks (among them the Zuni, Pescado, and Taos), from Taos in the north to the Piros in the south (near Socorro) and from Zuni to the west to the Galisteo basin and the eastern slopes of the Sandia and Manzano Mountains (the Salinas Pueblos) in the east. Located in or near ecosystem transition zones, with their more abundant wildlife, the central pueblos drew from the world's greatest natural cottonwood bosques (stands of trees), especially along the Rio Grande near modern Albuquerque. The Puebloans collected piñon and juniper wood and harvested piñon nuts and a bounty of other natural foodstuffs nearby. For weapons, they shaped obsidian, available in the volcanic landscape. They continued to rely on trade with Mexico and the plains, exchanging such items as turquoise and lead for pot glazing from deposits in the adjacent Cerrillos Hills. Their turquoise trade items were transported to the empires of central Mexico, probably via Paquime (near Nueva Casas Grandes, Chihuahua), the last great center of the Mogollon culture. When it collapsed by 1450, some of its people migrated north to join the Puebloans.

During the late 1400s and early 1500s, the Puebloan peoples overcame three centuries of droughts, want, and dislocation. They made their living conditions more stable, increased their harvests, and improved their social and cultural worlds. An estimated 150 large pueblos, each surrounded by fields and field houses, extended across northern and central New Mexico. Irrigation and dry-farming techniques ensured agricultural success, along with the ability to store the surplus in a dry climate. The Zunis practiced both creek-side and dry farming, probably like the Chacoans. Taos, which was too high in elevation and too cool for the cultivation of cotton or large crops of corn, relied more heavily on hunting and gathering. Pecos succeeded as a population center by harvesting a variety of foods from its irrigated fields and through trade with Plains peoples. Its location at the base of the mountain pass to the Rio Grande pueblos also made it the target of Plains raiders, who by the mid-1400s had forced the consolidation of peoples into the large house atop a high ridge overlooking the Pecos River. A wall separated the Pecos trade grounds from the pueblo—a tenuous boundary that also served as a defensive line in case nomadic traders might turn to raiding. Although the Pueblos lived in relative peace, on occasion, the possibility of attack from nomadic foot warriors wielding bows and arrows caused unified, though limited, Puebloan defensive action.

The Pecos Puebloans called these hunters and raiders from the high plains the Tagú-kerésh. Today, we think of them as the Apaches. These nomadic peoples provided the Pueblos with trade items, especially buffalo meat and hides, the latter made into clothing and shoes. Organized in small mobile bands and living in buffalo-hide or brush-covered pole-houses, these ancestral Apaches followed the buffalo, antelope, and other game across eastern New Mexico. They used buffalo, antelope, and deer hide for clothing, sometimes ornamented with delicate stitching or porcupine quills. Men hunted with long bows and arrows or spears, often decorated. They lacked livestock, but dogs carried their masters' belongings. These Apaches may also have adopted some farming methods from the Pueblos and grown small patches of corn, beans, and squash. More often, they traded the products of the plains for these foodstuffs produced by the Pueblos of the central Rio Grande region.

The Tagú-kerésh culture appears to have extended across northern New Mexico and into the plains by the time of European contact. The ancestral cultures of both the Apaches and the related Navajos have received much reconsideration and study over the past two decades. Although both spoke Athabascan languages that linked them to peoples migrating from western Canada, these two groups may have had multiple genealogies. During the Chacoan period, some ancestral Apaches and Navajos worked as nomadic traders within the classic Chaco sphere. Archaeologists suggest that during the long period of dislocation (1200–1400), these nomads incorporated into their evolving culture an infusion of peoples, including the migratory Athabascan from the north. The cultural repertoire of the first Navajos, for example, not only benefited from this infusion of Athabascan linguistic and cultural traits but also retained their Chacoan cultural heritage, including rituals, stories, and trade networks. Still, we know less about prehistoric nomadic groups than we do about the Pueblos.

In the multicultural world of New Mexico prior to the European arrival, Pueblo village life followed the agricultural seasons, each with its distinctive hunting activity, religious festivals and rituals, and games. Villagers flowed out to the surrounding landscape in spring for planting. Summer was for tending crops, fall for harvest, and winter for feasts, rituals, dances, and socializing. The diverse Puebloan lands grew corn, beans, squash, and gourds, as well as cotton, tobacco, and feed for domesticated turkeys. Small dogs and turkeys were kept in pens, but there were no large domesticated livestock. The Puebloan knowledge of seasons, planting, and harvest became encoded in religious ceremonies, kachina dances, and chants. Despite lacking a writing system, the Puebloans preserved their stories by passing them down through bearers of oral traditions. Men joined expeditions to hunt buffalo on foot, finding their prey along the Pecos River and in vast herds on the plains, and mingling or competing with the nomadic hunters there.

A Pueblo community may be compared to a medieval European community, with a central town surrounded by surplus-producing farmsteads, a trade network for obtaining necessary goods, and a rich religious life. The Puebloans lacked a class of feudal lords, having learned to live without creating a true elite among themselves or an expansive central governmental authority. Pueblo polities were more like city-states than feudal principalities. Some researchers believe this egalitarianism was fundamental to Pueblo survival and reflected group decision making among a relative small number of people.

By the mid-1500s, life in New Mexico was still hard by our modern standards, but the population continued to grow. A healthy birth rate indicates that the Puebloans had achieved a thriving agricultural society. Droughts still brought hunger, and conflict persisted between nomadic hunters and Puebloans over stores of food, captives, and domesticated animals. These conflicts would become more one-sided once the Apaches, Navajos, Utes, and Comanches acquired the Spanish horse in the seventeenth century. Even with such threats, however, this was a period of stability. Some consider it the Pueblo Golden Age.

CHAPTER 2

Early Spanish Exploration of New Mexico, 1539–1598

Accompanied . . . by my own Indians and interpreters, I proceeded on my journey until coming within sight of Cíbola, which is situated in a plain at the base of a round hill. The pueblo has a fine appearance. . . . The houses are . . . all of stone, with terraces and flat roofs, as it seemed to me from a hill where I stood. . . . The city is larger than the city of Mexico.

FRAY MARCOS DE NIZA, 1539

THE SPANISH ARRIVAL IN THE CARIBBEAN in 1492 triggered a period of exploration and conquest that had far-reaching consequences for the indigenous peoples of New Spain (present Mexico). Those at the far northern boundary of New Spain lived in a land Spain first called Cíbola (when they searched the land for the mythical Seven Cities of Gold), then La Nueva México, meaning "the other Mexico," and finally La Provincia de Nuevo México. Forty-six years after Columbus's first voyage, four shipwrecked Spanish castaways from an ill-fated expedition to Florida made their way overland from the Gulf Coast and through the northern edge of present Chihuahua on their way home to New Spain. Peering into the distance of the *tierra adentro* (the interior) beyond the Rio Grande, they wondered about stories they heard from Native traders about people, far to the north, who lived in houses, grew cotton, and were rumored to have great wealth. Once rescued, they told about what they had seen and heard. Before long, other Spaniards moved northward to explore the tierra adentro. By one lifetime after Columbus's landing, Francisco Vázquez de Coronado and his men were camped on the bank of yet another place: Tiguex, an Indian province in the large valley that now hosts Albuquerque, below the craggy mountain known to the Spaniards as Sierra Nevada, the Snowy Mountain. By the end of the sixteenth century, New Mexico had been explored, conquered, and settled by Spain. Over the intervening sixty years, explorers traveling north from New Spain visited nearly every pueblo in New Mexico and gathered invaluable information about them, their rich cultures, and their resources. The early cartography of New Mexico, based on exploration, encompassed an area extending northward along the Rio Grande Valley, westward to Zuni and Hopi, and eastward to the Great Plains. European mapmakers, who had never been to the tierra adentro, saw New Mexico through the eyes of explorers who had dared to enter the *terra incognita,* the unknown land, a place of mystery.

Abraham Ortelius, like other sixteenth-century cartographers, mapped the route of each Spanish explorer across the New World with the studied eye of a scholar-monk. Greek and Roman mythological figures, sea monsters, the four winds, and ornate compass rosettes illuminated his maps and enhanced the mysterious place-names of the real and imagined geography he recorded. Ortelius was among the first to become interested in the geography of North America's interior. Through interviews with explorers, and through study of their letters, diaries, and field maps, the famed cartographer received vague and varied descriptions of the New World. In 1587, he published his atlas of the world, which featured a map of the Americas. Because so much was known of the Atlantic coastline of the New World, Ortelius drafted it with great accuracy, as he did the Pacific Coast of southern South America. But the land north of Acapulco on the western Mexican coast was little known, as no more than five expeditions had been that far north. Ortelius, plagued with uncertainty, published a map showing western North America pocked with distortions and imaginary place-names. For example, Ortelius mistakenly showed the Río Nuestra Señora (the Rio Grande in New Mexico) draining into the Pacific Ocean.

Among sixteenth-century geographers and adventurers seeking their fortunes, however, the names on Ortelius's map raised many questions and piqued curious minds. His maps were marked with strange names like Acuco (Acoma), Cicuye (Pecos), Totonteac, Marata, Cíbola,

Tiguex, and Gran Quivira, the legendary kingdom of enormous wealth that the Spaniards sought in their explorations of the north. By the end of the sixteenth century, those names and others had earned a place in the annals of the history of the Americas and European folklore. Their stories were intricately tied with Indian America, as is the name New Mexico. In 1521, the Spaniards wrested Tenochtitlan from the Mexica and renamed it Mexico. The search for another Mexico, *otro México,* inspired the name Nuevo México.

Through traders and slavers, the Pueblos received vague and varied reports of events along the Gulf Coast, Mexico, and interior lands south of them. Long before they beheld Coronado's bearded visage and heard the snort and neigh of a Spanish horse, the pueblos knew of the white man and his terrible weapons. One story they heard was different. It was about four men, the aforementioned shipwreck survivors, one of them "a black man," who had crossed the continent from the east to the southern end of the Rio Grande. The Spaniards knew well the story of Álvar Núñez Cabeza de Vaca, Esteban the Moor, and two other companions, who, lost for eight years, had crossed the wilds of North America from Texas to Sonora, where they were rescued.

Pressed for information by Spanish officials interested in new sources of wealth, the men searched their memories for details about the tierra adentro. Finally, Cabeza de Vaca submitted a *relación* (account) of his experiences in the wilds of North America to Viceroy Antonio de Mendoza. The *Relación* quickly became a primer for those interested in the tierra adentro. He recounted how, after Pánfilo de Narváez's expedition to Florida had failed, the men attempted to make their way back to Cuba or New Spain on makeshift boats. Following the coastline westward from Florida, the explorers seemed to be succeeding until they were thrust out to sea by the mighty rush of the Mississippi River as it emptied into the Gulf of Mexico. Soon, a storm scattered the fleet and 150 survivors—half of the expedition—made it to shore along the Texas coast and nearby islands. Out of touch with one another, the scattered bands of Spaniards attempted to regroup. Many had lost their weapons, provisions, and clothing to the sea.

It was a bitter winter, as northers on the mainland blew a mass of cold, humid air toward the islands. Few Spaniards survived the first winter, and were it not for friendly Indians, none would have lived to tell the tale of Narváez's ill-fated expedition. After the first year, Cabeza de Vaca could account for only fifteen enslaved survivors. If there were others, they had probably been captured by Indians and taken farther into the interior. Four years later, in 1532, Cabeza de Vaca, still a slave to a wandering band, could count only five survivors. He planned to escape with them, and in time, found a way to contact them. All but one accepted the challenge; the dissenter believed they would die in the attempt. To him, slavery was a means of survival. Sometime in 1535, under cover of darkness, Cabeza de Vaca, Esteban, and two others sneaked away from their captors. Three years later, they reached Sinaloa, where they learned of other Spaniards nearby.

As Cabeza de Vaca and his companions traversed the land, sometimes as free men, other times as slaves to different Indian groups, they were the first Europeans to glimpse North America's interior. They trudged the rolling plains of east and south Texas to the Rio Grande and the arid prairies on the edge of the Chihuahua Desert. Once past the Pecos River, they made contact with different Indian bands and may have crossed and recrossed the Rio Grande where it makes its sweeping "Big Bend" on its way to the sea, hundreds of miles away. Somehow, the four men survived the hot summer months on the northern edge of the Chihuahua Desert as they migrated westward toward the setting sun. Somewhere along the Rio Grande, probably in southern New Mexico, they learned about the pueblos of the north. By the time they crossed the northern tip of the Sierra Madre Occidental, they realized that they had become Indian-like. Later, once safe among the Spaniards of New Spain, they became vocal opponents of the Spanish treatment of the Indians. Yet it was Cabeza de Vaca's *Relación* that inspired the Spanish exploration of the tierra adentro.

Not long after the rescue of Cabeza de Vaca and his companions, Spanish officials in Mexico City authorized a small expedition to reconnoiter the tierra adentro. Cabeza de Vaca and his fellow Spaniards declined offers to go north again, but Esteban the Moor was easily induced to guide a small party beyond the northern limits of New Spain. Coincidentally, in the spring of 1537, the bishop of Mexico, Juan de Zumárraga, brought a fellow Franciscan, Fray Marcos de Niza, to the viceregal palace in Mexico City. Niza, who had served at Santo Domingo in the Caribbean and recently arrived from Guatemala with tales the bishop desired to share with Viceroy Mendoza, had also spent time in Peru and had conversed with Francisco Pizarro, who was winning new kingdoms for the crown of Spain. Niza then traveled to Mexico City at the request of Zumárraga. From this interview Fray Marcos de Niza emerged as a leader in the viceroy's plan to explore and conquer the tierra adentro. In 1538, the viceroy commissioned Niza "to find a way to go on and penetrate the land in the interior." He was to make careful observations about the people, the land, the rivers, and the flora and fauna of the interior.

The bearer of these instructions to Niza was none other than the young governor of Nueva Galicia, Francisco Vázquez de Coronado, a favorite of Viceroy Mendoza's. The two men met for the first time on November 20, 1538, at Tonalá, a village near Guadalajara. At Culiacán, on the edge of the Spanish frontier, Niza assembled his expedition. Besides Esteban, a Franciscan priest named Fray Onorato and Indian friends of Esteban's who had accompanied him during his lost years formed the reconnaissance party.

By the spring of 1539, Niza and his retinue were on their way. On March 21, he made a fateful decision. Restless with the slow progress the expedition was making, Esteban proposed to go ahead as an advance scout and send back messages regarding his findings in the form of crosses. Esteban promised to wait for Niza near the pueblos so that they could proceed to Cíbola, the large kingdom they sought. Niza would never again see Esteban, for he was killed by the people at Hawikuh, a Zuni pueblo in the province of Cíbola.

In the meantime, Niza's progress was slow because he had been instructed to gather information about the land and people. Also, he sought to determine his proximity "to the sea." To do that, he took a detour away from Esteban's trail, which caused him further delay. The information he gathered, he believed, would be useful to Spaniards who were not clear on the coastal geography. They were unaware that Baja California was a peninsula, not an island, and that the body of water along the Sonoran coastline was a gulf, not the Pacific Ocean. Niza's information failed to clarify the subject and was useful only to determine the distance from the Sonoran coast to wherever Niza's route lay in the interior. Throughout, Niza continued to receive crosses from Esteban's Indian messengers. When he received larger ones, his anticipation heightened because he thought the larger crosses signaled that Esteban had discovered a rich city of gold.

Once out of the Valley of Sonora, Niza entered the *despoblado* (desert) of southeastern Arizona. There, in one of his lonely camps, Niza learned that Esteban was dead. What happened next has baffled historians for centuries. Apparently, most of Niza's followers deserted him, but despite the desertions and the ill tidings regarding Esteban's death at Hawikuh, Niza continued northward until he got within sight of Hawikuh, which he called Cíbola. In his account, Niza did not write that he saw a city of gold; instead he wrote:

> I proceeded on my journey until coming within sight of Cíbola, which is situated in a plain at the base of a round hill. The pueblo has a fine appearance, the best I have seen in these regions. The houses are . . . all of stone, with terraces and flat roofs, as it seemed to me from a hill where I stood. . . . The city is larger than the city of Mexico. . . . When I told the chieftain . . . how . . . impressed I was with Cíbola, they told me that it was the smallest of seven cities, and that Totonteac is much larger and better than all seven, that it has so many houses and people that there is no end to it.

Returning to Compostela, Nayarit, Niza reported to Governor Vázquez de Coronado. Later, on September 2, 1539, Niza met with Viceroy Mendoza in Mexico City and retold his story, this time with some exaggeration. Convinced by Niza's stories, Mendoza decided to explore the north in hope of discovering another Tenochtitlan. In 1540, Vázquez de Coronado left Compostela on the west Mexican coast, leading a large expedition of more than 1,100 Spaniards and Indian allies and nearly five thousand sheep, goats, cattle, and horses. Many of the Indian allies on the expedition took their wives and children with them. At least three other women listed by name accompanied the expedition: Francisca de Hozes, wife of Alonso Sánchez, who brought their young son with them; María Maldonado, wife of Juan de Paradinas, a tailor; and Señora Caballero, the Nahua-speaking wife of Lope de

Caballero. In later battles fought by the expedition, María Maldonado organized the care for the wounded, while Francisca de Hozes donned armor and fought alongside her husband. She later testified against Vázquez de Coronado, accusing him of having mismanaged the expedition, leading to its failure to find the Seven Cities of Cíbola.

In northern Sonora, Vázquez de Coronado divided his force, so that he and an advance guard could move faster to the pueblos of New Mexico. Along the San Pedro River valley, they veered northward through the mountain ranges of eastern Arizona until they reached the Zuni village of Hawikuh. Near Hawikuh, far from their supply line and suffering fatigue and near-starvation, Vázquez de Coronado and his party avoided an ambush set by Pueblo warriors. Then at Hawikuh, they met hostile warriors who refused to let them enter the pueblo. The cause of their hostility remains unclear: perhaps the Spaniards had intruded on a sacred event at Zuni, perhaps the people of Hawikuh feared that the Spaniards had come to avenge the death of Esteban, or perhaps they simply saw the Spaniards as a hostile party. Desperate lest his men perish for lack of food and water, Vázquez de Coronado attacked Hawikuh.

Once in possession of the pueblo, the Spaniards explored to the north, reaching the Hopi pueblos in northeastern Arizona and the Grand Canyon. At Zuni, Vázquez de Coronado received emissaries from Pecos far to the east, led by a man they dubbed Bigotes, who brought gifts, among them a buffalo hide. Curious about the animal, Vázquez de Coronado sent Hernando de Alvarado to explore as far as the present panhandles of Texas and Oklahoma.

Marching eastward, Alvarado and a small party, led by Bigotes and his Indian guides, passed by Acoma, a fortress pueblo on a high plateau; their guides called it "Acuco." A few days later, they reached a large Pueblo province called Tiguex, within present Albuquerque. From there, they went to Pecos by way of the Galisteo Basin, where they saw several more pueblos.

Pecos, known to Alvarado as Cicuye, was a pueblo fortress on a high promontory on the edge of the Great Plains. Its residents traded with Plains bands and the Rio Grande pueblos. From Cicuye, Alvarado crossed the Pecos River and reached the "Buffalo Plains." Returning to Tiguex, Alvarado joined García López de Cárdenas, who had set up winter quarters there.

Meanwhile, Vázquez de Coronado had left Hawikuh along a southwesterly route. He approached the Rio Grande at a place called Tutahaco, perhaps near present Socorro. From there, he followed the river northward past Isleta to Tiguex, where he rejoined López de Cárdenas and Alvarado, who told him about Cicuye and the Buffalo Plains.

The winter of 1540–41 proved disastrous for Spanish-Pueblo relations. Unprepared for frigid weather, the Spaniards traded for or confiscated Indian blankets and supplies. In one incident, a Tiwa claimed a Spaniard had molested his wife. Pedro de Castañeda, a member of the expedition, wrote that the incident "occurred before Vázquez de Coronado arrived at Tiguex, when the army was camped at the pueblo of Alcanfor. A Juan de Villegas left the pueblo, hoping to gather clothing and other items. At a nearby pueblo, Villegas spied a woman. He called her husband down below," wrote Castañeda, "and asked him to hold his horse by the bridle while he went up"; and, as the house was entered from the top, the husband thought he was going to another place. While the native held the horse, a commotion occurred, then Villegas came back, took his mount, and rode away. When the husband climbed to the upper part, he learned that [Villegas] had ravished or attempted to ravish his wife." What actually happened is unclear. Some Indians said that the soldier had tried to have relations with the woman. At other times, it seemed they indicated "by their signs that he tried to take a blanket from her."

Outraged at the offense, the man, accompanied by other prominent persons from his pueblo, went to the governor's quarters to complain. Vázquez de Coronado ordered all soldiers and persons in his company to appear before him. The Indian reviewed the lineup but could not identify the offender. Failing that, the Indian said he would recognize the horse because he had held it by the reins during the incident. After inspecting the horse herd, he saw a blossom-colored horse covered with a blanket. The owner of the horse, said the Indian, was the offender. "The owner denied it," wrote Castañeda, "saying that the Indian had not recognized him in the lineup, and perhaps he was mistaken also in the horse." After a lengthy debate, the governor determined that there was insufficient certainty in the identification of the animal to warrant punishment of the horse's owner. As far as the husband and his pueblo were concerned, however, justice was not served. In another incident, the Spaniards had taken two Indians from Cicuye, mistreated them in order to intimidate them into revealing the location of the gold they were sure must exist, and held them prisoner in one of the Tiwa villages. The Tiwa protested the imprisonment of Zuni foreigners in their villages, but to no avail. Pueblo resentment against the Spanish festered, adding a further chill to the already cold winter. By midwinter the Tiguex War had broken out. When Pueblo warriors killed and wounded several Spanish black and Indian servants as well as several horses, the Spanish attacked the Tiwa villages of Moho, Arenal, and Alcanfor and mounted a lengthy siege.

Several years after the expedition had returned to Mexico, Spanish officials held an inquiry into these and other controversial matters. As for the confiscation of Indian clothing, Castañeda reported that the governor, "seeing that winter was setting in very severely and that some of the Indians and *negros* who were with him had frozen and died, ordered this witness and others to go in different directions through the pueblos to ask the Indians for some clothes in order to be able to withstand the winter. Some of the Indians gave some clothing of their own will, and others against their will, although they were not at all ill-treated on this account, nor was it permitted." Regarding the alleged rape, Castañeda reiterated that Vázquez de Coronado "tried to apprehend the soldier who had done it in order to punish him; that it was never established that Villegas was the one who attacked the Indian woman, nor was anyone else found guilty." Vázquez de Coronado, López de Cárdenas, and others were tried for their abuse of Indians in the Tiguex War. López de Cárdenas was found guilty and sentenced to seven years imprisonment, but Vázquez de Coronado was absolved. Colonial authorities did investigate and record the actions of the expedition, rather than denying they had ever occurred; still, the Natives never saw anyone punished for the misdeeds.

Despite the Tiguex War, Vázquez de Coronado sent his men to explore in all directions from the Rio Grande. One expedition got as far as Uraba (Taos Pueblo), and another revisited Tutahaco, claiming they reached a point where the Rio Grande disappeared belowground, probably near present El Paso. Other explorers went west toward Chia (Zia) and Hemes (Jemez). Almost every pueblo in New Mexico, save those east of the Manzano Mountains, was visited by the expedition.

When the spring of 1541 came, the expedition moved to Pecos. From there, Indian guides, one of them called El Turco, who apparently hoped to lose the Spaniards in the vastness of the Great Plains, led them in a hopeless search for the elusive, rich civilization of Gran Quivira. Having constructed a bridge across the Pecos River, the expedition entered the Llano Estacado of eastern New Mexico, followed the Canadian River, and moved southeast to Palo Duro Canyon near present Amarillo, Texas. Along the way they met Apachean groups who followed buffalo herds from sunrise to sunset, hunting with stone projectiles, as they had for thousands of years. The Querechos (an Apachean people) and the Teyas (perhaps related to the Wichitas), who traded with Pecos, confirmed the existence of Quivira, in the direction of the rising sun. Following their compass north across present-day Oklahoma, the expedition reached central Kansas. There, they saw the disappointing Wichita huts and decided to return to Tiguex, after executing El Turco for leading them on a fool's errand.

Although Vázquez de Coronado's expedition failed to find Quivira and alienated the Pueblos along the Rio Grande, it did succeed in gathering information related to a large geographic region of North America. The explorers had gathered much knowledge about flora and fauna as well as the ethnography, albeit through colonial eyes, of the Natives in the area, both Puebloan and Plains peoples. The region explored by the expedition stretched from eastern Arizona to the Great Bend of the Arkansas River by way of present-day Sinaloa, Sonora, Arizona, New Mexico, Texas, Oklahoma, and Kansas. At the same time, two other expeditions explored North America: Juan Rodríguez Cabrillo sailed along the California coast as far north as southern Oregon, and Hernando de Soto explored from Florida and Georgia to the Mississippi River and eastern Texas. The three expeditions gave Spaniards a glimpse of the vast extent of North America from coast to coast.

Stories about the expedition circulated far and wide. Some years afterward, Francisco Peralta, who had been on the expedition, left

Mexico to visit Italy. While in Rome, he visited a wealthy official and saw, hanging on the wall, a tapestry picturing landscape images of Cíbola, just as Peralta had seen and remembered it. The Italian official said that a Spanish prince had presented it to the Duque de Sajonia along with a large buffalo hide, similar to those Peralta had seen on the plains of Cíbola and Quivira.

For nearly forty years after Vázquez de Coronado's expedition, the Spaniards did not think much about it. In that time, the Indians of the tierra adentro transformed their encounters with the first wave of Spaniards into an oral tradition with a portent. For the most part, the Spaniards turned their attention to expanding the Spanish frontier line northward along the profitable silver-mining districts of the central Mexican corridor. Yet from time to time, as the frontier extended north into southern Chihuahua, Spanish slavers would cross the Rio Grande chasing "thieving Indians." Looking northward into the *despoblado* (uninhabited lands), they wondered about what lay beyond them. At Santa Barbara, on the edge of the Spanish northern frontier, they told tales of the despoblado and speculated about the rumors of mysterious cities beyond it.

Finally, in the late 1570s, a group of men, among them Francisco Sánchez, nicknamed "Chamuscado" (singed) for his red beard, met in Santa Bárbara near Parral, Chihuahua. For more than two years they planned a journey into the tierra adentro. An Indian had told them that far beyond Santa Bárbara "was a certain settlement of Indians, who had cotton and made cloth with which they clothed themselves." Another leader of the group was Fray Agustín Rodríguez, a Franciscan who had gone beyond the Río Conchos, a Chihuahuan tributary of the Rio Grande, to minister to the Indians there. Having read Cabeza de Vaca's *Relación,* Fray Agustín had a different view about the "people who made cloth." In 1579, he petitioned the viceroy for authority to explore and convert the settlements of the tierra adentro. Although King Felipe II of Spain had forbidden new *entradas* (explorations), except with royal permission, Rodríguez received approval from the viceroy and permission from the Franciscan father provincial to go to the tierra adentro with a small party not to exceed twenty men and to carry some articles for barter.

On June 5, 1580, Fray Juan de Santa María, Fray Francisco López, Fray Agustín Rodríguez, and eight soldiers led by Francisco Sánchez Chamuscado left Santa Bárbara. They went northward to the Río Conchos, then eastward to the Rio Grande. Near the river, they met a group of Indians who told them that "there were more settlements beyond."

For three weeks, they went upriver until they came to a pueblo they called San Felipe, south of present-day San Marcial. Aside from possibly unrecorded illegal expeditions, Sánchez Chamuscado and his companions were the first Europeans to travel officially through the area since Vázquez de Coronado's men had ventured that far south in 1540. Hernán Gallegos, a member of the expedition, wrote that San Felipe "had been inhabited by a large number of people, who must have been very advanced." He remarked that "said pueblo was walled in; and the houses had mud walls and were built of adobes, three stories high." It appeared to have been abandoned for a long time. The expedition camped at San Felipe that night.

The summer sun rose early over the ruined pueblo as the explorers departed it northward along the Rio Grande. Shortly, they came to another pueblo, which they surmised had been hurriedly abandoned the previous day. The pueblo, which they dubbed San Miguel, had many "houses three stories high." At the pueblo they found turkeys, much cotton, corn, and many decorated pots, large clay jars, and flat pans. Surrounding it they saw scattered fields of corn, beans, calabashes, and cotton. To signal that they did not intend any harm to the people, they did not take anything from the pueblo or the fields. Their description of the pueblo, albeit seen through Spanish colonial eyes, provides an idea of the typical pueblo on the lower Rio Grande of New Mexico.

The Spaniards spent the rest of the day trying to make contact with the pueblo's people. When some returned, the Spaniards explained their peaceful intentions so that the rest of the pueblo would come out of hiding. Gallegos wrote that the friars showed them to make the sign of the cross as a sign of peace and "the news that we were coming in peace spread."

Traveling beyond San Miguel as far as the large valley of the Rio Grande in present-day Albuquerque, the Spaniards encountered people who lived similarly, yet spoke different languages. The Piros of the southern Rio Grande and the Tiwas (or Tiguas) in the area of present Albuquerque appeared only subtly different to the Spaniards, though modern-day tribal members and ethnographers recognize differences in material culture. Gallegos wrote that all the pueblos grew corn, beans, calabashes, and cotton. The people also made corn tortillas and *atole* (a corn gruel), as well as pottery and blankets. The buildings he described were generally two, three, or four stories high, and the distinctions he made among the pueblos were generally based on their size. "The further one goes into the interior," wrote Gallegos, "the larger are the pueblos and the houses, and the more numerous the people."

The Spaniards observed many details of the Indians' attire and appearance. Some men cut their hair short and left "on top . . . a sort of skull cap formed by their own hair." Others wore their hair long, to their shoulders. Some wore colored cotton cloth, with which "they cover their privy parts. Over this they wear, fastened at the shoulders, a blanket of the same material . . . which reaches their knees, like the clothes of the Mexicans." Others wore cotton shirts and sandals or moccasins. Gallegos noted that women "combed their hair in a Spanish style. They wore colored and embroidered" cotton skirts. Like the men, they wore a blanket over their shoulders, which extended below the waist. In the "fashion of Jewish women," the Indian women tied the blanket around their waists with an embroidered cotton sash adorned with tassels. The Spaniards described the Puebloans as "handsome, and fair skinned" and as "very clean people."

Only the men worked the cornfields and bore heavy burdens. Women carried smaller loads such as firewood and water. Aside from their maternal and household duties, women prepared the food, made and painted pottery for storing food and water, ground corn with metates, and were "the ones who spin, sew, weave and paint." The Spaniards observed that "girls do not leave their room except when permitted by their parents." Generally, women were "given husbands when seventeen years of age and they married for life."

Moving north beyond Tiwa country, they heard of pueblos to the east of the river, including a place they called San Mateo, in present Galisteo Basin south of Santa Fe. Preparing to visit San Mateo, Sánchez

Chamuscado made Puaray, one of the Tiwa pueblos in the valley, his headquarters. The friars remained there while the soldiers explored to the east, beyond the Sierra de Puaray (in the present Sandia Mountains), a mountain sacred to the Pueblos. At San Mateo, they learned of mines with "coppery steel-like ores." The Pueblos, however, were quick to add that similar ores could be obtained from Indians "in the region of the buffalo." The people of San Mateo surely hoped the Spaniards would go to the plains and never return. They did indeed go, in search of the mineral wealth Spain was perpetually in search of to support its empire, but returned unharmed and disappointed. They reported that the peoples of the plains did not have houses, hunted and ate mostly buffalo meat, were enemies of the pueblos, traded buffalo meat for corn and blankets, and were warlike.

Returning to San Mateo, the curious Spaniards asked the Puebloans why they "lived so far from the [buffalo] herds, and they replied that it was on account of their corn fields and cultivated lands, so that the buffalo would not eat their crops." The soldiers learned that during certain times of the year, the buffalo were only two days' journey away. The Puebloans were keenly aware that the Indians who followed the buffalo were brave hunters and able bowmen who would not hesitate to kill them. Thus, the Spaniards gained insight into the delicate relationship between the Pueblo and the Plains Indians. Other pueblos on the edge of the Great Plains formed a line from Taos in the north to Picuris, Cicuye (Pecos), and the Salinas pueblos to the south.

While at Galisteo, Sánchez Chamuscado learned that Fray Juan de Santa María had left for Santa Bárbara to report to his superiors about the great possibilities for religious conversion in the pueblos. Using his recently acquired geographical knowledge of the tierra adentro, Fray Santa María took a shortcut south behind the present Sandia-Manzano Mountains, hoping to reach the ford at present El Paso in less time. Later, Natives informed the Spaniards that the priest had been killed by Indians "in the sierra." At Puaray, meanwhile, Fray Agustín and Fray Francisco were making little headway in their efforts to convert the Natives.

When the soldiers returned, Sánchez Chamuscado was restless and determined to go to Acoma and Zuni. The freezing temperatures and snow forced him and his companions to turn back to Puaray, however, so instead they decided to explore behind the Manzano Mountains to the southeast, where they "discovered" some pueblos and a series of dried-up salt lakes. Heavy snowfall again forced them to return to Puaray, to recover from the numbing cold and wait for the weather to lift.

The soldiers had seen enough of the land and its people, and decided to return to Santa Bárbara. The Franciscans, however, ever hopeful of spiritual conquest over the Tiwas, decided to stay, even at the risk of martyrdom. Therefore, Sánchez Chamuscado and his men headed south without the priests. Somewhere in the northern Chihuahua Desert, the expedition leader fell ill and died, and his soldiers buried him with a prayer that his soul rest in eternal peace.

Nearly a year after the expedition had begun, the tired and dust-covered soldiers returned to Santa Bárbara. By May 1582, Hernán Gallegos and others had traveled to Mexico City to present their reports of the tierra adentro to the viceroy's notaries. Their testimony raised concern for the welfare of the two priests, particularly in light of Fray Juan's death. Although sparse in any mention of riches in that land, their reports excited speculation that soon was twisted into rumors that the land of the pueblos contained rich mineral deposits, if only one knew where to look. Several entrepreneurs stepped forward, pledging to risk life and fortune to go and rescue the two friars (which provided a convenient excuse for a prospecting expedition).

Antonio de Espejo, who had been in New Spain for eleven years, offered to outfit a small military escort, provided he be permitted to explore the tierra adentro for signs of mineral wealth. Espejo was a successful cattleman until one day his brother Pedro shot it out with two ranch hands who had refused to work during a cattle roundup. Don Antonio was charged with complicity in the homicide of the ranch hands. Pedro was convicted and received a heavy punishment, but Antonio, refusing to pay the fine levied against him, fled northward with whatever assets he could take. Thus, using his influence with the mayor of Cuatro Ciénegas, south of Santa Bárbara, and hoping for a pardon, Espejo gained authorization in the name of the king to accompany, at his own expense, Fray Bernardino Beltrán.

On November 10, 1582, the expedition set out from the Valley of San Gregorio bound for "Nuevo México." Aside from Espejo, Father Beltrán, and three of his brethren, there were fourteen soldiers and servants carrying quantities of munitions and provisions and driving a herd of 115 horses, mules, and cattle. The expeditionary force did take on one unusual feature, when Miguel Sánchez Valenciano departed the party to escort another priest who wanted to join the group. Upon returning to Santa Bárbara, Sánchez was confronted by his wife, Casilda de Anaya, who demanded to go on the expedition. Two days later, Sánchez rejoined the party with Casilda; his oldest son, Lázaro; and two younger sons, Pedro, almost four years old, and Juan, then twenty months old. Two others of the family also joined them. Although Casilda became pregnant during the expedition, she and her children stayed with the expedition until it returned to San Bartolomé eleven months later.

Suffering hardships, the expedition reached the Rio Grande in December. By mid-January, they explored a part of the Rio Grande called Las Vueltas "because here it starts to wind as far as the settlements (pueblos)." There, in the vicinity of present El Paso, the party camped for a week. Eight days later they had moved north to a point near present Elephant Butte Reservoir, one day's journey from Sánchez Chamuscado's San Felipe. After a few days' rest, the expeditionary force and its livestock stood on the edge of the volcanic *malpaís* near San Marcial. They had seen the abandoned pueblo of San Felipe, and now proceeded upriver to the Piro villages.

Somewhat more observant than the men of the Sánchez Chamuscado expedition, Espejo's people reported new details of Piro life. They pointed out, for example, that "they have earthen jar stands on which they keep their water jars." The doorways, they remarked, were "shaped like a U so as to allow only one person to go through at a time." Noticing their weapons, Diego Pérez de Luján, the chronicler of the expedition, reported, "These people do not seem to be bellicose, because they fight with flint-edged clubs and hide-wrapped stone bludgeons about a half a yard long. They have few and poor Turkish bows and poorer arrows." Regarding their "shoes," Pérez de Luján observed that "they wear shoes of tanned buffalo leather and tanned deerskins fashioned like boots." Notably, they described two significant features of the pueblo, aside from the multistory design: the plaza and its attendant kivas, which they called *estufas*. "In each pueblo, in the center of the plaza," wrote Pérez de Luján, "are some very large cellars two and one half estados deep, with an entrance in the shape of a trap door and a step ladder. They are all whitewashed and provided with some benches all around. Here the people perform their games and dances. On one side are their *temascales* [sweathouses] where they bathe." In every pueblo they visited, Espejo's men continued to notice the kivas, the plazas, and the Native weaponry.

By mid-February 1583, the small Spanish party had reached the valley of the large Sierra Morena (Sandia-Manzano ranges). They were impressed with the number of pueblos that stretched from one end of the valley to the next. Upon entering Puaray, which was virtually abandoned, they learned that the Tiwas had killed the two priests. They also confirmed that Fray Juan had been killed in the Sierra Morena. Pérez de Luján reported, "The inhabitants of all these settlements had fled the sierra because all had taken part in killing the friars. Some Indians soon came to find out what we wanted to do, and we sent them to bring the others in peace. There was one among them playing an instrument resembling a flageolet."

Espejo and seven men went to the sierra with the Indian messengers to bring the people back. Some came down, and by means of signs they agreed to return to their pueblos because their families were suffering greatly from the cold. Many others refused to return for fear of Spanish reprisal. The memory of Vázquez de Coronado's attack on their pueblos forty-one years previous was still fresh in the lore of the pueblos of the Rio Grande.

Meanwhile, the Spaniards inspected the abandoned pueblos and provisioned themselves with corn, beans, green and sun-dried calabashes, and other vegetables, as well as poultry. They also took some pottery that they needed. Frightened of the Spaniards, some Indians offered them gifts and information about other provinces to appease them and draw them away from Puaray.

By February's end, Espejo had visited San Felipe and Cochiti pueblos and traded hawks' bells and small iron articles for buffalo hides, corn, tortillas, turkeys, and pinole. In their view, these pueblos differed little from Puaray. From there, the expedition went to Zia and Jemez, while a disconsolate Father Beltrán prayed for his fallen brethren. From Jemez, they traveled to Zuni via Acoma. Just east of Mount Taylor, they picked up the trail to Acoma, arriving there as the weather turned colder. From Acoma, they pushed westward until snow forced them to camp on the malpaís (present El Malpais National Monument) in a large pine forest that protected them from the snowfall. "We slept in the woods because it snowed so much that we were unable to proceed," recalled Pérez de Luján. For water, they melted snow in their pots and pans, and they called the area El Helado (the frozen place) because of the extreme cold they suffered. It was March 11, 1583, when they reached a place they named El Estanque del Peñol (the pond at the rock). In the shelter of the sandstone promontory of present El Morro National Monument, they camped just as Indians of yore and probably as some of Vázquez de Coronado's men forty years before had done. Although thousands of passersby have camped at this waterhole over the centuries, leaving inscriptions ranging from pictographs to signatures in flowing script, no members of the Espejo expedition seemingly bothered to engrave their names in the rock.

Once rested, Espejo and his people marched westward. A few days later they reached Zuni. At Hawikuh, Alona, Cana, Quaquina, and Mazaque, they found well-constructed wooden crosses. "Here," wrote Pérez de Luján, "we found a book and a small trunk left by Vázquez de Coronado." They also met Mexican Indians, a number of them from Guadalajara, whom Vázquez de Coronado had left behind. Although they served as translators, they spoke Spanish with difficulty, as they had been absent from New Spain for four decades. Still, their influence was evident in the crosses and in other signs the Spaniards saw among the Zunis. Three of the Indians, Andrés of Coyoacan, Antón of Guadalajara, and Gaspar of Mexico, told Espejo about the land and its people.

At Zuni, Espejo and the friars argued over continuing the expedition. As far as Father Beltrán was concerned, the expedition's purpose—to rescue Fray Agustín and Fray Francisco—had been fulfilled at Puaray when it was learned that they were dead. Espejo departed Zuni with four soldiers to explore westward into present Arizona. After traveling more than two hundred miles, probably as far as present Prescott, Espejo returned to Zuni and found Father Beltrán and the others still there. Again, the two leaders argued as some of the soldiers took sides. The rift between them was irrevocable. Father Beltrán and his faction returned to Mexico by way of the Rio Grande.

Not long thereafter Espejo and eight loyal soldiers returned to the Rio Grande, where they skirmished with the people of Puaray. With Puaray up in arms, they could not remain along the river, so they marched east, beyond Pecos, through a forest of white pine and juniper. They marched through rough terrain to get to the Pecos River. Fleeing down the Pecos, they spent two months trekking to San Bartolomé in Chihuahua. It had been a long year for the explorers, who had come home empty-handed, lucky to escape the tierra adentro with their lives. As autumn gave way to the winter of 1584, Espejo, the friars, and the soldiers had many tales to tell of their adventures and the exotic people of the north—stimulating the imaginations of those who would dream of conquering the tierra adentro. It was only a matter of time.

Meanwhile, in Nuevo León, south of Texas, a drama unfolded that would have far-reaching consequences for the settlement of New Mexico. In 1590, the Holy Office of the Inquisition jailed Luis de Carbajal, governor of Nuevo León, for secretly practicing Judaism. Gaspar Castaño de Sosa, his lieutenant governor, decided to move the colony at Nuevo León to another place within the large land grant they believed included New Mexico. Despite the viceroy's warnings that the expedition was illegal, Castaño de Sosa and several hundred men, women, and children departed for New Mexico in late July 1590.

Driving herds of livestock, the expedition reached the Rio Grande near present Ciudad Acuña on the U.S.-Mexico border six weeks later. Crossing the despoblado to the Pecos River, they followed the river northwestwardly. In December, Spanish scouts reached Pecos Pueblo. Soon after, the settlers reached Pecos in a snowstorm. The Indians denied them entrance.

On December 31, 1590, after six hours of trying to persuade the pueblo to surrender, Castaño de Sosa realized his people would perish in the freezing cold without shelter. Finally, he attacked the pueblo, which fell after several of the warriors were killed. The expedition entered Pecos and settled there for several months. By March 1591, the Spaniards had moved from Pecos to the Galisteo Basin pueblos. From there, they explored the Rio Grande and settled at Santo Domingo. During that year, they traded with the pueblos along the river valley.

In spring 1592, the viceroy sent Juan de Morlete to arrest Castaño de Sosa for having led an illegal expedition to New Mexico. In the end, his settlers were forced to return to Nuevo León. After a trial, Castaño de Sosa was convicted and sentenced to perform duty in the Philippines, where he died in a slave uprising a few years later. Meanwhile, Castaño de Sosa's fate served as a warning to potential leaders of expeditions that their actions had to be approved and sanctioned by the viceroy of New Spain as the king's representative.

From time to time, illegal expeditions entered the tierra adentro. In 1593, Captain Leyva led a group of soldiers from southern Chihuahua in pursuit of marauding Indians who had fled northward. The expedition having completed its mission, Leyva unexpectedly proposed to explore the tierra adentro. Six soldiers refused to go, but the others were curious about what lay ahead. Leyva and Antonio Gutiérrez de Humaña led the horsemen to the pueblos of New Mexico. After spending several months there, they moved to the far northern pueblos, probably Taos or Picuris. There they made another crucial decision.

While trading with Plains Indians at Taos or, possibly, at Pecos, they learned about the Great Plains. Hoping to discover a great civilization similar to the Aztec kingdom, they decided to go to the plains. Believing that previous expeditions had not gone far enough in the correct direction to find it, Leyva and Gutiérrez headed northeastward into what is now Kansas. Somewhere on the plains, Leyva and Gutiérrez argued, and in the fight that followed, Gutiérrez killed his captain. He now found himself in command of the troops in hostile territory. Moving northerly for eighteen days, the expedition may have reached the Nebraska plains—farther than any European had heretofore ventured into the North American heartland. There, several Indian guides deserted him. One of them, Jusepe, who was soon captured by Apaches, later escaped to Pecos Pueblo. Soon after Leyva's death, Plains Indians ambushed Gutiérrez and his men, attacking at daybreak under cover of a grass fire. All the Spaniards and their Indian allies were slain.

In an attempt to put a stop to further illegal expeditions, Spanish officials in Mexico City decided to plan the long-term settlement of New Mexico. In 1595, fearing that other restless frontiersmen would dare strike out on their own and possibly ruin conditions for a royal enterprise, the viceroy authorized Juan de Oñate to settle New Mexico.

Having suffered long delays and personal losses, Oñate on January 26, 1598, led nearly six hundred settlers out of the Valley of San Bartolomé. Aside from Spanish-born settlers, mestizos, mulattos, and Nahua-speaking Indian allies, some with their wives and families, joined the expedition. Driving thousands of sheep, pigs, goats, cattle, mules, and horses, the settlers crossed Chihuahua headed toward the Rio Grande. For months, the eighty-*carreta* (cart) caravan wended its way toward New Mexico.

Instead of taking any of the familiar but circuitous routes eastward along the Río Florido or the Río Conchos to their confluence with the Rio Grande, Governor Oñate sent his nephew Vicente de Zaldívar with scouts to move directly north and find a route with water, which they did. That route, blazed by Oñate and his settlers from Santa Bárbara to El Paso, became the segment of the Camino Real de Tierra Adentro (Royal Road of the Interior) known today as La Ruta de Oñate (Oñate's Route). By the end of April, Oñate had reached the Rio Grande near where the mountains formed "the pass of the river and the ford." They named the crossing Los Puertos, later popularly known as El Paso del Norte (the pass of the north).

At El Paso, a group of Indians approached Oñate's settlers in friendship. The almost nude natives contrasted with the well-armed European-attired Spaniards. The Indians "had Turkish bows," wrote one of the settlers, and "long hair cut to resemble little Milan caps, headgear made to hold down the hair and colored with blood or paint. Their first words were *manxo, manxo, micos, micos,* by which is meant 'peaceful ones' and 'friends.'" At El Paso on April 30, 1598, the Spaniards observed a day of thanksgiving. Marcos de Farfán staged a play, "Moros y Cristianos," for the entertainment of the tired settlers.

Ten days later they camped near present Las Cruces. There, Oñate and sixty horsemen rode out ahead of the slow-moving caravan to select a site for settlement far to the north.

Meanwhile, the caravan, hoping to avoid the many turns of the Rio Grande as it cut through a series of ranges and mesas, took an alternate route east of the present-day Organ Mountains. Leaving the river, the caravan entered the waterless flatlands of the Jornada del Muerto (dead man's journey). Proceeding northward, the expedition crossed the *jornada,* suffering great thirst and hardship until they arrived at a marsh below a plateau of black rock near present San Marcial. There they said mass and prayed for better luck. A day later they camped on the northern end of the jornada at a pueblo called Qualacu. Suspicious and fearful after previous encounters with the white man, the Indians had abandoned the pueblo. For travelers approaching from the south, Qualacu was the first pueblo on the Camino Real in New Mexico.

Far ahead of the caravan, Oñate and his horsemen rode past the abandoned Puaray to the Keres pueblo known as Santo Domingo. They knew of the pueblo because of the eventful arrest of Gaspar Castaño de Sosa by Juan de Morlete in 1592. There the Spaniards sought out two of the Mexican Indians, Tomás and Cristóbal, who had been with Castaño and had decided to remain at Santo Domingo. Oñate needed them as translators. Although Spanish activities in the area had been peaceful, Tomás and Cristóbal were taken by surprise and quickly impressed into service as interpreters.

Although the Santo Domingo Indians looked on with guarded displeasure, they soon realized that Oñate intended them no harm. Oñate, through his Mexican Indian interpreters, called a general council at Santo Domingo and invited the seven nearby pueblos to send representatives. Once the council was assembled, Governor Oñate, speaking through Tomás and Cristóbal, explained the purpose of the new Spanish presence among them and asked each leader to pledge obedience to the Spanish Crown, an act whose meaning he believed they comprehended. Then Oñate announced that Santo Domingo would be the site of a Franciscan convent dedicated to Nuestra Señora de la Asunción and that the patron saints of the pueblo would be Peter and Paul. Convinced that peace had been established among the pueblos of the Rio Grande and the Spaniards, Oñate departed Santo Domingo in a northward direction.

Seeking a place to settle, Oñate and his men pushed their horses along the upper Rio Grande between Cochiti and Taos Pueblos. En route, Oñate passed the pueblo called Bove, which he named San Ildefonso in honor of the expedition's father commissary, Fray Alonso Martínez. Passing much of the land described by Castaño de Sosa, they reached the confluence of the Rio Grande and the Río Chama. On July 4, 1598, Oñate set up camp at a small pueblo called Caypa. He renamed the pueblo San Juan de los Caballeros and ordered the *maese de campo,* Juan de Zaldívar, and a small contingent of soldiers to return to Nueva Sevilla and bring up the settlers, who arrived there in mid-August, after seven months on the trail.

Next, Governor Oñate undertook an inspection of New Mexico and took time to find Jusepe, who told him about the fate of Leyva and Humaña's illegal journey to the Great Plains. He visited the northern and eastern pueblos. At Taos (known to the Spaniards as Braba, Tayberon, or San Miguel) and at Picuris Pueblo, Oñate got his first look at the Plains Indians, a group of whom had rendezvoused to trade there. From there, he wended his way southward to the Galisteo Basin and stopped at a pueblo called San Cristóbal. Moving northeast, Oñate visited Pecos before returning to San Juan at the end of summer.

In September 1598, having learned of the huge herds of buffalo, Sargento Mayor Vicente de Zaldívar and his men marched past Galisteo to the plains. From there they went southward, past the Sandia Mountains to the Salinas Pueblos. The people of Salinas rebuked Zaldívar and his troops, who had been gathering the Indians' foodstuffs on their march to the plains. Once out on the plains, along the Canadian River within the Texas Panhandle, Zaldívar found many buffalo. He visited the Querechos and Teyas and hunted buffalo for fifty-four days.

Zaldívar, the consummate explorer of the Great Plains, returned to San Juan. There he learned that his brother, Juan de Zaldívar, had been slain in an ambush at Acoma. The Acomans had challenged the Spanish right to rule over them. Threatening the other pueblos with violence, the warriors from Acoma urged other pueblos to join them

Spanish sketch of a buffalo, 1598. ("Dibujo de un bisonte," fecha de creación 1598, Archivo General de Indias, ES.41091.AGI/16418.9//MP-ESTAMPAS, 1)

in their defiance. Having earlier witnessed Spanish military power at Pecos and the Rio Grande pueblos, they refused. Instead, they adopted a wait-and-see posture should the Acomans be successful.

Meanwhile, Oñate planned to explore westward to the Pacific Ocean to find a harbor from which to supply New Mexico. Following the Rio Grande southward from San Juan de los Caballeros to Santo Domingo Pueblo, the Spaniards traded Spanish goods with the pueblos. Eastward from Santo Domingo, Oñate visited Galisteo on his way south to Salinas, where salt beds were located near present Willard, New Mexico. It was mid-October when Oñate and his men left the Manzano Mountain pueblos through the pass he called El Portuelo, later named Abó Pass. They crossed the Rio Grande at Isleta, where they traded for more supplies, and headed west. At Acoma, they stopped to trade for food with the resentful residents, who watched their food supply dwindle as winter approached.

Hoping to kill Oñate, the Acomans invited him to their pueblo atop the *peñol* some 220 feet high. Oñate and some of his men made the difficult climb by using foot holes carved into the rock. Against the better judgment of others among them, some of the warriors planned to isolate Oñate and kill him. When they invited the Spanish governor into one of their kivas, he declined. They tried to persuade him to enter another one, saying that he would see something wonderful inside. Looking into the dark kiva, the wary Oñate sensed a trap, while his men urged him not to go inside. In the kiva, armed warriors waited to kill him the moment he stepped into it.

Before departing Acoma, Oñate sent a rider with a message for his nephew Juan to join the expedition to the Pacific. Although some Acomans were relieved to see Oñate go, others argued that it was necessary to drive the Spaniards out, warning that if they did not attack the Spaniards, the pueblo would surely be destroyed. Confident of victory, the warmongers argued that they had much to gain. The decision to attack the Spaniards caused much debate among the Acomans. As Oñate and his men marched away, the Acomans looked on with mixed opinions. They would wait for another opportunity.

Oñate reached Zuni and waited for Juan to join his force. Oñate wondered about Juan's delay and sent scouts out from his camp to determine his whereabouts. Shortly, he moved the expedition to Tusayán to wait for him. Still no word from Zaldívar. As the fall weather turned colder, Oñate, still at Tusayán, decided to return to San Juan for the Christmas holiday.

Moving westward to El Morro, Oñate and his men were overtaken by a heavy snowstorm in which they lost many horses. While they were camped near El Morro, hard-riding Spaniards from Zaldívar's command arrived from Acoma to tell him that his nephew and others had been killed in an ambush. A grieving Oñate led the expedition back to San Juan. There he would learn more of the details regarding the fight at Acoma and would make a momentous decision that would affect Spanish-Indian relations in New Mexico for the rest of the colonial period.

Survivors of the ambush at Acoma told Oñate that while Juan de Zaldívar and his men were camped at the bottom of the mesa at Acoma, some warriors came down and invited them to visit their pueblo. While Zaldívar and most of his men climbed the "stone ladders" to the top, other Spaniards stayed below to guard the camp and horses. As usual, Zaldívar and his men began to trade for food. This time, however, the warriors had devised a plan to divide the Spaniards. The Acomans fell on them, killing Zaldívar and twelve others and throwing their bodies over the escarpment. Helpless to come to their aid, the guard at the bottom could only watch as three men, in desperation, jumped from the cliff; one other died as he plummeted from the pueblo's edge. Having attended the wounded, Zaldívar's men split into three groups. One group went to San Juan to warn the settlers, another rushed to warn the friars at the missions, and the third party hastened to report the attack to Oñate.

While Acoma celebrated its victory, the settlers at San Juan struggled with an uncertain future. Gripped in fear, the Spanish settlers at San Juan believed that Acoma's success could signal a rebellion of all the pueblos. Upon their arrival in San Juan, Oñate and his men found the settlement heavily guarded. As the settlers mourned the dead soldiers, Oñate called a council of war. Those who had been with Juan de Zaldívar at Acoma told their side of the story. The members of the council of war recognized that prompt action should be taken to show Acoma and the other pueblos that defiance of Spanish authority would not be tolerated. From a military perspective, the Spaniards knew they could not permit Acoma to get away with the attack, lest the other pueblos interpret Spanish inaction as a sign of weakness. During the council of war, Oñate consulted his captains and the friars about the best course of action. All agreed that Acoma be made an object lesson if the Spanish settlement at San Juan was to survive. One priest wrote that "peace was the principal end for which war was ordained." They urged Oñate to attack Acoma in order to reestablish peace and control.

Oñate had planned to command the seventy troops along with their Mexican Indian allies. However, Sargento Mayor Vicente de Zaldívar, whose brother had been slain at Acoma, claimed the right to lead the punitive expedition. Most of the troops agreed that he had the right to avenge his loss. Oñate agreed and gave him instructions to proceed to Acoma, "plant your artillery and musketry," and deploy the troops in "battle formation." That done, Zaldívar, with the aid of Mexican Indians, particularly Tomás, Cristóbal, and other suitable interpreters, must "summon the Indians of Acoma to accept peace, once, twice and thrice, and urge them to abandon their resistance, lay down their arms, and submit to the authority of the king, our lord, since they have already rendered obedience to him as his vassals." Dipping a quill in ink, Oñate signed the instructions to Zaldívar before his secretary, who notarized the document.

As instructed, Zaldívar approached Acoma and demanded that the residents "surrender the leaders responsible for the uprisings, and the murders." He assured them that they would "be justly dealt with." Zaldívar also demanded that the bodies of the dead Spaniards, along with their belongings, be returned. Zaldívar considered that if the Acomans resisted, he would decide whether to attack them or postpone the fight. The attack, furthermore, would be called off if the Indian strength was too great. Under that circumstance, Oñate had counseled, Zaldívar should call off the attack "for there would be less harm in postponing the punishment for the time being than in risking the people with you." If the Acomans wanted a fight, Zaldívar and his men were ready. Oñate's instructions to Zaldívar were clear. "Inasmuch," he ordered, "as we have declared war on them without quarter, you will punish all those of fighting age as you deem best, as a warning to everyone in this kingdom." Zaldívar's orders countenanced the possibility that the Indians would surrender those responsible for the attack. In that case, he was instructed to call for restraint in punishing Acoma. Still, the possibility of a war of "fire and sword" was an option if the Acomans refused to meet Spanish demands.

When on January 21, 1599, Zaldívar and his troops arrived below the mesa, the defiant warriors looked down from the mighty pueblo and greeted them with taunts, jeers, insults, and obscene gestures. With an odd calm, Vicente de Zaldívar deployed his men and artillery. Experienced in siege warfare, his scouts identified the best point for the assault on Acoma. Standing around a campfire on that cold day, Zaldívar and his men formulated a plan. The main force would feign an assault on one side of the pueblo by climbing up the main ladders. Meanwhile a detail of men would pull up a cannon to the rear of the pueblo. Once in position at each end of the pueblo, they would catch the warriors in a crossfire.

Before ordering the attack, Zaldívar and his interpreters would, as instructed, offer the prescribed peace gestures, "once, twice and thrice."

Despite pleas from some of their leaders, the leading warriors rejected Zaldívar's peace offerings. They made their intentions to fight known by jeering, shooting arrows, hurling wooden spears, and throwing rocks at the Spaniards. That freezing night, the Spaniards, trying to keep warm, camped below the pueblo and rested. The Indians, meanwhile, spent the night "in huge dances and carousals, shouting, hissing . . . and challenging the army to fight." The Spaniards reported that "the Indians all shouted loudly, raised their swords on high, and presented themselves in the coats of mail and other pieces of equipment they had taken from the dead Spaniards, boasting that they had killed ten Spaniards and two Mexicans, and that we were a pack of mongrels and whore mongers." Defiantly, the Indians kept shouting they wanted to fight. They shouted, as Zaldívar's translators told him, "why were we waiting, and why we did not fight, since they were ready for battle and were waiting for nothing but to kill us and then kill the Queres and the Tiguas and everyone at Zia because they failed to kill the Spaniards."

On January 22, about three o'clock in the afternoon, Zaldívar ordered the attack. Preparations had begun under cover of darkness the previous night when twelve Spaniards dragged the small cannon around to the rear of the mesa and hid themselves. When the attack began, the main body of troops climbed up the escarpment as planned. Turning their attention to them, the Acomans left the rear of the pueblo unprotected. Moving quickly, the twelve Spaniards reached the top, positioned the cannon and proceeded into the pueblo. Meanwhile, Zaldívar saw a warrior wearing his brother's uniform. The *sargento mayor* fought his way toward the Indian and killed him with his sword. Night ended the first day's battle at Acoma. Although many Acomans surrendered, a large body of warriors had hidden in the chasms of the mesa.

The second day of battle continued from early morning until five o'clock that afternoon. Zaldívar asked them to surrender. The warriors refused and the battle continued. In the midst of the fight, Zaldívar ordered that "all Indian women and children who could be found should be taken prisoners to save them from being killed by the Indian warriors." About five hundred young and old men and women were taken for that purpose. The warriors preferred that their women and children be killed than be taken prisoners by the Spaniards. Seeking to end the battle, Zaldívar ordered his men to proceed without quarter. They set all of the houses and provisions on fire. That day, Spanish arms and assault tactics overpowered the courageous and most feared warriors from Acoma. The fall of Acoma shook its inhabitants, but did not break them. Most of them escaped and returned to rebuild their pueblo. Undaunted, they continued to defy the Spaniards and challenged other pueblos to resist them. Later, in 1613, the warriors drove off a Spanish force that threatened to attack the pueblo.

Zaldívar and his force having subdued Acoma, on January 23, 1599, they took their captives to Santo Domingo Pueblo for trial. Under Spanish law, the captives had a legal status. Captain Alonso Gómez Montesinos was appointed as their attorney and guardian. On February 9, the Spanish settlers gathered to hear the testimony of those who had taken part in the battle of Acoma. Statements were taken from captured Acoman warriors. The next day, Captain Gómez Montesinos presented a petition to Oñate on behalf of the Acomans. He declared that some of those captured were not guilty, as they had been away from the pueblo when Juan de Zaldívar and his men were killed. Gómez Montesinos pleaded that they be set free. He also pleaded for others who were accused of killing the Spaniards in the ambush at Acoma. In the context of the times, Gómez Montesinos had competently pleaded the case, expressing, albeit in colonial terms, his compassion for the Acomans.

Other pleas for clemency were made by some of the settlers. After the three-day trial at Santo Domingo came to an end, Oñate read out the harsh sentence for the Acomans for "having wantonly killed Don Juan de Zaldívar Oñate" and twelve others and for having refused the peace offered them by Vicente de Zaldívar. "I must and do sentence," he pronounced, "all of the Indian men and women from the said pueblo under arrest." Boys and girls under twelve years of age whose parents were involved in fighting against the Spaniards were placed under the guardianship of the missionaries. Of them, those between twelve and twenty-five years of age were sentenced to twenty years of servitude. The elderly men and women were freed but entrusted to the Querechos, Indians from the Great Plains, who "may not allow them to leave their pueblos." Governor Oñate ordered that twenty-four of those responsible for the murder of Juan de Zaldívar, and the other Spaniards who were with him, would each be severely punished by having a foot cut off. Although the sentence was to be carried out on twenty-four Acoma males at Santo Domingo and at other nearby pueblos on separate days, no record or mention of the execution of the sentence was made to verify whether it actually occurred. Nevertheless, upon hearing the severe sentences, some colonials not only helped some of the convicted Indians to escape but also brought charges against Governor Oñate and Vicente de Zaldívar in 1613 for their excesses at Acoma and for other cases of abuse toward Spanish settlers. By then, Oñate and Zaldívar had been gone from New Mexico for several years. Still, they were found guilty, heavily fined, and not allowed to return to New Mexico. They lost all of their landholdings and investments in the conquest and settlement of New Mexico—a heavy price for a colonial to pay. To Oñate and Zaldívar, however, the swift and severe punishment of Acoma had evidently served its purpose. In time, other Indians defied Spanish rule in New Mexico. The legacy of the Battle of Acoma was not deterrent enough.

Oñate's tenure in New Mexico, however, was successful in other endeavors. Sometime in 1599, Governor Oñate moved the capital of New Mexico from San Juan de los Caballeros to San Gabriel, closer to the confluence of the Rio Grande and the Río Chama. Significantly, the *cabildo*, or town council, was created as the basic unit of government, first at San Juan in 1598, then transferred to San Gabriel in 1599. When Santa Fe was established as the new capital in 1610, the cabildo was moved there. During the Mexican period (1821–46), the cabildo became the *ayuntamiento de Santa Fe*, then reformed as the *asamblea del Departamento de Nuevo Mexico*. During the U.S. territorial period, the asamblea became the Territorial Legislative Assembly, and after statehood, in modern times, the New Mexico State Legislature became known popularly as the "Round House." During Governor Oñate's period, the cabildo comprised elected and appointed officials. Thus, the cabildo at San Agustín, Florida, established in 1571, and the cabildo of New Mexico predated the Virginia House of Burgesses (1619) and the New England town council (1620) by a number of years. Likewise, the cabildos in Puerto Rico (1497), Havana (1518), and Mexico City (1525) far predated them.

Further exploration of the area occupied Governor Oñate and his settlers. From 1600 to 1604, Oñate ordered other explorations of the Great Plains as far as the Great Bend of the Arkansas River. In October 1604, he took up his old dream of exploring to the Pacific Coast. On that expedition, Oñate and his men found no mines, saw no gold or silver, and, once on the Colorado River in western Arizona, located no pearl fisheries as he had hoped. Disappointed, he turned back to San Gabriel. On passing El Morro (Inscription Rock), he paused long enough to leave a message for posterity. The inscription reads: "Pasó por aquí el Adelantado don Juan de Oñate del descubrimiento de la mar del sur a 16 dia del Abril año 1605" (The Adelantado don Juan de Oñate passed by here from the discovery of the South Sea, on the 16th day of April 1605). In New Mexico literature, the words *pasó por aquí* came to represent the metaphorical idea that humanity since the beginning of time has and continues to pass by here. Many other inscriptions at El Morro repeat those words. The waterhole at El Morro has hosted Indian, Spanish, and Anglo-American travelers over the centuries. Since Oñate, some three thousand historical signatories have passed by there, not counting those who did not sign their names on the rock.

The early explorers of New Mexico left behind a heritage in creating a body of literature in which the earliest descriptions of people and land were written and sometimes published. Indeed, Spanish frontiersmen often commented that they "read it in a book." The three reports, *La Relación (The Account), Naufragios (Shipwrecks),* and *Comentarios (Commentaries)* of Álvar Núñez Cabeza de Vaca were widely known. In 1539, Gonzalo de Fernández de Oviedo y Valdés incorporated them into his *Historia General y Natural de las indias, islas y Tierra-Firme del Mar Océano.* Other early sources included the many documents, diaries, and pieces of correspondence left by Vázquez de Coronado, Pedro de Castañeda's "Relación de la jornada de Cíbola" (1596), and accounts of the Sánchez Chamuscado and Espejo expeditions that were read by officials in the viceroy's archive. Portions of some of them were copied in reports to the Council of the Indies. In 1610, one of Oñate's officers, Gaspar Pérez de Villagrá, published *Historia de la Nueva México,* which recounted the route and events of the founding expedition to New Mexico and the first year of settlement ending with the Acoma war.

If explorers pointed the way to New Mexico between 1535 and 1593, the Oñate period in New Mexico (1598–1609) set the pattern for the effective Hispanic settlement of the province. Oñate and his settlers established a significant portion of the Camino Real de Tierra Adentro from Mexico City to San Juan de los Caballeros and San Gabriel. In 1610, Santa Fe, the new capital, became the terminus of the trail for the rest of the Spanish colonial period. Missionization of the pueblos began in earnest during the Oñate period and ran its course to the end of the colonial period. Governor Oñate's establishment of San Juan de los Caballeros and San Gabriel had, indeed, changed the course of history for the tierra adentro.

CHAPTER 3

Spanish Bureaucrats, Settlers, Soldiers, and Missionaries, 1598–1821

As soon as he may have arrived in the said provinces he shall inform himself of the state of the settlements there, endeavoring before all else to put into execution the founding and settlement of the Villa [Santa Fe] which it is intended and ordered to be made there so that they may commence to be and live with some system and permanence.

VICEREGAL INSTRUCTIONS TO GOVERNOR PEDRO DE PERALTA, 1609

NEW MEXICO'S HISTORICAL PERIOD began with explorers searching for rich civilizations. Following them came Hispanic frontiersmen seeking trade and arable land for settlement. During the period 1598–1680, as they established themselves among the Indian pueblos existing since pre-Columbian times, these settlers established the essential nucleus of colonial-period New Mexico. Then the Pueblo Revolt drove the Hispanic settlers out, and New Mexico became autonomous Indian territory for roughly a decade. From 1692 to 1821, exploration and settlement continued as settlers expanded westward from the Rio Grande and northwestward from Santa Fe to western Colorado. In this time they explored as far northwest as the Great Salt Lake of present-day Utah. By the second decade of the nineteenth century the province of New Mexico claimed land as far north as the Yellowstone River. Some New Mexicans had settled the Denver-Loveland area. Others chose to seek their fortunes on the Santa Fe Trail and headed toward the Missouri and Mississippi rivers.

Settlement was the dominant theme of the period from 1598 to 1680, the first phase of Spanish occupation and mission building in New Mexico. The establishment of towns and farms, structures of governance, a Spanish legal system, and a colonial culture developed at a

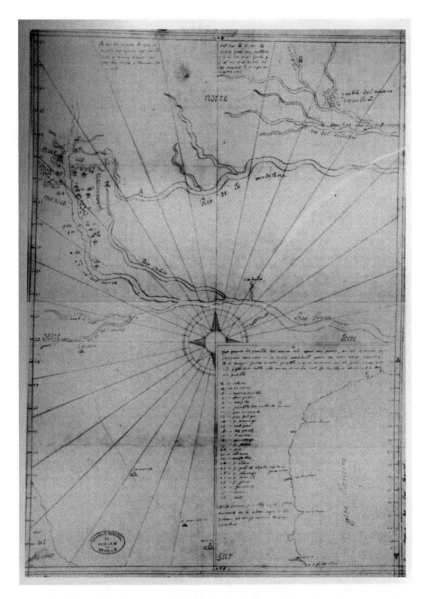

The province of New Mexico, as mapped by Enrico Martínez circa 1600.
("Mapa del Nuevo Mexico c. 1600," in AGI, Mapas y Planos, ES.41091.
AGI / 16418.17 / / MP.Mexico, 49)

pace that surprised Native groups. From the days of Governor Juan de Oñate on, New Mexico was governed in accordance with the laws of Spain. In the Americas, the Laws of the Indies (Recopilación de las leyes de los Reynos de las Indias), a compilation of applicable laws, royal decrees, and ordinances, was mandated as a guide for governing the New World. In accordance with the Laws of the Indies, each province, called a kingdom (*reyno*) or a province (*provincia*), had a governor to oversee executive, legislative, and judicial functions. Initially, the governor bore the title of captain general and commanded the military within his province. Later, when the Comandancia General de las Provincias Internas was organized in 1776, it established a separate military jurisdiction that reported directly to the viceroy. Among the governor's powers, he executed laws and policies, served as chief magistrate, approved and gave land grants, appointed officials to the cabildo (town council) or other offices, and handled Indian affairs.

By the time of the U.S. annexation of New Mexico following the Mexican War, more than three hundred land grants existed, the majority having been conferred by the governor in the name of the Spanish king. These large tracts of land were granted to individuals, families, or communities for the purpose of settlement and development of territories in colonized areas of the empire. Under contract the grantees were obligated to use the land for a stated purpose, most commonly for farming and raising small herds of livestock but sometimes solely for ranching or raising horses or mules. In all cases the Laws of the Indies required that settlements be located near water, pasturage, and wooded areas. The people were charged with caring for the land as stewards, thus inaugurating a concern for the environment and sustainable use for future generations.

The modern legacy of the land grants is that the farming communities on former grant lands serve as cultural enclaves preserving Spanish colonial-period linguistics, religion, law, literature, local political organization, and lore of seventeenth-century Spain. *Dichos* (proverbs), folktales, medicinal cures, husbandry, dances, and songs or ballads were among the cultural activities that persisted and evolved throughout the subsequent Mexican territorial and Anglo-American occupations. Sustainability is a part of that legacy, for the network of *acequias* (irrigation ditches) that exist today, along with the practices for administering them, date from that period. The descendants of land grant families continue to preserve the values born in Spain and modified in the theater of the Spanish colonial and Mexican territorial periods. Today, despite the passage of time, that tie remains relatively unbroken.

Overall, a top-down administration oversaw the daily or occasional events in the towns and countryside. The chain of command ran from the king of Spain in Madrid to the viceroy in Mexico City to the provincial governor of New Mexico. In time, the provinces were divided into *alcaldías mayores,* jurisdictions akin to modern counties. An *alcalde mayor* was either appointed by the governor or elected by the cabildo to serve as the head administrative officer of each alcaldía, reporting to the governor. *Alcaldes mayores de indios* were appointed by the governor to oversee the political business of Indian pueblos. Each governed a large Indian district, such as the Jurisdicción de las Salinas behind the Manzano Mountains. Today its history and heritage are interpreted and preserved at Salinas Pueblo Mission National Monument in Mountainair, New Mexico. Whether in Spanish towns or Indian pueblos, the alcaldes managed ordinary civil and criminal matters, and together with the provincial *alguacil* (sheriff), also appointed by the governor, were the chief law enforcement officials in their territories. The alcaldes, furthermore, carried out economic and political policies set by the governor and the cabildo. In larger or more important towns, a municipal council called the cabildo or, in the late Spanish colonial and Mexican periods, the *ayuntamiento,* ruled the citizens. Large towns had one or more *alcaldes ordinarios* who exercised the same functions in their municipality as the *alcalde mayor* in the larger districts. Smaller towns and villages did not have a cabildo but did have an alcalde ordinario who served as magistrate.

Sometime about 1605, Juan de Oñate apparently approved the establishment of an outpost called San Francisco de Santa Fe, Real Campo de Españoles (the Royal Spanish Outpost of Saint Francis of the Holy Faith). Juan Martínez de Montoya led a group of settlers south from San Gabriel (near the confluence of the Rio Grande and Río Chama) to set up an encampment. Over time, the location of Martínez de Montoya's outpost became blurred, but Spanish colonial chroniclers, including Friar Alonso de Benavides in 1626, equated it with the Spanish capital of New Mexico: Santa Fe. The official founding of Santa Fe did not, however, occur until 1610.

Meanwhile, Juan de Oñate, seeing that his fortunes were waning, and having been exiled by the viceroy for his harsh treatment of settlers and Indians, resigned as governor of New Mexico. Simultaneously the Spanish crown decided to take the New Mexico province under its royal wing, and Don Pedro de Peralta was appointed governor and captain general of the province. On March 30, 1609, Viceroy Luis de Velasco handed Don Pedro instructions to follow in establishing his administration as royal governor and in strengthening defenses within his jurisdiction. The viceroy also authorized Peralta to establish a new villa that would serve as New Mexico's capital. At that time the viceroy did not mention the existence of any town named Santa Fe, instead identifying the main settlements as being in the San Juan de los Caballeros–San Gabriel area. Upon receipt of his orders, Peralta organized his expedition and departed Mexico City sometime that summer. With Peralta and his soldiers were Fray Alonso Peinado, the new *padre comisario* (father commissary) of the missions, and eight friars. The caravan—numbering at least thirty carretas, a large herd of livestock, servants, teamsters, and a mounted escort—traveled north on the trail to Nuevo México.

Once in New Mexico, Peralta quickly acted to found the Villa de Santa Fe and move the settlers there from San Gabriel. Another of his instructions was to take measures to protect the pueblos and the villa from the Apaches and Navajos, a provision which prohibited exploration and trade on the Great Plains. To that end, Peralta hoped to concentrate the Spanish population at Santa Fe and likewise move the Pueblo Indians into fewer and larger towns for their protection. Before Peralta could establish his governorship on a sound footing, he found himself embroiled in a conflict with the Franciscans over the administration of the pueblos, a quarrel that continued under succeeding governors as well. The missionaries had hoped to establish New Mexico as a mission frontier. Settlements had taken root on the Rio Grande and along the Santa Fe River, and Peralta's administration stood in the way of expanding the mission programs. The Franciscans wanted a free hand to convert the pueblos, establishing missions that would be exempt from taxation; the governors, for their part, demanded their right to collect the annual tribute called the *encomienda* in return for Spanish men-at-arms protecting the pueblos against Apaches, Navajos, and other raiding tribes. If this tax in the form of bushels of corn or blankets for trade could not be paid, the value of the amount due would be converted to service or labor under the *repartimiento*. Both institutions were throwbacks to feudal Europe where lords collected tribute from their serfs or converted the debt to labor. In either case, labor was taken from Indian villages and used for public works or personal service. Spanish settlers also paid a yearly tax called the *diezmo,* one-tenth of their crops, mainly paid in wheat seeds. The diezmo was allocated to support the missionaries and the churches. Miners paid the *quinto real* (royal fifth), which was a tax payable to the crown and equal to one-fifth the value of extracted mineral wealth. The missionaries argued that the encomienda and repartimiento system interfered with the missionizing process.

The New Mexico mission field was named the Conversión de San Pablo in honor of the conversion of St. Peter, which in the colonial church calendar was celebrated on January 25. They adopted St. Peter as their patron because many incidents associated with him had occurred in New Mexico's brief but already full history. The religious conversion of New Mexico began when Governor Oñate visited all the pueblos in 1598 and assigned friars to them. Deep in the Manzano Mountains Padre Comisario Alonso Peinado began working as the sole friar among the Tiwas at Chililí in 1613. Indeed Fray Alonso heavily influenced the pattern of the mission field in New Mexico, expanding the *doctrinas* by assigning priests to work in areas rarely visited by missionaries. Under Friar Peinado, the incipient stage of mission expansion extended down the Rio Grande to Sandía Pueblo. In 1612, travelers passing Sandía Pueblo noted that it was the "primer convento de este Nuevo México" (the first mission residence one comes to in New Mexico). In late 1612 or early 1613, Fray Juan de Salas founded the mission at Isleta, which replaced Sandía as the southernmost mission. Salas remained there until 1630, over which time Isleta continued to grow in importance as a stopping place for weary travelers coming from Mexico or departing New Mexico along the Camino

Real de Tierra Adentro. By the time Friar Estevan Perea took over as padre custodio of the New Mexican mission field in 1617, Franciscan friars were scattered over a large area along the Rio Grande from San Ildefonso in the north to Isleta in the south, and from Jemez in the west to Galisteo in the east. Perea intensified his predecessors' efforts such that by the time of his death in 1638 the conversion of New Mexico's pueblos was in full bloom. Before mid-century, Isleta surrendered the title of southernmost mission to Senecú, near Socorro.

With the supply caravan of 1626, Fray Alonso de Benavides arrived with twelve other missionaries, bringing the number of friars in the Conversión de San Pablo to twenty-six. Benavides's arrival signaled a new beginning for the New Mexican missions. As custodian, he worked tirelessly to convert more Indians and expand the mission field. At the time of his arrival, Chililí, Tajique, Las Humanas, Quaraí, and Abó already had missionaries who had been working in their midst since the early 1620s. The padre comisario reported that "fourteen or fifteen pueblos in the area, which must have more than ten thousand souls," were being served by friars who were working to establish "six very good convents and churches" among them.

From a modern perspective, Benavides is more significant in New Mexico's history for his prolific quill, which made him one of its most prominent chroniclers. His magnum opus, the *Memorial of 1630,* was written as a report to the king, exalting the prospects for the province of New Mexico. The viceroy, the archbishop, and other church officials in Mexico City encouraged Benavides in his promotion of New Mexico. It suited the state's objectives concerning the pacification of the northern frontier and it dovetailed with the church's quest to save souls and spread the gospel. Before the seventeenth century was out, his *Memorial of 1630* and the revised version of 1634 had been published in at least five languages.

From 1626 to 1629, Fray Benavides also served as prelate and agent of the Holy Office of the Inquisition in New Mexico, responsible for ensuring strict Catholic orthodoxy among the settlers. In that capacity, he pursued cases against Spanish settlers for crimes against the church, such as superstition, witchcraft, and demonology. Established in Spain in 1478 and in the West Indies in 1520, the Holy Office of the Inquisition was

Spain's attempt to strengthen Catholicism in the face of the rising threat of Protestant heresy and the ongoing presence of Jewish and Islamic minorities in the country. The Inquisition in fact continued in Spain and the empire for centuries until its abolition in 1820.

Indians were exempt from the Inquisition's power because they were as yet imperfectly converted to Catholicism and thus not part of the congregation. Although religious conformity was their goal, the friars realized that the conversion of Indians to Christianity was often imperfect, as often they continued to practice their spiritual ways in their pueblos. In his glowing account of successful conversions, Benavides omitted a crucial perspective, that of the anti-Spanish Indians throughout the pueblos. The Pueblo Indians viewed Spanish colonial institutions, both religious and civil, as a threat to their cultures. They often expressed this view as a rejection of the missionaries. When passive resistance failed, the Indians turned to coordinated, armed rebellion. Less than a century after missionization began, a coalition of pueblos succeeded in overthrowing the colonial regime, driving the Spaniards out for more than a decade.

In the interim, however, Benavides worked hard to expand the missions to the rest of the frontier pueblos and to put the existing ones on better footing. The *Memorial of 1630* indicates that as of 1628 twenty-five missions served the pueblos, with one or two friars and several Indian assistants at each one. Of Santa Fe, Fray Alonso mentioned that 250 Spanish families lived there. His figures accounted for nearly 1,500 settlers within the jurisdiction of the villa, including those who lived in the many haciendas and ranches already established within the province. Settlers tended to own two houses, one in Santa Fe and another wherever their ranch or farm was located. As yet, there were no Spanish towns other than Santa Fe, where the majority of Spaniards lived, although settlers had begun to expand into the large valley along the Sandia/Manzano Mountains. Spanish settlements stretched from Taos in the north to Socorro in the south. Santo Domingo, south of Santa Fe, served as the ecclesiastical headquarters of New Mexico and directed the expansion of missions and the pacification of tribes.

Of all the pueblos Benavides visited, the Salinas pueblos seemed to tantalize his fertile imagination the most. Showing their supreme indifference to Indian cultures, the Spaniards referred to these people as Jumanos, lumping them together with the Caddoan-speaking Wichitas and at least one other distinct Indian group. Perhaps Benavides felt a close affinity to the people of Salinas because they had little prior experience of indoctrination. It was he who could claim the conversion of one of their principal pueblos, Las Humanas, a place-name denoting where the Jumanos came to trade and sometimes live among their pueblo friends. The present-day ruins are known as Gran Quivira, a unit of Salinas Pueblo Mission National Monument, located in Mountainair, New Mexico.

Another aspect of the Jumanos in which Benavides took a great interest concerned the appearance of María de Jesús de la Concepción, a mystic nun of the order of St. Francis from Agreda in the Spanish province of Burgos. The investigation of this mystery took up much of Benavides's time and involved a great deal of travel. The story goes that María de Agreda "miraculously bilocated" herself from her convent in Spain to New Mexico to preach to the Indians. Mysteriously appearing to the Jumanos on the edge of the plains as a Lady in Blue, she had inspired them to convert. The story of the apparition of the Lady in Blue first surfaced when Jumanos from the plains crossed the large mountain east of the Rio Grande to Isleta Pueblo on the Abajo River. For several summers, they reportedly returned annually to "beg" Fray Juan de Salas to visit their land and baptize them.

When thirty new friars arrived in New Mexico in 1629, they bore a missive to Benavides from the archbishop of Mexico, authorizing him to undertake an inquiry into the apparition, which by now "was common news in Spain." Until Benavides saw the letter, he had never thought to ask the Indians why they sought conversion. Dazzled by the contents, Benavides said he thought that the Jumanos' plea "for friars to go and baptize them must have been through inspiration from heaven." Shortly after receiving the letter, Benavides noted that, four days sooner than in previous years, the Jumanos had returned to Isleta to make their request.

This time Benavides asked them about their request for baptism. Gazing at a portrait of Mother Luisa in the convent at Isleta Pueblo, they said, "A woman in similar garb wanders among us over there, always preaching, but her face is not old like this, but young." When asked why they had never before mentioned it, they answered, "Because you did not ask us, and we thought she was around here, too." Dumbfounded, Benavides sought to verify the story.

Soon thereafter, Fray Juan de Salas and Fray Diego López, led by the Jumanos, departed Isleta bound for the plains of New Mexico and Texas. The priests had no idea where they were going. They traveled for many days across the buffalo plains, past the land of the brave Apache *vaqueros*, to Jumano country. When they reached the Jumano *rancherías*, the people came out "in procession carrying a large cross and garlands of flowers." From them, the priests learned that the nun in blue had taught them about the cross, had helped them decorate it, and had even instructed them on the processional march. After spending several days among the Jumanos and other tribes, instructing them in the catechism and in prayer, the friars set up a large cross and, promising to return, departed the ranchería for Isleta to report to Benavides.

Benavides returned to Spain, where he received permission to visit Mother María de Jesús, abbess of the convento of La Purísima Concepción at Agreda, which he did on the last day of April 1631. Friar Benavides was impressed with the Lady in Blue, who reported that her transportations to New Mexico "by angels" took place "from the year 1620 to the present year, 1631." She told Fray Alonso "all we know that has happened to our brothers and fathers, Fray Juan de Salas and Fray Diego López, in their journeys to the Jumanos, and confirmed" that she had asked them "to go and call the priests, which they did." Perhaps Benavides asked leading questions, but he was able to get detailed descriptions of the priests and Indians she claimed to know. "She told me so many details of this country that I did not even remember them myself, and she brought them back to my mind," he wrote. She told Benavides that "she had been present with [him] at the baptism at the Piros . . . [and] had helped Father Cristóbal Quirós with some baptisms, giving a minute description of his person and face." Astounded, Benavides was convinced that Mother María de Jesús was gifted with powers of bilocation, and that indeed she had often visited the Jumanos.

The story of the Lady in Blue fit perfectly with Benavides's promotion of New Mexico as a mission field. Impressed by Benavides's reports, his superiors pledged renewed support for new missions in the province. Under him, special attention had been given to the Tewa, Manzano, Tiwa, and Tompiro pueblos. Friar Benavides also encouraged the resumption of work in the Jemez area, where the Pueblo de la Congregación de San Diego was reestablished. New missions were founded among the Piro and at Acoma, Zuni, and Hopi as the Franciscans spread their influence throughout New Mexico after Benavides's tenure.

In the seventeenth century, the history of colonial New Mexico was largely one of church-state conflicts. The disputes were fundamentally between missionization and economic policies of colonialism. In the 1640s and 1650s, discord among governors and missionaries became apparent, largely over who would control the Pueblo Indians for religious conversion or civilian purposes under prevailing Indian policies. The Franciscans used the Holy Office of the Inquisition as a political weapon against New Mexico governors to discipline them and thwart their opposition to missionary efforts. Missionaries wanted sole control to convert the Pueblos without interference from civil authorities. The governors, on the other hand, wanted a free hand to collect tribute (encomienda), employ Indians under the repartimiento laws, or use them as allies against raiding Apache, Navajo, Ute, and later Comanche warriors who attacked pueblos and Spanish settlements. Each charged the other with abuse and exploitation of the Pueblos and other friendly Indians. Witnessing the discord and division among missionaries and civil authorities, many of the pueblos became increasingly restless. Indian rebellions occurred throughout the period, but they were small and easily quelled by Spanish militia. As for the Pueblo Indians, decades would pass before they could muster their forces for a successful revolt in 1680.

Several factors led to the Pueblo Revolt. The oppressive colonial regime enforced the yearly tribute of the encomienda and forced labor under the repartimiento; although by law workers had to be paid, abuses were common. Meanwhile, the power struggle between Franciscan missionaries and the civil government created disunity in the colony, causing dissension among the Spanish settlers, who were forced to choose sides.

Meanwhile, the Indians witnessed the squabbles and sometimes encouraged them by reporting abuses to one side or the other. They used the Inquisition to testify against settlers and governors that the missionaries accused of religious infractions, while resisting conversion efforts in their pueblos. The fight between governors and priests ran deep. Many governors were ousted from New Mexico. Others were sent in chains to Mexico City for trial by the Inquisition.

By the mid-1600s, Pueblo Indians were openly expressing their hostility to the colonial system imposed on them through military force. Spanish-Indian relationships were not exclusively antagonistic, however. In the eighty years since Oñate's establishment of New Mexico, intermarriages and religious kinships had been established. Friendships and social associations had been formed among Spanish frontiersmen and their Indian counterparts. But such relationships were not enough to soothe Indian resentment against the injustices of Spanish colonialism.

Some pueblos plotted with the Apaches to drive out the Spaniards, but most of these plans were discovered before they happened. In many cases, Indian relatives or friends told their Spanish kin about the planned insurrection. In 1675, Spanish officials quelled a rebellion in San Juan, hanging three conspirators and imprisoning forty others. Escaping prosecution, one of the leaders, Popé, fled to Taos and resumed plotting. Even though his accomplices swore not to reveal the plan under penalty of death, two days before the revolt, informants from Taos, Galisteo, and Pecos reported the impending trouble to Governor Antonio de Otermín. Nevertheless on Saturday, August 10, 1680, the feast day of San Lorenzo, the Indians unleashed their fury, killing as many Spanish farmers and their families as they could. Again, loyalties were not black and white: some Spanish families were spared because of their familial relationships with certain pueblos.

Spanish settlers along the Rio Grande south of Santa Fe fared better than their counterparts in the capital. More than 120 Spaniards were killed, but 1,500 escaped with the assistance of the lieutenant governor, Alonso García, who lived in the area. García sent messengers to Santa Fe, but none got through. He concluded that Santa Fe had fallen with no survivors. Similarly, when Governor Otermín's messages to García went unanswered, he assumed that the entire province had perished.

Meanwhile, settlers around Santa Fe fled to the capital and barricaded the town, besieged by Indian forces. By August 15, the Pueblos cut off the water supply to the acequia and gave Governor Otermín two choices, to be signified by a white or a red wooden cross. The white cross meant that Otermín would abandon the country forever and leave in peace; the red cross that the Spaniards intended to fight to the death, in which case all would be killed without mercy.

Otermín and his settlers decided to fight their way out. Facing starvation and thirst, they suddenly attacked the unprepared Pueblo warriors; 300 Indians were killed, 47 were captured, and an estimated 1,500 fled to the surrounding hills. For the Spaniards, the situation was still desperate. As they fled Santa Fe, they saw the havoc wreaked in the countryside by Pueblo and Apache warriors. Along their escape route toward the *bosque grande* (the large riparian forest of the Rio Grande between Bernalillo and Isleta), they witnessed desolated farms and many families who had been killed.

Otermín and his fellow refugees, numbering about a thousand men, women, and children, moved southward down the Rio Grande. For seventy miles, the Indians followed them to make sure they kept going. On passing present Las Cruces, Otermín saw fabulous spirals on a mountain and named them "Los Organos," the Organ Mountains. Beyond there lay El Paso del Norte, where they met up with the refugees under García. Otermín declared El Paso to be the official headquarters of New Mexico. Thus, El Paso served as New Mexico's fourth capital, from 1680 to 1692. There, the settlers recounted their experiences and mourned the nearly five hundred men, women, and children, along with twenty-one Franciscan missionaries, killed in the uprising.

The Pueblo Revolt of 1680 resulted in the displacement of New Mexican families to El Paso del Norte and towns farther south. Some families returned to New Mexico after the rebellion was quelled, others did not. At least twelve families with close ties to the pueblos did not flee New Mexico, but remained to live among their Indian relatives. From time to time between 1680 and 1690, Spanish officials in El Paso ordered sorties into New Mexico to gather information about the status of the revolt. Some expeditions reached Cochiti Pueblo, but determined that an effort to retake New Mexico was likely to fail. Meanwhile, officials in Mexico City viewed the rebellion with great concern, fearing that if they left it unpunished, they risked the danger of encouraging other revolts.

In 1690, the viceroy of Mexico appointed Diego de Vargas governor of New Mexico, with a mission to retake Santa Fe. Setting out from El Paso del Norte with three hundred men in August 1692, Vargas headed north to Santa Fe. By September 13, he and his army had surrounded the town and cut off its water supply and all communications. Vargas demanded that the Pueblo warriors surrender. By this time the alliances that had enabled the Indians to defeat the Spanish before had broken down, and the pueblos had suffered through a seven-year drought, leaving them in a far weaker position. Despite some blustering and threats, they surrendered before nightfall. Having retaken Santa Fe, Vargas toured the entire province, visiting pueblos from Taos in the north to Zuni and Hopi in the west. Although he touted the *reconquista* of New Mexico as bloodless, the reality was that Pueblo and Apache warriors resisted the Spanish return, and the people subsided into sullen acquiescence while awaiting better opportunities to rebel.

Aware that the peace was tenuous at best, Governor Vargas decided to bring nearly one thousand Spanish settlers north from El Paso to consolidate his position. After long delays, Vargas started north for the permanent reoccupation of New Mexico. By mid-December 1693, the colonists had arrived on the outskirts of Santa Fe, seemingly without opposition. When they tried to enter the town, however, the Indians refused to vacate it and forced the colonists to camp nearby. All were suffering from the bitter winter weather that swept down from the Sangre de Cristo Mountains. Vargas ordered his men to assault the town. Before the second day had ended, the Indians surrendered. Seeking to assert Spanish supremacy and instill fear in the recalcitrant Indians, Vargas executed many of the Native warriors as an object lesson.

Other rebellions flared up at the end of 1693 as the Pueblos attempted to shake off Spanish control before it could be reestablished. Most of the central and northern pueblos were in rebellion throughout the next year. Vargas used diplomacy, Pueblo allies, and increasingly severe force to keep them in check. In 1696, fourteen pueblos rose in another mighty rebellion, killing missionaries and Spanish settlers in a smaller-scale reenactment of the Pueblo Revolt. Taos, Picuris, Cochiti, Santo Domingo, Jemez, and Acoma were among the pueblos that led the revolt of 1696. Vargas responded quickly and harshly, putting down open revolt but leaving simmering resentment.

Governor Vargas realized that Pueblo sentiments were divided over continued rebellion. Prolonged resistance inevitably meant ongoing death and destruction. Many recognized that they would never rid themselves of the Spanish settlers and sought accommodation. As always, not all relationships were antagonistic for there were new intermarriages and friendships. Both Pueblo Indian and Spanish settlers were farmers who had more in common than their animosities. Still, the colonial regime stood in the way of a harmonious relationship. One of the positive outcomes of the Pueblo Revolt from the Indian perspective was that the encomienda and the repartimiento were not reinstituted in New Mexico and the Indians gained some freedom to preserve their social organization and cultural practices within their pueblos.

As the sentiments for rebellion quieted, Vargas saw the opportunity to reestablish the mission system in New Mexico. By the end of 1694, the missionaries were able to establish mission programs in nearly eighteen pueblos, and missionization proceeded steadily. When Bishop Tamarón visited New Mexico in 1760, he confirmed that more than 14,000 Christian Indians lived there, inclusive of those in the El Paso mission district. Still, long-standing bitter feelings between the missionaries and traditional Pueblo Indian elders and headmen did not go away. Franciscan missionaries struggled to overcome the power of these traditional leaders. Too, the missionaries remained adversarial to civil authority and became embroiled in arguments with Spanish officials over control of Indian jurisdictions.

Governor Vargas expanded the settlements along the Rio Grande from north to south. Three years after the start of the reconquista, Vargas authorized seventy families to establish the Villa of Santa Cruz de la Cañada, some thirty miles north of Santa Fe. Other towns were established at Bernalillo and Cerrillos, with farming communities at Angostura, Atrisco, Los Padillas, and other places. Vargas offered land grants to entice settlers to leave the security of Santa Fe and establish farms and ranches along the river. Because fear of the Apaches was deterring settlement of new lands, Vargas warred against Apache raiders and pursued them into the Sandia Mountains.

After Vargas's death in 1704, the new governor, Francisco Cuervo y Valdes, founded several other settlements. Among them was the Villa de San Francisco de Alburquerque, soon renamed San Felipe de Alburquerque in honor of the newly crowned King Philip and the viceroy the Duke of Alburquerque. With a slight spelling change, Albuquerque (modern local spelling and pronunciation without the first *r*) has grown today into the metropolitan center of the state of New Mexico. The eighteenth-century Villa de Alburquerque served as a center of governance with an ayuntamiento, a small garrison, and a church that attracted many settlers to the area. The town, however, offered little protection against Apache raiders who followed a plunder trail through Tijeras Canyon a short distance to the west in the Sandia Mountains. To deter raiding, a land grant was offered to anyone willing to settle the mouth of the canyon at Carnuel. In time other land grants with names like Alameda, Los Ranchos, Los Griegos, Los Candelarias, Los Poblanos, Corrales, Pajarito, Los Padillas, and Armijo dotted the entire valley from north to south. Surviving periodic raids and slowly beginning to thrive, many of these communities persisted intact into the twenty-first century.

Meanwhile, settlers petitioned the governor for greater protection for their families, lands, and livestock. Prior to the founding of Albuquerque, the Santa Fe garrison, numbering eighty men at full strength, was the only substantial military presence north of El Paso. Smaller units of five or six men, called *compañías volantes* (flying squadrons) because they were designed to be mobile, were stationed in places like Jemez, Laguna, Cochiti, and Santa Clara. For the most part settlers depended on civilian militias recruited from the various communities and on Pueblo Indian allies to secure their safety. Travelers on the Camino Real de Tierra Adentro between El Paso and Santa Fe took their chances against Apache raiders. After 1770, thirty soldiers were stationed at Robledo, at the southern end of the Jornada del Muerto north of El Paso.

Throughout the eighteenth century, the Apache threat loomed large along the Camino Real and in the many Hispanic villages that sprang up along it. To the west, Navajos often raided land grant communities east of the Sierra de Cebolleta (today's Mount Taylor) and on the west side of the Villa de Alburquerque. Settlers far to the north in the Española Valley feared raids by Utes, and, in the northeast, Comanches hit as far south as Pecos and Galisteo. By the 1790s both of those areas had seen significant population declines. Pecos, for example, had a population of nearly 2,000 in the seventeenth century; by 1760, the number had dropped to about 600; and by 1797, it had dwindled to 189 residents. In the context of the period, Spanish officials were essentially powerless to stop the Apache, Ute, Navajo, and Comanche hit-and-run tactics. Punitive expeditions of Spanish militia and Pueblo allies sallied forth annually to track down raiders, but often had little success against Natives who were adept at disappearing into rugged country.

At the start of the eighteenth century a new peril appeared on the eastern plains in the form of French traders selling weapons to Plains peoples bordering Spanish New Mexico. Having moved southward from the Canadian Great Lakes to Louisiana during the seventeenth century, the French began to eye Spanish Texas as a possible addition to the French Empire. In 1680, René-Robert Cavelier, Sieur de La Salle, attempted a settlement in eastern Texas. After he was murdered by his own men, the French outpost at Fort St. Louis fell prey to the Karankawas and other local Natives. A few survivors escaped toward the Spanish settlements in Coahuila south of the Rio Grande. Two of them, Jean L'Archevêque and Jacques Grolet, made their way to El Paso in 1693, where they joined Diego de Vargas and his settlers on their march to New Mexico. The murky French threat became more real in 1706, when Juan de Ulibarri, one of the founders of Alburquerque, led an expedition against the Utes and Comanches. At a place called El Cuartelejo in southern Colorado, he heard tales of Frenchmen among the Pawnees. Between 1719 and 1721, French traders under La Harpe traveled from Natchitoches in western Louisiana and reached Santa Fe.

To upset the growing French influence on the Great Plains, Governor Antonio Valverde led an expedition in 1719 against the Utes and Apaches along the Arkansas River and beyond as far as El Cuartelejo. There Apache informants told him that they had fought a battle with Pawnees who were equipped with French firearms and that Frenchmen were living among various Native groups along the Platte River.

In 1720, Valverde sent a second small expedition, numbering forty soldiers from Santa Fe, sixty Pueblo Indian allies, and a few others, under Captain Pedro Villasur. Among them was Jean L'Archevêque, who served as an interpreter. Villasur's orders were to spy on the French and report back on their activities. Marching northeastward as far as the junction of the North and South Platte in central Nebraska, Villasur failed to locate any French traders. On the morning of August 13, as Villasur and his men were breaking camp to return to New Mexico, a large Pawnee war party fell upon them in a surprise dawn attack, wiping out nearly the entire expedition. Only thirteen men survived to tell the story. When the news reached New Mexico, the entire colony was thrown into a panic. Believing that Frenchmen had orchestrated the Pawnee victory, New Mexicans prepared for the worst. So fearful were the settlers that many considered abandoning the province.

Meanwhile, in Europe, matters between Spain and France came to a head and the two countries made peace in 1721. Among the issues of contention was Spanish encroachment toward the northeast from New Mexico and Texas. Spain agreed to halt its expansion and prohibit Spanish subjects from trading on the Great Plains, concessions that favored French control over Plains peoples. New Mexicans were not about to cede control to the French, and the provisions of the agreement of 1721 went unenforced.

The French did not back off. In 1739, the Mallet brothers with a small group of men crossed from Missouri through present Nebraska and Kansas, reaching Taos and Santa Fe. The Mallet brothers demonstrated that the Great Plains could be crossed despite the dangers posed by hostile Plains bands. The following spring, they returned to Louisiana and reported to the commander at New Orleans, briefing him about trade opportunities and conditions in the Provincia de Nuevo México. The Mallet brothers had opened the door to New Mexico. French officials in Louisiana took great interest in the possibilities of opening up trade with Santa Fe. Between 1741 and 1752 other trading parties visited Santa Fe. Some French traders created problems for Spanish officials. In 1749, for example, a trading party under Pierre

Satren along with two other French deserters sold firearms to Plains peoples on their way west. On arriving in Santa Fe, they stole horses and mules from New Mexicans and traded them to Comanches who were raiding northern New Mexican villages. Such activities caused Spanish officials to consider all traders as personas non gratas and trespassers. In 1752, officials in Santa Fe promptly arrested Jean Chapuis, who had come from Fort Chartres in Illinois, confiscated his goods, and sent him and his men to prison in Mexico City and Spain.

The French and Indian War in North America (1754–63) pitted the British colonies against the colonists of New France. As the conflict spread to Europe, launching the Seven Years' War, Spanish-French relations underwent a change. In 1762, realizing that they were about to lose the war with England, the French Bourbons quickly negotiated a land transfer to their Spanish Bourbon cousins. The result was that Spain inherited French Louisiana. Under the terms of the 1763 Treaty of Paris, England emerged the victor with newly won possessions in the Caribbean.

Meanwhile, New Mexico continued to be beset by Plains raiders. In order to pacify them, Spanish officials in Santa Fe developed a policy to control trade on the plains by befriending and creating alliances with certain bands. Although the policy did not stop the raiding, the last quarter of the eighteenth century was a period of comparative peace. The Utes did form alliances with New Mexicans, but Apaches on the lower Rio Grande continued raiding farms and villages, such as Socorro, from their strongholds in the Magdalena Mountains. Other Apaches still menaced travelers on the Camino Real between El Paso del Norte and the Villa de Alburquerque. In northern New Mexico, the Comanches, raiding from southeastern Colorado, dominated the area from the Arkansas River to mountain villages from Taos to Mora, Las Trampas, Pecos, San Miguel, and Villanueva. Comanche warriors raided at will, took captives, and killed whoever stood in their way.

Far away in Mexico City, Spanish officials formulated plans to stifle aggression from England, which had, between 1775 and 1790, encroached on Spanish claims to the lower Ohio and Mississippi river valleys. The plan aimed at blunting Indian attacks in a wide arc from Sonora northward through present southern Arizona, northern New

Mexico, and Texas along with the provinces of Chihuahua, Nuevo León, and Coahuila in present northern Mexico. To do that, Spain militarized the entire frontier.

The first phase of the plan called for an inspection of all frontier military outposts and towns that could support a militia. Similar inspections had taken place in 1726–28 under Pedro de Rivera and again in 1765–66 under the Marqués de Rubí. Each inspector had visited every town and outpost for months on end and had presented recommendations for making the frontier defenses more efficient. Rubí's report resulted in the *Reglamento de 1772,* which reorganized the frontier, instituting a set of policies and plans that turned the outlying frontier area into a large military jurisdiction called the Provincias Internas (Internal Provinces). The Reglamento designated a new frontier line of defense running from Texas to California that was supervised by one commander, the *comandante general de las Provincias Internas,* based in Ciudad Chihuahua. The comandante general was appointed by the king and independent of the viceroy, insulating him from New Spain's politics. He oversaw all political, military, and financial affairs within the Provincias Internas, with the governor of each province reporting directly to him. Judicial matters remained under the jurisdiction of the courts (*audiencias*) of Mexico and Guadalajara. Teodoro de Croix, "El Caballero de Croix," became the first comandante general. Deeming Apache and Comanche raiders a threat to the prosperity of the northern provinces, he proceeded to wage war against them. Still, despite some small successes, the raids continued.

The Spanish lack of success with Plains tribes was in part attributable to profound cultural misunderstandings between them. Despite the animosity between the two, the Spanish never doubted that they were more civilized than the Plains Indians, but they did fear and respect them. Indeed, since the days of Juan de Oñate, succeeding Spanish governors had prohibited trade with Plains tribes unless explicitly licensed. Violators suffered penalties. Recognizing the warrior culture and the tribes' athletic abilities in warfare, Oñate, as early as 1599, believed that they were so strong and numerous that they could overrun New Mexico if antagonized. Eventually, the same policy was applied to the Utes. Accustomed to a strictly hierarchical political organization, most

Europeans rarely recognized that nomadic and seminomadic peoples such as the Apaches, Utes, and Comanches lived in small, mobile, largely autonomous bands. Although not always successful, Spanish settlers, along with Pueblo Indian allies, led punitive expeditions against them, often tracking specific Navajo, Apache, and Comanche raiders to their campsites. Sometimes, such engagements triggered revenge killings by Plains Indians honor bound to avenge their dead. That, in turn, provoked Spanish counterattacks, and so the cycle continued. Still, throughout the colonial period, Spanish and Pueblo Indian farmlands and animals, along with women and children, were easy targets for raiding warriors. Similarly, Spanish settlers took Plains Indian women and children as hostages to trade for their captured Hispanic kin. Trade fairs, called *rescates,* were held at Taos, Picuris, and Pecos for such purposes. Some New Mexican captives were rescued as far away as San Antonio, Texas. Others were never seen again. Tactically, Europeans, with their long guns, were accustomed to certain maneuvers on the battlefield, whereas Indian warfare, at least among their adversaries on the northern frontier of New Spain, resembled guerrilla hit-and-run tactics. Indian raiding was not a warfare tactic per se, but, in the long run, it became a desperate attempt by roaming peoples to survive the pressures of American westward expansion as Plains tribes pushed one against the other toward New Mexico.

Finally, in 1779, New Mexico governor Juan Bautista de Anza, a seasoned frontier commander, pursued the Comanches relentlessly until he trapped them at the Arkansas River. There in a bloody afternoon fight, he defeated them. With the death of Chief Cuerno Verde, the Comanches ceased their raids into New Mexico for a long period.

During the 1770s and 1780s, Spanish officials in Santa Fe also turned their attention toward making contact with settlements in Texas, Louisiana, and California. Finding an overland route to the California settlements, nearly cut off from the rest of New Spain except by sea, became a priority, however. New Mexicans reasoned that the recently established missions and towns in California offered rich trading possibilities, but range after range of rugged mountains separated them from the coast. Exploration of western Colorado and Utah as far as the Great Salt Lake had taken place since the 1670s. New Mexicans, seeking

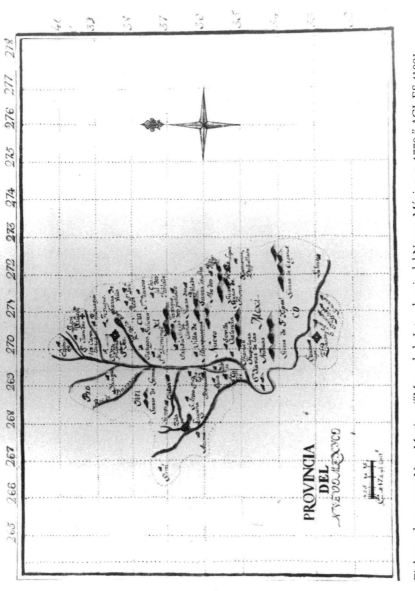

Eighteenth-century New Mexico. ("Mapa de la Intendencia del Nuevo México, c. 1770," AGI, ES.41091. AGI/16418.17/MP-Mexico, 268)

a mythical place called Teguayo, where the Pueblo Indians ostensibly had originated, crisscrossed many of the Indian trails in the area. In 1765, Juan María Antonio Rivera led two expeditions through western Colorado as far as the Colorado River. He spent a summer prospecting for silver (*plata*) in a mountain range they called Sierra de la Plata, today's La Plata Mountains. In July 1776, Franciscan friars Atanasio Domínguez and Silvestre Vélez Escalante led an expedition to locate a route to the California coast. Their route meandered northwest into Colorado and Utah as far north as present Grand Junction, Colorado. Crossing the Green and Colorado rivers the expedition headed westward, where they made contact with the Timpanogos, who lived near the Great Salt Lake. From there they traveled southwestward to a point near Cedar City, Utah. From there they could see snowcapped mountains and decided to return to New Mexico. Exploring through the mazes of the Grand Canyon, the expedition made its way to Oraibi and other Hopi pueblos. Eventually, they reached the Rio Grande below Albuquerque. On January 3, 1777, the explorers entered Santa Fe and reported all they had seen to the governor. Their route would inspire the successful route blazed in 1830 by Antonio Armijo from Santa Fe via present Kanab, in southern Utah, to Los Angeles.

In 1788, Pierre Vial, a French trader from Louisiana, led a small party from San Antonio to present Wichita Falls. From there he followed the Red and Canadian rivers to New Mexico and made his way to Santa Fe. Known as Pedro Vial to the Spaniards and as Manitou "the Great Walker" by eastern Plains Indians, Vial was a trailblazer who opened a route from Santa Fe to St. Louis, Missouri. His partner, Francisco Fragoso, ran another route from Santa Fe to New Orleans via northern Texas. Such trails, though feasible, were not practical and were soon forgotten. In the nineteenth century, other, more successful trails, such as the Santa Fe Trail from Missouri, would revolutionize trade from New Mexico via the Great Plains of Texas to Missouri.

In 1800, Spain found its entire empire threatened, not by external enemies, but by internal foes who began to talk about independence from the mother country. Recognizing its weaknesses, in terms of being able to defend its empire against Great Britain and the United States, Spain decided to return Louisiana to France in exchange for lands in

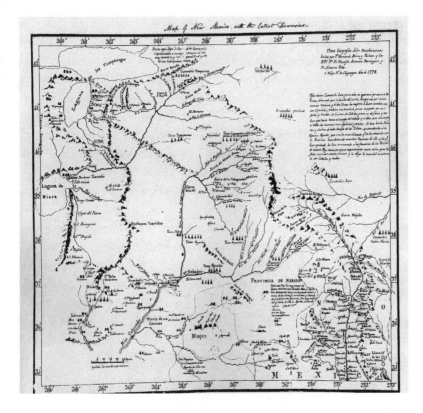

New Mexico Province in the late eighteenth century, mapped by Bernardo Miera y Pacheco. (Facsimile made in 1970 by Meriden Gravure Co. of "Plano geográfico de los Descubrimientos hechas por dn. Bernardo Miera y Pacheco y los RRs Ps Fr, Francisco Atanasio Domínguez y Fr. Silvestre Veles. Año de 1778"; archived in the Yale Collection of Western Americana, Beinecke Rare Book and Manuscript Library, Yale University, New Haven.)

Tuscany, with the hope that the French government would establish a buffer to protect Spain's sparsely populated northern frontier. Spanish and French officials signed the Treaty of San Ildefonso (1800), exchanging Louisiana, at a palace near Segovia, Spain. The Spanish plan was thwarted when Napoleon Bonaparte, in need of money and hoping to retake Louisiana later by force, sold the territory to the United States in 1803. Three years later, he stationed 20,000 French troops in Haiti with the intent of invading Louisiana, but the Haitian rebellion led by Toussaint L'Ouverture in 1806 squelched that plan.

Meanwhile, Spanish officials in Mexico saw the United States as a threat. While the eastern boundary of Louisiana was established along the Mississippi River, the western boundary was unclear. How far west did Louisiana extend? Did it include Texas? Spain argued it did not. Thomas Jefferson said that the boundary could reach as far as the "Stoney [Rocky] Mountains," and claimed it was the manifest destiny of the United States to extend all the way to the California coast. As Santa Fe was at the southern end of the Rocky Mountains, New Mexicans had reason to be concerned about Jefferson's claims.

In July 1803, following the Louisiana Purchase, Meriwether Lewis met in St. Louis with Carlos Dehault Delassus, the last Spanish governor of that city, who stated that he could not permit Lewis to proceed any farther. Delassus warned Spanish officials, "I believe that his mission has no other object than to discover the Pacific Ocean, following the Missouri." Meanwhile, General James Wilkinson, an officer simultaneously in the U.S. and Spanish armies, gave Spain information about the Lewis and Clark expedition (the Corps of Discovery). As a double agent, Wilkinson advised Spanish officials in Louisiana that they should arrest Lewis and Clark and oust Daniel Boone and his Missouri River settlers from Spanish territory.

In New Mexico, Spanish officials received notice of the Lewis and Clark expedition. At the time, Santa Fe was the center of concerns about possible encroachments by the British and by Anglo-Americans, especially the latter since their acquisition of Louisiana. All Anglo-American expeditions were watched closely by Spanish officials, ranging from the minister in Washington to the viceroy in Mexico. Meanwhile, much correspondence flowed between Spain and its North American possessions. From St. Louis, Delassus suggested that the only course for Spain was to arrest Lewis and Clark, whose expedition "can hardly avoid passing among the neighboring Indian nations of New Mexico through their forts or villages." In the past, the routes French traders had blazed from Louisiana and Illinois had crossed the Great Plains to New Mexico. Delassus warned officials in Texas and New Orleans that Anglo-American settlers claimed that the boundary of the United States included the Rio Grande, inclusive of Santa Fe. He cautioned that these settlers might begin setting up posts for contraband trade into Mexico.

The Spanish foreign minister in Spain issued warnings about this danger to the governors of Coahuila, Chihuahua, and New Mexico. In the summer of 1804, Governor Fernando Chacón of New Mexico sent Pedro Vial to alert Plains tribes allied with Spain to monitor movements of the Lewis and Clark expedition should they attempt to cross the Great Plains. Vial had orders to arrest Lewis and Clark if he encountered them.

At Taos Vial was joined by twenty New Mexican frontiersmen and Pueblo warriors. By September 3, they had reached the Río Chato (Platte), and three days later they arrived at the Pawnee villages. They did not find the trail of Lewis and Clark's party, but they did meet some twenty Frenchmen from Illinois who reported that Lewis and Clark had sufficient men and supplies, and that they had befriended various Indian tribes, whose chiefs had given them Spanish medals, flags, and *patentes* (commissions) in exchange for Anglo-American patentes and flags. Only the Pawnees had refused to ally themselves with the Anglo-Americans. Vial returned to Santa Fe and made his report. On a subsequent search for the Corps of Discovery in 1806, Vial and Juan Lucero and their men were attacked by a party of about one thousand Indians, who pillaged two-thirds of their supplies. The Spanish repulsed the assailants, but Vial, finding their supplies dangerously depleted, returned to Santa Fe at about the same time that Lewis and Clark reached the mouth of the Columbia River. Other expeditions were sent out without success.

Spanish officials in New Mexico did not give up their search for Lewis and Clark until late 1806. That year, Facundo Melgares and six hundred men, including Pueblo auxiliaries from New Mexico, had journeyed to the eastern end of the Arkansas to trade and discuss alliances with the Osage and Pawnee. The Arkansas River was recognized as the boundary separating New Spain from the United States. Melgares was ordered to keep an eye out for the Lewis and Clark expedition, which Spanish officials believed had crossed the continent via the Great Plains of Nebraska and Kansas. Instead, Lewis and Clark followed the Missouri northward to the Mandan villages and then turned west to the Pacific coast, arriving at a point near present Portland, Oregon. They returned by the same route. Melgares never came near the expedition, which had already returned to Louisiana several months earlier.

Upon his return to Santa Fe, Melgares was instructed to lead an expedition north from Santa Fe to arrest an intruder named Zebulon Montgomery Pike south of Denver, near present Colorado Springs. Pike knew well that the Arkansas River was the boundary, because Thomas Jefferson had instructed him not to cross it. What he was not sure about was where or at what point the boundary line ran north of the Arkansas. Seeking a safe haven, he and his frostbitten, fever-ridden men marched northwestward in the snow toward present Pikes Peak, which he could see in the distance. If Anglo-Americans were unsure of the boundary, Melgares knew that Pike was within Spanish territory and arrested him for trespassing on Spanish soil. In effect, Melgares rescued Pike's party from certain death in the winter of 1807. Pike and his men were escorted to Santa Fe for interrogation, then subsequently to Ciudad Chihuahua for further questioning and possible execution. Eventually, they were released by way of San Antonio, Texas. Pike's release and the publication of his diary sparked renewed interest regarding Spanish New Mexico. As a result, between 1807 and 1818, the United States pressed Spain for a clarification of the vague boundary line between their territories.

The winds of war that would sweep the Spanish Empire presented an advantage to the United States in boundary negotiations with a weakened Spanish government. The turmoil began in 1808 when France invaded Spain, forcing the Spanish king and his son to abdicate, imprisoning them, and imposing Joseph Bonaparte as monarch. A Spanish opposition government in exile that included representatives from the Americas was established at Cádiz, serving as a regency for the absent monarch. New Mexico's representative was Don Pedro Baptista Pino. New Mexicans aptly observed that despite the drafting of a new, liberal constitution by the Cortes, nothing changed for Pino or New Mexico during his tenure in the Cortes de Cádiz. Indeed, when it was all over, New Mexican frontiersmen quipped, "Don Pedro Pino fue, Don Pedro Pino vino" (Don Pedro Pino went, Don Pedro Pino returned.) He did, at least, either write or assist in the publication of an endearing description of New Mexico that was presented to the Cortes de Cádiz entitled *The Exposition on the Province of New Mexico, 1812*. It remains a significant narrative of daily life, cultural practices, and political issues in New Mexico at the end of the colonial period. Meanwhile, during the throes of the French occupation of Spain, Father Miguel Hidalgo raised the flag of revolution in Mexico in 1810, triggering the Mexican independence movement that finally ended in success in 1821.

These developments put the United States in a good bargaining position during the 1818–19 boundary negotiations leading up to the 1819 Adams-Onís, or Transcontinental, Treaty. The western limits of Louisiana, which had never been resolved following the Louisiana Purchase, remained a point of contention between Spain and the United States. Many Anglo-American frontiersmen claimed Texas as part of the Louisiana Purchase. Meanwhile, Andrew Jackson had demonstrated that the United States could easily take Spanish Florida by force. Armed with information gained from Jackson's invasion of Florida, the United States persuaded Spain of its weaknesses in North America and proposed an agreement. Spanish officials were perturbed but eventually compelled to reevaluate Spain's hold on Florida. Debilitated by rebellions at home and in Latin America, Spanish officials perceived that losing Florida would be inevitable. Reluctantly, in 1819, they agreed to cede Florida to the United States.

The treaty of 1819 finally established a western boundary line for the Louisiana Territory and settled issues regarding Florida. For several decades, raiders from Florida had been causing property damage to landowners in the United States, totaling more than $5 million. When the Americans demanded compensation for this property damage, Spanish negotiators agreed to cede Florida to the United States in exchange for the latter's assumption of the $5 million claim. Along similar lines, Spanish officials agreed to relinquish all previous claims to Louisiana and Oregon if the United States would give up claims to Texas. The new boundary ran from the mouth of the Sabine River, on the present border between Louisiana and Texas, to the 32nd parallel, then north to the Red River, west along the river to the 100th meridian, then north to the Arkansas River and along its right bank to its source. From there, the new boundary zigzagged north along the Rockies to the 42nd parallel. Then it turned west to the Pacific, separating Oregon from Spanish holdings in California and giving the United States its long-sought extent from coast to coast.

During this period, New Mexicans, not aware that the Treaty of 1819 had been concluded, continued to pursue expansion of the province and gather information to define and verify the boundary. In 1819, the Spanish commander in Santa Fe, Facundo Melgares sent a map along with descriptions of the land between Santa Fe and the upper Missouri to Mexico City. This map shows Santa Fe at the bottom, South Pass, Wyoming, at the top, the full extent of the Missouri River to the Yellowstone, and the three rivers that flow into it (which Lewis and Clark named the Madison, the Gallatin, and the Jefferson), as well as the full extent of the Arkansas River from the Rockies to the Mississippi. In his letter to the viceroy, Melgares promised, "As soon as the weather warms, I will lead an expedition northward." In 1820 he did in fact order an expedition northward by way of present Denver to the Yellowstone River. In the end his efforts came to naught when the United States prevailed on the western boundary issue and came closer to gaining California as its prized possession.

That did not stop the New Mexicans from consolidating their hold on northern New Mexico. Abiquiú quickly became a jumping-off point for settlement. From there settlers pushed northward to a perilous Ute-Navajo frontier at Tierra Amarilla, Ojo Caliente, and Chama. They also occupied the Española Valley with settlements at and surrounding Los Luceros. East of there, New Mexicans founded the mountain settlements of Peñasco, Ojo Sarco, Las Trampas, and Truchas. Other settlers in the early nineteenth century pushed the frontier line from Mora to La Cueva and, eventually, south of there to Las Vegas. Everywhere along the line of settlements were land grants covering millions of acres.

Agriculture and stock raising were New Mexico's main industries. In the rugged frontier zone of northern and central New Mexico, valleys with freshwater for irrigation and supplies of wood for building, cooking, and fuel to keep home fires burning through the cold, unforgiving winters were prerequisites for survival. Corn, wheat, beans, squash of all kinds, chile, and fruit, such as apples, apricots, and pears, were grown on the arable lands along the waterways. Acequias drew water from nearby rivers and crisscrossed farmlands for miles, supplying settlements and farms. Mules, burros, cattle, horses, and sheep were raised in great numbers. Barnyard fowl were also raised to supplement the settlers' diets. Local industries centered on producing trade items such as furniture, crafts, textiles, and pottery.

The Spanish colonial period in New Mexico was significant in many ways. It saw the establishment of a Spanish population, a system of governance and laws, a dominant religion, and documentation of the people, flora, and fauna across a broad geographic area stretching from Nevada to the Mississippi River and from South Pass in Wyoming to the crossing at El Paso. The development of the Camino Real de Tierra Adentro (designated as a National Trail by the U.S. Congress in 2000 and as a World Heritage Site by UNESCO in 2010) established a trade and immigration route that served to transmit western culture northward to merge with the Indian heritages of the present U.S. Southwest. In the waning days of the Spanish Empire, New Mexicans were preoccupied with survival. Their agriculture, irrigation systems, stock raising, and trade sustained them, but their conflicts with raiding tribes often pulled them away from their livelihoods. Exploration continued throughout the Spanish period as New Mexicans traveled as far north as the Great Salt Lake of Utah, through northern and western Colorado, and eastward across the Great Plains as far as the Missouri-Mississippi drainages. By 1781, New Mexicans had caught glimpses of a new power: the United States of America. In the previous decade Spain had aided the American cause by sending troops to the Gulf Coast to prevent Britain from attacking from the south. Residents of northern New Spain—New Mexicans, along with Californians, Sonorans, Chihuahuans, Coahuilans, and Tejanos—had contributed money, blankets, and horses to the American Revolution. In the end, as Spanish power gave way to U.S. encroachment and later an independent Mexico, New Mexicans became absorbed into a new order and acquired a new identity.

CHAPTER 4

Mexican Administration of New Mexico, 1821–1848

As of today, it is thirty-four days that I have the honor to govern you, and already I can count thousands of examples of your gentleness, your love for order, your submission to justice, and a true complement of many civic and moral virtues which God has joined here so as to illuminate His Omnipotence in this majestic retreat.

GOVERNOR ALBINO PÉREZ TO NEW MEXICANS, JUNE 23, 1835

FOR CENTURIES, NEW MEXICO, as a remote colony of Spain, had been a distant outpost from the center of power. That aspect changed little under Mexico. In October 1821, the Mexican government sent a circular throughout the nation calling for the immediate celebration of independence. Although they were aware of Mexico's struggle for independence from Spain, New Mexicans heard only rumors about the creation of a new government, until late December 1821, because the rugged terrain between Mexico City and Santa Fe made overland mail service along the Camino Real de Tierra Adentro slow and dangerous.

Finally, a mounted courier passed through the Villa de Albuquerque and other villages of the Río Abajo on his way to Santa Fe. On December 26, 1821, at the Palace of the Governors, the courier dismounted and handed a mail pouch to Governor Facundo Melgares. The pouch contained official correspondence demanding that New Mexico's governor and other officials take an oath of allegiance to the recently established Mexican government. Five days later, New Mexicans celebrated the event despite the cold weather that had blown in over the Sangre de Cristo Mountains.

Two festivities in the Plaza de Santa Fe, a week apart, marked the event. The first gathering took place on December 31, 1821, to commemorate the significance of the revolutionary goals known as the Tres-garantías (the three guarantees)—Religion, Union, and Independence. The event, organized by Governor Facundo Melgares, was called a *loa*, a sort of dramatic presentation in which, in this case, three designated individuals praised the three guarantees. A stage was constructed in the plaza near the portal of the Palacio del Gobernador (Governor's Palace), as it was then called. The postmaster, Don Juan Bautista Vigil y Alarid, planned the construction of the stage and artwork, in conjunction with various Santa Fe artisans. Vigil left no detail unattended. Nailed high in the center of the plaza was a white flag with a tricolored heart, easily seen by everyone there.

The stage was designed with careful attention to the symbolism that the presenters of the loa would highlight in their homage to the new sovereign. Adorned with the finest draperies of taffeta and various exquisite clothes, the stage had a backdrop painting with three symbols. The first, a lamb and a lion in an embrace, signified Union. The second illustrated a tree of liberty watered by four streams fed by a cloud; and the third was a likeness of Mexico's founding father, Agustín de Iturbide, portrayed with a crown of laurels. The flag of Mexico was raised high above the stage. From the stage, Santiago Abreu paid homage to the independence movement, Juan Tomás Terrazas spoke about religion, and the presidial chaplain Fray Francisco de Hozio proclaimed the significance of the Mexican union. Governor Facundo Melgares reported that the celebration was a quiet and somber affair.

The second event, occurring about a week later on the feast day of Los Reyes (the Magi), January 6, 1822, was much different. In the dead of winter, New Mexicans braved freezing temperatures to celebrate into the wee hours of the night. The celebration included parades, orations, patriotic dramas, music, masses, ringing of church bells, firing of muskets, Pueblo Indian dancing, and a ball in the governor's palace. Thus originated the New Mexican tradition of commemorating Mexican Independence (Diez y Seis de Septiembre).

Thereafter, New Mexicans received other official notices concerning political reform throughout Mexico, with new laws largely regarding the reorganization of political and economic institutions. For the most part, the structure of the budding Mexican nation affected the political organization of settlements as participating units in national politics. Anxiously, New Mexicans wondered how New Mexico would fit into the larger picture of Mexican rule, having no idea at the time that this period would evolve quickly in a brief but active twenty-five years or so.

Already New Mexico was poised between two different countries. Only two long roads led to Santa Fe in 1821. One, the Camino Real de Tierra Adentro, passed from Mexico City through the Central Plateau of Mexico via extremely rugged terrain. Travelers often endured long, lonely stretches of hostile and empty land marked by deep canyons to reach the next Mexican village. The other road, the Santa Fe Trail, came from Missouri in the United States. It connected in Santa Fe with the Camino Real, later becoming known as the Santa Fe–Chihuahua Trail. Established by William Becknell in 1821, the Santa Fe Trail was not only a commercial route for Anglo-American and New Mexican merchants, but also an immigrant trail used by U.S. citizens. Thus, U.S. citizens also took an interest in the changes made by the Mexican national government in areas like Texas, New Mexico, and California.

In 1829 Antonio Armijo with a small group of men blazed a third trail from Santa Fe to Los Angeles, California, via southern Utah. This trail, known as the Old Spanish Trail, became a migrant and trade route connecting with the Santa Fe Trail and the Camino Real in Santa Fe. New Mexican products, primarily blankets, made their way over the Old Spanish Trail from New Mexico to California, and from there by sea to the Sandwich Islands, today's Hawaii. Similarly, mules from New Mexico, Sonora, and California eventually made their way to Missouri. The Missouri mules were actually Mexican mules. The Santa Fe–Chihuahua Trail became significant in the history of New Mexico, especially early in the War with Mexico in 1846, when the Army of the West invaded and occupied New Mexico.

Change was in the wind as Mexico turned to nation building. Under Spain the chain of command was top-down from the king to his viceroy in Mexico City to the governors of the provinces, such as New Mexico. Cabildos, or local town assemblies, such as the one in Santa Fe, voiced their concerns and made recommendations on issues of community interest. Such measures could be approved by the governors or, if needed, by the viceroy. Mexican officials would redefine the system of governance to support the sovereignty of the new nation.

During the first years of transition from Spanish colonial to Mexican national power, the Mexican government defined its authority throughout the country. The Mexican Constitution of 1824 was modeled after the U.S. Constitution of 1787 and similarly established legislative, executive, and judicial branches as constituting the "supreme power" of the new nation. The Constitutive Act, passed on January 31, 1824, provided for the election of representatives to the National Congress. This act stipulated that the territories of Mexico would be directly subject to the national government in Mexico City. The country was divided into internal states of the east, west, and north, the last of which encompassed the provinces of Chihuahua, Durango, and New Mexico. Subsequently, the Mexican Congress created large states, all containing provinces within them.

Six months after the passage of the Constitutive Act, the Decree of July 6, 1824, created the Mexican territory of Nuevo México, with its capital at Santa Fe. The state was divided into two districts (*distritos*), each subdivided into *partidos,* or subdistricts. In the first district, partido capitals were located at Taos and San Ildefonso (not the Indian pueblos, but nearby Hispanic settlements with the same names). In the second district, Alburquerque served as the capital of the first partido, and Los Padillas, some fifty miles to the southwest of Santa Fe, as the capital of the second. Alburquerque and Los Padillas each had an ayuntamiento and an *alcalde constitucional* who administered the respective partidos. To the south, El Paso del Norte served as capital of a partido administered from Ciudad Chihuahua that encompassed Las Cruces and surrounding towns in modern southern New Mexico.

In all land grants and towns established during the Spanish period in New Mexico, the settlers elected members to the local council and made decisions regarding the administration of the partido with the approval of the ayuntamiento and the alcalde constitucional. Occasional elections were held for district delegates who would represent their constituents in the ayuntamientos. Each partido was subdivided into *manzanas,* or blocks, for the purpose of identifying voters. Thus, Hispanic villagers depended on the political influence of their representatives in the ayuntamientos.

Under Mexican rule, New Mexico—like other outlying provinces and territories such as Alta and Baja California, Texas, and the extreme fringes of the north Mexican states and the Yucatan Peninsula—would seemingly be treated as an equal within the legislation of new laws. Unfortunately, Mexican officials did not regard those areas as nationally significant.

As the Spanish colonial period gave way to the development of independent Mexico, Mexican officials for the most part merged old ways with new policies. Land tenure issues greatly concerned New Mexicans. They feared that Mexico might make changes in the Spanish legal system that would affect them, their land grants, and their towns. They realized that the Mexican government was unlikely to revoke any land grants, but landowners would have to learn how the new Mexican political system and the chain of command worked in order to survive. On the older Spanish land grants, land transactions typically occurred among family members, close friends, and extended clan relations of the original grant owner, by means of conveyances, donations, and land sales. Once a transfer of land was completed, the contracting parties would take the documentation to be validated by the alcalde constitucional, located in the partido capital.

Spanish colonization laws pertaining to settlement and land tenure carried over into the Mexican period. Particularly in Texas, the earlier Spanish colonial policy had allowed—in fact, encouraged—Anglo-Americans to enter and settle in Spanish territory. Attracting colonists served Spanish goals of populating the far northern frontier with what they hoped would be loyal settlers and of having a sufficient permanent population to develop and bolster local defenses and secure the area against Indian raiders. The Colonization Law, enacted on August 18, 1824, awarded land grants to entrepreneurs, called *empresarios,* who promised to colonize the northern frontier. Anglo-American pioneers were allowed to become empresarios and settle within Mexican territory, provided that they convert to Catholicism, settle a prescribed number of families on the land, and show progress toward cultivating the land. Such policies significantly influenced New Mexico's settlement and economic patterns.

New Mexico remained a territory under the Constitution of 1824 until the new constitution of 1836 provided that the Congress could create departments or states. With the decree of December 29, 1836, the republic was divided into "departments" (a new label for the territories), and New Mexico, among other former territories, effectively became a department. Santa Fe, of course, hosted the departmental junta, the highest council. The Department of New Mexico was divided into two districts, each governed by a *prefecto,* and each district further subdivided into two precincts, or *partidos,* overseen by subprefects; below them, at the local level, common councils and justices of the peace formed the governing authorities. Cochiti Pueblo served as the point of division for New Mexico's two districts, the Río Arriba district extended north of Cochiti, the Río Abajo south of it. Each partido had a seat of government where the ayuntamiento and alcalde constitucional resided; these capitals remained at San Ildefonso and Taos (the Hispanic settlements) in the north, and at Alburquerque and Los Padillas in the south.

Although New Mexico, like other outlying departments, was, on paper, treated as equal to the more central departments under the laws of Mexico, Mexican officials did not regard those areas as nationally significant, so they carried little clout. Mexican officials did not regard those areas as nationally significant, so they carried little clout. For example, the central government reserved the right to make the appointments to political office. Each department nominated three individuals for the post of governor, but in the case of frontier departments such as New Mexico, the central government was not obligated to consider the nominations and could appoint its own choice without any other consultation.

The powers of the governor were defined under the decree of December 29, 1836. It stated that governors "shall be appointed by the latter [that is, the central government in Mexico City] . . . and shall hold office for eight years and may be reelected." The duties of the governor were to attend to "the preservation of public order," to comply with all decrees and orders of the central government as well as those of the departmental junta, and to transmit "all enactments of the departmental junta to Mexico City." Within his jurisdiction, the governor had the power to appoint prefects, to approve the appointments of subprefects, to confirm appointments of justices of the peace recommended by the departmental junta, and to remove any official "after first having heard the opinion" of the departmental junta. With the consent of the departmental junta, the governor could suspend common councils in the districts or prefectos of the department. With regard to elections of common councils, he served as arbiter in case of a contested election or as the deciding vote in case of a tie in an election, and could accept or reject resignations of council members. The departmental junta proposed laws chiefly related to taxes, public education, industry, commerce, and municipal administration. It could also propose amendments to the national constitution in conformity with constitutional law. Within the department, the junta was charged with establishing schools for primary education in all towns, providing for school funding out of municipal revenues, and levying moderate taxes if no municipal funds were available. It also had the power to establish "institutions of learning and public charity as well as those dedicated to promoting agriculture, industry, and commerce," but approval from the Mexican Congress was required if "these provisions should in any manner prove burdensome to the towns." The junta was also charged with opening and maintaining roads and establishing moderate tolls to cover their cost. All accounts, particularly those dealing with municipal revenues, were to be examined and approved by the junta. With the governor, the junta was to formulate municipal ordinances governing common councils, as well as regulations pertaining to law enforcement in the department, subject to congressional review. In sum, the departmental junta was "to promote, through the medium of the governor, everything that may contribute to the prosperity of the department in all its branches; and to the well-being of its towns [and] . . . advise the government on all matters on which it may require [advice]."

The central government warned governors and members of departmental juntas that they could not levy taxes without congressional approval. According to the decree of December 29, 1836, tax revenues could be used only for the purpose for which the tax was enacted. The governor and the departmental junta were also prohibited from raising an armed force without the express authorization of the central government. These changes would have profound implications for the frontier Department of New Mexico, which was now subject to the same rules governing all departmental juntas. As frontier residents not accustomed to intense regulation, New Mexicans resented perceived government interference and, as would their counterparts in Sonora and California, began to evaluate the rebellious path already taken by Yucatan and Texas.

Although the position of local prefect was a fairly minor office within the department, it was a coveted and jealously guarded position. Indeed, local prefects could become quite powerful because they directly affected the lives of those over whom they held power. As described later, New Mexicans rebelled in 1837, in part incited by the power held by prefects. The law of March 20, 1837, empowered prefects to "regulate administratively and in conformity with the laws, the distribution of common lands [*tierras comunes*] in the towns of the district, provided there is no litigation pending with regard to them, [in which case] the interested parties reserve the right to apply to the governor, who without further appeal, shall decide what is most proper, with the concurrence of the departmental council [junta]."

In 1843, the departments underwent one last revision before the end of the Mexican period. The decree of June 13, 1843, created *asambleas,* or departmental legislative assemblies composed of seven to eleven members, to replace the departmental juntas and perform the functions of that body. Members, who had to be at least twenty-five years of age, were to be elected by the outgoing juntas so that their terms would be staggered, some members serving two years and the others four. Eleven alternates were also nominated to serve the remainder of a member's term in case of a sudden vacancy.

The electoral process had evolved quickly during the early republic. Caleb Cushing, U.S. envoy to China, passed through Mexico on his return from the Orient in 1844 and recorded some observations about Mexico's social and political conditions. Cushing's explanation offers a glimpse of the political ambiance throughout the Mexican Republic in the 1840s. Cushing wrote that popular elections were held throughout Mexico every two years in the months of August, September, and October. Throughout the republic, the adult male inhabitants of each partido, generally consisting of at least five hundred people, voted for one primary elector ("*de primer voto*" in Cushing's words). Married males could vote at age eighteen; unmarried males had to be twenty-one years old. The primary electors, in turn, met to choose secondary electors ("*de segundo voto*") who collectively constituted the electoral college of each department, responsible for electing the deputies to the National Congress and the departmental asambleas. In the heavily populated areas of Mexico, at least, the primary electors "choose secondary electors, in the proportion of one secondary to every twenty of the primary electors." Cushing reported that the department assemblies elected the president of the Republic and two-thirds of the senators. Thus, in national politics as well as in local affairs, the partido was the basic unit of government.

The asambleas were charged with levying taxes subject to congressional approval, regulating spending, and appointing necessary employees. In regard to property, the asambleas also regulated the acquisition, alienation, and exchange of property through legislation in accordance with colonization laws. A priority was attending to the departmental infrastructure, including opening and maintaining roads. Other responsibilities included the promotion of public instruction, the recruitment and maintenance of the army and an urban and rural police force, the establishment of municipal corporations, the promotion and regulation of public health, the encouragement of agriculture and industry, and the establishment and regulation of superior tribunals and inferior courts. At the end of each year, the asamblea prepared an annual statistical report and an annual estimated budget—both to be presented to the National Congress. Congress retained the right to review and, if need be, annul legislation or actions by the asambleas. The asamblea was required to consult the governor on all issues regarding the administration of the department. The oldest officer of the asamblea also served as acting governor should the need arise.

The decree of 1843 also reduced the governor's term from eight to five years and tweaked his responsibilities. For example, the governor was chief of the public treasury of the department and served as an ex-officio member of the asamblea with authority to vote only for deciding ties. He had eight days to review and comment on decrees passed by the asamblea to ensure they were in conformity with laws and policies. He also nominated superior magistrates, judges, attorneys, and government employees in the department for review by the National Congress.

Governors still reported directly to the central government. They were appointed by and served at the pleasure of the president of the Republic, although the departmental asamblea had the right to nominate candidates for the post. To assure the governor's direct involvement and communication with the central government, the decree of 1843 stipulated that "Governors are the only and necessary conduct of communication with the Supreme Authorities of the Republic" with the exception of accusations of malfeasance against them.

In sum, during the Mexican period (1821–48) the relationship between the central administration in Santa Fe and the local municipal councils retained similarities to the old Spanish system. In the Mexican period, the Spanish-period cabildos headed by alcaldes mayores were transformed into ayuntamientos presided over by an alcalde constitucional, a legally empowered magistrate. The main difference between the Mexican and Spanish periods was that the alcalde constitucional was elected and made decisions in consort with the ayuntamiento. In contrast, Spanish-era alcaldes mayores were appointed and held judicial, executive, and legislative powers in large districts. Alcaldes mayores also exercised military functions as *capitanes de guerra*. Prior to the establishment of the ayuntamiento, the alcaldes mayores made decisions or recommendations on their own as judicial officers without benefit of a council. As appointees, the alcaldes mayors were obligated to carry out orders from their governors without question. For example, more than once Francisco Trébol Navarro, alcalde mayor of Albuquerque, was overruled by Governor Pedro Fermín de Mendinueta. In contrast, during the Mexican period the alcaldes constitucionales seem to have developed enough local political strength and support from their local ayuntamientos to overrule their governors. In part, this may have been the result of longevity in power, as alcaldes constitucionales generally tended to remain in office longer than the governors did. Given the elective character of government under Mexico, the local political system played a greater role in the administration of judicial and economic matters as well as the distribution of land.

Between 1830 and 1840, the political atmosphere created by vigorous Mexican assertion of authority in a frontier context proved stressful to New Mexicans. Frustrated and angry about changes that appeared abusive to them, New Mexicans openly rebelled against the centralist Mexican government in 1837. The governor of New Mexico at the time was Albino Pérez, who had been appointed by Mexican president-dictator Antonio López de Santa Anna in 1835.

A native of Veracruz, Pérez was an experienced military officer who gave his unquestioning loyalty to the central government. He arrived in New Mexico in April 1835 with high hopes of transforming New Mexico from an outlying provincial frontier territory to a department integrated into the Mexican state. Unfortunately, as an outsider to Santa Fe politics, Pérez succeeded only in fomenting resentment and public opposition against him among local New Mexicans. Pérez's actions inspired opposition from New Mexican frontiersmen who interpreted the change to mean that they would surrender local power to a distant central government. Consequently, an explosive political dispute over home rule undermined his mission.

Soon after his arrival at Santa Fe, Pérez toured northern New Mexico in order to assess the situation there. On his return, Pérez gave a speech that in patriotic and romantic terms told the people of the "patience of a truly paternalistic government, proud of its Mexican origin and . . . heroic . . . because it is supported by the unanimous vote of the nation." His speech, published and circulated throughout New Mexico, was received with indifference.

Meanwhile Pérez went about the business of implementing the departmental model of government. The departmental plan was part of Santa Anna's plan to quickly transform Mexico from a federal republic to a dictatorship. Early in 1835, the National Congress in Mexico City revoked the departments' previous powers of self-government. Each department thereafter was permitted a five-member junta that reported directly to the Congress. In November 1835 a provisional junta met in New Mexico in conformity with the congressional directive. The convocation of this body signaled New Mexico's preparation to evolve from territorial to departmental status. Seven months later the first permanent junta for New Mexico was recognized under the Constitution of 1836. By that time New Mexico had been divided into districts and partidos administered by prefects and subprefects with judicial and political powers who were appointed by Governor Pérez.

Thus, the prefectos reported to the governor, who in turn was directly responsible to the National Congress. Subsequently, the prefect system established a chain of governmental command directly from the local level to the central government.

Controversy shrouded the department system in New Mexico, and Pérez's leadership became the focal point of dissent among New Mexicans. Chief among the causes of discontent were direct taxes that the Pérez administration imposed on the inhabitants of New Mexico. Another area of complaint was Pérez's demands that the people assist in protecting themselves against marauding Indians, whereas the people felt that the central government owed them military assistance.

Don Albino's activities, albeit practical, became increasingly unpopular. On October 16, 1835, for example, Pérez announced legislation regulating trade with Indians in an attempt to curb the lucrative illegal trade that was supplying Comanche, Apache, Ute, and Navajo raiders with weapons and horses that enabled more frequent attacks on Spanish settlers. Traditionally, trade with Indians was permitted only with a license issued by the governor. The October law prohibited *estrangeros,* meaning Anglo-American mountain men, from trading with Indians in New Mexico, and no one of any nationality could trade arms and ammunition to Indians. Mexican citizens, furthermore, required a license from the governor in order to trap beaver, and were prohibited from trapping beaver for Anglo-Americans. Violations of these laws were punishable by fines, confiscation of goods, and imprisonment. Pérez reckoned that monies from fines and confiscations could be used to outfit troops for combat against Indian raiders. New Mexicans, however, viewed the law as an example of Pérez's role as an agent of the centralist government bent on destroying home rule.

Eight months later, in June 1836, Pérez rashly signed into law more regulations. One targeted foreign merchants. This law, weighty with details, levied taxes on each wagon hauling foreign merchandise into Santa Fe, on each animal involved in freighting, on each horse or mule brought into New Mexico for sale, and on each head of cattle or sheep driven through the streets of Santa Fe. The foreign traders promptly passed their new tax burden on to their customers by raising prices on trade goods. Josiah Gregg, an American trader in Santa Fe, noted

New Mexicans' resentment, saying that although it was "necessary for the support of the new organization to introduce a system of direct taxation . . . the people . . . would sooner have paid a *doblón* through a tariff than a *real* in this way." Other regulations instituted a license for cutting timber, and imposed fees for attending theaters and dances. Far-reaching in scope, the June legislation also mandated that anyone residing outside of Santa Fe, whether a foreigner or native of New Mexico, had, under penalty of fine, to report to the alcalde within three days after arriving in the capital, and to state his occupation and reason for traveling to the city. Although the earlier October law and the June regulations may have been intended to address legitimate concerns, they affected many facets of the New Mexican economy and New Mexicans' daily lives.

Meanwhile Pérez turned his attention to other local problems, including education. He did not have to go far to find examples of illiteracy, for the 1836 report of the ayuntamiento de Santa Fe recorded that two of the seven deputies of the departmental junta could neither read nor write. Describing the state of education in the department as deplorable, Pérez stated that children who were running in the streets, as well as youths who were given to "evil dispositions, abandoned to laziness, and practicing vices," ought to be in school. Moreover, he described the prevailing "thievery immorality, desertion, and poverty as the most humiliating shame of the city." On July 16, 1836, Pérez proposed a remedy: the establishment of two schools in Santa Fe devoted to primary instruction. Henceforth, all children ages five to twelve were to attend school under penalty of fines ranging from one to five pesos, double that for the second offense, and triple for the third. Anyone who could not pay the fines was to be jailed for a minimum of three days, the length of the term to increase with each arrest.

Failing to acknowledge that the people were already feeling oppressed, Pérez detailed how his compulsory education system would work. Commissioners of public instruction were stationed in every block of Santa Fe and charged with making lists of the inhabitants and keeping track of school-age children and their attendance in school. Aside from making monthly attendance reports, the commissioners selected students for academic or vocational programs. Under the law they were obliged to inform each parent that school attendance was mandatory and that the family henceforth had a financial responsibility to support the school by paying fees determined by the schoolmaster. Performing their duties under penalty of law, commissioners followed additional instructions to seek "idle and suspicious" individuals and give them notice to find employment. To do this, they kept records of the population within their sectors and reported the whereabouts of people who moved out of their blocks. Commissioners who failed to perform their duties satisfactorily were subject to penalties.

On the regional level, Pérez also ordered the prefects to keep lists of all the inhabitants within their respective districts and their occupations. Unemployed individuals who could not prove that they had a legal means of subsistence were to be punished. Justices failing to comply with the requirements of the law were to be censured, fined, and removed from office.

If any doubt existed concerning Pérez's legal authority to impose taxes within the department, it disappeared with the decree of April 17, 1837. Sent from Mexico City, the decree spelled out the role of *jefes políticos* in directing their departments toward improved fiscal efficiency. Granting investigatory, advisory, and appointive powers to governors, it authorized Pérez to supervise treasury officials by signing off on their monthly and annual cash statements, to police for omissions and abuses. Furthermore, he was empowered to report and suspend employees who did not perform their duties in an exemplary and loyal manner. In the same way, control of customhouses fell to jefes políticos throughout Mexico. The decree of 1837 not only increased Pérez's power but added greater sanctions to his law of October 1835 and the June and July 1836 regulations.

An undercurrent of opposition to Perez's accretion of authority swiftly gained strength, gathering the discontented and opportunistic elements of New Mexico's political society. The optimism described in Pérez's inaugural speech began to evaporate, and his political enemies gradually revealed themselves. One of the first to do so was Juan Estevan Pino, a wealthy associate judge. Pino used his office to openly critique the few local New Mexican political cronies with whom Pérez surrounded himself. Pino's opposition to the appointment of Francisco Sarracino, another Pérez favorite, to the office of subcomisario forced

Sarracino's removal in 1836 on charges of embezzlement. In response to the charges, Pérez audited Sarracino's account books and found them to be correct. Yet Pino was not about to let Sarracino get off so easily, and joined forces with postmaster Juan Bautista Vigil and interim subcomisario Manuel Armijo to press his case.

Unwittingly, Pérez had intruded on a local political feud that would negatively affect his relations with all involved. The Pino-Sarracino rivalry was long-standing and had reached a breaking point late in October 1835 when Sarracino, under orders from Pérez, investigated charges that Juan Bautista Vigil was mismanaging the mail service. Vigil stood accused by Miguel Sena, a loyal follower of Pérez. Upon Sarracino's recommendation, Vigil was removed from office. Vigil appealed the decision, finding able support in Manuel Armijo, who wrote a counterbrief to Sena's complaint. Consequently, Vigil regained his position, and became an invaluable ally to Armijo, whose friendship with Judge Pino was personal as well as political.

This bitter history came to a head in 1836, when Sarracino was removed as subcomisario and Manuel Armijo replaced him. The following year Sarracino was brought to trial, even though Pérez had found the books to be in order. Presiding over Sarracino's trial, Juan Estevan Pino expeditiously found him guilty of embezzlement. Completely disregarding the verdict, Pérez reinstated Sarracino to his position, but acting subcomisario Manuel Armijo refused to give up the office. Perhaps Armijo was reluctant to give up a position paying four thousand pesos a year, but controversy also swirled around whether Pérez had the authority to override Pino's verdict.

The opposition to Pérez gathered momentum. The Sarracino episode had defined the factions; the compulsory education law, new taxes, and restrictions on people's movements had focused the locals on the issue of outside interference; the decree of 1837 had demonstrated the power of the central government; and local feuding supplied the emotion required to make the situation explosive. When Armijo was appointed *administrador de rentas* to oversee policies related to the collection of revenues, then summarily dismissed by Pérez, the disgruntled former public servant took a strong stand. Armijo denounced the power of governors. He and his allies found much to criticize about Pérez's administration. Objecting to all the obnoxious forms of taxation, they speculated on the possible precedents the law had set, ranging from a tax on poultry to the eventuality that "husbands would be taxed for the privileges generally attaching to connubial bliss." At the heart of the unrest was opposition to the departmental plan.

Meanwhile in the hinterland of northern New Mexico, more trouble brewed for the Pérez administration. A seemingly obscure court case in out-of-the-way La Cañada de Santa Cruz began a chain of events that led to a political confrontation with the governor. Presiding over a trial involving his relatives, Judge Juan José Esquivel acquitted them. The case was then reviewed by Ramón Abreu, a supporter of Pérez, who not only overturned the decision but had Esquivel arrested for refusing to comply with the reversal. Public sympathy soon rallied around the jailed Esquivel. A mob formed outside his cell, liberated him, and absconded to a mountain stronghold. Commenting on the situation, Josiah Gregg noted it was "an occurrence that seemed as a watchword for a general insurrection," and indeed it became the pretext for rebellion. On August 3, 1837, a revolutionary junta was formed, consisting of twelve persons who called their district the Cantón de La Cañada. The position statement they drew up said nothing about the Esquivel incident:

> Long live God and the Nation and the faith of Jesus Christ. The principal points which we defend are as follows:
>
> To be with God and the Nation and the faith of Jesus Christ.
> To defend our country to the last drop of blood in order to attain victory.
> Not to permit the Departmental Plan.
> Not to permit a single tax.
> Not to permit the bad order of those who are trying to effect it.
>
> God and the Nation. Santa Cruz de la Cañada. August 3, 1837. Encampment.

Gathered at the "encampment" with their counterparts, "the principal warriors of all the northern pueblos," the Hispanic rebels signaled that the rebellion had begun.

When word of impending trouble reached Pérez, he hastened to gather a militia but could muster only "150 men, including the warriors of the Pueblo of Santo Domingo." With his small force Pérez left the capital on August 7, 1837, to suppress the rebellion. While en route they were attacked by the rebels, reported Francisco Sarracino, "in a disorderly manner . . . giving us a lively fire. . . . Colonel Pérez approached the cannon and said to me these words 'Friend Sarracino, do not abandon the cannon.'" Needless to say, the cannon was abandoned, the battle lost, and most of Pérez's men either were captured or defected to the rebels. Pérez was chased back to the outskirts of Santa Fe, where on August 9 he was caught and brutally murdered. Josiah Gregg gave a secondhand description of the mistreatment of Pérez's corpse: "His body was then stripped and shockingly mangled: his head was carried as a trophy to the camp of the insurgents, who made a football of it among themselves.'" Gregg furthermore claimed to have witnessed the death of one of Pérez's associates, Jesús María Alarid: "I saw them surround a house and drag from it the Secretary of State, Jesús María Alarid, generally known by the sobriquet of El Chico. He and some other principal characters who had taken refuge among the ranchos were soon afterwards stripped and scourged, and finally pierced through and through with lances."

The rebellion gathered strength. Two thousand strong, almost all Pueblo warriors, the rebels marched on Santa Fe. Preparing for the worst, the inhabitants fortified themselves in their homes. The rabble entered the city and elected a governor, José Gonzales. Two days later, Gonzales and the rebels left to subdue the villages surrounding Santa Fe.

News of the rebellion reached the Hispanic villages on the Río Abajo (the lower Rio Grande south of Cochiti Pueblo). Despite their dislike of the Pérez administration, the people of the Río Abajo, which formed the second district of New Mexico, could not or would not support the rebellion. On September 8, 1837, members of the second district held a meeting at Tomé, south of Albuquerque, and called for the suppression of the rebels, who by then had established themselves in Santa Fe. Sensing that the tide of sentiment had turned against rebellion, Manuel Armijo, who lived in Old Town Alburquerque, denounced the uprising. At the meeting at Tomé, Mariano Chaves nominated

Armijo to be leader of the army opposing the rebels, saying, "I know of no one better qualified to lead our army than Manuel Armijo."

Armijo reported the situation to Mexico City and asked for reinforcements. Mexican officials sent three hundred more men under a certain Colonel Justiniani in command of the Veracruz Squadron, along with presidial troops from Chihuahua, but they did not arrive until the end of the year. As soon as the reinforcements arrived, for he could muster only a fighting force drawn mostly from the second district, Manuel Armijo, who had appointed himself governor, attacked the rebels just north of the Santa Cruz Valley. On January 27, 1838, at the Battle of La Cañada, Armijo captured and executed Gonzales, thus crushing the revolt. Reporting to the central government that the situation was under control and there was no need to send more troops, Armijo petitioned for the governorship and received it. With that concession, the government of New Mexico was restored to its native sons.

The next few years, Governor Manuel Armijo entrenched himself as sole ruler of New Mexico, governing the department with an iron hand. With Armijo in charge, New Mexicans could ignore directives from the central government in Mexico. Santa Anna's government had already been weakened by political and military defeats in Texas and California in 1836. Instability in Mexico allowed New Mexico to revert to its customary pattern of isolation. In effect, throughout the 1840s New Mexico went through a laissez faire period during which Mexican officials kept their distance as long as Manuel Armijo controlled affairs within his jurisdiction.

Among oral traditions and historical records, the ballad "Año de mil ochocientos treinta y siete desgraciado" (O Unfortunate Year, 1837) presents a nineteenth-century personal perspective on the death of the hapless jefe político. In the twentieth century the tragic event received renewed attention when, on Saturday, June 15, 1901, a group of New Mexicans met in Santa Fe to dedicate a monument to the memory of Albino Pérez. Leading the parade were the First Cavalry and the New Mexico National Guard Band, followed by the Daughters of the American Revolution, some members of the Rough Riders, firefighters, and a contingent of interested citizens. The paraders marched from the plaza to a point along Agua Fria Street and stopped near the spot where Governor Pérez had fallen sixty-four years before. As they gathered for a commemorative ceremony, gusts of wind and dust swirled around the spectators, while overhead clouds began to darken the late-afternoon sky. As a storm approached, a marble boulder was unveiled. Polished on one side, it bore the inscription:

On this spot, Governor Albino Pérez
was assassinated August 9, 1837

The paraders listened to speakers while wind and dust disturbed them and the rain clouds became ever more menacing. After a round of introductory remarks, Demetrio Pérez of Las Vegas made a brief, apologetic presentation punctuated with "forgive the brevity of my remarks." Demetrio Pérez, son of Albino Pérez, expressed his appreciation for the honor extended to the memory of his father. As he ended his speech, a driving hail storm scattered the crowd and cut short the ceremony. The administration of Governor Albino Pérez was, figuratively speaking, like the gathering storm that broke over the paraders on that June afternoon of 1901.

In the wake of rebellion, a strange event took place that would solidify Armijo's powers with the central government in Mexico City. Tending their sheep and farms, New Mexicans were unaware that their lives would be touched by a historical event that historians would later call the Texas Invasion of New Mexico and that would solidify Armijo's standing with his own people and the central government in Mexico City. Unbeknownst to New Mexicans, a group of adventurers in Texas decided to invade New Mexico and make the eastern half part of Texas. They claimed that the treaty Santa Anna had signed designated the Rio Grande as the boundary of Texas, and that the entire east bank, from the Gulf of Mexico to the San Luis Valley, belonged to the Lone Star Republic. In general, the Texans theorized that New Mexicans were awaiting an opportunity to declare independence from Mexico, and it was no less than their duty to release them from Mexican tyranny—at least those of them living east of the Rio Grande. The Texans also had opportunistic motives, hoping that if the invasion were successful, the Santa Fe–Chihuahua Trail trade could be diverted through Texas.

In the spring of 1841, President Mirabeau Bonaparte Lamar, without the support of the Congress of Texas, approved an expedition of about three hundred men in six companies under the command of Colonel Hugh McLeod. Three commissioners accompanied the expedition to proclaim the advantages of freedom from Mexico. Other men accompanying the expedition were traders, adventurers, and travelers who did not understand its purpose. The anonymous author of a note to the *Journal of the Santa Fe Expedition* by Peter Gallagher, a member of the ill-fated fiasco, described it as follows: "This 'wild goose chase' was sponsored by President Lamar for the express purpose of territorial expansion, of acquiring control of New Mexico—by peaceful means if possible; by military force if necessary. The expedition was assembled within the shadow of the Texas capital and with the advice and aid of the Texas President himself."

Pretending to be traders along the Santa Fe–Chihuahua Trail, McLeod and his men left Brushy Creek, fifteen miles north of Austin, on the morning of June 19, 1841, bound for New Mexico. Poorly supplied and equipped, they planned to live off the arid lands of west Texas. After a week, the expedition had reached unfamiliar land. By the first week in September, they had reached the vicinity of present Amarillo. The men, fatigued from the long march across treeless plains, were discontented and wanted to abandon the expedition. One had committed suicide, a few others had suffered fevers, some had been killed by Indians, and morale was low. By the time the expedition reached New Mexico, the survivors were near starvation, dehydrated, ragged, and dirty.

On September 17, New Mexicans arrived in the expedition's camp with messages that electrified the men. Gallagher's entry for that date reads: "About 8 o'clock, one of the Mexicans . . . together with three others from New Mexico, arrived in camp bringing letters informing us that all was right and that we should destroy all that we could not bring and take those Mexicans for guides to the settlements." The next day, seven wagons and all unnecessary baggage were burned. The Texans followed the guides through the waterless Llano Estacado for nearly two weeks. On October 4, a fully armed Mexican escort commanded by Colonel Damasio Salazar met them at Laguna Colorada to demand the Texans' surrender. Lieutenant Colonel Juan Andrés Archuleta presented the terms of capitulation: (1) that the Texans would lay down their arms; (2) that their life, liberty, and personal property would be protected; and (3) that they would be escorted to San Miguel, several days hence. Believing that their arms would be returned to them, the Texans capitulated.

On October 6, 1841, they camped at a point on Pajarito Creek. There the officers were separated from the men and taken to San Miguel. Two days later, after marching sixty miles, they arrived at Anton Chico, where they were fed and incarcerated in an old house. The next day they marched twenty miles to San Miguel del Vado. There, they were again kept under guard. Women came to sell them food, which they traded for the buttons off their shirts.

Meanwhile, Governor Armijo appointed Prefect Antonio Sandoval from Albuquerque as acting governor in Santa Fe while he personally attended to the invasion. Armijo had already informed New Mexicans that the Texans' intent was to "burn, slay, and destroy" on their march through the department. At first, Captain William P. Lewis, the expedition translator, tried to persuade Armijo that they were merchants from the United States. Having dealt with merchants along the Santa Fe–Chihuahua Trail, Armijo pointed to the star and the word "Texas" on Lewis's uniform. Turning to the Texans, he said, "You cannot deceive me: United States merchants do not wear Texas uniforms." Armijo's ire was evident; his patience thin. To save himself from imprisonment and possibly a firing squad, Lewis betrayed the Texans.

Armijo dealt with the invasion for what it was. Some Texans were executed. The majority of them were sent to Mexico City for trial and imprisonment. Damasio Salazar was the officer in charge of the prisoners. He marched them south from Santa Fe along the old Camino Real to Albuquerque. Many Hispanics felt sorry for them, gave them food, and—making the sign of the cross—wished them well and prayed for them. *Pobrecitos* was the word the Texans heard repeatedly as they headed south.

George W. Kendall, a Louisiana newspaper reporter who was one of the prisoners, recalled that about noon on October 22, they entered Albuquerque, "famed for the beauty of its women, besides being the largest place in the province of New Mexico, and the residence of Armijo a part of the year." He continued, "As we were marched directly through the principal streets the inhabitants were gathered on either side to gaze at the *estrangeros*, as we were called. The women, with all kindness of heart, gave our men corn, pumpkins, bread, and everything they could spare from their scanty store as we passed." Kendall wrote that after they departed Albuquerque, they passed through a succession of cultivated fields and pastures, undoubtedly those of Atrisco, Los Padillas, Armijo, and Pajarito. Of the route near Atrisco, a short distance from Albuquerque, Kendall wrote, "After leaving Albuquerque, we continued our march through a succession of cultivated fields and pastures until we reached a small rancho called Los Placeres, and here we camped for the night." By the evening of October 24, 1841, they had reached Valencia. Settlers all along the Camino Real approached the prisoners and gave them food, mostly corn and bread, and water for sustenance. The march continued past Isleta to Socorro.

The road to Mexico City was filled with death. Those who could not stand up and march were executed; the ears of the dead were cut off as proof that the prisoners had not escaped. Once past Socorro, lack of water and food and the desert heat took their toll on the Texans as they were forced to march through the Jornada del Muerto to El Paso. Having been brutally treated by their captors, the Texans arrived thirsty, starving, fatigued, and beaten. In El Paso, as in the valley of Albuquerque and later in Ciudad Chihuahua, compassionate people came out to give them food and water. Finally, the survivors made it to Mexico City, where many of them were released. Others were found guilty of sedition and treachery and imprisoned in the dungeons of the Acordada in Mexico City or at San Juan de Ulloa, the island in the harbor of Veracruz. Among them was José Antonio Navarro, who had supported the Texas rebellion against Mexico. He was treated as a traitor by President Santa Anna and imprisoned for nearly four years.

As for Governor Armijo, he emerged as a patriot for his heroic handling of the invasion, which prevented any loss of life among New Mexicans. Santa Fe Trail merchants kept away from the prisoners lest they be identified with the invaders. Within three weeks after the attempted Texan invasion, New Mexicans read a circular dated November 10, 1841, in which Armijo justified his actions. In it, he declared that it was necessary to delude the Texans, apprehend them, and manipulate their surrender with minimal risk to New Mexicans and thereby protect Mexico's honor. He emphasized that the nation's integrity had been challenged by Texans who wished to extend their claim to include New Mexico. In this instance and in all future relations, Armijo kept a wary watch on all foreigners.

Outside of New Mexico Kendall's biased writings told the story from the Texans' perspective, portraying the Mexicans as barbaric and unjustifiably cruel. He began a historiographical legacy that would malign and stereotype Armijo. Still, Mexican authorities had long anticipated an invading army from Texas. They had issued warnings about the possibility and had sent reinforcements to Chihuahua against such an eventuality. In the aftermath of the Texan incursion, Governor Armijo's superiors and citizens praised him for the way he had handled the situation. Armijo confiscated Captain McLeod's order book, which revealed the Texans' plan, and based on this evidence, later historians acknowledge that Armijo appropriately handled the attempted invasion for what it was.

Just prior to the U.S. occupation of New Mexico, the distribution of land took on a history of its own. Beginning with the Colonization Law of 1824, Mexican departments were directed to enact laws consistent with national policies providing for the colonization of lands within their respective boundaries. Mexican law prohibited the granting of lands within twenty leagues of an international boundary and ten leagues of coastlines without consent of the central government in Mexico City. No individual, furthermore, could receive more than eleven square leagues of land.

In New Mexico, especially during the 1840s, New Mexican officials used land grants to influence private enterprises and create defensive barriers against marauding Indians, Texans, and Anglo-American intruders. New Mexicans were encouraged to settle along river valleys on the northeastern and eastern peripheries bordering the Republic of Texas. Governor Armijo, one of the more profligate grantors of New Mexican land during the Mexican period, ostensibly gave away 16.5 million acres of the 31 million acres of available land between 1837 and 1846. In 1841 Guadalupe Miranda and Charles Beaubien requested and received from

Armijo lands east of the Sangre de Cristo Mountains along the Cimarron and Canadian rivers. They had planned to ranch, cultivate cotton and sugar beets, cut timber, and prospect for minerals. That grant later became the subject of one of the largest land grant claims when Beaubien's son-in-law, Lucien Maxwell, claimed nearly the 2 million acres (2,680 square miles) in northeastern New Mexico and southeastern Colorado.

Cautiously selecting land grant recipients to reinforce New Mexico's defenses, Armijo generally chose foreigners who either had married Mexican women or had lived in New Mexico since the 1820s. Most foreign grantees had New Mexican partners. In 1845, for example, the French Canadian Gervasio Nolan and two New Mexican partners received lands neighboring the Beaubien-Miranda Grant on the Canadian River. Charles Beaubien's thirteen-year-old son, Narciso, and a partner, Stephen Louis Lee, a fur trapper from St. Louis, received the Sangre de Cristo Grant in the San Luis Valley straddling the present New Mexico and Colorado border. Cerán St. Vrain and Cornelio Vigil received the Animas Grant along the Cucharas, Huerfano, and Apishapa rivers in eastern Colorado; and John Scholly and his Mexican and Anglo-American partners received a grant northwest of Las Vegas.

The large amounts of land granted to foreigners apparently alarmed New Mexicans. One of Armijo's more vocal opponents was the celebrated cleric Father Antonio José Martínez of Taos. In February 1844, when the ailing Armijo stepped down briefly as governor, Father Martínez jumped on the opportunity, urging interim governor Mariano Martínez to annul the Beaubien-Miranda grant because Beaubien, a naturalized Mexican citizen, had Charles Bent, who was a foreigner, as a partner in the land grant. Arguing that the Colonization Law permitted foreigners to acquire property anywhere in the Mexican Republic except in departments contiguous with other nations, where they required special permission, Father Martínez persuaded the interim governor to oust Beaubien from his land. In late spring 1844, Governor Martínez ordered Beaubien to vacate his grant. Father Martínez's victory was short-lived, however, for the next governor, José Chaves, reinstated the rights of Beaubien, Bent, and St. Vrain to settle foreigners on the Beaubien-Miranda Grant. In 1845, General Francisco García Conde, a representative of the central government on an inspection tour of New Mexico, ordered all foreigners in the

Cimarron area to vacate their lands. Yet Manuel Armijo, who had once again assumed the governorship of New Mexico, encouraged the foreigners to ignore the order. Motivated by his one-fourth interest in the grant, Governor Armijo supported foreign settlers in their desire to remain on the Beaubien-Miranda land grant.

The Mexican government actively sought to colonize the northern frontier with settlers in order to secure it against Indians and encroachment by foreign governments. Anyone who would swear allegiance to the Mexican government, become a Roman Catholic, and promise to bring additional settlers into the area was welcomed. Buoyed by this policy Armijo's giveaway land grant policies attracted new immigrants into New Mexico. In 1821, New Mexico's population was estimated at approximately 42,000; by 1845, on the eve of U.S. annexation, the number had reached virtually 65,000 inhabitants. Armijo remained governor of the politically fragmented Department of New Mexico until the U.S. invasion of 1846. With the government weakened by nine years of political strife, many leading New Mexicans desired separation from Mexico and annexation to the United States. When Stephen Watts Kearny and his Army of the West marched into Santa Fe in 1846, during the War with Mexico, members of New Mexico's upper class welcomed him. A new, troublous era then began for the Hispanics of New Mexico.

The Mexican period was a time of change, mainly administrative, that demonstrated the adaptability of New Mexicans to a new political system. Mexico's heroes became their heroes and they celebrated their country, even as they resented the tighter chain of command and heavier taxation that came with integration into the republic. A well-documented Mexican Independence Day event in Santa Fe on September 16, 1844, reflected the spirit of New Mexico's citizens and their participation in the political culture of Mexico. President of the assembly Tomás Ortiz and his committee organized the refreshments, balls, and opening ceremony on September 15. Juan Bautista Vigil y Alarid oversaw the organization of processions, church festivities and a mass, fireworks, and public events on the plaza, including a bullfight. Captain Donaciano Vigil's committee arranged for military salutes, cannonades, and proclamations by the governor.

The Mexican Independence Day celebration came off as one of the grandest ever held in the department. In only twenty-three years, New Mexicans had by 1844 embraced liberty from the Spanish crown and the evolving political system of Mexico. Very shortly, however, contemporary events far to the east, particularly the U.S. presidential campaign in the fall of 1844, would turn New Mexico's world upside down. Subsequent events would transform the region from part of Mexico's far north in 1845 to part of the American Southwest by 1848. New Mexicans' novitiate in Mexican politics prepared them for the next cycle of change.

CHAPTER 5

Shifting National Identities, 1846–1850s

As I see things over here, this Department [of New Mexico] will have to belong to the neighboring nation of the North that tolerates all religions. For some time it has coveted this area, and, according to what I observe, our rulers disregard these perils pretending not to believe what they are told, even though the time of the change of sovereignty is near.

PADRE ANTONIO JOSEPH MARTÍNEZ, TAOS, SEPTEMBER 2, 1845

MEXICO HAD LONG KNOWN that the United States had designs on acquiring Mexican lands. Since the Louisiana Purchase in 1803, American expansionists had dreamed of what Thomas Jefferson called an "Empire for Liberty" extending to the Pacific Coast. Early in the nineteenth century, with the help of General Andrew Jackson, the United States nibbled away at the Spanish Empire's Gulf Coast lands from Texas to Florida. By Mexican Independence in 1821, the United States abutted the newly independent country and had a presence in the Caribbean. Once elected president, "Old Hickory" Jackson sent emissaries to Mexico on a bungled mission to buy San Francisco harbor, Alta California (encompassing much of modern California and Mexican territory west of New Mexico), and perhaps New Mexico. He also cheered on the revolution in the Mexican province of Texas in 1836, but left office before he could push annexation of the Lone Star Republic through a less than enthusiastic U.S. Congress.

In the fall of 1844, Jackson's protégé "Young Hickory," James Knox Polk of Tennessee, ran for president on the Jacksonian expansionist agenda. His campaign promises—to settle the boundary dispute with Great Britain over the Oregon territory, to annex the Texas Republic, and to purchase New Mexico and Alta California from Mexico—appealed to nationalistic Americans who foresaw the culmination of a long-felt ambition. Shortly after Polk's inauguration, a journalist immodestly proclaimed that the United States had a "Manifest Destiny" in accordance with God's will to spread civilization across the continent, from ocean to ocean. To Mexico and Britain, the rumblings from Washington, D.C., were tantamount to declarations of war.

In 1836 Mexican President Antonio López de Santa Anna had under duress signed a treaty ending the Texas Revolution. This peace treaty recognized Texas as an independent republic and established the international boundary. Texans interpreted the boundary line as following the Rio Grande from mouth to source, making all lands east of the Rio Grande (including Santa Fe and present eastern New Mexico) part of Texas. Everything west of the river remained Mexican territory. The Mexican Congress had never ratified the treaty, however, and in fact, President López de Santa Anna had been overthrown and exiled for signing it. Consequently, subsequent Mexican governments repudiated Texan independence and vehemently opposed the claimed boundary line. The U.S. intent to annex Texas, New Mexico, and California constituted claims on Mexican sovereign territory. Although some expansionists, such as Missouri Senator Thomas Hart Benton, valued New Mexico for its trade and resource potential, and President Polk valued the transcontinental crossing that ran through it, New Mexico was far less important to expansionist Americans than Texas and California. New Mexico was in the path of American westward expansion.

In January 1845, the U.S. Congress passed a resolution favoring annexation of the willing Lone Star Republic, even though Mexican leaders threatened war if the United States did so. By summer the Texans had drafted a state constitution and formally prepared to join the Union as the twenty-eighth state, which they accomplished on December 29, 1845. Meanwhile, New Mexicans watched the impending crisis with divided loyalties. Mexicans such as Padre Antonio Joseph Martínez of Taos sought in vain to garner attention (and protection) from Mexico City, while the few Americans in New Mexico celebrated the news of annexation and announced to their *compadres*, prematurely, that they were now part of the United States. The building tensions manifested in a brawl in Santa Fe between Anglos and Hispanics, the first of many that spring of 1846.

Anglo traders such as Charles Bent favored a peaceful transfer of power to the United States as most conducive to their interests in protecting the trade along the Santa Fe Trail and with the Indians. To that end, a network of spies and dispatches kept the U.S. military informed of developments in New Mexico. For example, twenty-four-year-old Francis Preston Blair, Jr., son of a member of Polk's unofficial "Kitchen Cabinet," left Missouri to join Bent in Taos, "for his health," where he commenced a pro-annexation letter-writing campaign to the press and government agents. (He was nearly beaten to death in Taos for his efforts.)

As war loomed in the spring of 1846, Polk ordered General Zachary Taylor to move his troops in Texas south to the Rio Grande, which Mexico considered an act of war and invasion of its territory. The new Mexican president Mariano Paredes y Arrillaga sent forces to meet the advancing Americans. When U.S. and Mexican soldiers engaged in a skirmish north of the river, President Polk declared that "American blood had been shed on American soil." In Mexico's view, Mexican blood had been shed on Mexican soil. Seizing the opportunity, the United States declared war on May 13. The subsequent battles of Palo Alto and Reseca de la Palma, victories for Taylor, began more than two years of bloodshed. At the time, no one foresaw how lopsided the eventual Mexican defeat would be, and both sides were eager for battle. After all, during the 1840s Mexico had successfully fended off advancing Texas soldiers and twice taken back parts of the Lone Star Republic.

Historians have debated the causes of the Mexican War for the past 150 years. The traditional American historical interpretation placed the blame on Mexico and its unwillingness to agree to a Texan boundary through diplomacy. The Mexican view, by contrast, is that President Polk brought on the war of North American aggression by maneuvering to cause conflict with Mexico and then seize its lands. These simplistic interpretations have over the years been refined, as the complexities of internal politics in Mexico and the United States have gained greater prominence than their diplomatic and military actions. No Mexican government could accede to the U.S. annexation of Texas and expect to stay in power: the fact that López de Santa Anna had been ousted and exiled for signing the treaty in the first place served as a grim warning. On the U.S. side, Polk was pursuing a strategy of bluster and intimidation; although similar tactics had worked in the wrangling with Britain over the Oregon country, they failed in the Southwest.

The American battle plan was three-pronged. General Taylor would advance into the northeastern Mexican states and a second army would be sent into the heart of Mexico to capture Mexico City. A third column would occupy the lands of New Mexico and California. In May 1846, President Polk and Secretary of War William L. Marcy ordered Colonel Stephen Watts Kearny to prepare an army to take New Mexico and California, annex them, and set up governments there. The soon-to-be general raised 3,200 troops, a mix of regulars, volunteers from Missouri and other Mississippi Valley states, and 500 Mormons, called the Mormon Battalion. By July the lead force of 1,700, with sixteen cannon and a mile-long supply train—the largest army ever to enter the region—had reached Bent's Fort on the Arkansas River in modern Colorado. From there Kearny wrote Governor Manuel Armijo of New Mexico the self-justifying fiction that "by the annexation of Texas to the United States, the Rio Grande from its mouth to its source forms at this time the boundary between her and Mexico, and I come by order of the government to take possession of the Country."

In Santa Fe, Armijo had called for the raising of a volunteer militia, and ordered the assembly to convene in order to allocate funds for munitions and supplies. Assembly President Tomás Ortiz failed to get government funds because the treasury was bankrupt, so sought instead last-minute loans to raise $5,000 in emergency funds. Armijo also summoned his advisors, ranging from local politicians and military officers to the Roman Catholic clergy. The military, including second in command Colonel Diego Archuleta and officers from Chihuahua, called for war. Fearing the slaughter of the ill-armed New Mexicans, one of the priests suggested capitulation. The *alcaldes* (city mayors) and some merchants and traders favored waiting for reinforcements from Mexico City or states to the south. Americans in Taos and Santa Fe, such as Charles Bent, had favored Armijo's selection as governor partially because he had commercial interests that they hoped might sway him from engaging the enemy at the cost of New Mexico's economic ties with the Americans to the north. Bent also advised Kearny that Armijo would not fight without reinforcements from Chihuahua or

Sonora, which never materialized. Kearny sent a party of dragoons and friendly merchants to the capital to meet with the governor and extend an offer of a negotiated surrender, which was rejected. Armijo declared he would meet General Kearny on the field of battle. On August 14, with two thousand courageous volunteers, the governor marched out of Santa Fe to meet the invaders.

Kearny's advance was that of a master diplomat. He ordered his troops to treat the property and persons of New Mexico as they would U.S. citizens. He stationed troops to protect fields and corrals of live-stock along the way. He declared that "not a pepper, not an onion, shall be disturbed by my troops without pay, or by consent of the owner." He helped a Taos Indian find his wife, once a captive of the Plains Indians. He let Mexican spies inspect his troop strength, fed them, and then let them return to report to Armijo. As he marched deeper into New Mexico, he displayed his military might at Las Vegas, Tecolote, and San Miguel del Vado, while promising the gathered populace that he would protect them. At each village, his speech was reserved: "We come amongst you as friends, not as enemies—as protectors not as con-querors . . . I absolve you of all allegiance to the Mexican government."

As Kearny approached the main pass into Santa Fe, the alcalde of Pecos informed him that Armijo's troops, which had been gath-ered to fight at the nearby close quarters of Apache Canyon, had dis-banded, and the governor had fled south toward Chihuahua. Years later, Rafael Chacón, who had been a young cadet with Armijo, recalled that fateful decision at Apache Canyon: "What could Armijo do with an undisciplined army without any military training, without commissary resources, and without leaders to direct the men? He was a dwarf against a giant. Armijo was the imaginary hero of the epoch. Had he rashly rushed to give battle, it would have been the equiva-lent to offering his troops as victims of an invading army; the result would have been a useless effusion of blood, offering himself unnec-essarily to death." A few days later, one of the American traders wrote his partner that Santa Fe was now "as quiet and tranquil as if nothing had happened."

As the Army of the West under General Kearny occupied New Mexico, a new order was at hand. On August 19, 1846, in the Plaza de

Santa Fe Kearney addressed the people of New Mexico, saying that they no longer owed allegiance to Mexico; that he would respect their property and religion; that he, not Armijo, now served as their governor; and that he rejoiced in taking possession "without firing a gun, or spilling a drop of blood." But his words were upstaged by those of the outgoing acting governor, Juan Bautista Vigil y Alarid. Vigil's words echoed with a certain *tristeza*, a sadness, throughout New Mexico as he acknowledged that "no one in this world can resist the power of him who is stronger." Vigil y Alarid also countered with a token of *la resistencia*. Where Kearny said that New Mexico was now part of the United States and its people U.S. citizens, Vigil y Alarid replied they would let Washington, D.C., and Mexico City decide that. Looking at General Kearney Vigil y Alarid continued: "Do not find it strange if there has been no manifestation of joy and enthusiasm in seeing this city occupied by your military forces. To us the power of the Mexican Republic is dead. No matter what her condition, she was our mother. What child will not shed abundant tears at the tomb of his parents? . . . Today we belong to a great and powerful nation . . . we know that we belong to the Republic that owes its origin to the immortal Washington, whom all civilized nations admire and respect." With those poignant words, New Mexico slipped uneasily into the hands of the United States.

Kearny's mandate from President Polk included the establishment of a civil government, with the option to retain standing Mexican officials. A number of the elite *ricos* assisted him in forming a new government and drafting a set of laws. Several talented lawyers turned soldiers under his command wrote a set of laws, called the Kearny Code, which established a territorial form of government. Primarily the work of the well-schooled soldier Willard Hall and Francis Preston Blair, Jr. (Yale class of 1839 and Princeton class of 1841, respectively), both of whom later served in Congress, the code incorporated the most recent legal principles of government. Vigil y Alarid and Donaciano Vigil, a native nuevomexicano military officer, assisted with translation and with incorporating Mexican laws to promote a smooth transition. The 171 pages of the Kearny Code detailed, in Spanish and English, the new law of the land. It would stand for thirty years as the most enlightened legacy of the conquest.

Kearny moved quickly to establish a territorial government, appointing a slate of officers on September 22. At the local level he and his successors kept the local Mexican prefects (judges) and alcaldes in place where possible. (Sixteen of twenty-two such officials during the 1846–50 period of military rule were Mexican, including five of the first seven prefects appointed in 1846.) But at the territorial level, Mexicans were woefully underrepresented, occupying only three of the nine territory-wide posts: Donaciano Vigil became secretary (lieutenant governor) under Governor Charles Bent. French Canadian Charles Beaubien, a merchant and longtime resident of Taos, and Antonio José Otero, of the prominent Valencia County family, were appointed to two of the three judgeships. The remaining posts—one judgeship, U.S. attorney, U.S. marshal, treasurer, and auditor—went to Americans, mostly from Taos and Santa Fe and associated with Charles Bent.

Meanwhile, U.S. public opinion was sharply divided over the war between Mexico and the United States; the Massachusetts legislature even passed a resolution declaring the war unconstitutional. When news of Kearny's actions reached the east, opponents of the war used the general as a scapegoat to incite an outcry against Polk's administration and the war. The *Richmond Whig* newspaper declared, "How Napoleonic!" asserting that neither Kearny nor Polk had the authority to establish a government and declare New Mexico residents U.S. citizens; moreover, Kearny had named himself governor then appointed his own replacement.

In this era of increasing literacy and the growth of the penny press, the public eagerly sought news of the war. Eager to meet the demand, newspaper editors across the country published and reprinted letters and journals by soldiers serving in New Mexico. These at times sensationalized accounts of "exotic" lands—possibly helped along by editors eager to gain readership—contained shocking tales of women of loose virtue and regularly portrayed Mexican males as rogues and thieves. The same themes were echoed in popular literature of the period.

More valuable from a historical perspective were the unpublished personal journals of the period. Members of the Mormon Battalion commented on the villages with their prominent churches. Many wrote about the prosperous-looking fields, farms, orchards, and livestock. Most noted the *acequia* irrigation systems that created these islands of green. Azariah Smith wrote, "There is little or no rain in this country yet they raise very good wheat, corn and onions and have lots of goats, sheep, jackasses, cows, mules and oxen." One can speculate about how these Mormons' impressions of New Mexico might have influenced the later growth of their own irrigated Zion around the Great Salt Lake.

Most letter and journal writers noted the hospitality and unexpected warmth of the New Mexicans. A weary Private William Richardson, near Abiquiú, fed and treated well by a mother and daughter who embraced him on his departure, wrote: "I was thankful for the meal my hostess had provided for me, but the hugging was a luxury I did not anticipate."

Best known of the letter writers and journal keepers was eighteen-year-old Susan Magoffin. She gave a rare woman's view, concerned with domestic life; her merchant husband's associates; and the gracious, friendly, and welcoming people that she came to know, albeit briefly, in Santa Fe and along the Rio Grande. She noted Kearny's continued diplomacy with the New Mexicans, including that he attended a Catholic church, visited the grand haciendas, and hosted a ball at the Palace of the Governors. Among the attendees at the last was "Doña Tules," Doña María Gertrudis Barceló, the owner of a gambling hall and brothel in the capital, a self-made businesswoman of her time. To Magoffin, she was the ruin of wayward young men.

Poorly housed and fed, the U.S. troops badly needed the residents' hospitality. Large numbers of soldiers succumbed to scurvy and other diseases, and an estimated three or four hundred died in the winter of 1846–47. During the war more soldiers were lost to disease than battle. Even today Santa Fe residents near the heights of old Fort Marcy periodically come across the unmarked grave and skeleton of some Missouri farm boy who followed General Kearny. The occupied capital became, according to one soldier, a "grave-yard for many young and gallant men."

The numbers of U.S. troops in Santa Fe diminished when General Kearny departed for California in late September. At nearly the same time he sent Colonel Alexander Doniphan and his First Missouri

Mounted Volunteers to treat with the Navajos and then invade and capture Chihuahua. Doniphan defeated Mexican armies, first at the Battle of Brazito, near modern Las Cruces, on December 25, and then on February 28, 1847, at Sacramento outside Chihuahua City. Doniphan's victories are important for their role in helping to establish the location of the current international border with Mexico.

Kearny left Colonel Sterling Price and his approximately one thousand Second Missouri Volunteers in Santa Fe. Idle, unpaid, and poorly fed, Price's soldiers soon unraveled all the goodwill that Kearny had worked so hard to knit together with the native New Mexicans. Robberies and violence occurred far too frequently. During the fall of 1846 rumors of revolt swept Santa Fe. Colonel Price's men had captured an apparently incendiary petition en route to Mexico City, signed by 126 New Mexicans seeking help. Rumors spread of a priest from El Paso del Norte who visited Santa Fe to incite revolt among his brethren and to assure them that help would arrive if an insurrection began. According to hearsay, Diego Archuleta had attended clandestine gatherings in Río Arriba and Taos counties. Soldiers arrested another suspect, who carried a list of all former militia leaders. Governor Bent feared a revolt was gathering impetus in Río Arriba, Taos, San Miguel, and Santa Fe counties. Any spark could ignite an explosion of violence.

In early December Colonel Price received concrete information about a conspiracy that involved a plan to capture Governor Bent, kill Price himself, and overthrow the government. Tomás Ortiz would become governor and Diego Archuleta would take military command. On Price's orders troops searched houses in the capital and arrested more than twenty suspected conspirators. Ortiz and Archuleta vanished. Bent issued a soothing proclamation assuring the populace that the revolt had been aborted, that its leaders were in flight, and that after their defeat by Colonel Doniphan at Brazito, the Chihuahua militia would not come to the rebels' rescue. A quick military trial acquitted the supposed conspirators, many of whom took the oath of allegiance and joined the American ranks.

Believing that matters had settled down, Governor Bent took a break to visit his family and friends in Taos. A day out, a group of Taos Pueblo Indians confronted the governor, asking him to release

Pueblo prisoners held in the Taos jail. Bent's blunt admonition that they should let the law take its course may have been the spark that inflamed simmering resentment into revolt. In the early morning of January 19, 1847, a mob of Pueblo Indians and Mexicans, after freeing the prisoners and killing the sheriff, attacked Bent in his home, killing and scalping him. They then proceeded to murder other Americans and American sympathizers in Río Hondo, Questa, Mora, and other nearby freighter camps. Within a few days nineteen men were dead.

Men in Taos stepped forward to lead an insurrection. Pueblo leader and former alcalde Tomás "Tomasito" Romero joined forces with José Pablo Montoya, a participant in the 1837 revolt. A call went out for recruits to attack Santa Fe. An example proclamation of January 21, 1847, read: "To the Defenders of their Country: With the end to shake off the yoke bound on us by a foreign government . . . [w]e have declared war on the Americans and it is now time that we shall take our arms in our hands in defense of our abandoned country."

By the end of January some two thousand revolutionaries marched into Santa Cruz de la Cañada bound for Santa Fe. Here, Colonel Price with his cannon and a special volunteer force who called themselves "The Avengers," most of them Bent's friends, met the poorly armed New Mexicans. Cannon fire broke up the rebel forces. In a rout, Price's men gave chase, and at Embudo and Taos they put down the revolt. A second military detachment swept the Mora Valley, destroying every house and ranch. Attempts to reignite the revolution in the spring failed. After another brief uprising in June, Price's troops similarly leveled a small village near Las Vegas. Altogether an estimated four hundred New Mexicans lost their lives.

The subsequent trial of fifty prisoners received national attention. Tomasito had been killed by a guard after the battle at Taos, but Montoya appeared before a military tribunal, was quickly sentenced to death, and was hanged on February 9. Price decided to hand the remaining prisoners over to the newly formed civil courts to be tried for treason and murder. After fifteen were hanged and the seventy-five-year-old patriot Antonio María Trujillo, the father-in-law of Diego Archuleta, was sentenced to death, Padre Martínez protested the court proceedings. Eventually, President Polk sent a request for leniency toward Trujillo, and Secretary of War William Marcy advised that the charge of treason did not apply since Trujillo (and the other nuevomexicanos) were still citizens of Mexico and could not be convicted of treason for protecting their own country: it is "unconstitutional to try any native inhabitant of New Mexico for the crime of treason against the government of the United States, until by actual treaty with Mexico he becomes a citizen," he wrote. Acting governor Donaciano Vigil ordered Trujillo's release. In the subsequent trials, the jurors were predominately Hispanic, and most of the remaining defendants were acquitted. In a thorough review of the trials, law professor Laura Gómez notes that even though flawed, the trials of 1847 marked the beginning of a transition from a military government to a responsive civil court system. She suggests that "it may have been precisely the fact of Mexicans' participation that resulted in the successful imposition of American colonial rule in New Mexico during the coming decades."

For New Mexico, the outcome of what has become inaccurately called the Taos revolt was martial law and military domination. As with other emotional issues of the war, the charge of treason against Trujillo and Kearny's civil government were attacked nationally in the opposition press and by the Whig Party. An editorial in the March 18, 1847, St. Louis *Missouri Republican* is typical; it called both the Kearny Code and the treason trials illegal and unconstitutional. Secretary of War Marcy ordered Colonel Price to disband all but the essential components of Kearny's territorial government. Price was appointed military and civil governor, governing the region as an occupied military zone. He wisely kept the alcaldes, prefects, and court system in place (though he abolished the office of U.S. attorney). He also retained Donaciano Vigil as his advisor, eventually elevating him, with Washington's permission, to civil governor and second in command.

As secretary and governor between 1846 and 1851, Donaciano Vigil served a critical role in New Mexico's transition from Mexican to U.S. forms of government, an interpreter of New Mexico for the Americans and a bridge to the new country for nuevomexicanos. As an example, the alcalde of Taos sent him a request: "because I do not understand these laws [Kearny Code]. Please teach me to understand this new code." Although Vigil had stood disappointedly at Apache Canyon as Armijo fled, he decided to participate in transforming New Mexico to a U.S. territory because, as he put it, "pride pointed in one direction; duty in another." During the Taos revolt he expressed his (and others') viewpoint: "is it not gross absurdity to foment rancorous feelings toward people with whom we are either to compose one family, or to continue our commercial relations?" He summoned the first legislature, an advisory one, in 1847, and led in the efforts to form a civil government after the war.

Many New Mexicans' attitudes shifted in favor of the United States in the aftermath of the Taos revolt and as Mexico lost battle after battle as the war progressed. By September 1847 American troops occupied Mexico City. President Polk, frustrated with Mexico's unwillingness to surrender, ordered troops to take Baja California, Sonora, and Chihuahua, which Price marched off in December to accomplish. Polk elevated Price to the rank of general and appointed him military governor of Chihuahua. Although Price probably expected his campaign would earn him a place among the war's heroes, he was all but forgotten when his defeat of the Chihuahuans coincided with the final acceptance of an unpopular treaty at the end of an unpopular war. The Treaty of Guadalupe Hidalgo was signed by emissaries on February 2, revised by the U.S. Senate on March 10, and accepted by Mexico on May 30; peace was restored with the evacuation of U.S. troops, including Price's column, out of Mexico, in July 1848.

Colonel Alexander Doniphan and his Missouri Volunteers, who marched five thousand miles, became the only war heroes of the New Mexico campaign; in the United States Doniphan was celebrated second only to soon-to-be-president General Zachary Taylor. The national media portrayed Doniphan as a citizen-soldier, the heroic equivalent of the citizen-warrior of ancient Greece. Unfortunately for New Mexicans, some of the letters his soldiers had published in small-town newspapers now became popular books about the war, describing the New Mexico they had "conquered" with Kearny as a "bleak and hostile" landscape inhabited by foreigners portrayed in the most unflattering terms. New Mexico could have found no worse press agents at that critical time when its political fate came before the U.S. Congress.

To the United States, the Treaty of Guadalupe Hidalgo ended an unpopular war. To Mexico, the treaty removed occupation troops from its capital while annexing half its territory to the United States. For former residents of Mexico's far north, now the American Southwest, it ostensibly offered private property protections and rights of citizenship. The treaty required the United States to protect Mexico from Apache and Comanche raiders into her domain, an impossible task. It also required the United States to return any Mexican captives held by these Indians. Article V would, because of a faulty map, poorly define the new international boundary line; it was not far enough south for President Polk and other expansionists, but they acceded in order to end hostilities.

The United States paid $18,250,000 to an impoverished Mexico and $3 million to her debt holders in exchange for the ceded lands, encompassing what is now Texas, California, Utah, and Nevada; most of New Mexico, Arizona, and Colorado; and slices of Oklahoma, Kansas, and Wyoming. Because of the payment to Mexico for the cession of lands and claims, most Americans today see the treaty as one big real estate deal. Yet the acquisition of new territory brought on disputes in the United States about the expansion of slavery, leading to disunion and civil war within thirteen years. To Mexico, it was a cleaving and loss of half of its domain, a source of long-lingering hostility toward the United States.

In the first half century following ratification of the Treaty of Guadalupe Hidalgo, hundreds of state, territorial, and federal legal entities produced a number of conflicting opinions and decisions interpreting the treaty's provisions, particularly those dealing with citizenship rights of Hispanics living in the Mexican cession. At the onset, the provisions of the treaty conferring citizenship rights on Mexicans living in the ceded territories seemed clear. The evolving practice of denying or suppressing these rights would prove otherwise. In the context of the nineteenth-century United States, where ethnocentrism and racism enjoyed a long history vis-à-vis white-black relationships, Hispanics had to fight for their rights. The struggle took on many forms from armed resistance to alienation with Anglo-American society. Within a generation, Hispanics learned to use the court system to challenge perpetrators who violated their citizenship rights. In general, they hoped to gain recognition of the treaty in the courts in order to protect their land and water rights. In regard to land issues, Hispanics had filed a thousand claims by 1880, but the federal government had only considered 150 of them. Many cases were never appealed beyond the jurisdictions of the district courts, where, it appeared, justice was final. Hispanics' experiences in the court system encouraged the belief that the Anglo-American judicial system, administered by Anglo-American politicians, legislators, and judges, particularly at the district court level, worked against Hispanic interests. Thus, property and voting rights of former Mexican citizens in California, Arizona, and New Mexico, proved vulnerable to interpretation by district and territorial courts.

Returning to the immediate aftermath of the treaty, the Santa Fe *Republican* in May 1848 published a copy of the Treaty of Guadalupe Hidalgo for all to read. In New Mexico, the immediate questions revolved around the articles promising a civil government, property rights, citizenship for residents who chose to remain, and repatriation of those who chose to return to Mexico. Article VIII provided citizens one year to elect to retain their Mexican citizenship or automatically become U.S. citizens. Those retaining Mexican citizenship could either remain in the Southwest or move south of the border to new homes.

In 1849 and 1850, commissioners from Chihuahua encouraged nuevomexicanos to relocate south. Meanwhile local New Mexico authorities, including the new military governor Colonel John M. Washington (Price's replacement) and Governor Vigil, did everything they could to discourage the out-migration of Mexicans. They argued that the move would result in great inconvenience, suffering, and misery, pointing out that settlers would lack protection from either government against Apache raiders, because they would be living in isolated areas north and south of El Paso. During that first year, 900 New Mexicans petitioned the Mexican government to move to Chihuahua, and an estimated 1,500 to 2,000 people eventually underwent the trauma of relocation. Overall, however, the depopulation of New Mexico failed to materialize due to Mexico's bankrupt recolonization program; the people's strong tie to the land, their *patria chica;* and for some, an optimistic desire to work within the new order.

Article IX provided for the protection of nuevomexicanos' property rights, including honoring land grants (parcels of land that Spain and Mexico had awarded for service to the crown or republic). In the turmoil of the war's aftermath, governor and acting registrar Vigil attempted to register land grants, a haphazard process until a U.S. surveyor general could be appointed for the territory; however, the U.S. Congress did not fill the position until 1854. Like a thread woven through the entire history of New Mexico, land grants reappeared in controversy after controversy down to the present (land grant issues will be taken up in subsequent chapters).

The treaty provided New Mexicans the option to retain their Mexican citizenship while continuing to reside in the newly acquired U.S. territory. Unfortunately, there was no process for recognizing individual decisions. Almost immediately, the issue became controversial when former members of the Mexican military or participants in the Taos revolt desired to return to or remain in New Mexico. In the fall of 1848, Diego Archuleta returned home, receiving a pardon from the acting military governor, as all combatants did. However, one of the judges who presided over the Taos trials sought to have him and others arrested as conspirators in the murder of Governor Bent. The military governor intervened to protect them.

Governor Washington, without guidance from his superiors, decided to require that all New Mexicans wishing to remain citizens of Mexico go to the nearest prefect and declare their intention by May 30, 1849, the one-year anniversary of the treaty signing. From later events, it is obvious that some if not most of the two thousand or so residents who decided to retain their Mexican citizenship did not realize that they gave up the right to vote, serve on juries, or hold political office in the U.S. territory of New Mexico. This became a major problem in territorial elections during the 1850s. Hispanic and Anglo political factions of the evolving territory repeatedly tried to disqualify their opponents' "Mexican citizen" voters, while turning a blind eye to those "Mexican citizens" who voted for their candidates. The opposing factions stationed individuals at the polls to check names against Governor Washington's list of "Mexican citizens," turning away prospective voters or challenging their ballots.

The disputed 1853 election of a New Mexican delegate to Congress finally brought the issue of Washington's process to the territorial court. The court ruled and was upheld that his process for declaring Mexican citizenship (and thus denying enfranchisement) was illegal and therefore null and void. Only the U.S. Congress had authority to define the system or process for granting citizenship, which it never did. Congress tacitly approved the court's decision by recognizing Miguel Otero as the elected delegate in 1855, over the protests of incumbent Padre José Manuel Gallegos, who claimed Otero was elected by "Mexican citizens." In effect, those on Governor Washington's list were now no longer barred from voting.

The issue of Mexican citizenship continued to be a problem in the courts however, especially in cases involving Anglo-Americans. For example, as late as 1858, when one George Carter was convicted of intent to murder a Hispanic, his lawyer demanded a retrial on the basis that the grand jury foreman, Anastasio Sandoval, had previously elected to retain his Mexican citizenship. A jury containing a Mexican citizen, he claimed, violated Carter's right to be tried by his peers. However, at a subsequent hearing Sandoval was declared a U.S. citizen. On appeal Carter's lawyer brought up the specter of distrust of people having a foreign (that is, Mexican) language and customs, portraying Mexicans as disloyal perpetrators of the Taos revolt, in an ultimately unsuccessful attempt to persuade judge Kirby Benedict to overturn the verdict.

As the judge's gavel came down, it resounded not just for Carter, but for Hispanics. The price, of course, was confirmation that some nineteenth-century Anglo-Americans in New Mexico harbored intense disdain and distrust of Hispanics, and would continue to question their loyalty to the United States (even in court). The negative fallout of the war between Mexico and the United States and of the Taos revolt would linger long in the collective memories of New Mexicans. Hispanics of New Mexico would not acquire the full rights as U.S. citizens promised them under the Treaty of Guadalupe Hidalgo until statehood in 1912.

The rancor was, however, most evident at the top. The military governors—General Price (1846–48), General Washington (1848–49), and Colonel John Munroe (1849–51)—did not serve the people well. Each administration clashed with the local populace over outrages in the military courts, abuses of citizens by troops, and corruption in the ranks, especially in the quartermaster's department, which tried to control local politics. All government officials served at the pleasure of the military governor, not by the vote of the citizens. Despite outcries against these abuses and calls to end military rule, Congress failed to act. A frustrated editor of the Santa Fe *Republican,* cursing the congressional inaction, declared on March 23, 1849, "We claim for the people of this territory, in the terms of the treaty by which it is ceded to the Union, at least equal privileges with the inhabitants of [other territories]. . . . We are a part of the United States, and the moment we became so the constitution spread its wings over us. . . . The young, at least, of the United States believe that this is a government of equal rights. Tear not the veil from their eyes. It is a wholesome deception."

To his credit, General Zachary Taylor, elected president in 1848, determined to create the new states of California and New Mexico out of the Mexican cession and to award full citizenship rights to their Hispanic residents. He sent secret emissaries to help California, and later New Mexico, initiate grassroots statehood movements. By late 1849, Californians had held a constitutional convention, elected a congressional delegation, and launched a state government, with congressional approval expected to follow. In late 1849, Taylor next had the secretary of war instruct his emissary to New Mexico that "should the people of New Mexico wish to take any steps toward this object [statehood] so important and necessary to themselves, it will be your duty and the duty of others with whom you are associated [meaning military governor Munroe], not to thwart, but advance their wishes."

The president's emissary arrived at Santa Fe in March 1850, and the various political factions quickly moved into action, calling together a constitutional convention; electing delegates; drafting a constitution; and holding an election to ratify it, elect new state officials and members of the legislature, and elect delegates to the U.S. House of Representatives and Senate. All this was completed by July. Merchant Joab Houghton, appointed by Kearny to be one of the judges, led one faction. A bible-thumping Baptist, a product of the Second Great Awakening and its crusade against slavery, Houghton ensured that the constitution would ban African slavery in the proposed state. The convention included Catholic clergymen—the previous September, in 1849, Padre Martínez had presided over a similar but less organized convention which passed a pro-statehood resolution—who continued to protect the church while working within the framework of constitutional religious freedom. *Ricos* endorsed the proposed constitution because it protected the peonage labor system and limited taxes. The convention gave the franchise to all white males, except active-duty soldiers—a reaction to the abuses of the military government.

The hopeful U.S. senator-elect from New Mexico, Richard H. Weightman, raced to Washington, D.C., with the constitutional proceedings, acting governor Manual Alvarez's address to the legislature, and other documents. Weightman was a typical political insider: a former captain of artillery under Kearny and son of the mayor of Washington, D.C. Unfortunately, by the time he arrived in September, he was too late to serve New Mexicans. President Taylor had died of gastrointestinal illness on July 9, 1850. Just as catastrophic for statehood, while Weightman was in Washington Congress passed the Compromise of 1850, a package of bills designed to maintain a balance of power between slave and free states.

The Compromise of 1850 temporarily tamped down conflicts over slavery and delayed the Civil War by a decade. Among the complex compromises was a bill determining how to divide up the Mexican cession, specifically whether the states created within its boundaries would remain free or allow the expansion of slavery. Southerners demanded slavery extending along the line of the Missouri Compromise all the way to the Pacific, which would have severed California in two. But in exchange for stronger fugitive slave laws, they acquiesced to California's entry as a free state and agreed that the remaining land would become territories whose slavery status would be deferred until they sought admission as states, when residents would decide the matter by popular vote. On September 9, Congress created from the remaining domain the territories of Utah and New Mexico. Texas, which had already been admitted as a slave state, had claimed land as far west as the Rio Grande and had attempted to establish counties in New Mexico, threatening to send troops into the territory if its claim was not recognized. As part of the compromise, Texas accepted a boundary at its present extent in exchange for the federal government assuming its pre-annexation debts.

Congress allowed Weightman an audience, and he eloquently argued for revision of the bill to accept New Mexico into the Union, but that would have upset the delicate balance of the compromise, and Congress was not about to revisit the issue. Weightman returned to New Mexico, where he was elected the territory's delegate to Congress, a nonvoting member of the U.S. House of Representatives, to continue championing the cause of statehood. New Mexico would repeatedly seek statehood, but that outcome seemed more distant than ever— sixty-two years away, to be exact.

As every resident of the territories quickly realized, their status made them second-class citizens. They could not vote in national elections for president or vice president. With only a nonvoting delegate to Congress, they had little say over territorial affairs at the national level. The president appointed the highest ranking officials in the territory, including the governor, secretary, and supreme court justices (who also presided over the district courts). These officials had to be confirmed by the U.S. Senate and were paid from the federal treasury. Although the territory had a popularly elected legislature, Congress could annul any of its acts.

The territorial governor's salary of $3,000 (which would have been less except that he also served as superintendent of Indian affairs) was generally too low to attract experienced, competent men to the post. Other officials received far less pay. One appointee as U.S. attorney, after complaining of the $250 annual salary, concluded that "the office is not worth the having." The early territorial governors and federal officials were either political hangers-on who expected some plum appointment in return for their loyalty to the president's party, or an odd lot of schemers who expected to speculate on and profit off the territory. Being typical western carpetbag appointees, they rarely served for their full terms. Not until 1894 was one a New Mexico Hispanic, a reflection of their lack of political access to the White House. In his final speech before Congress on leaving office, Delegate Weightman denounced the party spoils system which, together with the prejudices of the time, effectively ensured that no local Spanish-surnamed person was appointed to any federal post, not even postmaster.

During the 1850s, the executive chamber in the Palace of the Governors had many occupants. The first governor, James Calhoun, died in office after serving barely a year; Colonel Edwin V. Sumner appointed himself acting governor until the sixty-three-year-old mayor of St. Louis, Dr. William Carr Lane, arrived to serve as second governor in 1852–53. Both Lane and his successor, David Meriwether (1853–57), were embroiled in conflicts with the local Hispanic elites and various American Indian groups. Abraham Rencher (1857–61), a Southern Democrat, was crippled by the impending crisis of the Civil War era. Governors were frustrated by lack of support from Washington, which appointed then ignored them. Some may have had good intentions of addressing issues of improving education, the economy, and relations with various Indian groups, but their authority and financial resources were too restricted to carry out any program. Almost constantly in conflict with the legislature, made up of the old guard, they all resigned in exasperation.

On September 3, 1851, Governor Calhoun called the first legislature together, which included ricos Juan Perea, Ramón Luna, Miguel Otero, and Padre Antonio Joseph Martínez among the predominately Hispanic membership. Martínez had grown up under three different regimes, but his calling was the Roman Catholic Church, where he played major roles in the spreading of the gospel, in education, and in influencing Mexican politics. In the legislature, Padres José Manuel Gallegos, Tomás Ortiz of Santa Fe, and Martínez would act as the conscience of the nuevomexicano Catholic Church during the transition to the new order. Perea, Otero, and Luna represented the wealthy landowners of the region. They were joined by Mexican-era leaders such as Diego Archuleta of Los Luceros, a ten-term member of the legislature. As one Anglo member recalled, "whatever they said must be . . . they controlled the legislature down to 1859, after which date other influences came in."

This did not mean they were always united, since their factional feuds continued as of old. As historian Howard Lamar concluded, the antebellum New Mexican political system was not American and liberal but conservative and traditional, with power concentrated in fifteen to twenty wealthy families and their protégés. "Instead of serving as an instrument through which American law and government might come to New Mexico, it expressed instead the ideas of a conservative and traditional society."

The first legislature enacted laws based on traditions handed down from the Spanish in areas of water rights, court and legal systems, land, and even mining laws. The various early legislatures set up systems to administer the territory via new, locally controlled county officials. The legislature slowly restructured the court system to give the most power to the county probate judges, the equivalent of the old alcaldes. With the sheriff, the judge (alcalde) ran the county government, which also controlled elections. These positions were usually held by ricos or their political allies.

After Richard Weightman left office, Padre José Manuel Gallegos, Manuel Otero, Francisco Perea (son of Juan Perea), and J. Francisco Chaves represented the territory in the U.S. Congress as delegates in nine of the next ten sessions. All were hampered by their lack of political and other connections needed to gain influence within the club known as the U.S. House of Representatives. Respected in New Mexico, they were largely ineffective in Washington, with the possible exception of Otero, who had married a well-connected Southern belle, which helped him court the Southern delegation with enough success to get congressional funds for postal routes, wagon roads, and other projects in the territory. His influence on the territorial legislature's passage of a slave code for New Mexico pleased the South, but had little real effect because of the nonexistence of plantation slavery in New Mexico. More important was legislation protecting master and servant contracts, which ensured that the peonage system of indenture would continue as before.

By the mid-1850s, the territorial government was firmly in place. The top appointed federal officials, all short-term Anglo residents, for many reasons either failed to or were frustrated in their efforts to do more than nominally govern. As the elections of 1853 and after demonstrated, the Hispanic populace became increasingly informed and eager to participate in politics. The voters ousted all but a few of the Anglos who had held positions initially, replacing them with Hispanics in the offices of delegate to Congress, members of the territorial legislature (all but two were Hispanic by the mid-1850s), and the local county offices and courts. By the late 1850s, the elasticity of the U.S. system allowed Hispanics to control and shape their local government framework, as they simultaneously shifted their national identity from Mexican to U.S. The Hispanic elites would retain control of the territorial legislature and local political machinery for the next quarter of a century, longer in the northern counties.

A fixture in the new legislature was Donaciano Vigil, who had stepped down as territorial secretary in March 1851, with the establishment of the new civil government. Voters elected him to the house of the territorial legislature (1852–53), then to the upper chamber (1857–59), where his peers selected him as its president, the highest elected office within the territory. He would influence its proceedings through the Civil War years. Respected by Americans and Hispanics alike, he also advised the new Anglo hierarchy, especially with regard to lawyers, courts, and documents in land cases. For himself, he acquired two large land tracts. In 1854, he moved his family from Santa Fe to a tract along the Pecos River on the former lands of the Pecos Pueblo. He began farming fields adjoining the river, improved the acequias, built a grist mill, and expanded ranching on pasturelands. He led efforts to build the community's Catholic church, still standing, and its school, where at age seventy he served in his last elected office, as school commissioner of San Miguel County. He became a legend for his accomplishments and talents, which helped create an enduring nuevomexicano community.

CHAPTER **6**

Nuevomexicano Homeland, 1850s–1876

This early American era is a time of major geographic expansion [for
the Hispanic population], continuing an outward movement that had
been gathering momentum during the Mexican era. It was powered
by a search for pastures, water and patches of arable ground. . . . As a
result of this spontaneous unspectacular folk movement an indelible
cultural stamp was imprinted upon the life and landscape of a broad
area of the Southwest.

D. W. MEINIG, *THE SHAPING OF AMERICA*

THE SPRAWLING NEW MEXICO TERRITORY at 1850 extended
from Texas west to the Colorado River. It included the headwaters of
the Rio Grande in modern Colorado; a triangular section, now the
southern tip of Nevada; and all of Arizona except the lands south of the
Gila River (which were added to the territory along with New Mexico's
boot heel via the Gadsden Purchase in 1854). The majority of the settled population, primarily Hispanic and Pueblo, resided along the thin
green ribbon of land adjoining the upper Rio Grande and Pecos River,
especially north and south of the modern Albuquerque area, along
the tributaries in the Sangre de Cristo Mountains above Santa Fe,
and in small outposts along the Santa Fe and Chihuahua trails. One
of Donaciano Vigil's last official duties prior to transferring his office
to Governor James S. Calhoun was undertaking the arduous duty of
counting the dispersed residents for the 1850 census.

The 1850 census, though an undercount and excluding the many
nomadic American Indian groups that controlled most of New Mexico,
provides a profile of New Mexico that contrasts sharply with the stereo-
typical image of the nineteenth-century West. The enumerated population of 61,547, excluding the military, was less than 1 percent Anglo
(the term used to describe Americans, Canadians, and Europeans of

non-Spanish descent). Only twenty-two African Americans lived in the territory, a statement about the impracticality of plantation slavery in such an arid environment largely unsuitable for agriculture. The majority of soldiers in the territory were European immigrants, Irish or Germans primarily. Ninety-two percent of the population was Hispanic, while Pueblo Indians accounted for 6 percent. The cultural geographer Richard Nostrand described New Mexico's upper Rio Grande region as a "Hispanic Homeland."

The largest community was the capital at Santa Fe. It was the army headquarters and a major supply center besides being the seat of government and having a small farming and ranching population. With more than five thousand inhabitants in 1850, it was the second largest town in the Far West, recently surpassed by a rapidly growing San Francisco, California. Santa Cruz de la Cañada (modern Española) had a farm population second only to the Río Abajo region, where a string of farming communities lined the Rio Grande Valley from Cochiti through Albuquerque to Socorro. Taos was long a commercial hub for the fur and Indian trades. San Miguel del Vado, at the Santa Fe Trail crossing of the Pecos River, was the largest community in eastern New Mexico, but would soon be outgrown by Las Vegas. No permanent Euro-American settlement existed in far eastern or western New Mexico.

The settlers of the Río Arriba and the Río Abajo farmed using techniques brought with the Spanish. A regulated system of acequias watered long, narrow plots of corn, beans, hay, and forage. Chiles were nutritious and the universal spice, and many an Anglo discovered their delights with blazing hot mouth and watering eyes. In some areas, such as around Socorro, the river bottomland was farmed using floodwater techniques similar to those practiced along the Nile. The surrounding lands were used to graze sheep, cattle, and other livestock. The traditional Spanish land system during colonial-era settlement, continued in the Mexican era, had set aside nearby lands for a home garden and surrounding acreage for pastures.

The sixty-some Pueblo Indian villages listed in the census of 1600 had been reduced to twenty by the 1850s. Indian farmers worked their fields, orchards, and surrounding pasturelands like their Hispanic counterparts. The Pueblo population had dwindled to an estimated eight thousand

View of Santa Fe in the 1860s, showing San Francisco Street with the plaza at the left and the Catholic church in the distance. (Courtesy of Palace of the Governors Archives, NMHM/DCA, negative no. 11329)

(although the census enumerators failed to canvas all the pueblos). The Pueblos had their own governments recognized by the New Mexico governor, who initially also served as superintendent of Indian affairs for the territory. Governor Calhoun and his assistant spent much time settling disputes between the Pueblos and the Hispanics, especially relating to encroachment on Pueblo lands.

New Mexico had a stratified society, with the *rico* landowners and merchants at the top and the *peones* (poor) at the bottom. The ricos owned or controlled extensive landholdings centered on the *hacienda,* an architecturally simple, square, flat-roofed adobe structure with a central courtyard, built with an eye on defense as much as tradition. The extended families of the ricos helped protect the hacendado institution throughout the territorial period and ensure these families' political and economic dominance. For example, the Chaves/Chávez family of

Valencia County during the early territorial period contained prominent merchants, soldiers, and politicians: merchant Felipe Chávez, delegate to Congress J. Francisco Chaves, and Civil War colonel Manuel Chaves.

Peones worked the farms and herds, usually in payment of debts to the landowner. Some of them would be able to break from indentured servitude through the *partido* system. The rico would loan the peon a certain number of sheep, expecting that number plus a small percentage more in return after a season. The peon could keep any extras to build his own herd. Although bad weather or loss to Apache and Navajo raiders might wipe out any profits, the partido system still gave peones the opportunity to rise within the social structure. Not unexpectedly, there were cases of exploitation of the unwary, especially as the old system lingered into the twentieth century.

At the bottom of society were a large number of Indian slaves—women and children captured during raids on the *indios bárbaros* (wild Indians). They became servants and ranch or farm laborers, but also might become part of the family through either marriage or long-term residence. The census showed that in the village of Limitar nearly every household had a Navajo captive as a servant.

The census shows that unlike in other parts of the Trans-Mississippi West, New Mexico had nearly a one-to-one male-to-female ratio. This percentage was more typical of the settled Midwestern farm communities of Illinois or Indiana than of the frontier. For example, gold rush California in 1850 had eight men to every female, while gold rush Colorado a decade later had a ratio of fifteen men to every female. Not even Utah, with its Mormon families, attained such an equal ratio.

Women of New Mexico were more independent than their counterparts in the eastern states. They might run ranches or be successful businesswomen, like the aforementioned Doña Tules (see chapter 5). They enjoyed far greater rights to divorce, own property in their own right, and manage their affairs than their American counterparts. The richest woman of the period, the widow Doña Perea, managed vast ranchlands in Bernalillo County. The period literature abounds with characterizations of Hispanic women as attractive and alluring, but without morals—Yankees were entranced by their loose clothing, fandangos, and cigarillos. In truth they were devoted to family and church, but were simply allowed to live differently. Deana González's study of Santa Fe Hispanic women of the period shows that relationships with American men were rare; typically they "refused the favor" of the new arrivals. Many factors, including an intricate courtship system, stymied intermarriage. The few that did marry Anglos found that that was not a route to upward social mobility.

Because Hispanic New Mexico had a fairly equal male/female ratio—except during the railroad boom of the 1880s—its population growth came about less by immigration than by its healthy families (despite high nineteenth-century mortality rates of children), steady birth rate, and longevity. During the 1850s and even more so in subsequent decades, the expanding Hispanic population settled new regions beyond the Rio Grande Valley. Two decades of good crops, limited epidemics, and military protection triggered expansive growth out of the Rio Grande core in all directions, into the Río Bonita, Río Frisco, Tularosa Basin, and San Luis Valley. Usually, stockmen from the established plaza communities would start temporary settlements of *jacales* (brush huts), which gradually became more permanent through migration—from San Miguel del Vado and Las Vegas east into the Canadian River valley, from Taos and Abiquiú north into the San Luis Valley, and from the Río Abajo west to resettle the Río Puerco. By the 1860s they were moving east along the Canadian River into the Texas Panhandle, and west into the middle Gila River valley and the headwaters of the Little Colorado River in present Arizona.

The Mesilla Valley, on the lower Rio Grande extending from roughly modern Hatch to Las Cruces, attracted settlers from the core as well, quickly igniting controversy. Before long the Mesilla Valley was in the national news and Mexico and the United States were again on the brink of war, all due to a cartographic error. Article V of the Treaty of Guadalupe Hidalgo had specified the location of the new international border and stipulated that the Mexican–United States Boundary Commission be created to survey the exact boundary line on the ground. In the summer of 1849 the U.S. and Mexican surveyors had staked out the western portion of the boundary from the Pacific across California. But when they arrived in El Paso to map the eastern segment, a nasty surprise awaited. The treaty had set the boundary at a spot on the Rio Grande roughly eight miles above El Paso del Norte (modern Ciudad Juárez). Because the map included in the treaty (Disturnell's *Map of Mexico*, New York, 1847) was inaccurately drawn, however, the latitude and longitude coordinates labeled on the map as corresponding to that spot lay well to the north and somewhat east, somewhere in the modern White Sands Missile Range.

The surveyors were in a quandary. The Mexicans were willing to adjust the border west to the Rio Grande but at the specified latitude, north of modern Hatch, while the fiery U.S. surveyor demanded the survey begin at the point on the river eight miles north of El Paso. John Bartlett, head of the U.S. Boundary Commission, offered a compromise that would place the Mesilla Valley in Chihuahua pending resolution of the discrepancy by the two governments.

By 1853, Mexico considered the boundary question settled. However Southern expansionists in the Senate were seeking a feasible route for a transcontinental railroad across the South, which the current Mexican cession did not seem to offer, and they withdrew their support of the Bartlett survey compromise. In New Mexico newly appointed Governor William Carr Lane took matters into his own hands. Learning that Governor Ángel Trías of Chihuahua planned to colonize the Mesilla Valley, Lane traveled south and issued a proclamation that the Mesilla Valley had always belonged and continued to belong to New Mexico Territory. Trías issued a counter warning and prepared to raise troops to enter and hold the region. When Trías issued several land grants in the valley, Lane ordered the commander of Fort Fillmore, near Las Cruces, to move in troops to secure the valley for the United States. The commander wisely waited for word from Washington, and when President Pierce caught wind of what was going on, he recalled Lane to Washington and sent David Meriwether to replace him. During the spring of 1853, the national media waited with bated breath to learn of a clash of troops.

While sending General John Garland to New Mexico to assess the situation, President Franklin Pierce dispatched an ambassador to Mexico City, ostensibly to settle the dispute peacefully. Thanks to the Southern lobby, James Gadsden, a railroad man from South Carolina, was selected for the post of minister to Mexico. Officially, Gadsden was to purchase the disputed strip of land to enable a southern transcontinental railroad corridor to the Pacific. Gadsden's hidden agenda was to buy as much of northern Mexico as he could. In Mexico, President López de Santa Anna, who had regained power, made the Mesilla Valley a cause célèbre, and forcing the United States to pay for the valley his public purpose. Meanwhile, the U.S. government played down the Mesilla Valley confrontation, even to the point of issuing press bulletins stating that the valley had little value.

López de Santa Anna made it clear he had no interest in relinquishing any substantial acreage beyond the area in dispute. However, to prop up the cash-strapped Mexican government, he accepted $10 million for a strip of land subsequently known as the Gadsden Purchase, which gave the boot heel of New Mexico and all of present Arizona south of the Gila River to the United States. To New Mexicans, the inclusion of the Mesilla Valley within the purchase was never a question. By April 25, 1854, when the treaty was ratified by the Senate and signed by President Pierce, some 2,500 settlers had moved to Mesilla from Chihuahua, becoming U.S. citizens.

By 1854, too, a party of U.S. Army topographical engineers was crossing the newly purchased territory, surveying a proposed route for a government-sponsored wagon road, earmarked for eventual expansion into a railroad route. Since the California gold rush of 1849, overland travelers had sought a quick and safe route to the Pacific. The Gila Trail, along the river of that name, traversed rugged terrain. The Old Spanish Trail, crossing northern New Mexico and Arizona along the 35th parallel had the drawback of passing through the lands of the Navajos, Utes, Apaches, and Mojaves, who intermittently blocked passage during the 1850s and 1860s. The route mapped out by the surveyor and improved by the federal wagon road makers became the primary southern route to California, through west Texas to El Paso, up through Mesilla, then west via Tucson, Yuma, and into California. By 1858, the Butterfield Overland Mail operated a stage line with mail and express service from St. Louis to San Francisco via the southern route. With the Butterfield stage came a new string of frontier outposts across New Mexico.

The main corridor of commerce continued to be the Santa Fe Trail, from Independence, Missouri, across Kansas, parts of Colorado and Oklahoma, and into New Mexico. Use of the trail as a lifeline for supplies and stage connections to the East peaked in the 1870s. Military supplies and goods consigned to merchants in rising Las Vegas, Santa Fe, and elsewhere in New Mexico accounted for most of the freight wagon haulage to the territory. German Jewish merchants like the Spiegelbergs of Santa Fe—especially ones connected to the wider markets as far as New York City and Europe—came to dominate this trade. Traffic did not stop at Santa Fe. From there goods continued south along the former Camino Real de Tierra Adentro, or Chihuahua Trail, to the Río Abajo and Mesilla Valley to El Paso. The military road crews improved these trails until high-wheeled freight wagons pulled by oxen, some able to carry 15,000 pounds, were now seen across the desert jornadas or straining over the rugged mountain passes of Glorieta or Raton.

During the 1850s, among the major uses of the trails was to drive sheep herds west to the California goldfields. Such well-known mountain men as Christopher "Kit" Carson and Felix Aubrey served as guides, while the wealthy sheep owners, the Lunas, Pereas, Chavezes, and Oteros, profited greatly from a markup of more than $18 per head in California. In essence this was a shift in the direction of trade: from the miners of Chihuahua and Durango, Mexico, pre-1846 to the miners of California. The economic boom was short-lived, however. In the 1860s, the trade rapidly declined due to the Civil War and the increase of sheep herds in California.

A major portion of the freight into New Mexico served the expanding military presence. Forts constructed within the territory received their forage, surprisingly, from distant suppliers in Texas or Kansas. To avoid sending the returning wagons back empty, such suppliers looked for profitable backhaul freight. For example, the mayor of San Antonio, Texas, and his partners reopened the Santa Rita copper mine, near modern Silver City, hired experienced miners from Chihuahua and German metallurgists, and began backhauling copper to the port of La Vaca, Texas, a thousand miles away. The economic development of the southern part of New Mexico in the 1850s was directly related to Texan economic expansion into the territory.

The Compromise of 1850, which finally established the territory of New Mexico, did not, as hoped, end the national split between the slaveholding South and the aggressively industrial North. With the election of Abraham Lincoln as president in November 1860, Southern leaders voted to secede. South Carolina was first, with the solid South following, including Texas on February 1, 1861. Residents of New Mexico initially deemed it best to remain neutral. As Congress called troops back east and diverted resources to the Civil War, however, the frontier infrastructure began collapsing as military posts closed, the Butterfield stage line was suspended, and a new pro-Union federal administration was installed in the territory. These factors combined to tip public sentiment toward the North. An attack from the Texas Confederates would push them wholeheartedly for the Union.

Lieutenant Colonel John R. Baylor of the Confederate States of America and his troops brought the Civil War into the territory. In the spring of 1861, shortly after the organization of the Confederacy, they marched up the Rio Grande from El Paso. After capturing Fort Fillmore in the Mesilla Valley, the Confederates forced the Union soldiers in southern New Mexico to surrender at San Augustin Pass (on present U.S. Highway 70 northeast of Las Cruces). On August 1, 1861 Baylor declared Mesilla capital of the new Confederate Territory of Arizona, splitting New Mexico territory in half on the 34th parallel. The few Southern sympathizers in the territory rallied to the Southern banner, many in part because he promised protection from the Apaches.

In response, the newly appointed Union governor, Henry Connelly (1861–66), a longtime resident and merchant who had married into the Chaves family, organized the New Mexico Volunteers, which quickly mustered in Hispanics to defend their homeland. Colonel Kit Carson was tapped to lead the volunteers, with Lieutenant Colonels J. Francisco Chaves and Manuel Chaves (the governor's stepson and cousin, respectively) as seconds-in-command. Organized into infantry and mounted units, the volunteer ranks were filled by September, and most were deployed to forts and posts along the Rio Grande.

The regular army was under General Edward R. S. Canby, a lifelong but untested frontier commander. He incorporated the volunteers into his Department of New Mexico, which prepared to defend against further military advances from Texas. His strategy was to remain holed up in Fort Craig along the Rio Grande and let the land fight the advancing Confederates. This course was unpopular to the volunteers, who expected to protect farm and family, not leave them open to Rebel raiders. Canby's plan, arrogance, and unfamiliarity with the New Mexico recruits—combined with a lack of pay—brought dissent among the ranks. He proved the wrong leader to defend New Mexico.

Meanwhile Confederate General Henry H. Sibley, a former U.S. officer, had pleaded the cause of a southwestern empire for the Confederacy. President Jefferson Davis, one-time U.S. Secretary of War, grasped the importance of the trails through New Mexico to California's ports as a supply route. In Texas, Sibley raised a brigade to capture New Mexico, as well as possibly the Colorado goldfields and southern California. With three thousand troops he began the march through west Texas and up the Rio Grande, where he was celebrated at the Rebel capital Mesilla. His intent was to capture Fort Craig, Santa Fe, and Fort Union. Rumors were rampant that New Mexicans would rally to the Confederacy, and Sibley's Brigade expected an easy victory over Union forces.

The first major battle, the Battle of Valverde on February 20–21, 1862, occurred within cannon shot of Fort Craig, where Canby awaited the advancing Confederates. Outmaneuvered by the Rebels, Canby's soldiers were forced to retreat to the confines of Fort Craig. Realizing that the Confederates had suffered heavy casualties and were short of supplies, Manuel Chaves's troops went before the advancing army to destroy supplies at Albuquerque and Santa Fe. Sibley's Brigade took Albuquerque in February and Santa Fe on March 10. The Rebels moved into the Palace of the Governors and hoisted the Stars and Bars in the plaza. Sibley appointed former surveyor general William Pelham as the interim governor of the proposed Territory of New Mexico, CSA, a short-lived appointment.

Governor William Gilpin of Colorado Territory had similarly called for recruits to join the Colorado Volunteers. Under Colonel John P. Slough the First Colorado Volunteer Regiment headed for New Mexico on a forced march. The soldiers arrived at Fort Union on March 10, where Slough took command and awaited Canby's orders, which were, predictably, to stay put. After learning of the defeat at

Civil War battles in New Mexico Territory, 1861–62. (Map by Catherine Holder Spude)

bloody Valverde, Slough disobeyed orders, deciding to advance and engage the Rebels, who had bypassed Canby at Fort Craig and were heading north. Manuel Chaves and his New Mexico Volunteers met the Coloradans on the Santa Fe Trail and helped guide them to the mountain pass of Glorieta.

On March 26–28, 1862, at Apache Canyon and later at Pigeon's Ranch, a wayside inn on the Santa Fe Trail belonging to Alexandre "Pigeon" Valle, the Rebel forces under Lieutenant Colonel William Scurry and Major Charles L. Pyron met the Coloradans and New Mexicans. Initial skirmishing in Apache Canyon west of the pass was followed at Pigeon's Ranch by the most significant engagement during the campaign, a battle sometimes called "the Gettysburg of the West." Valle had a grand hacienda, pastures, and fields in a narrow confine on the east slope of Glorieta Pass. On the morning of the 28th, Union forces under Colonel Slough stopped to rest at the ranch, only to immediately meet the advancing Confederate forces, prepared in attack formation. Intense back-and-forth fighting on what later became known

Pigeon's Ranch, Santa Fe trailside inn and site of the Civil War battle of
Glorieta, March 1862. (Photograph by Ben Whittick. Courtesy of Palace
of the Governors Archives, NMHM/DCA, negative no. 115783)

as Sharpshooter's Ridge and south of the ranch forced the Union forces
to retreat, pushed back by Rebel fire. The Rebels captured Slough's
headquarters at Pigeon's Ranch, as well as Valle and his family, turning
the ranch to a field hospital.

The rebels were left holding the field of battle around Pigeon's
Ranch, where the most intense fighting occurred. But in the meantime,
Manuel Chaves was guiding a Union force over the mesa for a flank
attack and came across the poorly guarded Confederate supply train,
which the soldiers burned. With their supplies destroyed, a large force

of Colorado Volunteers before them, and no response to requests for reinforcements from Texas, the Sibley Brigade began a retreat down the Rio Grande. Canby, after leaving the confines of Fort Craig, gave chase, engaging the enemy in a brief skirmish at the Battle of Peralta, where the greatest loss was the town and Governor Connelly's hacienda, all reduced to rubble. By summer a much-reduced Sibley's Brigade straggled back into Texas.

The advance of the Confederate troops across New Mexico was devastating to the settlements. After the Battle of Valverde, New Mexico volunteers, who had not yet been paid, deserted in great numbers to protect their families and plant their spring crop, although they arrived home too late to prevent a lost harvest. Since Canby's strategy for defeating the Rebels did not include protecting the river villages, the Confederates easily advanced, confiscating supplies and war material from the mostly Hispanic residents. Union forces acquisitioned what provisions remained. This left the villages in a crisis, particularly in war-torn Socorro, Peralta, and the Pecos Valley, where foodstuffs became scarce commodities.

General James H. Carleton, who replaced Canby in September 1862, was a steely-eyed veteran dragoon who pushed his troops hard and bullied civilian officials. He had been in New Mexico Territory before. During the mid-1850s he participated in campaigns against the Jicarilla Apaches and Utes, groups already feeling the pressure of new settlements in New Mexico, Utah, and future Colorado that drove them away from the best lands. In 1854, guided by mountain man Kit Carson, Carleton mounted a winter campaign to defeat a Jicarilla band when they were hungry and suffering, a cruel method that he would use again. The Utes, defeated during the same campaign, would become military auxiliaries fighting with Carleton in future campaigns.

Carleton declared martial law, ruling with an iron fist (Governor Connelly became but his puppet). He began to confiscate property in southern New Mexico from any individual whom he considered a likely Confederate sympathizer. Arrests of prominent citizens in Mesilla, along with confiscation of goods and material, further damaged the economy and the morale of New Mexicans. For the duration of the war New Mexico's home front resembled the occupied South,

Brigadier General James Henry Carleton, military commander
of the Department of New Mexico in the Civil War and architect
of the Navajo Long Walk. (Courtesy of Palace of the Governors
Archives, NMHM/DCA, negative no. 22938)

impoverished and bitter toward the Union general in command. It
slowly recovered but full recovery—overcoming drops in population,
food sources, the economy, transportation systems, and morale—
would take nearly a decade.

As the potential for conflict with Confederates waned by late
1862, Carleton turned his attention to the Apaches, Navajos, and
Comanches. The militias called up for Civil War duty provided him
with more troops than ever before in the territory, up to 6,000 soldiers. Taking advantage of the fact that his movements were being
ignored by superiors because of the battlefield slaughter in the East,
he launched a dark, devastating period for nomadic Indians. His Civil

War became a war against the Indians of New Mexico. He first attacked the Apache band that had earlier surprised his advancing troops in Apache Pass, Arizona, where the volunteers founded Camp Bowie. Previously, during the 1850s, the Chiricahua Apaches under the great leader Mangas Coloradas (Red Sleeves) had been promised a reservation in southwest New Mexico, but the U.S. Senate failed to ratify the treaty. Instead the conflict was exacerbated by increased American settlement, the building of the Butterfield stage stations, and the opening of mines. In a campaign against Mangas Coloradas's people near modern Silver City, Carleton sent General Joseph West to establish a post in the Apache heartland and break the band's resistance through continued attack. According to miner Daniel Ellis Conner, members of his prospecting party tricked Mangas Coloradas into capture and turned him over to West's troops, who murdered the Apache leader, supposedly while he was attempting to escape. Later, his severed head was sent back east for scientific study. Carleton's troops did not bring peace; rather, the betrayal of Mangas Coloradas further inflamed Apaches' feelings against Americans.

Carleton next turned his troops to the Mescalero Apaches, a band being squeezed by the new settlements of southern New Mexico and Plains tribes. In a swift, take-no-prisoners campaign in the winter of 1862–63, troops led by Colonel Kit Carson captured up to five hundred Mescaleros and relocated them to Bosque Redondo (Round Grove of Trees) in central New Mexico within the barren, flat landscape along the Pecos River. Fort Sumner was built at the forty-square-mile reservation to direct a grand experiment to have the Indians peacefully convert to a more sedentary life by teaching them to build irrigation ditches, plant fields and orchards, and graze livestock. Conveniently, too, it would rid the settlers of the "Indian problem."

At the same time, Carleton sent word to the Navajo leaders that they too were to surrender themselves. In April 1863 two peaceminded chiefs, Barboncito and Delgadito, met with him, where he bluntly ordered them to move their people to the reservation at Bosque Redondo. Two months later he made the same demand, but added that if they had not congregated for removal to there by July, he would send troops into their strongholds.

The Navajos lived in what is now the Four Corners region, in a varied landscape, parts barren and sterile, others well watered with pine-covered mountains and valleys. In the canyon landscape at the heart of their country was Canyon de Chelly, a deep cut into the sandstone of the Colorado Plateau, where they kept orchards, raised herds of sheep, and tended fields. To a military exploring party in 1850, the Navajos seemed more like the settled Hispanic communities on the Rio Grande than the *bárbaros* they had been portrayed as.

The Diné (People), as they called themselves, had a complex clan-based, social and religious system misunderstood by the Spanish, Mexicans, and Americans who followed them. The most misunderstood aspect of the Navajo economic and social system concerned incessant raids on both Hispanics and other Indians for the purpose of taking livestock, primarily sheep and horses, as well as captive women and children to be sold or assimilated into the tribe. At the same time, Hispanics raided the Navajos and took captives to use as slaves. In its effort to protect settlers, the U.S. army interceded in the ongoing raids and counter-raids. The standard response throughout the 1850s was a succession of military campaigns, followed by tenuous peace treaties which too often were soon ignored.

By 1863, Carleton believed the removal of the Navajo to Bosque Redondo on the middle Pecos River would serve to convert them into the pastoral, non-warring society Americans expected. The combination of a bottomless supply line, virtually limitless troops to sustain a prolonged campaign, collaboration with Ute and Pueblo auxiliaries (lifelong enemies of the Navajos), and the New Mexico Volunteers under Kit Carson's command—New Mexicans were just as eager as the Americans for a major campaign and the spoils of war—gave Carleton an unequaled advantage over the Navajos. After a devastating winter campaign during which the troops destroyed their crops and cut down their orchards, the Navajos were starved into submission. The survivors were marched in the infamous Long Walk four hundred miles from northwest New Mexico to the Bosque Redondo reservation, far from their homeland within the four sacred peaks into the lands of their historic enemies, the Apaches. The story of the Long Walk is one of exposure to the elements and harsh treatment causing grave suffering and loss of life. It is one of the darkest chapters in New Mexico history.

Large numbers of Navajos remained in hiding, slowly surrendering to Carleton's experiment over the next several years, but there were at least six thousand Navajos on the reservation by 1865. The experiment at Bosque Redondo, however, was a massive failure. To the Americans, there was little difference between Navajos and Apaches, and they never realized the two peoples were mortal enemies. The small area was pitifully short of firewood and potable water, causing disease, suffering, and death. The expected self-reliant farmers experienced repeated crop failures because of insect infestation, plant diseases, and drought. Animosity flared between the Mescaleros and Navajos until a feud motivated the former to slip away back to their home in the Sacramento Mountains, where they later settled on a reservation. The Navajo herds were easy prey to the Comanches and other Plains tribes who took advantage of their plight. Added to all this, the Hispanics continued taking captives and enslaving young Navajos.

After the Civil War, a shift in Indian policy brought General William Tecumseh Sherman to New Mexico in 1868 to investigate the situation at Bosque Redondo. What he found was a catastrophe. The Navajos had been slated for removal to Indian Territory (present Oklahoma), but Barboncito and other Navajo leaders eloquently expressed their desire to return to their homeland and live in peace; influenced by their words, Sherman rescinded that order. Sherman drafted a treaty that closed Bosque Redondo, guaranteed them a reservation in their homeland, promised herds to their people, and an end to child enslavement. The veteran commander allowed the Navajos to return to a new reservation in northwest New Mexico. In June 1868, the Navajo began their joyful return.

The year 1868 marked the beginning of the collapse of the so-called Comanche Empire, which covered the southern Plains, including New Mexico. Four years before, Carleton had sent Kit Carson to lead an attack on the Comanches in their winter campgrounds. At Adobe Wells in the Texas Panhandle, Carson encountered an unexpectedly large band of Indians, numbering in the thousands. Carson is credited with managing to get himself and most of his roughly three hundred men out alive in one of the largest battles on the plains. Left uncontested because of shifting Indian policy, the Comanches regained their power through raids across the southern plains. The horse people had long thrived on bison hunting, raiding, and trade among the New Mexico settlements. But as bison herds were being depleted, they had come to rely more and more on plundering ranches in west Texas, selling the captured stock to Hispanic traders known as Comancheros. Comancheros had a long, honorable tradition of trading goods from the Rio Grande Valley with Comanche in exchange for bison meat, skins, and other trade items. Because of the illegal activity that disrupted the Texas settlements, Texans cursed the valued trade network between the New Mexicans and the Comanches.

By the late 1860s and early 1870s, recovering cattle stolen from Texas became the pretext for retaliatory raids by Texans not only against the Comanches but also Hispanics. During one military-supplied raid upon the Hispanic villages on the east side of the Sangre de Cristo Mountains, Texas cowboys claimed stolen stock as their own. In response, the New Mexico governor asked for federal protection. The Comanche raids and the ongoing plains warfare brought the full wrath of the military down on the southern Plains Indians. From the Battle of Washita in Oklahoma in 1868 to the Red River War of 1874–75 in Texas, the U.S. army relentlessly pursued the Plains tribes, driving them onto reservations in Indian Territory. The collapse of the Comanche Empire, and their removal to reservations eliminated the nomadic tribes as major players in the once-widespread warfare within the territory. Skirmishes and outbreaks from the reservations continued over the next decade or so, but the once-powerful Indian populations no longer kept New Mexico Hispanics confined to the Rio Grande Valley.

The reformers and abolitionists who envisioned America's future as slave-free did not overlook New Mexico. The system of peonage—technically not defined as slavery for life, but a system of servitude to pay off debt easily manipulated into a lifelong condition—became a cause for reformers, as did the long-held tradition of American Indian enslavement—particularly of Navajo women and children. In the 1860s, Superintendent of Indian Affairs Felipe S. Delgado defended the taking of captives because it served the benevolent purpose of raising and transforming "heathens" into good Christians. In 1866, Congress took another view and passed legislation banning all forms of slavery as well as servitude based on debt, including peonage. In 1868, the U.S. marshal was ordered to arrest all citizens holding captives or peons. In Taos and Santa Fe counties some sixty-five arrests were made, freeing all of the slaves and releasing all but one peon from his owner's grasp. Ethnographer James Brooks has shown that though legally these institutions were ended, Hispanic families practiced debt peonage and held Indians captive well into the twentieth century.

The leader of the Roman Catholic Church was an important force in the effort to promote reform in New Mexico. Jean-Baptiste Lamy, one of the most influential men of the early territorial period and the model for Archbishop Latour in Willa Cather's *Death Comes for the Archbishop,* was born in France and ordained in Rome before being assigned to churches in Baltimore and the Midwest. He was sent to Santa Fe in 1851, as much to help improve the impoverished state of the church in New Mexico as to effect its transfer from Mexican to American administration. Lamy first introduced schools, few in number but important toward the overall goal of "modernization." He quickly encountered opposition from local Hispanic clergy. Compounding their animosity, Lamy reformed longstanding religious practices—reinstituting tithing, cracking down on the Penitente Brotherhood, and censuring priests whose lifestyle was too worldly. He tactlessly removed dissident Hispanic priests who opposed him, Father Martínez of Taos the most prominent among them. Lamy excommunicated Martínez and other clergy for various questionable causes, which forced a schism with Hispanic parishioners—and put the church and Lamy front and center of territorial politics.

In the 1850s, the territorial legislature led by former priests sent a resolution to Rome to have Lamy's policies investigated, without effect. In 1878 Santa Fe was elevated to an archdiocese, with Lamy as its archbishop. Under Lamy the Catholic Church greatly influenced the politics, elections, and economic activities of the majority of the new territory's population and brought an end to the old practices.

For example, Lamy decried Navajo enslavement while readily allowing captives to be baptized into the faith.

Initially, Lamy was equally intolerant of the Penitente Brotherhood, devout Hispanic Catholics who organized a religious society that practiced penance and administered mutual aid. The society's rituals, including self-flagellation, harkened back to the feudal church from which the current Roman Catholic hierarchy wished to distance itself. Lamy succeeded in largely forcing the Brotherhood underground, but because of their strength and widespread influence, he tempered his public criticism (he issued a rule for their guidance in 1857). Jesuit historian Thomas J. Steele noted that Lamy maintained an uneasy truce with the Penitentes. During the 1880s, the pope decreed an end to self-inflicted personal injury, and Archbishop Salpointe (Lamy's successor) led the effort to control the Penitentes. The Protestant press and widely read writers like Charles Lummis sensationalized not only their activities but also the schism between the Penitentes and Lamy's more traditionalist church. In the 1940s, the Penitente Brotherhood reconciled with Rome, and it continues to exist today in rural northern New Mexico and southern Colorado.

Mixing elements of American Indian ceremony into European Christianity was commonplace in New Mexico. But New Mexico's feudal image was never more pronounced than when Indian religion crossed over into what Anglos perceived as witchcraft. In 1854, a Pueblo man killed a witch who had cursed his family, and was convicted in a noted trial. Much to the consternation of the church, the Indian agents, and the territorial court system, witch purges within the American Indian community continued well into the 1870s.

The predominance of the Catholic faith, the prosecution of "witch" killers, and the persistent use of the Spanish language and Mexican customs attracted criticism throughout the remainder of the territorial period. The negative rhetoric dated back to the war with Mexico, when as in all wars, the popular press painted dark pictures of the enemy in order to justify the cause of conquest. W. W. H. Davis, Mexican War veteran, U.S. attorney for New Mexico, and for a time acting governor of New Mexico, wrote an account of his time there entitled *El Gringo; or New Mexico and Her People* (1857) that exemplifies the negative characterizations of native New Mexicans, depicted as either lazy or scheming, dangerous or conniving, and their women as beautiful but immoral. He waxed on how badly modernization was needed, promoting "scientific husbandry" to improve the condition of agriculture. He decried the people's lack of education, and faulted the electorate and jurors as "too uneducated to make decisions." Such dark images—along with a healthy dose of xenophobia—influenced public and popular media perceptions of the region throughout the territorial period. Even into the 1880s, Davis's book and its depiction of a backward people was cited as reason for denying New Mexico statehood.

At the same time the negative stereotype was taking shape, writers discovered an audience for Western hero adventure stories. Kit Carson, Davy Crockett, and Daniel Boone became fictionalized in countless dime novels, Sunday newspaper supplements, and—years later—on the silver screen, portrayed as adventurous young frontiersmen and heroes in the wilderness. Place-names like Taos became commonly known and synonymous with frontier adventures in the public mind. One of the first biographies by De Witt Peters, *The Life and Adventures of Kit Carson* (1858), gave the trapper a notoriety and a media identity far from reality. Early dime novels, beginning with *Kit Carson, The Prince of the Gold Hunters* (by Charles Averill, 1849) are morality tales as well as prescriptions on how to fulfill personal dreams of wealth and adventure by going West. Actually an illiterate backwoodsman, Carson the trapper and guide for explorers was re-created in mythic proportions, the image that prevailed into the twentieth century. By the second half of the twentieth century, as national awareness grew of the nineteenth-century near-genocide of American Indians, Carson's image was tarnished. His role in the 1860s war on the Navajos and Apaches was elevated (above Carleton's), and ever since he has been blackened as the worst of the Indian killers. From hero to villain, his many-storied life has only recently receive a balanced biography.

New Mexico's first gold rush followed the May 1860 discovery of Jacob Snively at Pinos Altos. Snively first gained notoriety in 1843 when he led a band of freebooters from Texas to raid the Mexican caravans traversing the Santa Fe Trail, aiming to take not only goods, but also the merchants' gold and silver. When gold was found in California, he followed the gold rush there, then prospected his way back eastward, repeatedly striking it rich then losing everything. His gold strike at Pinos Altos attracted a thousand or so stampeders who came in to work the claims, including a large number of *gambusinos* (prospectors) from Chihuahua and Sonora. The riotous life of gambling and saloons that stereotyped the hell-for-leather western gold rush boomtowns of the mid-nineteenth century were in stark contrast to the traditional Mexican mining communities. After three seasons, with the richest placer gold removed, Snively and most of the transitory prospectors were off to new gold strikes elsewhere.

New Mexico has a long tradition in mining, dating back to the late Spanish colonial period. Mines had been worked at New Placer south of Santa Fe during the 1830s and 1840s, but the California gold rush swept the mining population west in 1849. (According to census statistics, there were more New Mexican miners in California in 1850 than in New Mexico.) After the Treaty of Guadalupe Hidalgo, merchant speculators in concert with politicians acquired leases on some of the historic Mexican mines located near Santa Fe, in the Organ Mountains near Las Cruces, and in southern New Mexico at Santa Rita del Cobre near Silver City.

By 1860, Santa Rita was second only to the great Upper Peninsula of Michigan in the production of copper in the United States. The community of nearly a thousand had revived after a pair of Texas merchants acquired the mine. A manager from the mining regions of Chihuahua and his low-paid miners reopened the workings, while a German-trained metallurgist built the smelter. The merchants hauled freight in from San Antonio while return wagons carried shipments of copper to a port in Texas. According to the 1860 census, the Santa Rita camp appeared more like a Chihuahuan mining camp, with its large population of women and children, priest, and traders. The Civil War brought an abrupt end to these mining operations.

The next discovery of rich placers, in the Moreno Valley northwest of Fort Union, fostered the boom-and-bust camp of Elizabethtown. The gold strikes at Pinos Altos, Elizabethtown, and Baker City (now Baker Park) in the San Juan Mountains of southwestern Colorado prompted the territorial legislatures to appease the growing number of incoming "gringo" miners by creating new counties—San Juan, Colfax, Grant—with mining camps as county seats. The gold strike in the San Juans helped open transportation corridors in the Tierra Amarilla region. However, the county was lost to the new Colorado Territory after it was determined that the county seat was actually in what was then Utah Territory. The western mining rushes of 1859 and after, from the Rocky Mountains to the Comstock, shook up the region, resulting in the partial dismemberment of New Mexico into new territories—parts going to Colorado and Nevada, and its western half to create Arizona.

The biggest silver strike of the period, however, occurred in the far southwest corner of the territory. At the site of today's ghost town of Shakespeare, silver miners worked claims that promoted one of the earliest silver rushes in 1870, followed the same year by additional silver discoveries near a new camp called Silver City. These camps were settled by experienced miners from Colorado and California. Borrowed technology in mining and ore processing kept the regions productive. At Silver City, which became the seat of Grant County, new prospecting parties outfitted themselves and fanned out throughout the region, creating new satellite camps. The independent souls in the county were frustrated by Santa Fe's refusal to acknowledge their demands for improved mining legislation, reduced taxation, and greater support for transportation. Southern New Mexico's resentment of northern control—especially from Santa Fe—would remain a point of contention that caused various abortive secession efforts as well as a petition to Congress to be annexed to Arizona.

The expansion of the Texan cattle tradition into New Mexico grew in concert with the mining rushes. The territory became a crossroads for herds of cattle driven from the west Texas plains up the Pecos River to Colorado markets. The Goodnight-Loving Trail of lore and legend followed this route. Cattle kings like John Chisum followed the trail to begin ranching along the Pecos, an example that was increasingly emulated after the Bosque Redondo reservation created a ready market for beef. These early cattlemen introduced Texas longhorns onto the eastern prairie, homesteaded ranches and located waterholes, and grazed their herds on the open range. By 1870, Chisum ranged cattle on two million acres of the public domain, maintaining control through the use of skilled Texas cowboys, some of whom were reportedly of disreputable character. In time, newcomers to ranching tried to claim some of Chisum's rangelands. A classic cattleman's war resulted.

Access to land proved to be the biggest issue among local ranchers. The U.S. Congress provided for a territorial U.S. surveyor general in 1854 to, among many things, establish a survey system that would allow settlers to acquire more public domain. In conflict with this process, however, was the surveyor general's obligation to review all Spanish and Mexican land grants, and to recommend their approval or rejection to Congress. No lands within a claimed land grant could be acquired under the existing land laws until the claim was disavowed. Many original land grant claims were fraudulent (or at least undocumented), exceeded their stated boundaries, or had incomplete boundary descriptions. During the 1850s, Donaciano Vigil had aided the surveyor general, who knew neither the Spanish language nor the land law traditions of Spain and Mexico, in investigating land grant claims. To their credit, by the time of the Civil War disruption, they had recommended that three million acres of grants be approved. Vigil, sometimes with the full knowledge of the surveyor general, is known to have stretched the law in some cases. In the eyes of Kirby Benedict, a hardened territorial judge, Vigil had established a bad legal precedent that he feared younger members of the legal profession might exploit.

Since land grants had not been claimed in the Tularosa Basin or in the lower Pecos Valley, Texas cattleman, following Chisum's example, moved into the region. They came into direct conflict with Hispanics, who had preceded the Texans into the Tularosa area during the 1850s, building acequias and planting fields. The cattlemen built dams and ditches upstream of the irrigation ditches, thus cutting off their water supply. Military intercession calmed the situation, but blocked the Anglo ranchers, who took their cases to court. The court, however, settled in favor of the Hispanics. Continued efforts to construct new dams and ditches brought the conflict to a head. In a subsequent shoot-out, law officers arrested twenty-one Hispanics for the murder of one Anglo assailant. Fortunately, the accused were granted a change of venue to Las Cruces and were acquitted. However, familiarity with the new land laws enabled Anglos to push the Hispanic occupants off much of their land, which the Anglos then homesteaded themselves.

On the Río Bonito in the Sacramento Mountains the situation was even worse. A group of Hispanics built homes and acequias along the stream, prospering under the protection of nearby Fort Stanton. Incoming Texas cowboys used violence in attempts to drive out the settled population. The Harrell brothers' raid, followed by the Selman gang, brought murder, rape, and mayhem. Local Hispanics, under the leadership of local probate judge and sometime sheriff Luis Pino, countered and worked cooperatively to run the cowboys out. In 1876, a cowboy taking revenge for the Harrells murdered Pino. Into this power void rode two former California Volunteers, Lawrence Murphy and James Dolan, lead players in what would become known as the Lincoln County War.

The war evolved from a power struggle between newcomer Anglos over meager opportunities in Lincoln County. Murphy and his clerk, later business partner, Dolan had opened the only general store in the area, price gouging residents. Backed by crooked politicians known as the Santa Fe Ring, they secured contracts to supply beef and foodstuffs to the Mescalero reservation, which they underfulfilled to increase their profits. Trouble arose when newcomers John Tunstall and Alexander McSween, backed by cattleman John Chisum, tried to open a competing enterprise. Both sides recruited armed men to back them. When Tunstall was murdered by a gang at the behest of Murphy and Dolan, it unleashed a vendetta of violence and revenge killings culminating in a four-day gunfight in which McSween was murdered. Most prominent among the Tunstall faction was Billy the Kid, whose murderous ride became one of the best known tales about New Mexico.

Billy the Kid went by a variety of names—William Henry McCarty, Henry Antrim, and during the peak of his notoriety, William H. Bonney. He arrived in the territory as a child, and spent his youth in the boomtown of Silver City until he fled after being arrested for petty theft. Many authors have told of the Kid's wild ride and how in his late teens he stumbled into the Lincoln County War. A partisan and friend of Tunstall's, the Kid went on a murder spree after the Dolan-Murphy gang gunned down Tunstall. When Lew Wallace became governor, he tried to end the Lincoln County War with an offer of amnesty. Billy the Kid contacted him to negotiate for amnesty or pardon in exchange for his testimony, famously showing up with guns in both hands. His continued acts of violence, including the murder of two deputies during the infamous breakout from the Lincoln County jail, left law enforcement agents no options. On July 14, 1881, Lincoln County sheriff Pat Garrett shot The Kid in old Fort Sumner. But the Kid's legend was just beginning to grow, eventually reaching global proportions.

Novelists first picked up on the theme of the desperado who had to die in order for law and order to prevail in the West. Simplistic dime novel plots moved to the silver screen, where some sixty movies helped raise Billy the Kid's legend to international fame. Historian Paul Hutton, an expert on the Kid's image, says the greatest shift was from a villain to a misunderstood youth who had admirable traits: orphaned young, he killed only in self-defense or when pushed too far, was a defender of the victims of power or greed, and was a friend to the abused Hispanic community (he was fluent in Spanish). Hutton writes, "Bearing a crystal-clear vision of gunsmoke justice, he is the eternal youth refusing to compromise or sell out and never hesitating to ride out against justice." No wonder the Kid remains a Western icon and Hollywood golden boy, often used to publicize New Mexico. One of Governor Bill Richardson's final acts of office in January 2011 was to announce on the TV show *Good Morning America* that after careful review he, as governor, would one more time not pardon Billy the Kid.

During the Lincoln County War, Santa Fe lawyer Thomas Catron temporarily jailed cattleman John Chisum for unpaid invoices. His act exemplified how Catron, a supporter of the Murphy-Dolan faction, used the courts to sway the balance of power. From the late 1860s, the legal office of Thomas Catron and Stephen B. Elkins, two Missouri law school graduates, become the most powerful law office in Santa Fe. Like other young adventurers who had fought in the Civil War, Elkins and Catron were lured to the New Mexico frontier. Elkins had served in the Union army and quickly rose in the political hierarchy. In 1871, at age thirty-two, he was elected the delegate to Congress from New Mexico, the highest elective position in the Territory. Elkins enabled

Catron—a Confederate veteran—to rise in the political machine to the position of U.S. attorney general, the territory's most prestigious legal office. The two were well placed to influence legal, economic, and political activities in New Mexico. By the time of the Lincoln County War, they were supposed members of the Santa Fe Ring, had become deeply involved in land disputes, and exploited every opportunity to lay claim to Mexican and Spanish land grants.

The Maxwell claim is the best known example of the Catron-Elkins land grant manipulations. In 1844, Mexican Governor Manuel Armijo, in an obviously shady deal, granted a virtual kingdom to two Taos land speculators despite the outcries of Father Martínez. By the mid-1860s, the claim had come under the control of Lucien Maxwell, a former mountain man and son-in-law of one of the grantees. With Catron's and Elkins's assistance, the Maxwell grant assumed an "India rubber quality," as it expanded to two million acres, the largest contiguous landholdings in the United States. The grant was confirmed by the U.S. Congress, despite having an undefined boundary. Through the influence of Elkins's brother, a corrupt U.S land commissioner approved the grant, which encompassed much of north central New Mexico and part of Colorado, ignoring the formal protests of Hispanic residents. The claimants no doubt acted in haste because the rich gold mining camp of Elizabethtown lay in the center of their vast domain. Maxwell claimed the goldfields as part of the grant, then promptly leased mining privileges to miners for a fee under the threat of eviction.

Governors Robert B. Mitchell and William A. Pile, Chief Justice John Slough, and other high officials were among the opportunists who aided Maxwell, Elkins, and Catron in exchange for shares or opportunities for land speculation. Not unexpectedly, war broke out in Colfax County among the factions. Murders went unpunished and challenges to the validity of the grant fell on deaf ears throughout Elkins's term in Congress and President U. S. Grant's tenure in the White House. By the late 1870s, the heated Colfax County war abated, and Elkins and Catron sold their Maxwell Grant shares. The new owners, represented by the talented lawyer Frank Springer, used the courts to hold onto the grant, despite the continued protests of former Hispanic and Anglo land users. In 1887, the U.S. Supreme Court finally decided in favor of the Maxwell grant holders, but controversy over the grant was one of the factors motivating Congress to establish the Court of Private Land Claims.

Contemporary historians have written much about the Maxwell grant and the Santa Fe Ring. The "ring" was a group of lawyers, politicians, and speculators, mostly Republicans, who controlled much of the federal machinery from the late 1860s to the 1880s. During that time they were accused of defrauding the government through inflated army contracts, robbing the public till and, worst of all, championing land manipulation, all the while in cahoots with high-ranking government officals. Land grants were avenues to wealth; therefore, many members speculated in grants, mines, and cattle. The grants were easy to manipulate since few people other than savvy lawyers like Elkins and Catron understood New Mexico's early legal tradition. Men like Elkins and Catron took advantage of the situation. They could not have succeeded, however, without the support of other federally appointed officials. Much of the corruption and illegal dealing was exposed during President Grover Cleveland's administration but that was too late to affect the grants, like the Maxwell grant, that had already been confirmed.

Elkins and Catron enjoyed the support of the local community. Catron was legal advisor to many Hispanics who were unsure of the law. Catron also won several well-publicized cases pitting longtime Hispanic residents against Anglo newcomers. Catron won the respect of the Hispanic community for his tenacious fights to defend them against what many considered an unjust system. They regarded Catron as a *patrón*, or political father.

Conversely, Elkins, like many others in his profession, saw himself as an agent of change determined to modernize a backward territory. He helped found the first bank, incorporated several stock companies, and attracted capital investment into the territory. In 1876 he was New Mexico's delegate to Congress when the territory submitted an application for statehood. His hopes of becoming New Mexico's' first U.S senator were dashed when the resolution failed by two votes. He left the territory for West Virginia, where he became a U.S. senator in 1894, serving in Congress until his death in 1911. The same year, Catron won the election to serve as New Mexico's first U.S. senator.

CHAPTER **7**

Boom Times and Consequences, 1877–1897

The 3d of February 1879, marks the formal commencement of railroad transportation in New Mexico. . . . Five days from Santa Fe to
New York is an annihilation of space, which will be appreciated by
everybody who travelled hitherward prior to 1868, when stages still
connected with steam[boats] at the Big Muddy.

SANTA FE NEW MEXICAN, QUOTED IN MESILLA NEWS, FEBRUARY 22, 1879

RAILROADS DEVELOPED in a surprisingly short period and with
transformative effect on the country. The crude experimental first
lines of the 1830s in Maryland and South Carolina had expanded to
long-haul trunk lines from New York, Philadelphia, and Richmond
to Chicago, St. Louis, and Memphis by the 1850s. When the Atchison, Topeka & Santa Fe Railroad (commonly called the Santa Fe) completed the last twenty-five miles of track into New Mexico in 1878 and
opened a depot outside Raton (near the current Colorado border),
it replaced one of the last stretches of the Santa Fe Trail to the Missouri River settlements. This event marked the beginning of a period
of rapid economic, social, and political change. Every corner of New
Mexico was affected. During the four-year period from 1879 to 1883,
a phenomenal 1,200 miles of track were laid in the territory. For more
than three decades—from the late 1800s to the early 1900s—the railroads built new towns, transformed sleepy villages into cities, and
caused new businesses and boomtowns to flourish, at least for a while.
Between 1880 and 1900, New Mexico's population increased by nearly
65 percent, from 119,565 to 195,310 people.

Crisscrossing the continent with railroads became the national
dream shortly after the War with Mexico. In the 1850s, Secretary of
War Jefferson Davis sent topographical engineers to survey potential
routes west. Lieutenant Amiel W. Whipple surveyed the route along

the 35th parallel, which passed through Albuquerque. Concurrently, Lieutenant John G. Parke followed the 32nd parallel through Mesilla and across southern New Mexico, the favored route of Southerners. The Civil War slowed all transcontinental construction. But only four years after the war ended, on May 10, 1869, the first transcontinental line from Chicago to San Francisco via Promontory Summit, Utah, linked the nation.

New Mexicans, through the press and their congressional representatives, lobbied in support of a southern transcontinental railroad. In 1866, the U.S. Congress chartered two railroads to build lines to the west coast through New Mexico, via both previously surveyed routes. To provide a financial incentive for construction, Congress offered the railroad companies grants of every odd-numbered section of land along an eighty-mile corridor paralleling their routes through the New Mexico Territory. Potentially, the two lines, once completed, stood to receive a land grant equal to more than one-tenth the land mass of New Mexico.

The transcontinental railroad-building frenzy captured the attention of financial titans on Wall Street and in Boston. Thomas Nickerson and his Boston partners acquired the Atchison, Topeka & Santa Fe Railroad, then a modest Kansas railroad linking the capital of that state with the western prairies. With an aim to acquire the land grants Congress offered, the Bostonians planned to extend west to the Rocky Mountains then southwest across New Mexico to the coast. By November 1878 they had built to the top of Raton Pass, and within three years had traversed New Mexico, following the Rio Grande through Albuquerque to El Paso, Texas, where they connected with a line to Mexico City still under construction. In the process, the iron rails replaced the historic Santa Fe Trail and the Camino Real de Tierra Adentro. In March 1881, the Santa Fe built a branch to connect with the Southern Pacific Railroad in the southwest desert near the Arizona Territory at Deming. This, the country's second transcontinental railroad, was soon followed by a host of other transcontinental lines. New Mexicans could now travel to San Francisco in two days—seated within the comfort of a railcar.

The Boston backers of the Santa Fe soon had competition. In 1879 Jay Gould, a five-foot-tall, black-bearded financier known as the "Wizard of Wall Street," began to build his Denver & Rio Grande Railroad (D&RG) lines south into New Mexico, getting as far as Española in the summer of 1880, and southwest via Chama to the San Juan silver-mining region of Colorado, which it reached in February 1881. At the same time, Gould also constructed the Texas & Pacific Railroad from Fort Worth to a junction with the Southern Pacific near El Paso—completing the long-awaited 32nd parallel rail route. He also completed the Denver City & Ft. Worth line, which clipped northeastern New Mexico near Clayton. The latter two lines, acting like a giant funnel, collected cattle on the eastern plains of New Mexico and delivered them to the Texans in Fort Worth.

Gould joined forces with Nickerson of the Santa Fe Railroad and Collis Huntington of the Southern Pacific Railroad (SP) for a third ambitious project: the completion of the long-dormant Atlantic & Pacific Railroad (A&P) from the Mississippi Valley to California along the 35th parallel. Huntington, who had built his Southern Pacific across southern New Mexico in 1881, agreed to build the California portion of the A&P. Nickerson agreed to build his portion of the A&P west from Albuquerque to hook up with Huntington's line at the California border. They began construction from Isleta, thirteen miles south of Albuquerque. Tracklayers quickly built across northern New Mexico during 1880–81, founding the new towns of Grants and Gallup (now along the route of Interstate 40) along the way. On August 8, 1883, the Santa Fe joined SP's section of the A&P at the new town of Needles, California, on the Colorado River, completing the long-wished-for route along the 35th parallel—the nation's fourth transcontinental route and New Mexico's second within two years. Gould at the last minute backed out of building the eastern section of the A&P he had promised, from St. Louis to Albuquerque; as usual, New Mexico was a pawn in Wall Street deal making. Instead he built his D&RG to Salt Lake City, forming a transcontinental link to another of Huntington's lines.

The Santa Fe Railroad was the major rail system in New Mexico, with operational headquarters in Albuquerque and Las Vegas, and legal staff in Santa Fe, led by former territorial chief justice Henry Waldo. It profoundly influenced the territory's economic development. The regional rail hubs it created shifted commercial power

A Denver & Rio Grande Railroad mixed freight train crossing the Rio Grande near Española and heading north, c. 1890s. (Courtesy of Palace of the Governors Archives, NMHM/DCA, negative no. 35876)

away from Santa Fe to Albuquerque. In addition to being a rail hub and repair facility for the Santa Fe company, Albuquerque was also the land office for the railroad, offering buyers some of the 13,000,000 acres of land grants in Arizona and New Mexico the railroad had received for completing the line. Close association with prominent New Mexicans, especially the Miguel Otero family, kept the company in relatively good standing with the territorial legislature. The Santa Fe rail town of Las Vegas, to the east of Santa Fe, vied with both municipalities for recognition as the preeminent community in New Mexico. The small rail town of Las Cruces, which never competed with the northern centers, became the dominant community in southern New Mexico, eclipsing nearby Mesilla.

The New Mexico Town Company, a subsidiary of the Santa Fe Railroad, platted new townsites in New Town Albuquerque and East Las Vegas, creating new rail boomtowns. They quickly became the

Atchison, Topeka & Santa Fe Railroad promotional brochure for New Mexico, 1880s. (Robert L. Spude Collection)

largest communities in the territory, as well as commercial, banking, and industrial centers. Promoters in Albuquerque led a two-decade-long battle to move the territorial capital to their expanding burg, a prize coveted by all of the dominant regional cities. The bosses of the Santa Fe Ring, however, successfully defeated every effort to relocate the capital, outmatching the vote-buying and corrupt maneuvering of the Albuquerque lobby. Even Governor Edmund Ross, an Albuquerque New Town founder and booster with connections to the Santa Fe Railroad, could not break the ring's power. Trying to make Albuquerque the de facto center of the territory, Ross and others proposed that a dozen branch lines be built from the Albuquerque to the four corners of the territory, but they failed to influence the territorial legislature to pass the bonds necessary for rail construction.

The city of Santa Fe used county subsidy bond sales to complete a rail connection to the Denver & Rio Grande line. Promoters had hoped the capital would be on the main line of either the Santa Fe or the D&RG railroads, but when the first locomotive steamed into town on April 3, 1880, it was on a branch line of the east-west Santa Fe. Meanwhile, by 1880 the north-south route of the D&RG had been built only as far as Española, where Frank Bond had created a competitive commercial hub for the northern villages by combining his mercantile and wool trade with other businesses. Santa Fe businessmen, led by Thomas Catron, raised the funds to complete the D&RG narrow gauge, which finally reached Santa Fe in January 1887. At long last, the railroad gave the capital a direct connection to Denver—albeit via the slow and windy "Chili Line."

When the railroad finally arrived, Santa Fe was beginning to transform from Wild West town to modern city. St. Francis Cathedral, Bishop Lamy's architectural gem, was nearing completion, along with schools such as St. Michael's College and hospitals built for the church by French donors. The capitol building was completed in 1886, as was a new territorial prison. At the same time, the railroads stimulated the territory's basic economies, creating a boom in stock raising and mining.

The arrival of the railroads in 1879 enabled long-distance transportation, making it possible to graze cattle on New Mexico's grasslands and ship the fattened stock to market as far away as Fort Worth, Kansas City, or Chicago. In the 1880s the cattle herds grazing on the New Mexico open range rapidly multiplied, from 137,314 head in 1880 to between 800,000 and 1,000,000 head (depending on the source) five years later. The railroad was only one of the factors that enabled the cattle boom of the 1880s. Additionally, the open range was accessible and Texas cattle could easily be transported there. Meanwhile beef prices jumped to record levels when the national demand for beef doubled at the same time as the British government decided to supply its troops with

American beef. The opportunities for profit attracted wealthy British and American investors into the industry, sometimes on a small scale and other times in huge corporate-controlled enterprises.

New Mexico's ranching tradition is centuries old. Cattle accompanied the Spanish entradas. Francisco Vásquez de Coronado brought herds with him, as did Juan de Oñate and later Don Diego de Vargas. These were the long-horned, Andalusian *criollo* cattle whose antecedents came from North Africa to the New World by way of the Iberian Peninsula. Cattle herds ranged free, across the southern part of the territory and into Texas and Chihuahua. By the time of the American conquest, vaqueros and cattle were common sights. Travelers to the New Mexico Territory wrote descriptions of *rodeos* (roundups) along the Rio Grande.

In Texas the Spanish-African criollo came to be called the Texas longhorn. Longhorns, although tough and rangy, survived well in the arid, hot region and could be trailed for long distances. Their versatility compensated for their tough meat. Cattlemen from Texas began to herd cattle from the brush country into the territory's eastern prairie during the 1850s and 1860s. During the days of unfenced open range, such legendary cattle kings as John Chisum spread his herds across southeast New Mexico, along the Pecos River. But the arrival of the railroads changed the playing field. Like many ranchers, Chisum had overextended his cattle empire; as he lost grazing lands to newcomers, he went bankrupt to eastern bankers and meatpackers. Some cattle operations survived by introducing new breeds of cattle and using midwestern ranching techniques. The extension of credit and other banking innovations, along with enactment of laws favorable to corporations, helped the new generation of incorporated "cattle kings" to eclipse the days of the open range.

Highly organized joint stock companies bought cattle and land as well as sold stocks and bonds to easterners, while seeking additional open range on which to graze the herds. The Women's Endowment Cattle Company sold stock in a herd raised in the Pecos Valley to New York's high-society women. By the late 1880s, the corporate cattle industry ranged from the boot heel of southwestern New Mexico to the barrancas (hill country) of the Canadian River in the northeast. The biggest enterprise was the Diamond A Ranch, an empire established in 1882–84 by George Hearst of San Francisco and his partners. Based in Deming, the outfit spread from Socorro to the Mexican border across Spanish-Mexican land grants and newly claimed lands.

Investment promoters sometimes served as flamboyant go-betweens in the establishment of ranches. During the late 1870s and 1880s, U.S. Senator Stephen Dorsey became one of the most newsworthy. Civil War veteran Dorsey had served in James G. Garfield's brigade in Ohio before moving to Arkansas, whence he was elected to the U.S. Senate in 1872. In Arkansas he speculated in plantations and a railroad. When the reconstructed state's new constitution disenfranchised African Americans, he was unable to win reelection. Cursed as a Republican carpetbagger in Arkansas, he decided to move to the territories. In 1877, he purchased the 600,000-acre Uña de Gato Land Grant in the northeast of New Mexico with the assistance of former territorial delegate Stephen B. Elkins, his one-time congressional colleague. Over the next decade, he formed a series of stock companies to introduce cattle to that part of the territory. Next, Dorsey built a showcase prairie residence between Springer and Clayton, the latter a rail town he helped promote and named after his son. Dorsey hired Texas managers and cowboys to care for the ranch. After learning his land grant might be invalidated, Dorsey ordered his ranch hands to homestead all of the known springs, a controversial (and illegal) act that would ensure his exclusive use of the surrounding dry grasslands.

Like many of his contemporaries Dorsey overextended his reach. A drop in beef prices in the mid-1880s combined with increased railroad and packing company fees to cut profits. In response, he tried organizing a local packing company that failed. Finally, he fought the rail rates, but it was his outstanding loans for land purchases that brought his cattle company before bankruptcy court. The U.S. General Land Office also investigated his fraudulent land claims. By the time Dorsey's managers introduced new breeds of cattle that might have sold better on the market, it was all too late. Ranchers who were able to adapt to changing market demands, and secure water rights and additional lands, weathered the crisis of 1893. Dorsey was not one of them. Hounded by creditors, as well as accusations of involvement in the nationally sensationalized Star Route frauds (in which officials took bribes for awarding crooked mail delivery contracts), Dorsey left the territory for California. (He was eventually acquitted in the Star Route trials.)

Not all ranchers failed. Henry Porter organized the Cimarron Cattle Company in Colfax County in 1882 with $10,000. By shifting away from longhorns to more marketable breeds of cattle like Angus and Herefords, Porter's operation met changing demands in beef quality. He also mixed leasing property when buying homesteads to ensure the company controlled rangeland. He hired only experienced cowboys, and his crew boss forbade pistols in camp, an act praised by the local press. He worked with neighbors to reach compromises over range use, drift-fence construction, and water allocations. Seventeen years later, Porter sold out for $60,400, a respectable return on his investment. A ranching success in Colorado as well, the rancher left as his legacy Denver's Porter Adventist Hospital.

There were many other successful ranchers who built up their herds slowly, replacing the longhorn with European breeds, especially Angus and Herefords. They adapted to changing conditions as more ranchers moved into the region, entering compromises with neighbors over water use, grazing rights, and boundary issues. By the late 1880s, the range became overgrazed and Texas tick fever threatened to infect local herds. In response New Mexico ranchers formed cattlemen's associations that lobbied the legislature to enact appropriate regulations. Legislators established a territorial board to halt the introduction of the fever by assessing a $1.00 fee for every new longhorn brought into the territory. In the long run, ranchers survived the market ups and downs, the unpredictable environment, and the generally unstable world in which they operated.

The reminiscences of ranchers relate the challenges they faced. One of the best, Captain William French's *Recollections of a Western Ranchman* covers the period for southwest New Mexico. Two that rank with French are by women: Fabiola Cabeza de Baca's *We Fed Them Cactus*, and Agnes Morley Cleaveland's *No Life for a Lady*. Although about a slightly later period, they tell of the isolation and loneliness, of the cowhands and the herds, of town visits and schools, and of the power of family through the frontier era into the twentieth century. They add a colorful dimension to the dry statistics of the livestock industry.

New Mexico ranchers experienced continuous droughts in 1891–93, which inflicted losses of 50 to 75 percent in some herds. The panic of 1893 struck a staggering blow to ranchers. They gradually recovered, but never again operated in a bonanza-like style. Besides economic instability, the decades from 1870 to 1890 were fraught with open resistance and legal protests to changing land policies. Range wars, caused by increasing numbers of Texas cattle moving onto former Hispanic sheep-grazing lands, fomented these conflicts. Contested land and water rights resulted in clashes, the best known among them the early feuds in Lincoln and Colfax Counties (described in the previous chapter).

A classic range war between local sheepherders and Texas cattlemen broke out in Valencia and Socorro counties. These counties once extended from the Rio Grande Valley to the western boundary of New Mexico territory, encompassing the lush San Augustin Plain, the American Valley, and the forested high country of the Black Range and San Francisco Mountains. The then–Valencia County seat of Los Lunas was the ancestral home of the Luna brothers: Jesús, Tranquilino, and Solomon. The brothers were descendants of seventeenth-century settlers and owners of the Los Lunas Land Grant, which held approximately 150,000 sheep on pasturage extending to the west into present-day Arizona. (By 1880 New Mexico contained 2,088,831 sheep, making this the territory's biggest product.) The Luna family maintained dominance over local politics through control of the probate courts and sheriff offices. In 1880, Tranquilino was elected to the U.S. Congress, representing New Mexico as a nonvoting delegate for two terms. As the patriarchs of Los Lunas, they employed more than one hundred sheep herders and managed their rangelands using the partido system (in which they lent the herders sheep for a specified period in exchange a greater number of animals at the end of the time).

During these years, cattle ranchers moved onto lands claimed by the sheep men, the most prominent being John and William B. Slaughter of the famed Texas clan. Texas cowboys moved in their herds, staking claims to natural springs and watering holes previously claimed by the local Hispanic population and "tenderfeet" Anglo homestead-ers. They generally terrorized the Hispanic population of western Socorro County. One incident involved the legendary deputy sheriff Elfego Baca, who after arresting one of the Texans, single-handedly held off Slaughter's cowboys in Frisco Plaza. The notorious shoot-out on October 30–31, 1884, was one of the incidents that escalated the range war.

When Slaughter's cowboys began shooting sheep in retribution, they ran into the combined forces of the Baca-Luna-Otero-Chaves fam-ilies of Socorro and Valencia counties, along with small ranchers. One of the latter, an Anglo homesteader, ambushed and critically wounded William Slaughter. In response, Slaughter's cowboys destroyed some eight thousand of the Lunas' sheep in a feud over water. Rather than escalate the range war, a wise Solomon Luna took Slaughter and his American Valley Cattle Company to court. After negotiations with Thomas Catron, the lawyer representing the cattle company, the judge dismissed the case, but by then Slaughter had declared bankruptcy in the face of the blizzard of 1889, the droughts of the early 1890s, and the financial crash of 1893.

Meanwhile, Solomon Luna prospered and became the largest sheep owner in New Mexico as well as a territorial political power in the Republican Party. He defended himself against increasing compe-tition by securing title to valuable pastures and springs. He imported Spanish merino sheep in an effort to adapt to market demands. He varied his wool clip and mutton production in accordance with mar-ket prices. He cosponsored banks, of which he served as president, to ensure financial control. He was also patrón to the people of Los Lunas, where he maintained a grand residence. Luna condoned accommoda-tion with the new settlers, and did much to help in their transition to the diverse community, while simultaneously providing adequate pro-tection for Hispanics. As member of the state constitutional conven-tion of 1910, Luna is credited with the sections of the document that provide for greater equality between the English- and Spanish-speaking population in education, voting, representation on juries, and office-holding. At the time of his accidental death in 1912, he was one of the wealthiest and most respected men in New Mexico.

Luna represented the large owners, who had elaborately organized their ranches with a hierarchy of supervisors to oversee the work of the so-called *pastores,* shepherds who handled a flock of about two thousand sheep. On the other extreme were the herders who tended small flocks in northern New Mexico. They often co-owned the sheep in a partido arrangement with merchants, such as Frank Bond of Española and Charles Ilfield of Las Vegas. Through a system of loans, the herder was given credit to buy sheep, whose wool and mutton was used to repay the loan at the end of the season. This partido system indebted local shepherds to city merchants, but it also introduced a basic cash economy to the Hispanic villages of northern New Mexico. During this period, the villages were being forced away from the traditional subsistence economy toward a world economic market.

El Cerrito, on the upper Pecos River sixty miles southeast of Santa Fe, was typical of these small villages. The village was founded in 1830 by Hispanic shepherds, who continued their livestock business into the next century. They sold their wool, the major commodity of the village, though Las Vegas dealers. In 1900, only 136 people lived in El Cerrito. Most were in the livestock industry while some also farmed small, irrigated plots along the Pecos River. The ability to market wool, however, provided for the basic cash needs to sustain the village. Villages like El Cerrito stood in stark contrast to the booming railroad towns and cattle ranches that continually encroached upon their grazing lands.

On the other hand, Liberty represented the isolated cattle town on the Llano Estacado. The town had its saloon, merchants housed in the usual false-front buildings, and a dirt main street. The town, and others like it, became lawless spots for cowboys that worked on the nearby ranches to blow off steam and for cattle rustlers to hide out. Occasional dances, rodeos, and festivals enlivened what was otherwise a boring, solitary existence. Unlike El Cerrito, Liberty flourished barely more than a decade as new towns along the railroad line supplanted its function as a cattle town.

By far the most violent section of the territory paralleled the southern border from Lincoln to Las Cruces and beyond the territorial boundaries to Tombstone in Cochise County, Arizona. Organized bands of rustlers easily raided company herds, selling the stolen stock in Texas, Arizona, or Mexico. One function of the cattle growers' associations was to pool funds to pay for the ongoing capture and conviction of rustlers. In addition, formed under the auspices of the Lincoln County Cattlemen's Association, a band of "regulators" chased and arrested these wayward cowboys, bringing them to swift justice. Albert Jennings Fountain, a militia captain in Doña Ana County, led one group of regulators to Rincon and cleaned up the outlaw Kinney band. The rustler war was swift and thorough. In 1896, while crossing the White Sands on the way to serve a warrant to a cattle rustler, Fountain disappeared and was presumed murdered along with his young son. The suspected murderers stood trial, but were acquitted. Local cowboy and later western novelist Eugene Manlove Rhodes intended to write a fictionalized account of the murder but changed his mind when those who thought it best that the incident and its associated feud remain quietly in the grave warned the young writer to avoid the topic.

In 1881, at age thirteen, Rhodes moved with his family from his native Nebraska to the Tularosa Basin. He grew up a cowboy, and would have remained one except that he was a keen observer who told tales of ranch life to his fellow wranglers. He published his earliest works about New Mexico cowboys, range wars, and sheriffs—both good and bad—in the 1890s. By 1910, his stories appeared in the *Saturday Evening Post,* which gave him a national following. His *Pasó Por Aquí,* a tale about his old home, is among his best, although today his writing style is dated. He was the first New Mexico–raised fiction writer to attract a large audience.

Two of Rhodes's contemporaries also gathered impressive followings of readers. Charlie Siringo wrote the first and one of the most popular books about cowboy life and work on the range: *A Texas Cowboy* (1886). Much of the story takes place in south central New Mexico—Las Cruces, White Oaks, and Lincoln County—during the 1880s. After a stint as a Pinkerton detective, Siringo retired to Santa Fe.

Jack Thorp also arrived in New Mexico in the 1880s, where he ran cattle and broke horses in Lincoln County near San Andreas, the home of Gene Rhodes. Thorp gathered songs he had heard from old cowhands around the campfire and on the trail. While living in Estancia in 1908, he published *Songs of the Cowboy,* the first book of cowboy songs and poetry, which included "Cowboy's Lament," "Get along Little Dogies," "Old Paint," and "The Birth of New Mexico." The last tells how the devil created hell along the Rio Grande. Thorp attempted to clean up the more risqué versions of some songs. Still, later writers praised him for his efforts to capture the world of the working cowboy, one of the most legendary characters in the West today.

The railroads also attracted investors to speculate in New Mexico's mineral riches, real or imaginary, resulting in the mining boom of the 1880s. The railroads needed coal to operate their engines. Railroad companies were the first to open large-scale coalfields in Raton, Gallup, Carthage, and Madrid through contracting with owners, entering into leases, or purchasing outright. At Carthage (near the modern White Sands Missile Range), the railroads purchased coal and coke from the Compañía Mexicana de Carbón, organized by a group of prominent Hispanics from nearby Socorro. In Raton, the Santa Fe Railroad leased its coal-bearing land from the Maxwell Land Grant owners. Similarly, at Madrid and Gallup, the railroad company went into partnership with local mine owners. Raton became the most productive of New Mexico's coalfields. In 1880 and 1882, the Santa Fe built branch lines from Raton into Dillon Canyon and Blossburg, a typical coal town transplanted, along with its workers, from Pennsylvania.

At first, Anglos predominately worked the mines, but after they engaged in a series of strikes and labor disputes, Anglo underground workers were replaced by Hispanics. Later on, the companies imported Europeans, primarily Italians, Austrians and Slavs; fully 50 percent of the workers in the camps around Raton were European immigrants. After the strike of 1889 in Gallup, mine owners imported the first of many African Americans from coalfields in the South, as well as hiring Navajo laborers, making the New Mexico coal camps the most ethnically diverse population in the territory. Increasing demands for coal throughout the territorial period, enabled coal towns—especially Raton and Gallup—to emerge as major cogs in the economic engine that drove New Mexico's economy, politics, and diverse population.

New Mexico's placer gold rushes in the 1860s, and the short-lived high-grade silver rush in the early 1870s, had waned by the time Santa Fe

Railroad construction crews traversed Raton Pass, heading south. Silver City was a well-settled community when the railroad extended its branch line to the silver camp in 1883. Idle mines near Silver City—at Pinos Altos, Santa Rita, and in the Burro Mountains—were quickly reopened. Although the Southern Pacific bypassed Shakespeare in favor of the rail-side town of Lordsburg, it completed a branch line (which eventually ran through the town's main street) to reopen Shakespeare's silver/lead mines with a flourish. Meanwhile, flamboyant promoter J. Parker Whitney used Boston capital to reactivate the old Santa Rita del Cobre mine. He built a showcase mill and produced a respectable amount of copper, until the market collapse of 1884 left the operation idle.

The rush of the 1880s to the Black Range and the Magdalena Mountains in west central New Mexico was a classic frontier mining boom. Prospectors discovered silver and gold ores across the ranges, staked mining claims, then either operated on a small scale or sold out to outside mining corporations. Promoters organized mining stock companies, touted the richness of their claims, and sold stock—most of which was not worth a "hoorah in hell"—to the gullible. The more fortunate companies—those holding claims containing enough ore to produce some metal—built mills to crush and separate out the gold, silver, lead, and zinc from the waste rock. Boomtowns such as Chloride, Kingston, Hillsboro, Lake Valley, and Kelly rose up around these mines and mills. Typically, each camp had a resident population of a few hundred people and a row of gaudily painted false-front businesses, interspersed with a respectable number of saloons, along a crude Main Street.

Lake Valley, north of Deming, typified the boom camps of the 1880s. A local prospector made the discovery in 1878. The rich silver find attracted George Roberts, a promoter from Leadville, Colorado. Roberts organized the Sierra Grande Mining Company and a half dozen other "paper" companies. He also built a mill to begin working the high-grade bonanza, including the pocket of ore known as the Bridal Chamber. He sold stock to easterners—even the poet Walt Whitman owned shares—and convinced the Santa Fe Railroad to build a spur to the camp. Before he sold out and left the territory, Roberts claimed his companies held an estimated $144,000,000 worth of ore! This gross exaggeration validated what author Mark Twain, a one-time

Nevada silver miner himself, wrote: "a mine is a hole in the ground owned by a liar." The value of Roberts's mines proved to be inflated, causing the mining bubble at Lake Valley to burst. Stockholders lost their money, but new owners turned the Lake Valley mines into small but steady producers. Eventually, these claims produced a respectable $6,000,000 worth of silver. In his book *Black Range Tales* (1936), James McKenna recounts the many vicissitudes of mining in the Lake Valley–Hillsboro–Kingston region.

The impact of industrialization on New Mexico is best exemplified by the transformation of Socorro, founded as a small agricultural community on the banks of the Rio Grande. When the railroad arrived in 1880, the town contained 1,272 inhabitants. In no time, Socorro had become a major mining center with its own branch railroad leading to the silver/lead mines at Kelly and the cattle and sheep pens in Magdalena. The territorial census of 1885 reported a population of 4,047, making Socorro the third largest community in New Mexico. Moreover, the construction of a major smelter known as the Billings works transformed Socorro into a regional processor of ore. Combined, Socorro, Grant (Silver City), and Sierra (Hillsboro) counties produced nearly all the territory's gold, silver, and copper, the value of which increased from less than $1 million in 1878 to nearly $6.5 million during the banner year of 1886.

The government's decision in 1893 to demonetize silver—that is, no longer to purchase silver to back its currency—caused metal market prices to collapse, killing the silver boom. Socorro was especially hard hit when its smelter closed because of competition from new works in El Paso, the new regional hub. In time, Socorro's business leaders and the town's mining newspaper moved to southwest Texas. Socorro's mining era is no longer evident, except at the campus of New Mexico Tech, formerly the New Mexico School of Mines.

New Mexico's leading population centers—the mining communities of Socorro and Silver City; railroad hubs such as Albuquerque, Las Cruces, and Las Vegas; and Santa Fe, the territorial capital—all experienced growing pains. Each had vigilante committees that from time to time circumvented the legal process in the capture and conviction of wrongdoers. During the early 1880s, lynchings as well as other extra-official law enforcement activities were common. These lawless days in early New Mexico became the stuff of legend, fodder for the Hollywood movies and television shows of a later generation.

More significant conflicts followed because of issues concerning education and religion, public health and sanitation, and newly arrived Anglo Protestants clashing with the entrenched Hispanic Catholics. Predominantly Anglo-owned newspapers were quick to criticize their new home. The Santa Fe paper criticized the filth and garbage in the streets that potentially bred disease. The fiery editor of the *New Mexican*, Max Frost, called for a government clean-up and an end to corrupt elections and politicians. Education was also in need of assistance. Socorro's editor, for example, decried the absence of a government-supported educational system for all the town's youth. Delegate to Congress Harvey B. Fergusson helped to pass an act in 1896 that improved public education immeasurably. The Fergusson Act set aside one section per township of New Mexico Territory's public land for lease to generate income in support of education, in accordance with the Northwest Ordinance of 1786. In 1889, the territorial legislature also established a university in Albuquerque, a school of mines in Socorro, an agricultural college at Las Cruces, and a school for teachers, or "normal college," in Las Vegas.

One topic that dominates the narratives and reminiscences of writers like James McKenna, Captain French, and their contemporaries, was the persistent conflict with the Apaches. By the mid-1870s, the American Indians in New Mexico had all been removed to reservations. Unfortunately, corrupt Indian agents, inferior or spoiled rations and other subsidies, and a growing dissatisfaction with the lands on which they were forced to live inflamed Native resistance. In probably one of the crowning examples of ineptitude in government Indian policy, the Chiricahua and Mimbres Apaches lost their own New Mexico reservation and were removed to central Arizona where several bands staged a series of outbreaks, attacking prospecting camps, isolated ranches, and small parties of travelers.

During 1879–80, the Mimbres Apache leader Victorio led his people off the Arizona reservation to return to their ancestral home in New Mexico. Fueled by newspaper headlines announcing the killings of lone prospectors and the decimation of isolated ranches, communities over-reacted to the danger, organizing local militias in response. Victorio terrorized residents in Grant, Socorro, Sierra, and Doña Ana counties. A federal military buildup coincided with the outbreak, as routine patrols and scouting parties from Forts Bayard, Selden, and Stanton coordinated their efforts to protect the communities by pursuing Victorio's band. African American horse soldiers of the Ninth Cavalry engaged the Apaches in numerous skirmishes. Because of the hard-fought campaign, eight African American soldiers received the Congressional Medal of Honor for bravery in combat. Eventually, the U.S. Army chased the Apaches across the border into Mexico, where Mexican troops cornered Victorio's band and killed him in October 1880.

Nana led his band of Apaches on another series of raids, after which the army chased him into Chihuahua that fall. The famed Chiricahua medicine man Geronimo staged the next uprising. In 1883, Apaches captured six-year-old Charley McComas after killing his parents, Judge Hamilton McComas and his wife, Jennie, near Silver City. The event made national headlines. Such raids eroded any support from outsiders the Apaches may have had. Up to the time of the final capture of Geronimo and his followers in 1886, southern Arizona and New Mexico were frequently raided as the last of the renegade Apaches resisted assimilation and enforced reservation life.

General Nelson A. Miles's military campaign forced Geronimo's surrender at Skeleton Canyon in southeastern Arizona. On September 8, 1886, the defeated Geronimo and his Chiricahua people—including Apache scouts who had helped the army track down Geronimo—were slowly marched to the Bowie Depot, Arizona, where they boarded Southern Pacific railroad cars that would remove them from New Mexico and Arizona forever. Although warriors like Geronimo, Nana, and Victorio instilled great fear, in the long term their outbreaks had a negligible impact on the continued expansion of the railroads, cattle ranches, and mining camps that were reshaping the New Mexico landscape. Still, they have become symbols of resistance to the injustice this expansion brought to Native American peoples.

As it had done with the Chiricahua and Mimbres Apaches, the federal government also ordered the Jicarilla Apaches removed from their reservation. In 1878, they endured their own "long walk" from Tierra Amarilla in northern New Mexico to the Mescalero Apache reservation in central New Mexico. Although there were no violent outbreaks, the Jicarillas gradually abandoned the reservation for the mountains and plains in the north. Fortunately for them, sympathetic supporters lobbied President Grover Cleveland to issue an executive order on February 11, 1887, that reestablished a reservation for the Jicarillas in the Tierra Amarilla region. Once returned, the Jicarillas became sheep herders like the western Navajos.

During the early years after their return from Bosque Redondo, the Navajos focused on rebuilding the reservation economy. The ever-evolving size and shape of the reservation concerned the Diné, especially after prospectors discovered gold in the San Juan River, Mormons built irrigation ditches and planted fields along its banks, and cattlemen moved into their territory. Eventually, prime farmlands in the San Juan River Valley were dislocated from the reservation. In 1878, the reservation witnessed a witch purge, a political and traditional religious method for the Navajos to eliminate the old ways. Anglos avoided involvement, though they commented on the larger issue of the Navajos' social reconstruction after the traumatic experience at Bosque Redondo. In a more positive vein, the railroad bolstered the reservation economy by offering many Navajo men jobs as track layers and laborers.

The railroad also brought money and jobs to the pueblos. Many of the nineteen pueblos, and their more than eight thousand residents, were located on or near the railroad. The Santa Fe lines passed through several of the Pueblo tribal lands, entailing payment for railroad rights-of-way. The railroad's attorneys demanded that government Indian agents define more precisely the boundaries of the Pueblo reservations in order to determine the boundaries of railroad land grants that stretched from Isleta Pueblo to Zuni Pueblo. Ultimately, this protected Pueblo lands, while the railroads received transferable land script where they gave up land grant claims. As traders became more numerous on the reservations, trade goods greatly improved. Most important, the railroads brought passengers eager to buy Indian-made crafts, which rapidly increased business opportunities.

At the same time, the railroad introduced reformers whose goals were to "Americanize" the American Indians by instilling Anglo values toward education, family, and mode of life. Boarding schools were by far the most intrusive means of assimilation, with Indian children sometimes being forcibly removed from their parents "for their own good." Carlisle Indian School in Pennsylvania, established in 1878, was the nation's first Indian boarding school. A school in Albuquerque (1884) and another in Santa Fe (1890) soon followed. These government-run schools adopted the American-style formal classroom education with its factory-like regimen. Besides the three R's, the predominantly female faculty taught hygiene and etiquette, all part of the assimilation process. Because of their proximity to the pueblos, New Mexico Indian schools were in constant contact with Pueblo leaders and parents. Consequently, they had greater ability to influence the education there to incorporate Pueblo values, culture, and traditions. Reformers, however sincere their desire to do good, were at times misguided in their determination to "civilize" the Pueblo people and other Native American groups.

With the first large immigration of Anglos, New Mexico's political world began to change. This transformation is clearly reflected in the makeup of locally elected political bodies at that time. Voted in by their peers, Hispanics predominated in the territorial legislature before 1880. In cattle country, however, the voters elected more Anglos—usually southern Democrats—to the legislature and local offices. The legislature created new counties to avoid the Anglo-Hispanic divisiveness characteristic of older Hispanic centers. For example, in the southeast corner of the territory, called "Little Texas," they established Eddy and Chaves counties.

In other cattle regions and mining communities, the legislature carved out new counties—Sierra, San Juan, Guadalupe, and Union—from the older, predominately Hispanic counties of Mora, Río Arriba, San Miguel and Doña Ana. During the 1880–90 decade, Taos, Mora, and Río Arriba counties in northern New Mexico collectively lost population, while Grant, Lincoln, and Colfax counties—composed mostly of cattle ranches and mining boomtowns—more than doubled in population. By the mid-1880s, the number of Anglos holding seats in the territorial legislative body had increased to near parity with Hispanics. Though the body was more or less equal in ethnic representation, there were neither solid Hispanic nor solid Anglo voting blocs. Thus, feuds and conflicts between parties on issues did not follow well-defined ethnic lines. For example, both Hispanics and Anglos supported public education, but how to pay for it divided them, especially those opposed to taxing Hispanic-owned lands or railroad and mining properties. Harvey Fergusson, a young lawyer who arrived in the mining camp of White Oaks in the 1880s, helped resolve the dilemma in 1896.

Fergusson represented Democratic reformers who had arrived in the territory during the boom of the 1880s with a plan to loosen the Republican hold on the territory. Another like-minded politician was Edmund Ross, who as a U.S. senator from Kansas had voted against the impeachment of President Johnson in 1866, which brought an end to his career in the Senate. Afterward, Ross moved to Albuquerque and became a strident booster for the new railroad center. He soon sought the governor's chair. Newly elected Democratic President Grover Cleveland appointed a new slate of territorial officials from his own party, including Ross as governor. Governor Ross (1885–89) and fellow Democratic Governor William Thornton (1893–97), led the party effort to rid the territory of corrupt politics as exemplified by the boss-ridden Santa Fe Ring.

The two reform-oriented governors also targeted the Hispanic *patrones*. Ross hoped to re-create New Mexico in the model of the agrarian-minded Kansas homesteader and yeoman farmer. He proposed more schools, but with instruction only in English. The Spanish-language press, along with Anglos in tune with the *gente* of New Mexico and their culture, vilified Ross's vision as misguided. New Mexico poet Jesús María Hilario Alarid countered Ross's position with the popular "El Idioma Española," written in 1899:

> Hermosa idioma española
> ¿Qué te quieren proscribir?
> Yo creo que no hay razón
> Que tú dejes de existir.

Lovely Spanish
What? They want to banish you?
I believe there is no reason
For you not to exist.

Ross failed, even despite the infighting among party-line politicians, because his view of Americanization prescribed an English-only society with anti-Hispanic cultural overtones. Not surprisingly, the resident population never accepted the proposed reforms. Subsequently, the economic downturn that began in the late 1880s and culminated in a disastrous financial collapse known as the crash of 1893, hampered Governor Thornton's attempts at social and political reform. Although acknowledging his efforts as well intentioned, New Mexicans ardently criticized him for too adamantly seeking the death penalty for convicted murderers and for breaking the Pullman railroad strike by arresting the workers. The strongest objections were leveled at Thornton's ineffectiveness in opening up the political process. Both the Hispanic patrónes and the Anglo bosses would enjoy long and prosperous political traditions in New Mexico.

U.S. Surveyor George Julian was one of the more outspoken Democratic political appointees. Julian, a former congressman from Indiana who led the Free Soil cause (restricting the expansion of slavery) in the 1850s, had a set philosophy on public lands. His study of oversized land grants in the Midwest early in the country's history made him a strident opponent of large land grabs. He was a hero to the yeoman farmer. During Lincoln's presidency, the 160-acre homestead became not only law but the political war cry of the Free Soil Party. On arriving in New Mexico in 1885, Julian used his office and the national media to target the land barons by overturning earlier decisions on land policy. These changes furthered his agenda of making free land available to homesteaders. Toward that end, Julian asserted that 90 percent of all land claims in New Mexico were fraudulent.

General Land Office commissioner W. A. J. Sparks agreed with Julian. He sent special agents into the field to investigate fraudulent homestead claimants and bring them to trial. He ridiculed ranchers (both Anglo and Hispanic) for not adhering to the spirit of the homestead law by acquiring control of multiple parcels of grazing land.

(Recall Dorsey's and Slaughter's tactics of having subordinates acquire homesteads containing waterholes and springs, rendering the surrounding dryland useless.) Sparks also demanded that all fences on the public domain be removed, which President Cleveland formalized by executive order in 1885. These actions unleashed cries of protest and stinging editorials in opposition. In 1886, the New Mexico Wool Growers Association openly protested Sparks's actions. However, jurors were unwilling to convict any of the fraudulent claimants Sparks brought to court because other people besides the large "land grabbers" were involved.

Sparks also went after the railroads, declaring the A&P Railroad land grant invalid. James A. Williamson, land agent for the railroad, denigrated Sparks as "three or four removes from an idiot." Williamson, a former general who had served under Grant during the Civil War, was appointed commissioner of the Land Office in 1876 during Grant's presidency. But under the Cleveland administration, Williamson and the A&P (controlled by the Santa Fe Railroad) lost their fight to benefit from the potential acquisition of a land grant bordering the yet-to-be-built eastern extension from Albuquerque to today's Clovis. The commission did, however, guarantee an eighty-mile swath of land along the recently built line running west from Isleta to Arizona. Historian William Greever, in his assessment of the concession, concluded that it was less beneficial to the railroad than promoters had hoped. Meanwhile, the A&P continually lost money until it filed for bankruptcy in 1896.

Julian also questioned the validity of Spanish and Mexican land grants, many of which were by now in the hands of eastern investors. He reopened the Maxwell Land Grant case, demanding that the grant's nearly two million acres be substantially reduced. Because of its size, the Maxwell property had attracted an increasing number of new Anglo and Hispanic squatters. At the same time, Julian attacked Senator Dorsey's ranch and the Uña de Gato Land Grant he acquired as its centerpiece. He also challenged J. Parker Whitney's land grant in the Estancia Valley. Whitney's brother shot and killed Manuel Otero in a feud over the grant's boundary. Julian further pronounced Thomas Catron's Tierra Amarilla grant both oversized and invalid, accusing Catron of being in league with "land thieves." The Bell Ranch land-grant holdings of

Wilson Waddingham were the worst, Julian claimed, because they exemplified everything he opposed: immense tracts or grants seized by a handful of land barons rather than distributed among simple, honest farmers. Both Dorsey's and Whitney's grants were eventually invalidated. Existing claims to the Maxwell and Tierra Amarilla grants, and to Waddingham's Bell Ranch, were upheld thanks to the litigation abilities of corporate lawyers Frank Springer, who represented the Maxwell company; William J. Mills, Waddingham's son-in-law; and Thomas Catron on behalf of the Tierra Amarilla claimants.

Julian's activities agitated the local populace, none more so than the residents of Las Vegas. He considered the community land grant of Las Vegas to be invalid, arguing that much of it should be public domain and opened to new homesteaders. He instructed the government surveyor to stake Hispanic settlers' tracts of land, offering them only the acreage actually in use as theirs with fee simple title. The remaining "unused" portions of land (the *ejidos,* or common lands that historically all the settlers jointly used for grazing) would be opened to new claimants as private homesteads. As the surveyor's work progressed, he notified Julian as well as the public—mostly newly arrived Anglos—that new lands were available for homesteads. The new homesteaders staked their claims and built fences within the "common lands" of Las Vegas, keeping traditional users (Hispanics) out and thus exacerbating an already explosive situation. With the political transition in the White House, Julian was removed from office, but he had already lit the fuse to a powder keg that would soon explode.

Traditionally, northern New Mexico's Hispanic population had an agrarian-based economy supported by the communal lands that surrounded each village. They were falling on ever harder times. First, the farm and sheep products they routinely sold in local markets were now threatened by cheaper foodstuffs brought in from Midwestern farms by the railroads. The railroads also brought tools, clothing, machinery, and other eastern-manufactured goods that hampered local craft businesses. By the late 1880s, the Spanish press lamented the loss of "common lands" as contributing to the decline of the local economy, and cried for action. Julian's decision to take away the communal lands by allowing homesteaders to fence in tracts that traditionally were considered only for common use evoked a violent response. In other states and territories, fence-cutters who destroyed the new barbed-wire fences being strung across the pasturelands were considered outlaws. What evolved on the Great Plains was a classic feud that pitted the yeoman farmer against the land baron.

The feud in Las Vegas, however, had deeper and very different roots. The first U.S. surveyor general validated the 496,446-acre Las Vegas Land Grant and recommended its approval to the U.S. Congress. Congress failed to act, however, resulting in confusion over the land's status. Was communal land to be used exclusively by the heirs of the original grant recipients, or was it in the public domain and subject to government conveyance to newcomers? Julian had declared it public domain. Therefore, Anglo arrivals had already begun to purchase interests in the land before Julian made his decision to invalidate the grant. In 1889 the territorial court ruled in support of the land grant heirs by recognizing the communal nature of the grants, further confusing matters. In April of that year, as defendants prepared to appeal their case, Juan José Herrera and his younger brothers Pablo and Nicanor organized Las Gorras Blancas (The White Caps) in Las Vegas. A secret Hispanic mutual protection association, their goal was to protest against encroachment on Hispanic lands, especially the theft of communal lands by the large ranches.

Juan José Herrera had been a Union officer during the Civil War. He had also organized railroad workers into a union called the Knights of Labor. Through his leadership and organizational abilities, Las Gorras Blancas gained a following. What began as Hispanic resistance turned into two years of open violence. Las Gorras Blancas attracted territorial attention when they destroyed four miles of new fence belonging to a British-owned ranch. The raids continued throughout 1889–90. Activists burned telegraph poles, cut up railroad ties, and destroyed fence lines. In March 1890, fully three hundred Gorras Blancas rode through the streets of Las Vegas in a show of solidarity. In time, their membership grew to more than a thousand.

Governor L. Bradford Prince, who met with Las Vegas town leaders in August, issued a proclamation calling for "the white caps" to cease their violent acts. He found the community split, half sympathetic to the fence-cutters. The governor left law enforcement to the county, but encouraged the suppression of all wrongdoing. He also hired a Pinkerton Detective Agency spy to infiltrate the vigilante group. Although the Herrera brothers were later indicted, they were never brought to trial. In essence, all of the governor's bluster failed to end the revolt.

The town's Spanish-language newspaper, *El Voz del Pueblo,* championed the need for Hispanic solidarity against the rapidly changing political climate. Newspaper owner Félix Martínez sought a more peaceful means to confront changing conditions. In 1890, New Mexicans organized the Partido del Pueblo Unido, or Populist Party. It included supporters of Las Gorras Blancas and their goals. Composed of both Hispanics and Anglos, the new party sought to distance itself from the old Democratic and Republican machines. Weary of violence, the fence-cutters channeled their anger into the Populist Party, led by conservative residents William Mills and Félix Martínez.

Martínez, in fact, called for Hispanics "to rise in their might to squelch the land grabbers as well as the fence cutters." Taking up the Hispanic cause, the Populist Party briefly gained power in the territorial political arena. By the end of 1891, the violence subsided. Yet, when Congress passed the Court of Private Land Claims bill on March 3, 1891, to adjudicate the remaining land grant claims, the protest movement remained a factor. Though isolated cases of fence-cutting and "white cap" activism continued for the remainder of the territorial period, with the passage of this bill confrontations moved from the land to the courtroom, which began the long, drawn-out process of litigation.

From 1891 to 1904, the Court of Private Land Claims adjudicated suits brought before the United States involving a total land area of 35,491,020 acres, nearly half of New Mexico's total landmass. The claims confirmed by court decree amounted to only 2,051,526 acres, with 33,439,493 acres rejected. The court represented a unique tribunal, unknown to earlier settled areas in the East. In fact, its existence was anathema to a nation that had come to expect squatters' rights to predominate over grants made by a foreign nation. And the blatant land frauds exposed by the court brought close scrutiny to all claims.

A case in point is the 12,147,456-acre Peralta-Reavis Land Grant, which extended east from Silver City, New Mexico, to Phoenix, Arizona.

To gain the grant, James Addison Reavis, a former St. Louis street-car conductor, cleverly altered documents from Mexican and Spanish archives—so well, in fact, that railroad attorneys and land companies accepted his claim as genuine and paid him rent. In 1895, the court conclusively exposed his hoax, not only invalidating the claim but arresting Reavis and sentencing him to prison for forgery.

However, by the 1890s most of the major land claims were in the hands of Anglos, many backed by eastern speculators. Most claimants were people like Senator Dorsey and J. Parker Whitney, who bought claims of questionable authenticity from Santa Fe land grant lawyers, only to have the court declare them invalid because of faulty documentation. As land grant specialist Malcolm Ebright suggests, reopening these cases today would, if the courts' decisions were overturned, help the original Hispanic land claimants' descendants less than it would the descendants of eastern speculators.

Rarely did the court allow grants that were unsupported by historical documents. A signal case was the grant establishing the city of Santa Fe, the supporting documents for which could not be found in any of the early records. It took congressional action to award the city its land grant in 1900. By disallowing large parcels of fraudulent land grant claims, the territory offered new opportunities for settlement to both Hispanic and Anglo citizens. Because of the court's findings, New Mexico entered a decade during which the largest number of homestead applications were filed, triggering in turn the next growth spurt in the territory's population.

Although residents in general praised the efforts of the court, later generations have questioned some of its decisions. Most important was the court decision to reduce the size of some community grants based on the assumption that title went to an individual or group of individuals. In addition, community grants that had been acquired by speculators became private grants, with the tacit understanding that the new owners could sell off tracts dislocated from the original grant without consideration for communal users. Malcolm Ebright has shown the court process to be flawed. If it had convened in the 1850s, at a time when the U.S. government was seeking ways to dispose of the public domain, the court would have been far more lenient towards claimants with evidence of use and ownership. But convening as it did after the government had begun to withdraw large tracts of land to protect and conserve forests, antiquities, and water resources, the Court of Private Land Claims required a far more rigorous application and legal review process. The stringent requirement for substantive legal documentation generally favored the government's case in land grant disputes. As Ebright points out, the victims of this process were the original land grant settlers, the Hispanics of northern New Mexico, who waited too long for confirmation and consequently were forced to sell their claims to individuals—usually from the East—with the funding to fight the drawn-out court battles.

As the century came to a close, New Mexico was shaping into the diverse community that it continues to be today. The agricultural and pastoral traditions of nuevomexicanos were joined by the busy hum of the multiethnic transcontinental railroad hubs, silver or coal mines and mill towns, and ranching centers. The high mountain villages remained a Hispanic stronghold, the residents supplementing subsistence farming with temporary industrial jobs in distant locations. The Catholic heritage was as strong as ever, thanks to the efforts of Archbishops Lamy and Salpointe, the lay priests, and the Penitente Brotherhood. Though the low, flat-roofed adobe haciendas of Santa Fe and Mesilla stood in stark contrast to the multistoried, Victorian wood-frame structures that lined streets in the "new towns" of Las Vegas, Albuquerque, and Las Cruces, all were representative of the gradual merging of the two differing societies and economies.

The starkest social changes occurred in southern New Mexico, where Texan ranchers brought their Southern Democrat views and societal expectations, which often resulted in personal feuds. They pushed a competitive, individualistic Protestant ethic and societal norms abhorrent to the traditional communal, Catholic villagers. Roswell and Eddy, with their main streets of false-front mercantiles, resembled Texas or Kansas cow towns more than New Mexican adobe villages. The religious beliefs of Methodists, Baptists, and Presbyterians fostered changes in local laws to support concepts of representative government, congregational sovereignty, the abolition of hierarchy, personal and moral discipline, and protection of civil and religious liberties. The Bible-thumping newcomers from Texas believed their stewardship would ensure freedom and break down the old Hispanic ways. At the same time, however, the denominations' competition for souls contributed to acrimony, jealousy, and distrust. Religion in New Mexico was nothing if not a complex institution.

Into the mix came miners from the other western territories and states who built boomtowns and generated boom-and-bust economies. The mining community was in transition during the 1880s and 1890s, soon to be replaced by the corporate takeover of the mining districts—especially base metal and coal districts—by major eastern firms. These activities transformed the camps into company towns, although the occasional lucky strike—such as at Bland and Mogollon—caused a new boom reminiscent of the 1880s.

The biggest shift in the late 1890s was political. The dominance of the legislature and political offices had slowly been transferred to the incoming Anglo population. But with the return to prosperity by the time of William McKinley's election to the White House in 1896, New Mexico Hispanics were regaining control of territorial politics. That year, Solomon Luna bested Thomas Catron to become national Republican Party committeeman, a post he held for the remainder of the territorial period. His countryman, J. Francisco Chaves regained the power seat in the territorial legislature's council, while Luna's nephew Maximiliano Luna was elected Speaker of the Territorial House.

In 1897, McKinley appointed Miguel Otero as governor. From an old colonial-era family and a relative to Luna through marriage, Otero was the first Hispanic to be so appointed. At the next election for territorial delegate to Congress, New Mexico voters sent Pedro Perea of the prominent Bernalillo family to Washington, D.C. The *Roswell Record* of October 7, 1898, opined that Perea's election might mean the end of progress and "a return to the days of the Don and *peon*." The new Hispanic officeholders in power by the end of 1898 were however not opposed to progress as defined by American political institutions, commercial and technological innovations, and social services such as public education; they simply wanted their own people to control it. As historian Howard Lamar stated, when President McKinley appointed governor Otero he began a "minor revolution in New Mexico politics."

CHAPTER **8**

The Land of Sunshine, 1898–1924

The majority of you Rough Riders came from the Southwest. I shall
ever keep in mind the valor you showed as you charged up the slope
of San Juan Hill. I owe you men. . . . If New Mexico wants to be a
state, I will go down to Washington to speak for her and do anything
I can.

THEODORE ROOSEVELT, LAS VEGAS, NEW MEXICO, 1899

ON FEBRUARY 15, 1898, the U.S. battleship *Maine* blew up in Cuba's
Havana harbor. For the United States, the event led to war with Spain,
but for New Mexico it brought questions concerning the territory's loyalty. After the *New York Times* published an editorial discussing the need
to watch the former Spanish provinces that were now U.S. territory,
angry New Mexicans gathered in the larger towns to denounce the critics and voice support for the war. In Santa Fe, a committee made up of
a majority of Hispanics resolved, "That we heartily endorse every action
of the President and Congress to declaring and maintaining war against
the kingdom of Spain; that we pledge ourselves to honor every call the
administration may make upon us with our lives, our fortunes and our
sacred honor." Those present at the mass meeting added, "We are neither
Mexicans, Frenchmen, Germans nor Irishmen—we are all Americans."

Among the first to respond to the call for volunteers was a contingent of troops that came to be known as the Rough Riders. Half of its
ranks were filled with New Mexicans. Among the first troops to arrive
in Cuba in June 1898, the Rough Riders were predominantly Anglo
cowboys, bolstered by Taoseños, Yaqui Indians, old-family Hispanics,
and others, and were led by Colonel Leonard Wood and Lieutenant
Colonel Theodore "Teddy" Roosevelt. In his later account of the regiment, Roosevelt credited New Mexicans under Captains Max Luna
of Los Lunas, William H. H. Llewellen of Las Cruces, and Frederick

Muller of Santa Fe for placing the first guidons atop San Juan Hill after their famous charge. With the truce of August 12, the so-called Splendid Little War ended.

The war coincided with New Mexico's best chance up to that time for statehood legislation to pass in Congress. Governor Otero led a coalition of old families as well as new politicos who saw the war as an opportunity to prove the territory worthy of statehood, or as Otero declared, becoming an added star on the flag. Following the war, New Mexico's Rough Rider can-do image was reasserted at the regiment's first annual reunion held in Las Vegas, where then New York governor Roosevelt pledged support for statehood. In 1900, the Republican Party's national platform included a plank supporting statehood. That year, President McKinley visited the Southwest and was impressed with the increases in population, agriculture, and nascent industries. Following McKinley's assassination in September 1901, New Mexicans expected now president Teddy Roosevelt to "push for statehood," as he had once promised to do. But, as the congressional sessions began, Albert Beveridge, a junior U.S. senator from Indiana and protégé of Roosevelt's, led his colleagues in crushing the movement for more than a decade. As was all too common, biased and racist views of New Mexico Territory's population thwarted its hopes of statehood and contributed to misguided decisions in Washington, D.C.

At the turn of the century, New Mexico's editors, promoters, and politicians believed the territory had an image problem. Max Frost, the soft-spoken but hard-fisted pro-reform editor of the Santa Fe *New Mexican,* advocated the territory's need for a "progressive" image which, according to his definition, meant midwestern farm values and architectural traditions. He became the head of the territorial Bureau of Immigration in the 1890s, a position he held for more than a decade. While at the bureau's helm, he promoted New Mexico's healthy climate, long growing season and agricultural diversity, and potential for irrigation projects to ensure the development of the "Land of Sunshine." Beginning in 1896 railroad publicists eagerly adopted a series of promotional publications entitled "Ho! The Land of Sunshine"; in the first decades of the twentieth century the Land of Sunshine became the territory's slogan.

In the 1890s and early 1900s, large irrigation projects and the opening of new farmlands became a corporate and later governmental panacea to correct New Mexico's image and slow development. New Mexico's first major project occurred in the broad lower Pecos River valley under the leadership of James J. Hagerman. Hagerman had made a fortune in the Midwest and in the Colorado mines before tuberculosis forced him to move to New Mexico. While visiting the Pecos River valley, he saw the opportunity for a new bonanza in irrigated agriculture. In 1890, Hagerman purchased a financially strapped land and irrigation project in the Carlsbad area that had been organized in part by sheriff Pat Garrett and cattleman Charles Eddy. He funded the construction of dams on the Pecos and, through land deals, acquired broad stretches of desert along the river. Hagerman bought 185,552 acres for $284,076, and sold scrip to settlers. Nicknamed the "Fruit Belt," the project at first appeared to be a success, especially after Hagerman built a railroad into the region. The initial success of the Pecos project resulted in the founding of a series of new towns from Roswell south to the Texas line, attracting more proposals.

New Mexico's weather is fickle, however, and its water resources tend to be in either drought or flood mode. Numerous floods caused damage to the Pecos project, eventually leading to its restructuring. There was also a larger issue of water rights. In the Southwest, traditional water rights laws differed from those in the Midwest and the East. In the water-rich eastern United States, the riparian rights system, based in British common law, prevailed. Under that system, a landowner had the right to use water from any watercourse passing through his or her property. In the arid Southwest, where there was never enough water to go around, that system was impractical. Instead, the Kearny Code codified into law the traditional Spanish system of water rights allocation according to prior appropriation, meaning that the first user of a watercourse was guaranteed first use of its waters thereafter. This water right could be sold to new owners, including those distant from the land.

The whole issue of water rights became increasingly problematic after 1880, as a technological transformation swept over the territory. As happened in the Pecos Valley, irrigation companies acquired water rights and competed with the old acequia users for the free-flowing waters. The longest battle involved the middle Rio Grande, where traditional users fought the corporate owners, primarily Chicago investors operating under various corporate names. Confrontations and court cases exemplified the fight between Hispanic acequia users and farmers in the middle Rio Grande. Although Hispanics claimed their rights to land and water under the Treaty of Guadalupe Hidalgo, they eventually lost out to new interpretations of legal rights and the right of eminent domain—the right to take land for the public good for fair compensation. By the 1920s the water rights had been consolidated, but by then the Federal Bureau of Reclamation had stepped in to manage the waters of the Albuquerque area.

Although aware of acequia users' rights, the territorial legislature revised local water laws. In 1907, believing New Mexico needed a centralized authority for water administration, members of the legislature enacted a new code of water laws that were to be managed by an official territorial/state engineer. Governor Herbert Hagerman, James's son, authorized the code, which remains the foundation for water law in New Mexico today.

One of the most influential innovations of the Progressive Era was the creation of the Bureau of Reclamation. In a sense the Progressives were social engineers, seeking to make society better by means of thoughtful planning underscored by "progressive," meaning scientific, development—common words of the period. They believed engineering know-how could resolve all ills, but lacked the modern recognition of the importance of environmental protection. In fact, the cultivated areas of today's southern New Mexico represent to a large degree the triumph of irrigation system engineering. President Roosevelt authorized the Bureau of Reclamation in 1902 with the support of many New Mexicans. The Reclamation Act provided federal funds for the construction of major dams and irrigation systems that were to be repaid through local irrigation districts and land sales. After another flood devastated Hagerman's Pecos River project, the Bureau of Reclamation explored taking over the system. In 1904, Hagerman's undertaking evolved into the Carlsbad Reclamation Project, one of the first projects sponsored by the Bureau of Reclamation. The agency

ELEPHANT BUTTE DAM

LARGEST IN THE WORLD · · · RIO GRANDE VALLEY IRRIGATION PROJECT
©
A.J.Hendee

Pamphlet advertising the Elephant Butte Dam, which at the time of completion was touted as the "Largest in the World," 1917. (Art Gómez Collection)

rebuilt the faltering project's dams, improved the major canals, and sold more land in efforts to make the desert below Carlsbad green with bountiful new farms.

Concurrently, the Bureau of Reclamation began work on Elephant Butte Dam on the Rio Grande north of Hot Springs (now Truth or Consequences), at the time one of the nation's largest irrigation projects. As a result of this project, the Bureau hoped to manage the flow of the Rio Grande through the Mesilla Valley into Mexico. Previously, an underfunded British company had attempted to build a dam at the site, only to go bankrupt. Although the bureau revived the project, it was not without ongoing problems: consummating water treaties with Mexico, determining the allocation of water between Texas and New Mexico, and negotiating the purchase of a large tract of land on the reservoir site granted to the estate of George Hearst. Work finally commenced in 1907, but the first concrete was not poured at the dam site until 1913. Appropriately, undersecretary of the interior and future U.S. senator from New Mexico Andrieus A. Jones flipped the switch that opened the floodgates to release water into the irrigation system below the impressive structure in 1916. At the time, the reservoir was the largest irrigation storage lake in the world.

Besides building irrigation systems, New Mexicans tapped aquifers, especially on the eastern plains. At Roswell, engineers discovered a one-hundred-mile-long artesian basin and expanded the use of artesian wells there during the 1890s. By 1920, there were 1,082 wells pumping to satiate flourishing fields and orchards. But competition resulting in overuse prompted the earliest laws against waste (unused wells were capped) and over-appropriation. The series of laws regulated the wells from 1905 until 1927, when an even more rigorous statute effectively closed the fields to further drilling. By then, the Pecos Valley had become one of the most productive agricultural and stockraising regions in New Mexico.

Similarly, farmers in the Mimbres Valley exploited its aquifer to supply orchards, fields, and vineyards. During the half decade before statehood, more than 125,000 acres of homesteaded land in the valley near Deming became a potential provider of agricultural goods for the territory. Technological innovations such as electrical pumps further expanded the supply of groundwater, especially in the high plains that surrounded Portales. Throughout the extent of the Ogallala Aquifer (which underlies the Great Plains), the eastern edge of the territory was transformed into a verdant strip of farmland.

Each of these regions experimented with commercially exploitable crops. The now-famous New Mexico chile industry began growing after the completion of the Elephant Butte Dam provided water and experiments conducted at New Mexico State University identified the best commercial varieties. Cotton, too, became a lucrative commodity in the south. The agribusiness culture of the New South replaced the Hispanic acequia system of small farms. Hispanic farmers became tenants on the newly irrigated lands. The appearance of peanut farms, the introduction of varieties of pecans, and expanded cultivation of those "diamonds in the field," the lowly pinto bean, spurred regional agricultural growth.

Meanwhile boosters like Max Frost and Miguel Otero pushed not just for new crops but more rail lines as well. New Mexico benefited greatly from a third wave of transcontinental railroad construction during the early twentieth century. Americans of that era considered railroads the panacea for all economic ills; New Mexicans were no different. Small-town boosters eagerly supported rail lines, and their associated benefits. Not surprisingly, railroad mileage within the territory nearly tripled in one decade, from 1,200 miles in 1900 to more than 3,000 by 1912.

The Chicago, Rock Island and Pacific (CRI&P) built the first new transcontinental line. After the railroad prospered in the Midwest farm region, its promoters decided to create a new link to the Pacific coast. The line entered New Mexico diagonally from the northeast, resulting in the founding of Tucumcari as a railroad hub. At Santa Rosa, the line connected with the Phelps Dodge Mining Company's El Paso & Southwestern Railroad (EP&SW). Beginning as a small branch line from El Paso to Alamogordo, the EP&SW collaborated with the Rock Island to open the Golden State Route from Chicago to Los Angeles. In February 1902, the first Rock Island Line passenger train left Chicago bound for Tucumcari (where the Southern Pacific took over beginning in 1924), Alamogordo, El Paso, Deming, and eventually California.

The largest system, the Atchison, Topeka & Santa Fe, either built or acquired the most mileage within the territory. By 1917, the Santa Fe owned 1,426 of the state's 3,041 miles of track, as compared to the Rock Island and EP&SW combined total of 893 miles. The Santa Fe also acquired Hagerman's line in the Pecos Valley, extending it from Roswell through Portales and on to Amarillo, Texas by 1900. The Sante Fe's ambitious Belen Cutoff project, built across the desert from Clovis to Belen, was completed in 1906, offering a new route across the Southwest to California. The Clovis subdivision remains the busiest line in the Western Hemisphere to this day.

The Santa Fe promoted a series of "immigrant" cars to attract new settlers. By 1912, the Santa Fe scheduled twice-monthly "home seeker" trains from Chicago to New Mexico. The other major railroads, including the Rock Island line and Burlington system (which had acquired the line through Clayton), also published promotional literature and used immigrant trains to attract midwesterners to the plains of eastern New Mexico. The Rock Island's "Breakfast Bacon Special" visited 35,000 agricultural enthusiasts around the territory during the 1912 season.

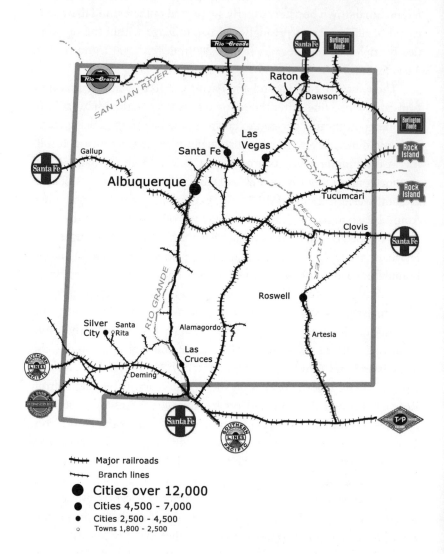

Major railroads
Branch lines

● **Cities over 12,000**
● Cities 4,500 - 7,000
● Cities 2,500 - 4,500
○ Towns 1,800 - 2,500

Fifteen largest towns and major railroads of New Mexico, 1910. (Map by
Catherine Holder Spude)

The agricultural "demonstration trains," taught the newcomers how to work the land.

In conjunction with New Mexico College of Agriculture and Mechanic Arts (now New Mexico State University), the Rock Island, Burlington, and Santa Fe railroads invited instructors such as Dr. Fabián García to ride "agricultural exhibit" cars, sharing information about successful farming techniques in the arid Southwest. Born in Chihuahua, García had attended New Mexico College before taking specialized courses at the University of Wisconsin and Cornell. After college, García began a long, productive career at the New Mexico Agricultural Experiment Station. His experiments greatly increased harvests of commercial crops, especially chiles, onions, and pecans.

New farming methods were also introduced. The Burlington system was the first to promote the new science of "dryland" farming, a technique that enables successful farming in arid climates with less water usage. To aid the dryland farmer the government in 1909 expanded land allocations under the Homestead Act from 160 to 320 acres. In 1916, Congressman Harvey Fergusson, the newly admitted state's first member of the U.S. House of Representatives, introduced legislation that increased homestead allotments to 640 acres, and reduced the number of years required to file from five to three. The numbers of homestead filings rapidly increased after 1905, peaking in 1916. From 1906 through 1927, an estimated 13 million acres of New Mexico public lands, mostly on the southern and eastern arid lands, were either homesteaded or transferred into private hands.

Not all homesteaders arrived by train. Many came by wagon on the old overland trails. The account of young Daisy Simpkins reveals that she, her husband, Payton, and two young children followed the Santa Fe tracks in traveling from central Oklahoma across the Texas Panhandle to a homestead near Mountainair. The movement of southerners from Texas and Oklahoma to the plains marked the largest migration into New Mexico since the Spanish colonial era. These southerners brought strong views on prohibition, a fundamentalist religion, and a tradition of populist dissent that would soon bring opposition to New Mexico's old-guard Republicans.

As thousands of immigrants flooded the plains and deserts, dry farming became the new dogma. New farming technology, a revised Homestead Act, massive promotion by regional railroads and their partners, increased global demands and rising prices for commodities, and an unseasonably wet cycle on the plains, facilitated the last classic land rush in U.S. history. The rush focused on the Great Plains, including the vast eastern and southern two-thirds of New Mexico. Of all the major land promotion schemes on the American frontier, speculation in the Land of Sunshine was not only the last effort but the least fortunate. The Dust Bowl would become the legacy of dryland farming and the rush of the teens.

In urbanized New Mexico, the railroads created jobs, contributing to population growth. Albuquerque, where by statehood the Santa Fe Railroad had concentrated its shops and state operational headquarters, benefited the most. The railroad paid some 2,000 workers a total of $100,000 in monthly salaries, further stimulating the growing community's economy. Fred Harvey built the Alvarado, the grandest of his Harvey house hotels along the Santa Fe lines, a tremendous benefit to Albuquerque's tourism economy. Similar construction of shops and offices in Clovis, Vaughn, and Belen stimulated local employment. The presence of Rock Island–built facilities in Tucumcari and the EP&SW shops located in Alamogordo could make or break these communities. For example, when the EP&SW transferred its workshops from Alamogordo to El Paso, it crippled the local economy for a full decade. Furthermore, the railroads attracted immigrant labor from Chihuahua and farther south in Mexico to work on track maintenance crews and at lower-paying jobs in the mines and lumber mills, especially while the Mexican Revolution raged south of the border. As a result, so-called Little Chihuahua neighborhoods arose in many New Mexico towns.

One traveling journalist referred to the railroad communities and the cities that arose from new water projects as New Mexico's "New Seven Cities of Cibola." Roswell, Carlsbad, Artesia, Alamogordo, Portales, Clovis, Carrizozo, Tucumcari, and others were all founded by railroad promoters. It might be said that railroads and water projects created modern New Mexico. The railroad companies either cosponsored or constructed communication networks such as the first telegraph lines and soon thereafter long-distance telephone service. Smaller towns finally received speedy and inexpensive mail service. The train also brought traveling entertainment, the theater, and the circus to these communities, thus reducing their isolation. Department stores in major cities were made easily accessible; train-delivered Sears & Roebuck and Montgomery Ward mail-order catalogues became an integral aspect of rural life.

Greater access to railroads also stimulated a population boom during the first decade of the twentieth century—the largest percentage increase in New Mexico's history. Between 1900 and 1910 New Mexico's population grew from 195,310 to 327,301 people, a 67.6 percent increase. Nearly 40 percent were born in other states, confirming the large migration that accompanied the railroads and opening of new homestead lands. Native-born Hispanics still predominated in the Rio Grande Valley and in the north central region, while most settlers on the eastern plains and in the southern counties were Anglo. Generally speaking, in cities with new town and old town divisions, such as Albuquerque and Las Vegas, Hispanics dominated the old towns while the predominantly Anglo newcomers flooded the new towns. The foreign-born population increased as well, by 8.6 percent, half of them from Mexico and the other half from southern Europe. Because the mining industry hired large numbers of immigrants, Grant, McKinley, and Colfax counties harbored as much as 25 percent foreign-born residents, as Mexican nationals, Austrians, Italians, Slavs, and others worked in the mines. Albuquerque had the greatest number of Italian neighborhoods, and Italians found themselves readily accepted into the Hispanic Catholic community as well as the Anglo commercial world. Italian immigration significantly diminished after World War I. African Americans represented less than 1 percent of the total population, but that group was growing rapidly.

For one of the few times in New Mexico's history, men substantially outnumbered women in the territory: 175,000 men to 152,000 women. This gap represented the greatest disparity between men and women in New Mexico since the first census in 1850, and was accounted for by the number of foreign-born males working in the mines, lumber camps, and other industrial centers. On the prairies and among the Hispanic communities, women were the dominant force in the home or homestead. According to Joan Jensen and Sarah Deutsch, both Hispanic and Anglo women were important in maintaining the family's claim to property ownership, particularly when their husbands sought seasonal employment in nearby urban centers or distant agrarian communities. One-third of New Mexico's population was age fourteen or under, the northern Hispanic counties supporting the largest number of children. This ratio of children versus voting-age Hispanics in 1910 suggests that although Hispanics were still in the numerical majority, Anglos represented the greater number of voting-age adults. This important demographic change would have an impact on state politics.

The ten largest towns in New Mexico were all situated on the railroad lines (see table). Albuquerque claimed 13,163 people and Las Vegas 6,934. The agricultural center of Roswell was third with 6,172, while the capital city of Santa Fe followed. Among the cluster having populations between 3,000 and 4,000 were the rail centers, mining towns and farm communities of Raton, Las Cruces, Clovis, Silver City, Dawson, and Deming. Today, the coal town of Dawson is a ghost town. Las Cruces, the state's current second largest city, was at the time overshadowed by the rail hub of El Paso. Housing 39,279 people and home to six major railroads, the west Texas town served as a principal commercial center for much of southern New Mexico.

Not surprisingly, in terms of population, the largest counties coincided with the largest towns. Bernalillo County, which included Albuquerque, was by far the largest, followed by San Miguel, which claimed Las Vegas. Chaves County, with Roswell as the county seat, came next. Rio Arriba, the fourth largest county, lacked a major urban center. Recognized for their numerous traditional Hispanic villages, Taos and Mora counties contained mostly numerous small, agricultural populations. In 1910, Wagon Mound, with nearly 2,000 people, bested Taos with 1,309 as the largest of the northern villages. Also contained within the various counties were the Pueblo Indian communities.

Ten Largest Towns, 1910 and 2010

1910		2010	
Albuquerque	13,163*	Albuquerque	545,852
Las Vegas	6,934*	Las Cruces	97,618
Roswell	6,172	Río Rancho	87,521
Santa Fe	5,072	Santa Fe	67,947
Raton	4,539	Roswell	48,366
Las Cruces	3,856	Farmington	45,877
Clovis	3,255	Clovis	37,775
Silver City	3,217	Hobbs	34,122
Dawson	3,119	Alamogordo	30,403
Deming	2,757	Carlsbad	26,138

*Includes "Old Town" and "New Town" sections

The territory's most dramatic population growth occurred in eastern New Mexico, especially Chaves County, nicknamed the "homesteader's paradise." The incoming homesteaders had changed the Pecos River valley from ranch country to farms that produced corn, beans, tomatoes, and fruit, as well as hogs and dairy products. The establishment of thirty-nine post offices and rural school districts in the county by 1912 was one clear indicator of growth. Ranchers changed their methods of operation in light of the increased productivity of well-watered farmlands and alfalfa fields, and greater acquisition of surrounding grazing lands, a move fostered by "nesters" who fenced in the open range then sold out.

The coal resources of Colfax County caused it to become the fifth most populous in New Mexico. Raton boomed early because of its coal-mining activities, then temporarily lost population as the result of shifting policy within the railroad industry. In 1906–1908, the Santa Fe redirected rail traffic to the Belen Cutoff, causing a long-term decline in the once-burgeoning rail center. Colfax County contained a large percentage of Italian and other southern Europeans imported to work in the mines at Dawson, Sugarite, Koehler, and other nearby camps. All were company towns with the requisite company-owned stores, meeting halls, schools, community churches and, in some cases, lodges representing the various immigrant groups.

In addition to foreign immigrants, increasing numbers of African Americans drifted into several of the coal towns, railroad centers, and lumber camps to find work. The U.S. Census of 1910 enumerated 1,628, a figure that swelled to approximately 10,000 during the next five years. According to school census numbers, African Americans also migrated to farming communities such as Blackdom near Roswell and Vado near Las Cruces. As one African American Vado resident stated, he moved to New Mexico seeking to "farm my own land, live in my own home, and put my kids through college," like everyone else. However, 1920 census figures indicated the number of African Americans had plummeted to a mere 5,733, and by 1930, the number had decreased below the pre-1910 figure.

There were a number of causes for this out-migration. One was the increasing availability of cheap labor from Mexico, especially at the beginning of the Mexican Revolution in 1910. The arrival to the Pecos River valley of southerners imbued with segregationist Jim Crow values was a more direct cause. Eddy County was the first to institute voting literacy tests in an effort to disenfranchise African Americans. Prairie schools were segregated, eventually influencing segregation of the state university at Las Cruces during the 1920s. An edict prohibiting African Americans from entering Artesia and other valley communities coincided with the rise of the Ku Klux Klan, headquartered in Roswell. "Little Texas" had become New Mexico's "Deep South." In 1912, a race riot broke out in Clovis, during which a group of infuriated whites rounded up African American railroad workers and ran them out of town on railroad cars. The governor sent the Mounted Police to quell the riot.

Subsequently, after it was alleged that an African American hotel porter was found in his room with a drugged white woman, townsfolk in Gallup gave African American miners twenty-four hours to leave town. As tensions flared, the coal mine owners, badly in need of African American labor, preempted their removal. In 1913, Albuquerque's African American community protested their exclusion from local businesses, theaters, and shops. City fathers ignored the complaints and did nothing on the rationale of not interfering in private business matters. Like the remainder of the nation, New Mexico experienced a shameful period of prejudice toward and segregation of African Americans that endured until well after World War II.

After many trials, New Mexico stood on the brink of gaining statehood in 1902. The powerful Pennsylvania senator Matthew Quay rallied forces in support of the territory. On previous visits to New Mexico, President Roosevelt had voiced his support as well. Governor Otero and the Republican majority relied on their friends in Congress to finally pass an omnibus bill enabling legislation for statehood for Oklahoma, New Mexico, and Arizona. A number of congressmen opposed the measure because they feared that adding the overwhelmingly Democratic Arizona along with Republican New Mexico as new states would upset the balance of power in the U.S. Congress. In a clever but outrageous maneuver, Senator Beveridge of Indiana, an influential member of the Committee on Territories, killed the statehood bill of 1902. Instead he introduced his own proposal for a joint statehood bill. Beveridge's plan was to unite Arizona and New Mexico territories into one state named "Arizona," but with its capital in Santa Fe. "Arizona the Great," he stated, would help "Americanize" Hispanic New Mexico through its unification with Anglo Arizona.

Politicians from both territories fought the measure, Arizonans more passionately because the more populous New Mexico would inevitably subsume Arizonans' political ambitions. In 1906, after years of political debate, Beveridge forced the joint statehood bill through Congress. Fortunately, the bill included a proviso that residents in both Arizona and New Mexico had to approve joint statehood. During the election, New Mexico surprisingly approved jointure, while Arizonans soundly defeated it. One historian, quoting Holm Bursum, head of the territorial Republican Party, argued that New Mexico agreed to joint statehood knowing that Arizona would defeat it, which might enable New Mexico to slip in among the ranks of the Union. As usual, territorial leaders were disappointed.

The fight over jointure, however, did cause Governor George Curry, a former Rough Rider and personal friend of Roosevelt's, to step forward along with the president to champion the cause of statehood. Throughout the political battle, Roosevelt had been lukewarm to the idea of joint statehood. As he prepared to leave office in 1908, Roosevelt endorsed separate statehood, but passed the issue on to his handpicked successor, William Howard Taft. Curry enjoyed Taft's favor because the two men had served together in the Philippines.

The struggle to get the bill through Congress was long and slow. But on June 20, 1910, President Taft signed the enabling legislation to create the new state. The last territorial governor, William J. Mills, issued a call to elect delegates and organize a convention to draft a constitution. On October 3, delegates representing each of the twenty-four counties met in Santa Fe. The constitutional convention was extremely partisan. Of the total one hundred delegates, seventy-one were Republican and twenty-nine were Democrat, allowing the former party to control the deliberations. The thirty-two Hispanics were all Republicans, which gave them powerful leverage over the Republican Party's votes and, thus, more influence on the convention than their numbers would suggest. Taft had called for a "safe and sane constitution"—meaning conservative and pro-business. With the conservative Holm O. Bursum and "old guard" Republicans like Thomas Catron, patron Solomon Luna, and railroad lawyer Charles Spiess in charge, that is what the delegates gave him.

On the other hand, Progressive Democrat Harvey Fergusson of Albuquerque proposed the idea of a voter recall of judges in an effort to assert some measure of control over judges. The revolutionary idea would greatly enhance local democracy. Republican legislators promptly either weakened or eliminated such "radical" proposals, including proposals for women's suffrage and prohibition, both supported by significant numbers of women. Women were however given the right to vote in local school board elections. Future Governor Washington Lindsey's wife, Amanda, is credited with encouraging her husband to insert this section into the proposed constitution. A college-educated Ohioan, she was a leader in the Woman's Christian Temperance Union, child welfare programs, and other family and gender reforms in the small eastern New Mexico town of Portales, where her lawyer-husband served as mayor.

The most striking part of the constitution concerned the territory's Hispanic citizens. In light of existing and expanding segregation laws and discriminatory practices against African Americans, Hispanic lawmakers pushed to protect their rights and traditions. In public schools they protected Spanish-speaking students from segregation. Also, they sought to preserve the citizenship rights awarded under the Treaty of Guadalupe Hidalgo. They ensured that voters could not be disenfranchised because of their religion, race, color, or ability to use English. Equally important to Hispanics was a clause that made it nearly impossible to amend the constitution. Future changes to the document required a three-quarter majority vote in the legislature. Republican Party boss Solomon Luna proved to be crucial to the passage of these proposals. It is said he had but "to raise a finger or an eye brow" to influence delegates' votes.

The convention concluded on November 21 with overwhelming approval of the drafted constitution. Diehard reformers like Harvey Fergusson, however, stood in opposition and refused to sign the document because it was not progressive enough. Governor Mills sent the constitution to the voters. Two months later, New Mexicans voted three to one to adopt the constitution. After the usual deliberations and a thorough review the U.S. Congress approved the constitution with some changes. President Taft authorized statehood and signed the proclamation on January 6, 1912. New Mexico became the nation's forty-seventh star.

In the meantime, on November 7, 1911, New Mexico voters had been allowed to vote for their first elected state officials. The growing number of New Mexico Democrats voted Harvey Fergusson into Congress. At the same time, they elected popular Republican former governor and statehood champion George Curry to the infant state's second allocated seat in the House of Representatives. Curry's tenure was more or less symbolic inasmuch as he served but a few months in the House. Owing to a reduction in the number of congressmen allowed from the state, the second seat was abolished and Curry could not run for reelection, which apparently suited the aging cowboy.

The first major political clash within the nascent state concerned the selection of two U.S. senators. The Republicans had gerrymandered

Political cartoon caricaturing New Mexico and Arizona as a happy
vaquero and a cowboy receiving their statehood diplomas, 1912. (Drawn
by Clifford K. Berryman. Robert L. Spude Collection.)

the voting districts during the state constitutional convention, that is,
divided them in a way that ensured their party's advantage. Hence,
Republicans largely dictated the makeup of the first state legislature.
The state legislature, in turn, selected the two U.S. senators (for the first
and last time, since new legislation took selection away from the too
easily bribed legislature and gave it to the state's voters). Among the
front-runners was Solomon Luna, who declined the position. His
abstention left William Henry "Bull" Andrews, the state's longtime

delegate to Congress, Santa Fe's Thomas Catron, and southern New Mexico power broker Albert Fall. The political contest was rife with accusations of bribery and influence peddling. The legislature voted Albert Fall as the state's first choice. Supported by the Republican old guard and local Hispanic politicos, the seventy-one-year-old Thomas Catron won the second seat and served as senator from 1912 to 1917.

In the first election for state officers, Democrats pulled an upset by voting William C. McDonald, a Lincoln County rancher, into office as the first governor. As Lieutenant Governor, Ezequiel Cabeza de Baca of Las Vegas joined with McDonald in an effort to get the new state government up and running. Because of some confusion regarding the term limit, they both served five years, which allowed them time to be effective. Inasmuch as Congress assigned twelve million acres of public lands to the new state to support education and public facilities, McDonald used profits from land sales or leases and other funding sources to finance the public schools, significantly improving the educational system. To his credit, McDonald targeted corporations for taxation, increasing tax rates for the railroads and large mining and timber operations by 20 percent or more. During his term as governor from 1912 to 1917, tax assessment evaluations increased from $59,248,881 to $329,869,888. At last, the corporations were paying their fair share.

Governor McDonald also proposed reducing salaries for state officeholders. During his five-year term, he established the State Highway Commission, expanded the Office of the State Engineer, which dealt specifically with water projects, and authorized a state Corporation Commission. An avid Wilsonian Progressive, McDonald instituted the first reforms to abolish corruption and vice. He used his veto to eliminate special-interest tax breaks. In 1913, he beefed up weak territorial legislation that outlawed gambling by adding enforcement power. He attacked prostitution, which had gone underground starting in 1910 after local communities began adopting ordinances making it illegal.

During this time, New Mexico experienced rapid political change because of the evolving demographics of the state's population. New ideas such as progressivism and socialism spawned new political parties. Though comparatively weak, their participation at times influenced the outcome of elections. Teddy Roosevelt's "Bull

Moose" Party split the Republicans in 1912. Socialist Party and later Farm-Labor Party candidates drew votes from the Democrats. The Prohibition Party was active, though narrowly focused. Reform-minded mayors of such plains towns as Portales and Roswell championed prohibition. The Woman's Christian Temperance Union and the Anti-Saloon League had both tried unsuccessfully to include prohibition in the constitution. Now, they led a slow, gradual acceptance of prohibition from one community to the next. Upon the death of Ezequiel C. de Baca, Washington E. Lindsey, the former mayor of Portales, became governor and made prohibition a statewide issue. In 1917, New Mexicans voted for the "grand experiment," which took effect on October 1, 1918.

At the time of statehood, the twelve counties on the Rio Grande and upper Pecos rivers were Hispanic and remained Republican strongholds. Political commentator Jack Holmes characterized the group as rooted in family values, placing great importance on formal education. Generally speaking, they were village-based and oriented to the Catholic faith. The prevailing political system was best defined as the *patron*, or boss, system, in which a paternal figure cared for the immediate needs of the local populace in return for votes and election to office. Importantly, the political boss (*jefe*), adept at political wheeling and dealing, assigned a high priority to the protection of the village, family values, and the church. For these reasons, the political bosses controlled the vote. The northern counties of Mora, San Miguel, and Guadalupe, for example, very often swayed a tight, statewide election with their bloc of Republican votes. Opponents, however, characterized San Miguel, controlled by resident patron Segundo Romero and its satellite counties, as a breeding ground for corruption and bossism.

"Little Texas," the six counties of eastern and southern New Mexico, maintained strong southern connections and, therefore, were mostly Democratic agrarian reformers. Also grounded in the church and strong family values, most were fundamentalist Protestants who took exception to interference from the Catholic Church in local politics and public education. Bernalillo County and its seat of Albuquerque held the greatest number of voters, but was often factionalized politically between Democrats and Republicans.

Another influential Republican faction was made up of lawyers representing corporate interests, specifically the mining companies and railroads. Prominent in the north were coal company lawyers such as Frank Springer in Colfax County and Charles Spiess in San Miguel County, along with a somewhat benign Santa Fe Railroad. Southern New Mexico was in the hands of attorneys representing mining giants Phelps Dodge (and its El Paso & Southwestern Railroad) and Chino Copper Company (and its subsidiary Gallup America Coal, about which more later). Chief among these were Otero County's Albert Fall and Socorro County's Holm Bursum, who served back to back in the U.S. Senate.

The elections of 1916 and 1918 underscored New Mexico's political schizophrenia. Because of a schism among Republicans, party leaders ousted Catron from his U.S. Senate seat. A well-organized coalition of Democrats, disaffected Republicans, and a number of independents elected Las Vegas attorney Andrieus A. Jones as Catron's replacement. Some historians suggest this surprising Democratic victory may have been achieved only because of the backroom antics of a disgruntled Catron. Jones, descended from an old Tennessee family of Southern Democrats, harbored Wilson's Progressive views and was notable for chairing the Senate Committee on Woman Suffrage. A powerful friend to the Hispanic communities of northern New Mexico as well as a supporter of the agrarian interests in Little Texas, Jones also earned the respect of the corporations, who begrudgingly gave him their support. His strong coalition of support enabled Jones to remain in Congress until his death in 1927.

In the 1918 governor's race, Octaviano A. Larrazolo managed to win the governor's seat by a slim margin, with 51.4 percent of the vote. A native of Chihuahua, Mexico, Larrazolo, a reputable Las Vegas attorney and editor, became an outspoken defender of the Hispanic community. He initially ran for office as a Democrat, but when his party failed to elect a single Hispanic to the constitutional convention, he switched to the Republican Party, denouncing the "element of intolerance" among Southern Democrats. He favored women's right to vote, national prohibition, and educational reform—in particular, teaching classes in Spanish. His biggest obstacle within the party was his connection to the large corporations, which were becoming more and more influential in politics.

At the behest of the corporations, for instance, Larrazolo declared martial law in McKinley County during the miners' strike of 1919. But, when he ordered a review of taxes paid by mining giant Phelps Dodge and its subsidiaries, he incurred their animosity. The increasing influence of the corporate world is best exemplified by Larrazolo's unsuccessful bid for reelection in 1920. During his term in office, Senator Jones, with the support of Governor Larrazolo, had pushed for a war profits tax on all state corporations. In response, state party leaders killed the governor's chances of reelection and replaced him with Bursum's recommendation, Judge Merritt Mechem of Tucumcari and Socorro. Thus, sponsoring the war profits tax in New Mexico, which failed passage in the local legislature, proved to be political suicide. One voter later claimed that the corporations' liberal distribution of money in certain counties kept Larrazolo off the ticket. Thus, Little Texas Democrats, Hispanic Republican, and Republican corporate politicians were the three controlling factors in New Mexico elections.

By the decade after statehood, another voting force emerged: women. The state constitution granted women the vote only in school board elections. In 1912 the good women of Wagon Mound were the first to use the franchise in a local election. New Mexican efforts to expand women's suffrage met stiff opposition from Senator Catron and the paternalistic attitudes of the Hispanic majority. Yet it was educator Adelina "Nina" Otero-Warren, from an old rico family, who led the New Mexico suffragette movement and chipped away at the opposition. Like their sisters in other states, New Mexico women celebrated the ratification of the Nineteenth Amendment in 1920. Otero-Warren promptly ran for Congress—the first woman to do so—and received most of the Hispanic north's vote, while the rest of the state opposed her. Not until 1947 did her peer suffragette and educator Georgia Lusk of Carlsbad become the first woman elected to the U.S. Congress from New Mexico.

When the legislature passed an act in 1921 allowing women to run for and hold state office, a group of suffragettes were elected into statewide positions, including Soledad C. Chacón of Albuquerque as secretary of state, Isabel Eckles as state superintendent of public schools, and Bertha Paxton as a state representative. Ella Becker of Lake Arthur became the first woman elected mayor. She had earned a reputation as a reformer a decade before by helping Carrie Nation wield her hatchet at saloons up and down the Pecos. Women were becoming a recognized political force within both parties.

When Francisco Madero publicly defamed the Porfirio Díaz regime in 1910, Americans could not have imagined the Mexican Revolution would bring the two bordering nations to the brink of war. What began as a social and political revolution in Mexico deteriorated into a civil war among revolutionary factions. One of the greatest challenges to Governor McDonald was how to deal with the Mexican Revolution that inevitably landed on his back doorstep. McDonald remained in constant communication with President Woodrow Wilson, whose administration orchestrated the relocation of thousands of Mexican refugees, supported lifting the ban on arms sales to the revolutionary combatants, and endured the last attack by a foreign army within the continental United States.

The Chihuahuan general known as Pancho Villa was one of the most renowned of the northern Mexico revolutionaries. A charismatic leader of his people, he had gained and then, at the hand of forces supporting Venustiano Carranza, lost national prominence as 1915 drew to a close. When the United States recognized Carranza's government in October of that year, Villa, who saw Carranza as a potential Díaz-style dictator, lashed out. Perhaps to gain national attention, to take personal revenge on the Americans, or on the advice of a German spy, Villa attacked the small border community of Columbus, New Mexico, on March 16, 1916. His predawn attack left seventeen Americans and ninety-three Mexicans dead. General "Black Jack" Pershing organized an ill-advised punitive expedition to hunt down Villa in Chihuahua, inciting international news coverage. Two captured Villistas were summarily executed in New Mexico before Governor MacDonald interceded to grant the remaining five captives a reprieve. Governor Larrazolo pardoned the five soldiers after three years of imprisonment. He reasoned that they were soldiers, forced to do their duty under penalty of death, and not the wanton thieves and murderers the popular press depicted them as.

Pershing's expedition in Mexico in 1916–17 proved to be a strategic failure in the field as well as a disaster to the image of the United States. Meanwhile, tension between Carranza and Wilson was at a high pitch. The well-remembered outrage of the American occupation of Veracruz on Wilson's orders in 1914, coupled with the intrusion of the Pershing expedition just as the Mexican Revolution appeared to be winding down, brought the United States and Mexico to the brink of war.

Compounding the problem, World War I had broken out in Europe in 1914. German submarines were attempting a blockade of Great Britain that included sinking noncombatant ships on the high seas, inflaming the international community. Realizing their actions were drawing the United States to the Allied side, Germany encouraged war between the United States and Mexico to divert the Americans' attention. According to intercepted diplomatic correspondence popularly known as the Zimmerman Telegram, the Germans offered to help Mexico regain the territory lost to the United States in 1848 as a reward for its joining Germany in the war effort. Deeming the offer impractical, Carranza declined. Pershing was recalled from Mexico in early 1917, and after the United States officially entered World War I on April 2, 1917, he was appointed to command the American forces, thus easing tension with Mexico and the new constitutional government. Villa continued his violent opposition to the Mexican government until 1920, when he submitted to a truce. Three years later, Villa was assassinated.

When the United States went to war, the New Mexico National Guard was removed from the international border and pressed into national service. One out of every twenty-two Americans served in the nation's first total war. In New Mexico, 17,000-plus patriots enlisted, and more than 500 never returned. Of the volunteers from New Mexico 60 percent were Hispanic. On the home front, women organized Red Cross drives and fundraising efforts to supply the troops and noncombatants. Bond drives blanketed the state, sometimes using a tank to demolish old buildings as a way to demonstrate the need for more bond purchases in order to buy war material.

Like other state governors, Governor Lindsey established a state council for defense to promote support for the war effort as well as monitor the activities of resident German and Austrian immigrants. The council created a wartime enemies list of all Germans and their families. No doubt New Mexico had the only Navajo on the national enemies' list—a woman who had married a German-born merchant living in Gallup. The state arrested a few German Americans whom overzealous, self-appointed patriots accused of criticizing the president. Fortunately, New Mexico did not experience the violent extremes that occurred in other western states during World War I.

But the state had to clean up the mess resulting from the Bisbee deportation of 1917. To break a miners' strike in that southeastern Arizona town, local vigilantes rounded up 1,185 men, loaded them onto boxcars, and dumped them in the Chihuahuan Desert south of Lordsburg without food or water on July 12, 1917. Exhibiting an unusual display of political courage, Governor Lindsey ordered the arrest of the anti-union thugs responsible for the hapless deportees. Next, the governor extended humane treatment to the deportees, transporting them to the nearest town to be fed and cared for. President Wilson ordered U.S. troops stationed in nearby Columbus to set up a tent camp and provide rations.

When the Great War ended on November 11, 1918, New Mexicans across the state celebrated the news. The boys were coming home and spontaneous parades reveled in the belief that the "war to end all wars" had saved the world for democracy. Just as the global conflict was coming to an end, however, news of a new and terrible killer spread throughout the nation—Spanish influenza. Hysteria spread as the disease appeared to be unstoppable. Albuquerque set up quarantine districts. People wore gauze masks in public, and town after town closed meeting halls, theaters, and other public gathering places, but to no avail. In December, the epidemic temporarily subsided but made a devastating comeback in early 1919, exacerbated by a shortage of doctors and nurses, especially in rural areas and on Indian reservations, and the absence of a state health department to coordinate a response. To this day, no one knows how many New Mexicans sickened and died, but more than 50,000 cases were reported (14 percent of the population). Nationwide an estimated half million Americans perished, ten times the fifty thousand American combat deaths sustained on Europe battlefields.

The Industrial Revolution both directly and indirectly drove new settlement of the West in the latter nineteenth and early twentieth centuries. By extension, the minerals industry became integral to regional development. Coal-fired industrialization and copper-enhanced technological innovation carried America into a new era of power and communication. New Mexico contains some of the nation's most abundant coalfields and copper mines. At the start of the twentieth century, huge undeveloped copper and coal deposits throughout the territory attracted large corporations headquartered in New York or other eastern cities. Their opening of mines and building of mills formed part of the great industrial colossus that characterized the United States during the early twentieth century. Industry, in turn, created a new labor class and social structures that affected the evolution of the fledgling state.

Phelps Dodge was one of the largest corporations operating in the territory, and by 1910 it controlled copper and coal mines in addition to timber lands and railroads. The corporation's arrival in New Mexico typified frontier development. Charles Eddy, the classic western entrepreneur, had built much of the empire that Phelps Dodge later acquired. A New Yorker who had come west in the 1880s to manage a cattle ranch on the Pecos, Eddy joined with partners to form the Eddy-Bissell Cattle Company and found the enormous Halagueno Ranch that sprawled along the Pecos north and east of present Carlsbad (initially incorporated as the town of Eddy). Hoping to attract new settlers, he and partners that included Pat Garrett and James J. Hagerman built an irrigation system and a railroad. A falling out with Hagerman caused Eddy to sell out and look for new ventures. In 1896, with New York backing, he organized the El Paso & Northeastern (EP&N) railroad and built a new line from the West Texas city into New Mexico with an aim to tap its natural resources. Eddy set up subsidiary companies to open coalfields in Capitan and harvest timber in the Sacramento Mountains near present Cloudcroft. He also acquired the extensive Dawson coalfield near Raton, using his rail system to link all of his enterprises. In

May 1905, New York–based Phelps Dodge and Company purchased all of Eddy's New Mexico properties and initiated full-scale resource exploitation.

Other local entrepreneurs profited in a similar fashion. August Hilton reopened the Carthage coalfields east of Socorro, then with his son Conrad, sold the mines to the Guggenheim-owned ASARCO smelter in El Paso (Conrad Hilton would later use the profits from this sale to finance and build his first hotel in Albuquerque). Maxwell Land Grant manager Frank Springer sold chunks of its coal-laden property to Rockefeller's Colorado Fuel & Iron Company (CF&I). In 1909, the Santa Fe Railroad organized the Victor American Fuel Company to operate its coal properties, while the Guggenheim-supported Chino Copper Company established the subsidiary Gallup America Coal Company (GAMERCO) to develop the Gallup field.

The Raton, Gallup, Madrid, Capitan, and Carthage fields combined produced one million short tons of coal per year at the turn of the century, and peaked at four times that amount in 1918. New Mexico ranked eighth among the forty-eight states in total coal production. Its coal towns and technology mirrored that of any Appalachian coal mining operation.

Phelps Dodge's Stag Canon Fuel Company and the nearby company town of Dawson were the largest operations. The railroads consumed 50 percent of the coal derived from the Dawson mines, while Arizona copper smelters devoured most of the rest, aside from a small portion for domestic use. Like many large corporations Phelps Dodge built a company town that provided the town's entire infrastructure but also exercised an effective monopoly over local goods and services, profiting from all the purchases miners' families made even as it might extend them credit at the company store during hard times. Dawson boasted a hospital, communal church, a school (with 1,200 students), and the Phelps Dodge Mercantile. Although the company promoted safety in its operation, the Dawson mines were the scene of some of western America's largest mine accidents. In 1913, an underground explosion killed 263 miners; in 1923, another explosion killed 122 more. For this reason, New Mexico posted one of the nation's worst coal miner death rates.

The mines supported spinoff industries. The growth of agriculture coincided with the mining boom. Also, the timber industry grew in direct correlation to the rising need for construction lumber, railroad ties, and shoring timbers to support underground mining. The American Lumber Company sawmill represented the largest industrial complex in the vicinity of Albuquerque. Owned by Michigan investors, the mill produced thirty railroad cars of timber per day, the timber mostly harvested from forested lands in the Zuni and Jemez mountains.

The abundant copper deposits of the Santa Rita del Cobre mine in southwestern New Mexico had been worked during the Spanish colonial and Mexican periods and sporadically during the territorial years. In 1905 John Sully, a young engineer recently graduated from MIT, investigated the Santa Rita mine and determined that it could be made profitable utilizing the new open-pit mining technology. But such an undertaking required big money, and Sully embarked on a search for backing. Four years later he attracted the support of Daniel Jackling and his partners—which included the Guggenheim family—who had recently opened the Bingham Canyon copper mine in Utah, turning it into a phenomenal producer. Jackling became president of the Chino Copper Company, making Sully manager. Using steam shovels, it took three years to strip away the overburden, mine the ore, build a mill, and deliver concentrates to the Guggenheim smelter in El Paso, before the mine showed a profit. In June 1913, the Chino mine paid its first dividend; at the end of 1916, the company had disbursed $7,177,335 in dividends from revenues totaling $19,219,767. The company had become the fifth-largest copper producer in the country and would remain near the top throughout most of the remainder of the century, at a time when the United States accounted for half the world's copper production.

Mine owners built the company town of Santa Rita on the edge of the pit, and the mill town of Hurley seven miles farther south. The workers also found housing in the satellite communities of Bayard and Central. The Chino mining operation supported some 9,000 people in Grant County. Because of its proximity to Mexico, and the long-standing tradition of employing Mexican labor, workers were predominantly Mexican nationals mostly from Chihuahua.

Miner holding ancient hide ore sacks and standing on a notched-pole ladder leaning against a steam shovel at the Chino Mine, Santa Rita del Cobre, 1915. (Courtesy of Palace of the Governors Archives, NMHM/DCA, negative no. 5255)

Hoping to imitate the success of the Chino operation, other companies probed New Mexico's mining districts. Phelps Dodge bought claims in the Burro Mountains southwest of Chino, opened mines, built a mill, and established the model company town of Tyrone. The New York–based New Jersey Zinc Company expanded its operation through a local subsidiary called the Empire Zinc Company, which purchased mines at Hanover, just west of Chino, as well as at Kelly, near Socorro. Meanwhile, Rockefeller's CF&I bought the iron mines at Fierro, near Hanover. All of these companies profited from high metal market prices during World War I.

During the summer of 1917, as the companies were enjoying unprecedented profits, laborers in the Gallup coal mines struck when the Chino-owned Gallup America Coal Company did not recognize their union contract. The United Mine Workers (UMW) ordered the strike to establish recognition for the union, increase pay, and improve working conditions. The operators in the district already controlled both the county's council of defense and the county sheriff's office. The latter appointed the company's guards as deputies in order to break the strike.

In a repeat performance of the Bisbee deportation but on a smaller scale, the council declared the strikers unpatriotic and a potential security threat, ordering the sheriff to deport all troublemakers. During the roundup of union representatives on July 31, a newspaper editor who favored the strikers and thirty-three other supporters were imprisoned. Later that evening, sheriff's deputies used a machine gun to march thirty-four Italian, French, Austrian, Spanish, Mexican, and American men—not all of them miners—to the depot where they were placed on a railroad coach and deported. After being abandoned in Belen, members of the group wired Governor Lindsey. Although the governor sent an investigator and the Mounted Police to Gallup, the company's "hired gunmen" had already successfully broken the strike. By the end of that summer, most miners had returned to work and the district's coal production exceeded that of all previous years. Federal investigators found the company at fault, but took no action against either management or local law enforcement. One Gallup newspaper declared: "Oh! Patriotism! What rank rot is carried on in thy name?"

Compared with the coalfield wars in Colorado and the infamous Bisbee deportation, New Mexico experienced few strikes. Historian Robert Kern credits John L. Lewis of the UMW with easing the tension. Lewis was present at the state constitutional convention to advise delegates on union labor demands. He helped sponsor the inclusion of mine inspection, regulation of hours, and anti-blacklisting laws in the constitution, and later legislation in an effort to protect union members. In the long run, Lewis's early influence on New Mexico labor laws limited the degree of violence that erupted in the state. Based on their collective experiences elsewhere, Phelps Dodge and CF&I established company unions for the purpose of bargaining and introduced social programs to enhance the quality of life for both the miners and their families. Physical upgrades in the appearance of the company town through the adoption of Spanish colonial and other southwestern styles were also designed to improve working conditions.

To no one's surprise, the companies used their economic clout to pressure local political leaders to support them over strikers in any labor disputes. They engineered the removal of Governor Lindsey during his reelection bid in 1918 and Octaviano Larrazolo two years later. Merritt Mechem chose to do the corporations' bidding. During the 1922 strike, Governor Mechem sent troops to Gallup and declared martial law in support of the operators. The 1,285 protestors had nearly won the bitter strike by convincing smaller operators in the district to recognize the union and support the proposed $8 per day wage. But socialist sympathies were widespread among miners, and in numerous labor disputes nationwide, company agents publicized rumors linking labor strikes to communist ideology, swaying public opinion against the strikers. Gallup was no different. Capitalizing on the inherent fear of Russian communism and its revolution, which pervaded the World War I era, opponents of the strike alerted political leaders to the potential revolutionary connection, motivating them to use force to quell the strike. The same strategy enabled mine operators to stifle the state's last, and probably its worst, major strike in 1933.

The miners, however, did have their champions who used the courts and existing legislation to improve labor conditions. Arthur Hannett, a tough Gallup lawyer, successfully brought damage suits against the coal companies on behalf of maimed employees. His successes influenced worker's compensation legislation in 1917. Because of his reputation as a champion of labor, Hannett, a Democrat, was elected governor, serving from 1925 to 1927. He helped secure legislation against the forced use of company stores, a profitable practice among the companies. He also favored regular pay days and stronger child labor laws that prohibited anyone under the age of sixteen from working in the mines. He strove to educate corporate leaders that, contrary to their inherent industrial capitalistic view, labor was not a commodity. Hannett served only one term as governor. The revolving door to the governor's office—no governor after McDonald served longer than a single, two-year term until Richard Dillon's reelection in 1929—testified to the power of the corporations and the willingness of the Republican old guard to bend to their wishes.

One politician who exemplified the old guard was Albert Fall. Fall was a tall Kentuckian who had honed his tough, frontier lawyer skills against cattle rustlers and desperados during his younger days in the Black Range mining camps near territorial Las Cruces. He was also notable for defending, and obtaining the acquittal of, the three accused murderers of regulator Albert Jennings Fountain and his son during the rustler wars. But his good fortune rose when he began to practice corporate law representing American business investors in Mexico. He wisely switched allegiance from the Southern Democrats to the Republican Party, within which he soon became a formidable political power. In 1912, he was elected one of the state's original two senators amid rumors of bribery and political manipulation of the legislature. As the Mexican Revolution brought ruin to American business interests there, the senator from New Mexico criticized the Wilson administration, demanding that it protect American investments across the border. The military's response after the raid on Columbus was in part Wilson's acquiescence. On the local level, the senator influenced state officials not to inhibit corporate activities. During his reelection campaign, President Wilson revealed his personal distaste for the New Mexico senator, which enabled Fall to easily win reelection at home in 1918.

When senate colleague and political crony Warren Harding was elected to the presidency, he offered Fall the position of secretary of the interior. Upon learning of Fall's appointment, U.S. congressman from New Mexico Benigno Cárdenas Hernández commented, "New Mexico has a friend in the secretary of the interior." Fall pushed Interior Department staff to resolve land issues to facilitate the transfer of the public domain to the private sector, to clear the path for irrigation projects, and to create new opportunities for business. At the time Hernández chaired the proposed Middle Rio Grande Irrigation Project, badly in need of Bureau of Reclamation support to get under way. After numerous delays, the costly project was approved in 1922.

When Fall was confirmed as interior secretary, Holm Bursum was appointed to fill the seat, and later won election in his own right. Bursum worked diligently to resolve disputes between Pueblo Indians and the whites who had squatted on Pueblo lands in New Mexico. With Fall's support and through his influence at the Bureau of Indian Affairs, Bursum proposed a bill to allow state courts (notoriously biased toward white settlers) to resolve disputes over Indian lands. The bill would have reduced the size of—if not completely eliminated—American Indian reservations, the last remnant of U.S. Indian removal policy. Fortunately, the proposal rallied national organizations fighting for American Indian rights. When the Pueblos got wind of the bill, delegates testified before Congress to protect their land. The opposition helped kill the Bursum bill, resulting in an important symbolic victory that evidenced changing attitudes regarding the protection of American Indian lands.

Soon thereafter, Fall became embroiled in the Teapot Dome bribery scandal that brought on his political downfall. Fall allowed oil tycoon Edward Doheny, a personal friend from New Mexico territorial days, to secure drilling rights to the Elk Hills Naval Petroleum Reserve in central California without a competitive bid, and did the same for Henry Sinclair, who sought production rights to the naval petroleum reserve at Teapot Dome, Wyoming. Fall and Doheny had both been impoverished miners in the 1880s territory. Through successful speculation, Doheny acquired vast oilfields in California and Mexico. In his quest to maximize his reserves, Doheny approached the newly appointed interior secretary to request leases on the government-owned oilfields. In 1921, Fall accepted various favors from Sinclair as well as an interest-free loan of $100,000 from Doheny. Many believed this money was in fact in exchange for the rights to the oil lands in California, a conflict of interest. A clever *Albuquerque Journal* newspaper reporter suspected fraud, which ultimately led to a formal congressional investigation, invalidation of both oil leases, and Fall's indictment for bribery. Tried and convicted for his failure to protect the public interest, Fall served a year in prison—the first presidential cabinet-level politician to do so—before his return to New Mexico in disgrace.

Fall's many loyal friends in New Mexico defended him, arguing that Doheny's monetary contribution was merely a loan. If anything, George Curry opined, Fall was simply "guilty of bad judgment and not of accepting a bribe." Divided opinions over Fall and his favoritism toward big business ended Republican domination in New Mexico by the mid-1920s. Political observer and strategist Bronson Cutting, elected to the senate as a Republican in 1928, eventually shifted his allegiance toward the Democrats.

A brief but severe agricultural depression jolted the entire United States in 1921. Although prosperity returned to enrich the lives of many Americans, who fondly recalled the 1920s as the "jazz age" or the "prosperity decade," the pall of hard times never lifted from New Mexico's agrarian sector. Twenty-seven of the state's banks failed in the 1920s. Farm commodity prices finally began to recover in 1929, only to plummet again with the onset of the Great Depression. Hard times caused many homesteaders to either sell or simply abandon their claims. During the early 1920s, the number of individual farm ownerships began a long, precipitous decline not only in New Mexico but throughout the country. The farm community of Johnson Mesa, east of Raton, was emblematic of the ominous change. Unemployed but optimistic coal miners from Raton began buying scrip for land to homestead the high mesa during the early 1900s. Although hundreds settled on the mesa and built schools and churches, the harsh climate severely limited successful farming. In the end, the farmers sold out, and the mesa was almost completely abandoned by 1930. Their dry farms were either consolidated into ranches or abandoned wholesale in what was to become a prelude to the Dust Bowl–era migrations out of the region.

By the 1920s, Will Barnes, a rancher turned forest ranger, wrote of the homesteaders near Taos: "One and all were looking for some stockman to come along and buy them out." The one-time fear among the ranchers that incoming homesteaders would spell the demise of the ranching industry was reversed. Ranchers purchased the homestead claims to expand their cattle operations. Twelve of New Mexico's counties—primarily those on the eastern plains—lost population during this decade. Curiously, New Mexico's overall population increased—from 360,350 in 1920 to 423,317 in 1930—despite a sustained population decline in the rural counties. After the homesteader boom of the early 1900s, the "bust" that followed in the 1920s continued unabated into the 1930s. On the southeastern plains Roosevelt County's fifty-nine post offices and their small rural homestead communities declined to no more than a dozen by 1930. Union County in the northeast part of the state lost nearly half its population between 1920 and 1950.

By 1930, New Mexico still had 15,664,121 acres of public domain available to homestead, most of it loosely managed by the General Land Office (GLO). But by then, the federal government was changing its management policy for western lands, influenced by the Progressive-era reforms in conservation and resource preservation on the public lands. In 1891, Congress passed the Forest Reserve Act, which allowed for the creation of national forest reserves; in other words, public lands to be removed from homesteading. Instead, use of the reserves would be "managed" so as to encourage reforestation and recovery of the rangeland while at the same time permitting beneficial use such as supervised timber harvests and grazing leases. Also "clear-cutting" practices were prohibited not only to protect natural water drainages but also to control flooding and soil erosion. The Pecos River Forest Reserve on the upper Pecos River was one of the earliest reserves created. Established on January 11, 1892, it was the precursor to the Santa Fe National Forest. President Teddy Roosevelt was the architect of forest conservation across the territory, aided by his appointees, such as Governor George Curry. By the time of statehood, Roosevelt had set aside eleven national forests containing 11,158,137 acres across the mountains of New Mexico.

Aldo Leopold, a young Yale graduate, became New Mexico's first forest ranger. Leopold's view's on wildlife management and land ethic philosophy, which greatly influenced the national conservation movement, began with his work experiences in the Carson, and especially, Gila national forests. At Gila, he implemented a new management system that went into effect during the 1920s, these were the first public lands to be managed as wilderness. In a *Sunset* magazine article published in 1925, Leopold asked his readers, "Is it unreasonable or visionary to ask the Forest Service to preserve the one remaining portion of unmotorized wilderness?"His philosophy would culminate in his classic book *A Sand County Almanac.*

When not in the field, Leopold spent his time in Albuquerque actively organizing hunting clubs; the ethic of the day did promote the killing of wild predators, but actually, the clubs were nascent conservation groups that saw the value of managed hunting as a way to ensure the continuation of the sport. Leopold married into the prominent Bergere-Otero family, which gave him access to political leaders. By the 1920s, in part because of Leopold's influence, the legislature had passed conservation and hunting measures, and other states were looking to New Mexico as a national leader in conservation and wildlife management legislation.

As in the natural resource conservation movement, New Mexico was also a leader in the protection of archaeological sites, at the time referred to as "antiquities." In the 1880s and 1890s, widely read authors Adolph Bandelier and Charles Lummis brought national attention to New Mexico's numerous archaeological ruins. Archaeologist Edgar Lee Hewett was the first president of New Mexico Normal School (today's New Mexico Highlands University) and later the founding director of Santa Fe's School of American Anthropology (now the School for Advanced Research). With financial aid from Frank Springer and political support from Iowa Senator John Lacey he played a vital role in the passage of the 1906 Antiquities Act. This act protected archaeological sites on public lands from looters, and allowed the president to set aside as national monuments sites of "nationally significant archeological, scientific or historic value for the good of the people."

Shortly after signing the act, President Roosevelt designated El Morro, the historic inscription rock located near Zuni, as the nation's second national monument. Gila Cliffs National Monument soon followed as did what is today known as Chaco Culture National Historical Park, also a UNESCO World Heritage Site (both established in 1907). By the early 1920s a half dozen new monuments had been established, including Carlsbad Caverns, the spectacular subterranean world that lies at the foot of the Guadalupe Mountains. When President Woodrow Wilson authorized the National Park Service in August 1916, New Mexico was well placed to become a national leader in the preservation of natural, prehistoric, and historic sites. The desire to protect these sites dovetailed with an aggressive state tourism industry endeavoring to call attention to them and the nascent era of automobile travel.

During the decade from 1910 to 1920, more and more New Mexicans were taking to the highway. In 1908, the year Henry Ford introduced the affordable Model T, a group of auto enthusiasts met in Santa Fe to organize a state Good Roads Association, intended to promote the construction and improvement of America's early auto roads. Lobbying for improved highways, they influenced legislation to create the territory's Good Road Commission, the precursor to the State Highway Department, established in 1912. The next year, the legislature required that all automobiles be licensed, and car owners licensed 1,898 vehicles during the first year. By 1917, automobile ownership rose to more than 12,000 licensed autos, and continued to increase until it approached 100,000 at the end of 1920. Concurrently, the U.S. Congress gave state highway construction a boost with its passage of the Federal Aid Road Act in 1916. The state received $1.2 million on a matching-fund basis the first year, with annual increases thereafter.

Boosters promoted the upgrading of cross-country roads, which began as rough, county wagon roads to become graded dirt roads in rural areas and paved roads in the city. During the teens, the Ocean-to-Ocean Highway traversing the southern part of the state, and the Old Trails Highway in the north (which partially followed the old Santa Fe and Camino Real de Tierra Adentro trails), saw vast improvements in the roadway and signage throughout the state. Governor Hannett, an avid highway booster, lobbied for a more efficient highway system.

Auto tour group at Lamy station, 1920s. (Courtesy of Palace of the Governors Archives, NMHM/DCA, negative no. 53651)

For example, by the 1920s, newly constructed national highways were to be enumerated. In 1926, the bureau established one of the nation's most celebrated highways, Route 66 from Chicago to Los Angeles. Without question New Mexicans had fondly embraced the automobile.

Pioneer motorists were an intrepid lot. Among the difficulties drivers faced were (1) acquiring sufficient fuel, which initially was available only through auto dealers or in hardware stores; (2) traversing rough roads that resulted in numerous blowouts, flat tires, and even engine damage that drivers had to repair themselves; and (3) the near-total absence of directional signs. When new roads opened, such as La Bajada Hill between Santa Fe and Albuquerque (noted as one of the most challenging sections of Route 66), enthusiasts celebrated with auto club outings. The wide expanse of desert in the south tempted locals to engage in cross-desert races, one of the earliest, known as the Race of the Speed Merchants, ran between Deming and Silver City.

By the 1920s, more and more "Tin Lizzie" tourists were arriving in the state, making recreational tourism a major industry. A trip to the

Carlsbad Caverns was on every itinerary. Increasing numbers of auto tourists frequented the state's forest lands and national parks, which created a need for auto camps, and later motels. In 1923, the highway commission introduced the *Highway Journal,* which featured articles on the various auto tours. The magazine, which soon evolved into a slick, tourist-oriented publication, was the predecessor of today's *New Mexico Magazine.* New Mexico had a long tradition of catering to tourists, but as the automobile made more isolated spots accessible, the number of tourist destinations multiplied. Resort hotels, dude ranches, and hot springs were already popular, thanks to the railroad passenger trains that served them. Beginning in 1910, the state marketed heritage as well, especially romantic tales about American Indians and Spanish conquistadors.

The Santa Fe railroad played a pivotal role in marketing the image of the Southwest, partnering with Fred Harvey to establish a series of elegant hotels and curio shops along the route so that tourists could travel in comfort. Charles Lummis called New Mexico the "Land of Poco Tiempo," a place where harried travelers could relax and let the time slowly pass by. Perhaps more than anyone, it was Lummis who influenced Santa Fe railroad officials to revise their southwestern promotional literature to emphasize the Spanish colonial and American Indian motifs. Most visible was the shift away from traditional territorial architecture to the increasingly popular California mission style in the design of the Santa Fe's train depots by the turn of the century. Not only the railroad depots, but also hotels and popular eating establishments, such as the celebrated Harvey Houses, in Las Vegas, Albuquerque, Clovis, and Portales, adopted the look of the former Spanish kingdom—or at least what was interpreted to be Spanish colonial design. Curio shops, generally located in the well-established railroad hotels, sold native crafts and American Indian artwork that highlighted the cultural diversity of New Mexico.

The railroad incorporated Pueblo architectural influences into its tourist hotels. After 1912, Santa Fe officially adopted the Spanish-Pueblo revival style as the preferred design for all future construction with the aim to create a new image for the state capital. Boosters had for years promoted the town as a tourist destination. However, with the establishment of the Museum of New Mexico in 1909, the restoration/renovation of the Palace of the Governors the following year, and the construction in 1917 of the Museum of Fine Arts (now New Mexico Museum of Art), modeled after Spanish mission church design, Santa Fe reaffirmed its resolve to become a national attraction. The Santa Fe Railroad assumed ownership of La Fonda Hotel on the plaza. They incorporated it into the successful Harvey hotel system and used it to promote the "Land of the Dons and Pueblos." The community's celebration of its Spanish past spawned the first Fiesta in 1911, a local attraction that has widespread appeal to residents and visitors to the present day. By 1919, the Fiesta—in full the Reconquista of Don Diego de Vargas—had become an established tradition within the Anglo as well as Hispanic communities. Early fiestas featured Pueblo dancers, a reenactment of Don Diego de Vargas's triumphant return to Santa Fe in 1692, and a host of festival parades and other celebrations of Hispanic culture.

The national obsession with the American Southwest, popularized during World War I by the slogan "See America First," coincided with a period of revolutionary advances for women. Most significant were gaining the right to vote and much improved employment opportunities. In addition, women's fashions dramatically changed from the restrictive corsets and long ruffled skirts to the routine wearing of knee-length attire and sports clothes such as slacks, once thought to be "shocking." The automobile, once dubbed the "mechanic's nightmare," liberated women more than ever. Erna Fergusson, daughter of Harvey Fergusson, New Mexico's first U.S. congressman, became a noted writer about the Southwest. She also operated her own tour business based in Albuquerque, but reaching beyond the Rio Grande valley deep into Indian Country. Her female guides—who wore riding breeches and khaki shirts, adorned with as much Navajo or Pueblo jewelry as could be worn—became part of the tour's attraction. In 1925, Fred Harvey bought her tour company in order to establish tours leaving from the Santa Fe Railroad depots, but left her to manage it. Other women gained financial prominence because of the lucrative tourist industry.

In the mid-1920s, New Mexico was a lively admixture of popular culture, art, and literature. Despite the tourism industry's attempts to make New Mexico into an exotic land full of Spanish Dons, it was much like any other region of the era. The embryonic state benefited from the many forms of cultural activities brought West with the railroads. Beginning in 1908, the remote rail town of Mountainair annually hosted an assembly of revivalists, temperance reform advocates, politicians, and lecturers that became known as Chautauqua meetings. A leading purveyor of popular culture in turn-of-the-century America, the Chautauqua movement represented a thirst for social and educational advancement within the farming communities. Meanwhile, local churches organized string bands, choirs, literary clubs, brass bands, and drama clubs. Traveling evangelists worked the circuit, sometimes in competition with socialist symposia seeking to inspire farmworkers and industrial camp residents.

Each town of any size had its own newspaper that carried local and national news as well as popular stories and poems. The rail towns generally boasted their own theater or opera house, a testament to their desire for culture. Traveling Shakespearean companies and vaudeville performers frequented the more accessible rail towns. Local city councils sometimes decreed that traveling shows be closed because of their "naughty" or "lewd" content, which might be nothing more than an actress appearing in tights. Local fraternal lodges used the opera house or other comparable main street locations to hold their meetings. The most common social and fraternal organizations included the Masons, the Knights of Pythias, the Elks, the Improved Order of Redmen, the Odd Fellows and any number of like-minded groups. Quasi-secret societies, fraternal orders counted among their membership an increasing number of middle-class businessmen. Women supported their affiliated lodges, church groups, and library societies. The Santa Fe Women's Board of Trade and Library Association, formed in 1893, maintained the central plaza and the library while they lobbied for city ordinances that promoted child and family services.

Spirit of community was very important to the Progressive era generation. This was especially evident in the immigrant neighborhoods and the mining and timber camps. Fraternal lodges transported from the Old World reinforced social values as well as keeping the immigrants in touch with their ancestral homeland. Italian miners established a reputation in the coal camps for having the best brass bands and making the most savory wine. The Germans, on the other hand, touted their beer gardens. Barbecues, baseball games, and community dances presented opportunities for folk traditions to comingle. African Americans in Blackdom and other segregated towns used their churches as vehicles for musical and other cultural expression. Like their Texas cousins, New Mexico's African American communities observed Juneteenth, one of the many originally southern traditions they introduced to the West.

Communities paid tribute to their pioneer ancestors by holding annual "old-timers" gatherings during the early decades of 1900s. Cowboys in Roswell or Deming might recall the days of the range wars. In 1915, Las Vegas reinstituted the Rough Riders' annual reunion with a festive celebration and rodeo. The New Mexico State Fair, held in Albuquerque since the 1880s, incorporated varied forms of entertainment into its program, including a grander rodeo that harkened back to the days of the Mexican vaqueros. Small towns staged their own regional fairs and festivals such as the Pinto Bean Days in Wagon Mound and Mountainair, the Melon Days celebration in Fort Sumner and Artesia, and Portales's Fountain Days. In the Pecos Valley, the resurrection of the Lincoln County War lionized Billy the Kid, raising questions about his reputation across the nation: Was he a folk hero or homicidal psychopath? Publications about El Chivato (The Kid) created a cottage industry locally. Old-timers, like Roswell banker John Poe, related purportedly "eyewitness" accounts. Sophie Poe's *Buckboard Days,* a realistic recollection of early life on the Pecos, exceeded the popularity of her husband's lurid tales about the adolescent outlaw.

The Hispanic community contained a complicated mix of cultures. Northern traditions dated back to the Spanish colonial era. Their culture differed markedly from that of new arrivals from Mexico, mostly Chihuahua, who settled largely in the southern sector of the state. Today, New Mexicans joke about the cultural distinctions that lead to variant Spanish words for the same item, the distinction between *farolitos* and *luminarias* (both candle lanterns lighted as Christmas decorations), or the taste preference for green chile versus red chile. As with other immigrant groups, Hispanics formed important self-help, or mutual aid, organizations. Fabián García of Las Cruces helped organize the Alianza Hispánico. Members contributed funds which were pooled to help families in need (mutual aid) and to improve education among the Spanish-speaking immigrants. The Catholic Church remained at the center of most cultural activities. The *parroquias* (parishes) celebrated prominent saint's days with festivals and parades. Mexican holidays such as Cinco de Mayo or Diez y Seis de Septiembre (Mexican Independence) were celebrated with as much fervor as the Fourth of July. Traveling artists, musicians, and even companies that sponsored bullfights targeted towns with large concentrations of Hispanics.

Some Hispanics wrote down and published oral histories of their ancestors and culture. Cleofas Jaramillo, a young woman from Taos who collected tales about early cultural traditions, remains one of the most widely read. Nina Warren-Otero's *Old Spain in Our Southwest* captured an experience of life on the large haciendas of the Rio Grande. Historian and lawyer Benjamin Read wrote an early state history from the Hispanic viewpoint, in part to counter the Anglo historical bias of Governor L. Bradford Prince and Las Vegas lawyer Ralph Emerson Twitchell. Twitchell's detailed *Leading Facts of New Mexico History,* which draws heavily on original sources, remains a useful reference for some topics today. Twitchell also edited the magazine *Santa Fe,* a popular historical journal that the *New Mexico Historical Review* replaced in 1926.

The Hispanic community also gained recognition for its weaving, carving, and religious art, especially after the Santa Fe Railroad's marketing campaign inspired a revival. Railroad promoters also encouraged Indians to modify their traditional crafts to increase their tourist appeal and to sell their wares at railroad stops to offer travelers an exotic cultural experience. The railroad, in conjunction with the Museum of New Mexico, created a market for pottery and artwork produced among the Pueblo communities. San Ildefonso potter María Martínez remains internationally recognized for her artistry today; however, artists from other pueblos contributed pottery and jewelry that enhanced the tourist trade.

The Santa Fe Railroad also supported the celebrated art colonies of Taos and Santa Fe. The colonies emerged about 1900 as result of a migration of artistic expatriates from what they regarded as the stifling socioeconomic atmosphere of the East. By 1920, the golden era of the movement, picturesque adobe communities of New Mexico teemed with resident artists. Ernest Blumenschein, Bert Phillips, Joseph Sharp, and a host of others created the prototypes for what was to become widely accepted as western style art—mostly landscapes and people (particularly Indians or Hispanics) whose culture representing the antithesis of modern industrial society. This handful of creative geniuses organized the Taos Society of Artists in 1915, an influential organization used as a means to market their own work. After World War I, scores of émigrés, including Gustav Bauman and Gerald Cassidy, joined the original cadre of painters. Foremost among those to arrive in the 1920s was Georgia O'Keeffe.

The artists found Santa Fe and Taos, both in a state of economic decline at the beginning of the twentieth century, inexpensive localities in which to live compared to the costly urban East. More important was the inspiration they derived from New Mexico's aesthetics, such as the incomparable natural landscape and the captivating multiethnic society. "Its environment and people," wrote historian Arrell Gibson, "attracted more creative people than any other area in the U.S." Artists, hoping to capture the Old West before its passing, depicted Pueblo Indian ceremonies and traditional Hispanic festivals. It was widely believed that American Indians were inevitably destined for extinction, or at least complete cultural annihilation. Concerned citizens joined in the cause to preserve American Indian culture and support their rights, establishing the New Mexico Association on Indian Affairs (NMAIA) in 1922 in part to fight the Bursum bill. Today, that organization has evolved into the Southwestern Association for Indian Arts (SWAIA), which promotes Indian artists and sponsors the noted Santa Fe Indian Market annual art show. The images of the Pueblos and the romance of the "Spanish American" villages attracted scores of enthusiasts to the Southwest. In return, Taos and Santa Fe tolerated the "temperamental eccentrics" and accepted their permissive lifestyle for decades to come. Santa Fe and Taos were among only a handful of artist colonies still in existence just before World War II.

Needing to earn a living, the artists not only marketed their works in eastern galleries, but also sold commercial illustrations to the Fred Harvey Company, the Santa Fe Railroad, and other corporations. National magazines published their work, and soon the Taos and Santa Fe artists appeared on the covers of *McClure's, Collier's Weekly*, and the *Saturday Evening Post*, which popularized their styles even more. The Taos Society of Artists also promoted their members through traveling exhibits.

With the completion of Santa Fe's Museum of Fine Arts, artists could exhibit and sell their compositions under the auspices of the Museum of New Mexico. The golden years in Santa Fe, also during the 1920s and 1930s, saw scores of artists visit or move to the community. The Santa Fe–based Los Cinco Pintores supported the tourism industry as well as the local museums, and participated in the local Fiesta activities with the introduction of a primal, almost pagan ritual. The product of artist Will Shuster's active imagination, the effigy burning of Zozobra (Old Man Gloom) has become a revered annual event. British artist and animal fiction author Ernest Thompson Seton also arrived about this time. Seton had lived in Clayton during the 1890s where he managed a ranch and wrote one of New Mexico's most famed animal stories about a wolf named Lobo. He eventually earned international fame as the author of forty-two books. Seton returned to Santa Fe late in his life to open his nature school and art institute on the edge of the town.

During the period between the two world wars, Taos and Santa Fe were renowned for their literary communities as well. Under the patronage of wealthy eastern expatriate Mabel Dodge Luhan, known as the "literary dowager of Taos" for her literary salons, luminaries such as D. H. Lawrence frequented New Mexico. In Santa Fe, Mary Austin stood out for her depictions of nature and knowledge of the Indians. She along with poet Witter Bynner were the town's most accomplished writers. Novelist Willa Cather, who befriended Austin during her many visits, authored the now-famous *Death Comes for the Archbishop*, perhaps the most popular book about New Mexico among American readers to date. Although contemporary readers can point out its many flaws and biases, the story still resonates with popular readers as a tale of accomplishment amid adversity. Similarly, Oliver

La Farge's Pulitzer Prize–winning *Laughing Boy,* the story of a young Navajo's determination to rise above personal hardship, won the hearts of its readers. LaFarge moved to Santa Fe and continued to write and to advocate for American Indian rights.

These works of art and literature transformed the image of New Mexico from that of the "Land of Sunshine," a region destined purely for economic exploitation, to the "Land of Enchantment," a place of romance, adventure, and profound natural beauty. Indeed, in 1934, the State Highway Department adopted the name Land of Enchantment for its tourism-promotion campaign. Both the name and the image prevail today.

CHAPTER **9**

Healing the Human Spirit
The Great Depression and the New Deal, 1925–1940

> It is not important that at one time we called our program work
> relief, at another CWA, still another Works Projects. . . . What is
> important is our increasing knowledge of the unemployed man's and
> woman's psychology that giving jobs is better than giving relief.
>
> NEW MEXICO EMERGENCY RELIEF BULLETIN, SEPTEMBER 1935

IN CONTRAST TO THE METROPOLITAN CENTERS of the eastern United States, throughout which the Wall Street "crash" of 1929 undulated like an earthquake, New Mexico initially experienced a more subtle advent of the Great Depression, but its effects proved to be equally devastating by 1932. Sparsely populated and predominantly rural, the nation's newest state was slow to experience the full impact of America's all-embracing economic crisis. State officials minimized the impact of the Depression at first. Official correspondence from Santa Fe in 1930–31 assured White House Republicans that even Albuquerque, the state's most populous municipality, had experienced "only moderate unemployment." The state's overall 4.6 percent rate of unemployment, the governor insisted, compared favorably to Michigan's 10.2 percent and New Jersey's 8.2 percent. Unlike more urbanized regions of the country, persistently agrarian New Mexico was not openly receptive to the embryonic federal relief measures initiated during the waning days of the Hoover administration.

By the time of President Roosevelt's inaugural address on March 4, 1933, New Mexico, like the entirety of the West and Southwest, had plunged deep into the morass of the Great Depression. The state's early economic achievements—grounded in the traditional industries of mining, railroad activities, timber, ranching, and agriculture—had experienced stunning reversals. Prices for agriculture and ranching commodities declined by more than 50 percent between 1932 and 1933. Mining productivity, valued at $8.3 million in annual income in 1929, plummeted to a mere $2.9 million in 1933. Meanwhile, the state's largest corporate taxpayer, the Atchison, Topeka & Santa Fe Railroad, saw its net income decline from $2.6 million in 1930 to $795,000 in early 1932. Worse still, New Mexico experienced the most severe drought of the century as unseasonable dust storms from neighboring Oklahoma, Arkansas, and Texas decimated agricultural and livestock productivity, especially in the eastern and southern sectors of the state. As the Great Depression reached its nadir, 60 percent of all resident New Mexicans could no longer pay their property taxes. In addition to being near starvation, most faced eviction from their homes. By March 1935 more than half of the state's population (totaling 423,317 in 1930) required some measure of economic relief just to survive.

Many turned to the myriad New Deal initiatives for salvation. Of paramount importance to New Mexicans were the thousands of jobs these federal and state subsidies created in an all-out effort to remove people from "direct relief" rolls in exchange for wage-paying employment. Projects, and the jobs they generated, were intended to restore some measure of human dignity among the downtrodden. In inaugurating the new work relief program in July 1935, Harry Hopkins, then director of the Works Progress Administration, issued this inspirational message:

> The purpose of the WPA program is to address problems growing out of widespread unemployment. The first of these problems is the suffering, demoralization, and debilitation of the unemployed and their families. . . .
> Only a job can answer the problem of the jobless man; only a wage will increase purchasing power for a basket of groceries. . . . Only through work can these people make their contributions to our national well being.

Unprecedented federal spending and innovative genius in Washington coupled with an unfaltering commitment at the state and local levels to mitigate the protracted human misery of the homeless and unemployed, eventually greatly abated not just New Mexico's but America's worst economic catastrophe to date.

Most historians generally agree that the adverse effects of the Great Depression were felt much earlier in the urban centers of the East and the Midwest. In contrast, in his 1994 architectural investigation of New Mexico during this period, David Kammer asserted that the state was on the verge of decline years earlier than commonly believed:

> For many, the Depression is viewed as a period beginning with the stock market's crash in the fall of 1929 and extending to 1941 when preparations for war began to restore prosperity. In New Mexico, a largely rural state dependent on small farming, ranching, mining and railroads, economic decline had become apparent much earlier. In fact, many indicators suggest that the state had been sliding into depression through most of the 1920s.

Kammer supports his argument that the agrarian-based economy was already deteriorating before 1929 with rather convincing statistics. "Farm values had declined from $224 million to $174 million during the five-year interval from 1920 to 1925," he wrote. The value of livestock, meanwhile, decreased more precipitously from $132 million just after World War I to a mere $61 million (nearly 46 percent) five years before the infamous Black Tuesday when the stock market plunged.

At the onset of the Depression, however, the economic reports emanating from the more populous urban centers sent mixed messages to administrators in Santa Fe, who were growing increasingly alarmed about the widespread depression. Clyde Tingley, the colorfully bombastic mayor of Albuquerque since 1922, beloved for his ungrammatical speech, issued reports to both the state capitol and the White House that unemployment in his city was "not acute," thanks to "continuing municipal and private construction." City relief rolls identified a paltry 550 out of 10,000 workers as "officially unemployed." The 1930 census bore out the mayor's claim, listing 6,573 laborers out of a total statewide workforce of 142,866 as unemployed. In Tingley's estimation, New Mexico's 4.6 percent unemployment rate was insignificant when compared with the rates in cities on the East Coast and the Midwest.

As Tingley implied, Albuquerque's municipal construction was indeed stronger than that in other western states. In 1930 city officials passed a $76,000 bond issue to install new gas lines throughout the greater downtown area in addition to designing and building several new structures on the University of New Mexico campus. Added to these civic improvements, the Hoover administration authorized construction of a new, modernized Veterans Administration hospital on the south end of town. The Reconstruction Finance Corporation (RFC), one of a handful of pre-Roosevelt attempts to mitigate the early effects of the Depression, provided the loan necessary for state and city officials to underwrite the ambitious project. Included in the inaugural federal financial package was sufficient capital to build a new downtown post office. Because it offered numerous opportunities for employment, Albuquerque attracted transient labor from the more depressed regions of the country.

Beyond Albuquerque's city limits, however, farming communities and small towns bore the brunt of prolonged drought and incessant winds that heightened the severity of the Depression. During the previous decade most of the state's farmers and ranchers had abandoned the more diversified practices of subsistence agriculture in favor of intensive, commercial production of a select number of cash crops. These practices, especially prevalent among the Anglo, Hispanic, and American Indian communities in the eastern and southern sectors of the state, resulted in acute overgrazing and critically depleted soils. When drought brought limited rainfall and unceasing winds, dust storms of unparalleled scale and intensity raged across the western plains.

The so-called Dust Bowl precipitated the evacuation of thousands of migrants from Arkansas, Texas, and Oklahoma. Lured by the myth of a prosperous and easy lifestyle, most were bound for the Pacific West. Those who remained on their ranches and farms suffered immeasurable hardship. In northwestern New Mexico and northeastern Arizona, persistent overgrazing on the Navajo reservation caused the federal government to unilaterally impose a stock reduction program that nearly decimated the sheep industry and economic livelihood of Navajo herdsmen. In the name of conservation, Bureau of Indian Affairs (BIA) officials indiscriminately destroyed 250,000 sheep and goats in addition to 10,000 horses between 1932 and 1936. Sadly, Washington administrators neglected to consult the Navajo people or consider the cultural damage of undermining a pastoral way of life before implementing the ill-conceived policy.

The one glimmer of light in an otherwise bleak economic forecast for New Mexico was the fledgling tourism and associated transportation industry. The catalyst for the unanticipated growth of these two industries was America's love affair with the automobile. Prior to 1920, New Mexico had established a reputation as a premier health destination. Well-publicized health spas that specialized in pulmonary diseases lured thousands of "health seekers" to what was popularly nicknamed the "Land of Sunshine." The AT&SF and Denver & Rio Grande railroads collaborated to establish luxury hotels and health resorts across the state to commercialize the scenic and recuperative attributes of the Southwest. The abundant mineral hot springs that dotted the New Mexico landscape added to its growing popularity as a health destination. Thermal waters found at Ojo Caliente (north of Santa Fe), Radium Springs (near Las Cruces), Las Palomas (later Hot Springs, then renamed Truth or Consequences in the 1950s), and Jemez Springs (north of Albuquerque) were among the most frequented therapeutic health spas in the state.

Of greater influence on early western tourism was the mass adoration of the automobile. According to one local study, "only 470 cars and trucks were registered throughout the state in 1910; a decade later, the number had jumped to 17,720, and by 1930 to 84,000, a nearly five-fold increase." More important, automobiles spawned road and highway construction, which in turn offered temporary employment to hundreds of New Mexicans. The two most prominent state highways at the time were U.S. 85 (present I-25), a north-south corridor connecting Raton (near the Colorado state border) to Albuquerque, and U.S. 66 (present I-40), an east-west, multistate roadway that bisected New Mexico almost exactly in half. In 1957, federal funding promoted the extension of U.S. 85 to Las Cruces, New Mexico, where it intersected with present Interstate 10 to create the nation's southernmost coast-to-coast corridor, thus forming a nascent interstate highway network. The jobs that government highway projects created helped hundreds of destitute New Mexico families endure the onset of the Great Depression.

As New Mexicans slid into the depths of despair, they turned to Santa Fe in hope that a solution rested with state government. To their profound dismay, the initial response from the state capitol was at best marginal, the politicians seeming to have only a vague idea of the true magnitude of New Mexico's economic troubles. As conditions worsened, Democratic challenger Arthur Seligman announced his candidacy for state governor and won. In an uninspired inaugural speech to the Tenth Legislature in 1931, the former banker and local businessman appealed to the electorate to support state officials in curtailing the looming economic crisis. In an awkward admission that state government seemed powerless to mediate the escalating crisis, Seligman said, "The governor of the state, alone, can not produce the desired results. The legislature is not sufficient unto itself to accomplish them. The people of the state are the power behind the government They are in fact the government. Those whom they elect are merely administrative officers."

Like his fellow administrators, Seligman mistakenly believed that New Mexico's rural population could sustain itself through the Depression based on its long-standing reliance on subsistence agriculture. What the governor failed to realize was that many small farmers and ranchers had long since abandoned their independent way of life to become wage earners. Historian Sarah Deutsch concurs with Richard Melzer, who wrote that "seven to ten thousand villagers from the Middle and Upper Rio Grande valleys had migrated annually to labor in the beet and potato fields of Colorado, the mines and smelters of Montana, and railroad and sheep camps of Utah and Wyoming." From all appearances, Governor Seligman was out of touch with his own electorate.

Born June 14, 1871, Arthur Seligman was the product of a frontier upbringing. His father, Bernard, and two older brothers had managed a wholesale and retail dry goods store in Santa Fe since 1852, shipping merchandise via the Santa Fe Trail. As a child he accompanied his mother, Frances, up and down the celebrated trail in an ox-drawn covered wagon. A proud graduate of Southmore College Prep School and

Pierce College of Business, Seligman returned to Santa Fe in 1891 to work in the Seligman Brothers Mercantile. He soon rose to an executive position, a post he held until his appointment in 1924 as president of the First National Bank of Santa Fe. He showed an early interest in municipal politics with his election as mayor in 1910. Over the next two decades Seligman served in various governmental positions, establishing a reputation as a progressive-minded civic leader bent on modernization. Through his influence the bustling capital benefited from paved streets, gas lighting, and the most up-to-date improvements available. It appears, however, that none of his experiences prepared the newly elected governor for the challenges wrought by the Great Depression.

Above all, Seligman was a self-professed fiscal conservative, as he underscored during his inaugural address in January 1931: "No state should obligate itself to expend more money than can be reasonably expected from its citizens. . . . New Mexico must live within her income, and it is my intention, insofar as it is possible for me to do so, to see that she does." From the day he entered office, Seligman valued a balanced financial budget over the deepening economic plight of his fellow New Mexicans. It was his firm conviction that putting more money into the hands of consumers through reduced taxation would enable local citizens to "spend their way through the depression."

In effect, Seligman's administration minimized the impact of the looming national crisis. Nationally, the number of jobless workers in the United States now exceeded ten million in just three and one-half years since the crash. Yet, corresponding with other executives regarding conditions in the various states, Seligman wrote that because New Mexico had virtually no industry, it suffered "no acute unemployment." Consequently, when the Reconstruction Finance Corporation (RFC) offered its first emergency loans to the individual states in the summer of 1932, New Mexico requested an anemic $240,000 for relief for the period from September 1932 to July 1933. It was soon apparent that this figure grossly underestimated the state's cumulative relief needs. Meanwhile, the average Hispanic family of six or seven in northern New Mexico was expected to survive on less than ten dollars a month.

An official economic assessment authorized by Seligman in 1932, titled "Report on Relief Survey in New Mexico," suggested that the relief situation within the state had become "far more serious than at any time known to the staff." Individual county estimates of people on "direct" relief rose to an unprecedented 152,000 cases during 1932. According to the report, "direct" relief consisted mainly of the distribution of commodities—basic food staples—to needy families and individuals. Other forms of relief included short-term employment on public works projects such as city street repairs, highway construction, and municipal parks improvements for payment "in kind."

The deteriorating economy saw no improvement under Andrew Hockenhull, the former lieutenant governor who assumed office after Seligman's unexpected demise in September 1933. The volume of wholesale business trade in New Mexico had declined 52.9 percent since 1929. Worse, salaries and wages decreased 25 percent during the same period. By March 1933, according to the Bureau of Child Welfare Report, "one-third of all New Mexicans required some form of relief merely to subsist." Nonetheless, Governor Hockenhull, in the tradition of his conservative predecessor, showed reluctance to request federal assistance through the RFC. Like Seligman before him, Hockenhull criticized the RFC stipulation that loans be paid back through a 20 percent reduction in the state's federal highway allocation. Traditionally, New Mexico depended on highway money as a perennial source of revenue. Thus, New Mexicans could anticipate little reprieve from their economic woes before the so-called New Dealers arrived on the national scene.

The comprehensive electoral sweep of the Democratic Party in 1932 predicted better days ahead as President Franklin Delano Roosevelt pledged to redress the nation's economic ills by promising all Americans a "new deal." The subsequent barrage of federal programs during FDR's first hundred days forged a mosaic of emergency work relief programs that included the Civil Works Administration (CWA, 1933–34), the Federal Emergency Relief Administration (FERA, 1933–38), the Works Progress Administration (WPA, 1935–39), the Works Projects Administration (WPA, 1939–43), the Public Works Administration (PWA, 1939–43), the Civilian Conservation Corps (CCC, 1933–42), and the National Youth Administration (NYA, 1935–39). While these "alphabet" agencies varied slightly in their specific function, their collective mission was to remediate the adverse effects of the Great Depression through the creation of jobs requiring vast numbers of unemployed workers and unprecedented expenditures of consumable goods and services.

In his electrifying inaugural address to the nation on March 4, 1933, president-elect Franklin D. Roosevelt uttered his now-famous assurance to the American people: "The only thing we have to fear is fear itself." Within weeks of this bold pronouncement Congress responded with a national economic recovery package that created the National Recovery Administration (NRA) to assist small businesses, the Soil Erosion Service (SES) to aid and advise the agricultural community, and the Civilian Conservation Corps (CCC) to undertake the arduous task of reinvigorating the nation's forested lands. Together with the aforementioned FERA, which addressed the immediate needs of the unemployed, all these programs would have a lasting effect in helping New Mexicans deal with ubiquitous economic collapse.

On the day that FERA began operations, Director Harry Hopkins, a longtime member of Roosevelt's elite "brain trust," wired all of the state governors, advising them to apply for federal relief funding. In the next twenty-four hours, Hopkins dispatched more than $5 million to needy states. By the end of the week FERA had distributed $51 million to forty-five states, the Territory of Hawaii and the District of Columbia. Suddenly, New Mexico had access to unimagined quantities of federal dollars. During the first year of the New Deal, for instance, the state received $5,792,000 for highway construction alone. Half of the allocation was to be spent on road projects outside municipal city limits, one quarter for street repairs within cities, and one quarter for designated "farm to market" secondary roads around the state. Margaret Reeves, newly appointed director of the state Bureau of Child Welfare, received $6 million in FERA money during 1933–34 for her agency as well. This was more than twelve times the amount of government funding ($495,000) granted by the RFC during Hoover's term.

The ebullient Clyde Tingley, at the time Albuquerque mayor, established an early reputation as an ardent New Dealer willing to spend all federal allocations that came his way. In time, Tingley became one of

Roosevelt's close personal friends. During his tenure as mayor— and later as state governor—Tingley visited the White House on numerous occasions to outline New Mexico's funding needs directly to the president. With the funds he secured, during his final days in City Hall Tingley modernized the interurban transportation system; beautified city parks and streets; expanded residential boundaries; and built schools, hospitals, airports, and other municipal buildings while putting thousands of destitute men and women back to work. So effective was Tingley in securing federal subsidies for Albuquerque—indeed, for all of New Mexico—that celebrated author Erna Fergusson later felt compelled to say, "As Augustus could boast that he found Rome a city of sun baked brick and left it a city of marble, Clyde Tingley might have boasted that he found Albuquerque a dusty little town and left it a city of paved and shaded streets."

A dusty little town it was in 1910 when Clyde Tingley arrived at the Albuquerque train station from his hometown in Madison County, Ohio. Born to a London, Ohio, working-class family on January 5, 1881, young Clyde found his earliest employment opportunities in the rail yards of Bowling Green, Ohio. His true calling, however, appeared to be in sales, as Tingley, not quite thirty years old, quickly rose to superintendent of the Graham Motor Car Company. He held that position when he first met Carrie Wooster, the beautiful, soft-spoken debutant of a prominent local family. Shortly thereafter, doctors advised Carrie, who had tuberculosis, to leave the damp environment of the Midwest and head to the more salubrious climate of Arizona. Clyde eagerly accepted the offer to accompany Carrie and her mother on the train ride west as their valet and chauffeur.

The trio never reached their final destination. Carrie suffered an acute bronchial attack en route that caused them to disembark in Albuquerque for treatment. Much to Mrs. Wooster's surprise, the unappealing and sparsely populated community harbored excellent physicians and reputable health-care facilities that enabled her daughter's recovery. Enamored with the scenic magnetism of the desert Southwest, Clyde and Carrie Tingley married on April 12, 1911, and made their home in Albuquerque. Within a decade, Tingley filed his petition of candidacy for the Albuquerque City Commission, thus beginning a remarkable political career that continued virtually uninterrupted until his retirement from public service in 1955.

Tingley's enormous success as mayor and his unwavering commitment to the state's economic recovery made him a likely candidate to enter the turbulent 1934 gubernatorial campaign. Even though most party-line Democrats favored Albuquerque lawyer and former New Mexico Supreme Court justice (1929–1930) John Simms, Tingley reckoned that he might rise above the political fray and "sneak in the back door" as his party's candidate. Naturally, the Democratic platform focused on the appalling state of the New Mexico economy, an issue that suited Tingley perfectly in light of his proven track record.

If elected governor, the feisty ex-mayor promised, he would not only shepherd the state to full economic recovery but also appropriate $50,000 to promote New Mexico as a regional tourism destination, pledging also to impose a suitable gasoline tax to be dedicated solely to statewide highway improvement. "Tingley's faith in New Mexico and its brilliant future was always winning—even in the midst of depression," noted one admirer. In the end, it was probably John Simms's unexpected withdrawal from the campaign the day before the convention that assured Clyde Tingley's nomination and subsequent election to his first two-year term in office.

Former U.S. Congressman Dionisio "Dennis" Chavez and his brother David, the incumbent mayor of Santa Fe, were among Governor Tingley's welcome though somewhat reluctant supporters. The elder Chavez, who lost his senatorial bid in a bruising slugfest with Republican strongman and self-proclaimed Progressive Bronson Cutting, had in recent years emerged as the new voice of the Hispanic faction within the New Mexico Democratic Party. Bronson Murray Cutting, having arrived from the East in 1910 seeking a cure for the inner-city scourge of tuberculosis, was the powerful, Spanish-speaking editor of the *Santa Fe New Mexican* and *Nuevo Mexicano*. He maintained a seemingly unbreakable Republican stranglehold on New Mexico politics, especially in the poverty-stricken, Hispanic-dominated counties in the north. Hard-line Democrats strategized (unsuccessfully, it turned out) in hopes that the fast-rising, youthful Hispanic from the Rio Abajo might unseat his formidable Anglo opponent and give the Democrats

Clyde Tingley, a former car salesman and newly elected governor of New Mexico, strikes a handsome pose in front of the Governor's Mansion in Santa Fe. (Photograph by the New Mexico State Tourist Bureau. Courtesy of Palace of the Governors Archives, NMHM/DCA, negative no. 050497.)

complete control of the state's three-member congressional delegation. In a twist of fate, Dennis Chavez lost the election, only to be appointed Cutting's replacement by Governor Tingley after a tragic plane crash near Atlanta, Georgia, on May 6, 1935, claimed the senator's life.

Although Dennis Chavez was a son of territorial New Mexico, his personal legacy is forever assigned to the twentieth century. He spent his early childhood in the rural, agricultural community of Los Chaves, where he was born on April 8, 1888. When Dennis was only seven, his father, David, moved the Chavez family to the industrial-driven, almost exclusively Hispanic barrio of Barelas in downtown Albuquerque. Under the political tutelage of New Mexico senator Andrieus Anson Jones (known to his constituents as A.A.), Chavez had an opportunity to advance his education as well as savor his earliest exposure to national politics as a Senate clerk. Once graduated with a law degree from Georgetown University in 1920, Chavez returned to his old neighborhood to open a law practice. While living and working in south Albuquerque, Chavez earned the reputation among local vecinos as a champion of the working class. The long-awaited acceptance of the Territory of New Mexico into the Union in 1912 left the then-teenaged nuevomexicano with a bitter impression. The fiercely ethnocentric Chavez attributed the sixty-four-year delay in granting statehood to two factors: an inherent prejudice in Congress against the territory's Spanish-speaking population (voiced most loudly by Indiana senator Albert Beveridge), and New Mexico's dilatory response to modernization. For these reasons the ambitious politico renounced his father's lifelong Republican Party affiliation to embrace the Democrats, the party of the working people, for the duration of his political career, which began with his election to the New Mexico House of Representatives.

Dennis Chavez first appeared on the national political scene when he was sworn into the Seventy-Second Congress on March 4, 1931. Chavez had defeated the venerable Albert G. Simms in the previous year's general election to become New Mexico's lone U.S. representative. Chavez gained valuable experience as chair of the House Committee on Irrigation and Reclamation. The New Mexico electorate returned him to the U.S. House of Representatives in 1932 for a second term. He resigned in 1934 to campaign against Republican Party boss Bronson Cutting for the U.S. Senate. After losing the election, then being appointed to the position upon Cutting's death, Chavez took his seat in the Senate on May 11, 1935. He was the first native-born Hispanic ever to do so.

As a freshman senator, Chavez etched his political imprimatur in Washington as a rabid New Dealer and fervent disciple of President Roosevelt. With Democrats holding the majorities in both the House and the Senate at the time, the outspoken "El Senador" won reelection to office in his own right in 1940. For the next twenty-seven years he served his beloved New Mexico as the state's most ardent champion. For the remainder of the Depression era the all-Democratic congressional delegation—Senators Carl Hatch and Dennis Chavez and Congressman John J. Dempsey—represented a powerful and exceptionally effective lobby for government subsidies on behalf of their home state.

As noted, New Mexico fared extraordinarily well among the less populous states in the West with regard to New Deal funding from Washington. The state ranked fifth behind Nevada, Montana, Wyoming, and Arizona in per capita expenditure of federal dollars from 1933 to 1939. David Kammer notes that New Mexico's apportionment resulted in "increased road construction, landscaping of several city and town parks, and repair or construction of several schools and other public buildings."

At this juncture, however, the state's most pressing need was to provide "direct relief" in the form of commodities and consumables to assist the long-term unemployed to survive the seemingly intractable depression. What began as a trickle of FERA funding ($100,000 in 1933) transformed into a stream of financial subsidies ($500,000 by the end of that year). During the initial phase of the New Deal, Margaret Reeves, appointed director of the renamed New Mexico Emergency Relief Authority (NMERA), instructed county administrators to certify thousands of "unemployables" for inclusion on state relief rolls. In January 1934, Congress appropriated $500 million to FERA for distribution as grants-in-aid to all forty-eight states and affiliated territories. The NMERA budget correspondingly "increased from $30,000 in 1928 to $465,000 by 1933."

More effective in ameliorating the calamitous impact of the Great Depression were the constellation of work relief programs authorized under the New Deal. The CCC was among the earliest programs (1933) to be introduced to New Mexico. Within America's general population, young men between the ages of fifteen and twenty-four were by far the most difficult to keep employed. Labor statistics from 1932 indicated that this age group represented 25 percent of the nearly five million unemployed citizens at the time of FDR's inauguration. Eager to rectify this worrisome problem, Roosevelt put forth a bold idea to his cabinet that linked unemployment imperatives to long-neglected natural resource conservation needs of the nation. Though his staff was not overwhelmingly supportive, the president underscored the importance of the proposal saying, "We can take a vast army of these unemployed [youth] out into healthy surroundings. We can largely eliminate . . . the threat that enforced idleness brings to spiritual and moral stability."

The immediate outcome was Executive Order 6108, bolstered by the Civilian Conservation Corps Reforestation Relief Act, which passed Congress barely three weeks after the inauguration. The latter authorized what Roosevelt called the Civilian Conservation Corps Reforestation Youth Rehabilitation Movement, later shortened to its more popular designation, the "CCC." According to one authority, the work relief program targeted young men between the ages of eighteen and twenty-five (later changed to seventeen to twenty-eight) who could document having at least one destitute family member. Physical requirements included "a height between 5 ft. and 6 ft. 6 in., weight exceeding 107 pounds, and at least three serviceable and natural masticating teeth."

President Roosevelt assigned organizational and supervisory responsibility for the CCC to the U.S. Army, with immediate induction of a quarter-million young men to be distributed among 1,330 camps across the country. Melzer notes that the army was not enthralled with the daunting assignment: "While it had taken three months to mobilize 181,000 soldiers at the start of World War I," he wrote, "the Army was now directed to mobilize 250,000 young men in no less a period of time." Still, the army met the challenge with characteristic fervor. First, it divided the nation into nine regions within which it began construction of the specified camps.

The CCC's first enrollee entered the program on April 7, 1933, just days after the president's inaugural. New Mexico officials reported sixteen camps in operation by June 1933, ranging north to south from Raton to Silver City and east to west from Clovis to Gallup. In addition there were CCC camps located in the Sandia Mountains near Albuquerque, and in Hyde Memorial State Park in the Sangre de Cristo Range north of Santa Fe. Enrollees were paid $30 per month, of which $25 was sent directly to struggling families back home. In the army's view, recruits did not need more than the remaining $5 for personal and recreational needs. All CCC enrollees were furnished lodging, three meals per day, shoes, clothing, and—most important— applicable job training. According to one authority, "An estimated $662,895,000 was paid out to familial dependents during the agency's nine-year existence."

The accomplishments of the CCC during its near decade of service were staggering. A recent publication by Santa Fe historian Kathryn Flynn lists the following national achievements: three billion trees planted; 46,854 bridges, 205 lodges—including the presidential retreat at Camp David—and museums constructed; 360 Civil War battlefields restored; capital improvements to 1,000 national, state and municipal parks; 138,000 miles of roads and trails built; 3,470 lookout towers erected; and six million man-days spent fighting forest fires. During its tenure, the CCC supplied virtually unlimited labor to the U.S. Forest Service, the National Park Service, the U.S. Fish and Wildlife Service, the U.S. Soil Conservation Service, the U.S. Bureau of Land Management, and the U.S. Bureau of Reclamation. By the time Congress finally ended the program in June 1942, more than 50,000 young men from the state and all across the country had passed through the 237 CCC camps built in New Mexico since April 1933.

Among the numerous contributions the CCC boys made to the state of New Mexico, some of the most enduring were the outstanding structures they built on behalf of the federal and state parks system. On January 18, 1933, two months before he left office, President Hoover declared the naturally occurring outcrop of gleaming white gypsum sand dunes near Alamogordo a national monument. The creation of the federal entity came none too soon, as the economy of southern New Mexico thereafter rapidly declined into total disarray. Nascent tourism, which promised a new source of revenue to the state during the late 1920s, was at a virtual standstill. The once-dependable farm and ranch markets in the East and Midwest had all but vanished, and the value of petroleum products derived from the southeastern oilfields plummeted to an all-time low.

In the view of New Deal officials in Washington, however, White Sands National Monument offered the perfect set of conditions for federally sponsored work relief. According to historian Michael Welsh, there were practical considerations as well, "The CCC [program] required no state matching funds, a factor crucial in New Mexico, where the entire state budget that year stood at only $8 million." Accordingly, site custodian Tom Charles requested a two-hundred-member CCC camp in September 1933 to commence roadwork and initial construction within the new federal preserve. One outcome of nearly four years of CCC labor were the roads and trails that made the park more accessible, thus facilitating the attendance of 4,650 visitors at the opening ceremony in April 1934. More impressive were the magnificent adobe office complex and outbuildings that are still in use today. Carlsbad Caverns, the universally recognized "underground wonder of the world" which became a national park in October 1923, similarly benefited from the New Deal. Most of the CCC-built structures, including the enormously popular underground lunchroom, are likewise actively used today.

Perhaps the single most recognizable CCC contribution to the National Park Service (NPS) was the 24,000-square-foot, former Southwest Region III headquarters building in Santa Fe. A classic example of Spanish–Pueblo Revival architecture and reputed to be the "largest known adobe office building in the United States," it was the vision of NPS Regional Architect Cecil J. Doty and Regional Landscape Architect Harvey Cornell. Built between 1937 and 1939 to facilitate the transfer of NPS Region III from Oklahoma City to a more centralized location in the Southwest, the building is currently acknowledged by the preservation community as a masterpiece of vernacular design.

Two hundred CCC construction workers from Camp 833, located in Hyde Park, peeled massive log vigas extracted from nearby stands of ponderosa pine, handcrafted and laid more than 280,000 adobe bricks, and fashioned all of the Spanish colonial–style furniture. They also crafted the building's light fixtures, which accentuated the interior walls along with traditional Pueblo, Navajo, and nuevomexicano artwork. Fifty years after completing their work, the now-aged recruits, many of them native Hispanics from neighboring communities in northern New Mexico, reflected with great pride on their splendid achievements on behalf of the CCC. Today, the building functions as the NPS headquarters in Santa Fe.

The civilian counterparts to the military-led CCC were a succession of public works agencies known variously as the Public Works Administration (PWA), the Civil Works Administration (CWA), and WPA (Works Progress Administration; Works Projects Administration). The principal differences between the PWA and its sister agencies

The Civilian Conservation Corps left its imprint on New Mexico and the rest of the nation, as evidenced in this photo of White Sands National Monument park headquarters. (Art Gómez Collection)

was the nature and complexity of the work performed, as well as the manner in which the projects were funded. According to one source, "During the early years of the Depression, the PWA distributed nearly $6 billion for the construction of roads, tunnels, bridges dams, hydro-electric power projects, public buildings and municipal water works and sewage systems." All of these undertakings were funded on a 30 percent federal and 70 percent state or local match.

Intended to stimulate the economy by putting substantial numbers of people back to work, the PWA fell disappointingly short of its goal. PWA projects required comprehensive planning and design, plus specialized labor that the bulk of the nation's unemployed were either ineligible or ill trained to perform. Nonetheless, one economist noted that the PWA accounted for 33 percent of all construction in the United States during 1933. It averaged nearly 140,000 workers each year and indirectly created more than 600,000 other jobs. The agency also allocated approximately $1.8 billion to fund such government agencies as the Bureau of Reclamation, Bureau of Public Roads, and the War Department. While its projects were praiseworthy, the long, complicated process of implementation did little to lessen the agony of America's unemployed, who numbered nearly ten million by the winter of 1934.

Conchas Dam, a 550,000-plus acre-foot concrete dam built near Tucumcari with the intent of converting 65,000 acres of semiarid desert into productive farmland, stands out as one of the stellar PWA contributions to New Mexico. The state's largest public works project authorized during the Roosevelt administration, Conchas was a model of New Deal multiagency cooperation. During its four years of construction (July 1935–November 1939) the impressive reclamation effort on the South Canadian River hired nearly 4,000 unemployed workers from Quay, Harding, Guadalupe, Union, Doña Ana, Grant, Bernalillo, Chaves, Curry, and San Miguel counties, as well as additional labor from the Panhandle region of West Texas. New Mexico Hispanics constituted 60 percent of the workforce, drawn exclusively from county relief rolls. According to one scholar, the massive work relief project could not have been more timely, as "50 percent of New Mexicans were unemployed by the summer of 1935, and only 1 percent of [the state's] irrigable land was under cultivation."

The road to the dam's completion, however, was far from easy. In the spring of 1935, as the U.S. Army Corps of Engineers began testing for an appropriate site for the projected reservoir, Governor Clyde Tingley lamented that the state treasury had no money to meet the PWA-required match. His admission caused Secretary of the Interior and PWA director Harold Ickes to question the overall viability of the project. Worse, Tingley had no idea where to secure the estimated $54,000 that the district engineer Captain Hans T. Kramer suggested the governor needed to purchase the right-of-way to the forty-square-mile Bell Ranch, judged to be the most suitable location for the dam site. Tucumcari Water District commissioner Arch Hurley believed Tingley would need an additional $100,000 to $234,000 for the outright purchase of the property.

With unbridled zeal, Tingley appealed to local farmers, ranchers, businessmen, and bankers to "open their pocket books" and pledge to the "Conchas Dam Fund." Although the governor successfully raised $40,000 from the dust-plagued communities of Las Vegas and Tucumcari, New Mexico, and Amarillo, Texas, it was clear he would fall desperately short of the required amount. To remedy the situation, Tingley once again made a direct appeal to the president, who at the time was dedicating the newly constructed Boulder (later renamed Hoover) Dam near Las Vegas, Nevada.

Tingley boarded a westbound train for Nevada, and after a forty-five-minute conference with Roosevelt, emerged with an agreement that the federal government would lend the money to pay for the right-of-way on the condition that the New Mexico legislature raised sufficient appropriations to purchase the Bell Ranch by January 1936.

After numerous threats of civil action on the part of both parties, the owners of the Bell Ranch surprised the governor with their decision to sell 34,000 acres, the amount estimated to be sufficient for dam construction, for $165,000 and guaranteed water use from the proposed reservoir. As construction moved forward, the complex project required the participation of nearly every New Deal program created by the Roosevelt administration. While PWA and WPA labor worked on the dam itself, the CCC built the recreational state park, permanent housing, and administrative complex.

The realignment of U.S. Highway 66 in 1933 was another PWA-sanctioned project that proved vital to the weakened economy of New Mexico. An estimated 210,000 immigrants bound for California used the highway (originally built in 1926) to flee from the Dust Bowl communities of Texas, Oklahoma, Kansas, and Georgia. Their tragic odyssey not only required substantial maintenance of the mythic roadway, but also demanded a more direct, linear path from Albuquerque to the Arizona border. While the story of Route 66 as a modern migration trail is well documented, less publicized is the importance of the thoroughfare to thousands of destitute unemployed workers who opted instead to remain at home and eke out a living within the fragile economy of the Southwest. Public roadwork proved to be a viable alternative to migration toward survival. As a result of their labor and commitment, the Chicago-to–Los Angeles highway was reported to be "continuously paved" by 1938.

Virtually all of the state's municipalities fared well under the New Deal public works programs. Prior to 1935, Albuquerque had benefited from federal subsidies from both the PWA as well as the short-lived CWA. The former granted $1.9 million for public works between 1933 and 1934. Most of the initial PWA funding underwrote improvements to the University of New Mexico campus, including Zimmerman Library, Scholes Administration Hall, an Olympic-sized swimming complex for Carlisle Gym, a biological science classroom building, an engineering laboratory, and a new student union (part of the present Anthropology Building).

Legendary architect John Gaw Meem designed all of the structures in Pueblo Revival style to make their appearance compatible. Economic historian Charles D. Biebel wrote later, "The University enjoyed unprecedented growth during what should have been hard times. More than $1.6 million in federal subsidies were allocated to UNM from 1934–1941." PWA and later WPA dollars paid for new construction or the rehabilitation of older structures on college campuses across the state, at New Mexico Military Institute in Roswell, New Mexico Normal School (present Highlands University) in Las Vegas, New Mexico A&M College (present New Mexico State University) in Las Cruces, New Mexico State Teachers College (present Western New Mexico University) in Silver City, New Mexico Tech in Socorro, New Mexico School for the Blind in Alamogordo, and present Eastern New Mexico University in Portales.

Meantime, on November 9, 1933, FDR signed Executive Order 6420-B, establishing the CWA; he then appointed longtime confidant Harry Hopkins as director. Unlike PWA chief Harold Ickes, Hopkins emphasized action over planning with the aim of putting as many of the unemployed back to work in the shortest time possible. According to one New Deal historian, "The CWA was authorized $800 million for distribution to the various states; 90% of all projects would be federally funded. . . . Hopkins planned to put four million unemployed Americans to work on short-term projects such as road construction, parks and playgrounds, and soil conservation projects."

In contrast to FERA, which paid in kind, the CWA paid its workers a nominal wage that would "go directly into the pockets of the employees." Director Harry Hopkins assigned New Mexico an initial quota of

8,250 workers a month to be granted work relief under the new, and as it turned out, short-lived CWA program. Six months later Washington raised the requirement to 15,240 per month, all of whom had to be NMERA certified as eligible for direct relief or determined to be unable to find a job. NMERA director Margaret Reeves issued a statewide call for "legitimate" projects.

Inasmuch as one focus of the CWA was to contribute money and labor to municipal landscaping and beautification projects, city officials were eager to respond. Albuquerque, to no one's surprise, headed the line of recipients. Among Mayor Tingley's pet projects were two midtown municipal parks designed for public enjoyment. One CWA-authorized undertaking was Terrace Park, a project encompassing two acres of city land plus eleven acres of leased Albuquerque Public School property. Newly elected Governor Tingley ordered the recreational area to be renamed Roosevelt Park to honor its principal benefactor.

More intriguing was the mayor's preoccupation with how to improve what initially began as a local flood-control project on the Rio Grande. During the summer of 1930, celebrated humorist Will Rogers visited Albuquerque and promptly received the mayor's highly touted personal tour of the city. The bellicose Tingley outlined a grandiose plan for a recreational complex centered along the Rio Grande. He envisioned a zoo, a baseball field, and a playground with plenty of picnic tables, all accented by a man-made lake for fishing. Rogers listened politely then responded, "Now Mr. Mayor, if you put some water in this river, you'd have something."

Coincidentally, Middle Rio Grande Conservancy engineer Joseph Burkholder had earlier suggested that a deep drainage ditch, already planned for excavation between Old Town and Barelas bridges, be widened to accommodate a small lagoon for swimming and perhaps even boating. Conservancy "Beach," later christened Tingley Beach in honor of the boisterous, insufferably ambitious city mayor, was the outcome of these early discussions. The popular contrivance remained a key recreational outlet through the remainder of the Depression and war years, eventually succumbing to the polio scare of the early 1950s. The beautification projects undertaken by the City of Albuquerque under initial New Deal programs inspired other communities—Santa Fe,

Roswell, Las Cruces, and Santa Rosa, to name a few—to follow suit using WPA funding.

With the arrival of the WPA in New Mexico in the summer of 1935, planning and implementation of public works clearly accelerated. Clinton P. Anderson, the Albuquerque insurance agent who replaced Margaret Reeves as the NMERA administrator in 1935, and New Mexico WPA director Lea Rowland announced Washington's bold new strategy to put 23 million unemployed men and women back to work immediately. They explained that the number of projects submitted for consideration would be virtually limitless as long as they were deemed "worthy." The maximum expenditure per project, however, could not exceed $25,000.

During the eight years that the WPA remained in operation, New Mexico benefited from more than four thousand public works endeavors statewide. Under the WPA, virtually every municipality enjoyed a new public building—a courthouse, post office, fire department, police station, or administration building—and either a new elementary or high school. Some communities—Raton, Las Vegas, Roswell, Clovis, Portales, Gallup, Willard, Las Cruces, Deming and, of course, Santa Fe and Albuquerque—were awarded two or more such projects.

Despite the obvious contributions of the various New Deal agencies, the work relief effort in New Mexico did not escape criticism. Program director Harry Hopkins virulently criticized the state's apparent reluctance to contribute "its fair share of matching funds." Hopkins sent Governor Tingley a terse telegram pointing out that in the preceding twenty months the federal government contributed more than $4.6 million toward unemployment relief exclusive of CWA funds. For New Mexico's part, "the state treasury had contributed only $6,189 and local governments $83,054, largely for the cost of work project materials." Hopkins made abundantly clear his intent to withdraw WPA money from New Mexico unless the governor agreed to contribute no less than $500,000, a sum Hopkins considered a fair and reasonable contribution. Once again Tingley turned to Roosevelt for a temporary reprieve to enable him to contribute his state's share.

Shortly after its arrival, the WPA divided the state into four quadrants of approximately equal size. Each constituted an administrative

The Eddy County Courthouse is an excellent example of Works Progress Administration construction still in use today. (Art Gómez Collection)

district with jurisdiction over eight or more counties. Naturally, the headquarters in each unit reaped early benefits from the WPA largess. Raton, the site of District I headquarters, for example, enjoyed a continuous flurry of activity from 1936 to 1940, resulting in the Colfax County Courthouse, City Hall, the National Guard Armory, and a new municipal airport. Similarly, the WPA contributions to Roswell, headquarters for District II, included the Chaves County Courthouse, the contemporary Museum and Art Center and Cahoon Municipal Park, considered at the time to be one of the premier public works achievements of the New Deal in New Mexico. Not to be outdone, Deming, the administrative hub for District IV, claimed a new U.S. post office, the Luna County Courthouse, the New Mexico Highway Department Headquarters, and the Deming Public Library.

Once again, Albuquerque, the state's largest municipality and District III headquarters, and Santa Fe, the legislative capital, fared exceedingly well under the WPA. In addition to the projects already mentioned, Albuquerque modernized the municipal airport; constructed the State Fairgrounds and Exhibition Hall, the Monte Vista Fire Station, and the Albuquerque Little Theater; and added new barracks and a runway to the recently designated Kirtland Army Air Field. Meanwhile in Santa Fe, Governor Tingley orchestrated several municipal improvements. The WPA accounted for many of the city's most recognizable landmarks: the Santa Fe County Courthouse, Fort Marcy State Park, the Galisteo Bridge across the Santa Fe River, and a completely remodeled museum at the Palace of the Governors.

Without question, the Tingleys' and the WPA's most cherished contribution to New Mexico during the 1930s was the Carrie Tingley Hospital, appropriately located in the historic health community of Hot Springs in Sierra County. During their many discussions with FDR about the state's employment needs, Carrie Tingley proposed a hospital specializing in the treatment of "crippled" children, many of whom, like the president, were polio victims. Citing the town of Hot Springs (later renamed Truth or Consequences, after the popular 1950s television game show) as "God's gift to health" in November 1935, the governor unveiled the plan to build a hospital "for the cure of infantile paralysis."

Governor Tingley promised to secure $100,000 from Washington to build the facility, plus an additional $100,000 to furnish it with state-of-the-art medical equipment. Next, he challenged the residents of Hot Springs to come up with an estimated $10,000 to purchase sufficient land to locate the massive structure. On the drive back to Albuquerque, the Tingleys chanced upon an old dirt road overlooking the town "with the craggy backdrop of the Black Range and a pastoral view of the tree-lined river below." It so happened that the site was the location of the town dump. Nevertheless, Tingley breathlessly proclaimed it "the perfect location for the new hospital."

Months later, *Sierra County Advocate* publisher Robert Coleman presented the governor with good news that "even in these most difficult economic times" the town's citizenry had raised $12,000 to purchase the property. Soon thereafter, to the Tingleys' utter delight, Congress appropriated $290,000 to build the ultramodern, hundred-bed facility. The original blueprints indicate that the building contained numerous terraces and sun porches for outdoor activity; a heated exercise

A jubilant governor-elect Tingley smiles at a portrait of his wife, Carrie. Mrs. Tingley established a reputation of her own as the founder of many children's hospitals across the state. (Courtesy of Palace of the Governors Photo Archives, NMHM/DCA, neg. no. 056514)

pool; and allocated space for radiology, surgery, medical treatment, and occupational therapy. There was even an ancillary building to manufacture leg braces. According to architect Willard C. Kruger, "the entire first floor of the hospital will be built on one level without stairs so that children can make their way about the building in wheel chairs." On February 13, 1936, three thousand celebrants watched the governor's wife ceremoniously turn the first spadeful of dirt to signal the start of construction. A year and a half later President Roosevelt acknowledged the hospital's completion with a note to the Tingleys that read, "You have done something with government money that will be a credit to you, to me, and to this administration."

For all of the good Roosevelt's New Deal endeavored to accomplish during the Great Depression, the federal government also demonstrated a dark side in the 1930s. As New Mexico congressional appointee Dennis Chavez stood up to take the oath of office on May 20, 1935, six of his colleagues turned their backs on the freshman senator and left the Senate Chamber in protest. Had Chavez antagonized his fellow congressmen when he demanded an electoral recount after Cutting's narrow victory in 1934? Or did they resent the Democratic upstart because of his political appointment to succeed Cutting after the latter's fatal accident? Or, as New Mexico–born historian Maria Montoya has argued, did the senators who turned their backs on Chavez "[resent] having a Mexican American, someone who many of them thought was below their station, in their elite midst"? The latter supposition may be closer to fact than conjecture, as the behavior toward Chavez in many ways mirrored the prevailing U.S. attitude toward the nation's Spanish-speaking population in general and New Mexicans in particular, as evidenced in the state's agonizing path to statehood.

More telling was the national disdain for the once-welcome Mexican immigrants, whom Americans, especially the jobless hordes, feared as competitors for whatever employment the New Deal offered. For this reason, both the Hoover and the Roosevelt administrations turned their heads as city and state government summarily targeted Mexican immigrants, and in some cases American-born residents of Hispanic and Mexican descent, for deportation. According to Montoya, while the actual number of people "repatriated" to Mexico is still unknown, "probably more than a half million people were torn from their jobs, homes, and families." Among the hundreds of thousands who were herded across the U.S.-Mexican border by panic-stricken, xenophobic Americans were U.S. citizens from Denver, Albuquerque, San Antonio, Tucson, and Los Angeles. One observer summarized, "it is inaccurate to use the term 'repatriate' in this instance inasmuch as native born Americans were unlawfully transported into a foreign country." The shameful event remains a dark stain in American social history

Indians of the American Southwest suffered a more subtle, government-induced form of racism under the well-intentioned but much criticized federal policy known as the Indian Reorganization Act of 1934 (IRA). At first glance, the IRA appeared to be a practical way to decrease federal control over American Indians by encouraging tribal self-government. In effect, the Roosevelt administration sought to create an "Indian New Deal" by enabling tribal political autonomy. The principal defect in the idealized strategy, according to critics, was that Indians themselves had little say in determining the nature of the policies that most concerned them. As with the previous disastrous policy to reduce the number of domesticated sheep, cattle, and horses on the Navajo reservation, the tribes were not directly involved in life-altering decisions.

Navajo, Apache, and Pueblo residents of the American Southwest were "voiceless" spectators, and ultimately victims, of misguided government policymakers. In summarizing the adverse changes imposed upon Indians during the 1930s, Donald Parman argued that "although the IRA was well-intentioned, its [policies] were frequently rushed and misunderstood; and thus led to unexpected or flawed results." The long-term consequence of shortsighted government actions toward American Indians during the Great Depression was that they, like their Hispanic brethren in New Mexico and the greater Southwest, were viewed as second-class citizens. These unfortunate circumstances would not begin to change until Hispanic and Indian veterans returned home after World War II.

In contrast to the ominous social and political climate of the times, the WPA-sponsored Federal Art Project elevated Hispanic and American Indian ethnicity to new heights. Nationally renowned artists and writers had long been attracted to the state, bringing economic and social benefits. At the urging of anthropologists like Edgar Lee Hewett and Jesse Nusbaum, reputable artists—Ernest Blumenschein, W. Herbert Dunton, and Bert Geer Phillips, followed by Gerald Cassidy, Will Shuster, Olive Rush, and Georgia O'Keeffe—journeyed to New Mexico, hoping to capture its alluring scenery on canvas. What one writer called the "commoditized West" followed in the form of mass-produced calendars, postcards, and photographs, which railroad companies, in turn, distributed nationally as a way to promote business. The profusion of these self-proclaimed "Bohemian" artists resident throughout the state dovetailed nicely with the long-term goals of the Federal Art Project, an ingenious New Deal program first introduced in August 1935.

The WPA Federal Art Project kept numerous New Mexico artists employed.
Here, Olive Rush works on her fresco in the Biology Building entrance
at State College (New Mexico State University) Las Cruces, New Mexico.
(Photograph by Ina Sizer Cassidy. Courtesy of Palace of the Governors
Photo Archives, NMHM/DCA, neg. no. 091578.)

The immediate objective was to put unemployed artists back to work presenting art to the public through traveling exhibitions, art education, vocational training in organized community centers, and enhanced public appreciation of the arts through the direct application of interior decorations in public buildings or exterior displays in municipal parks, schools, and playgrounds. The restored murals of Olive Rush in Santa Fe's Old Public Library and Peter Hurd's vibrant exterior wall designs on the former U.S. post office and U.S. Forest Service building in Alamogordo are just two of the numerous existing examples of decorative artwork produced during these years.

One of the true innovations of the New Deal arts program was the revival of traditional art in New Mexico. Before 1930, non-Hispanic artists Gene Kloss, Willard Van Dyke, Elizabeth Boyd, and others popularized nuevomexicano themes essentially through their own creations. Early attempts by Frank Applegate, Mary Austin, and Concha Ortiz y Pino to revitalize Spanish colonial artistic motifs foundered with their passing. With the advent of the WPA Federal Art Project, however, a cadre of young, talented Hispanic men and women established solid reputations as contemporary and traditional artists. The works of painters Esquípula Romero de Romero, Pedro López Cervántez and Juan Amadeo Sánchez, sculptor Patrocinio Barela, weaver Max Ortiz, tinsmith Ildeberto "Eddie" Delgado, straw appliqué specialist Ernesto Roybal, and santeros José Dolores López and Santiago "Sam" Matta emerged from the Great Depression as nationally acclaimed artists.

In similar fashion, local Indian artists, some of whom Dorothy Dunn and Geronima Cruz (Montoya) nurtured in their studio at the Santa Fe Indian School, experimented with both modern and traditional styles. Painters Pablita Velarde, Allan Houser, Quincy Tahoma, and Fred Kabotie, along with potters María Montoya Martínez and Julian Martínez, represented the best artists of their day. In the years to come, the creative genius of the 1930s would set the standard for a new generation of exceptionally gifted men and women who today proudly represent the ethnic artistic community in New Mexico.

The monetary and physical contributions of the New Deal from 1934 to 1942 left an indelible legacy in New Mexico and across the nation.

In the process, federal subsidies aimed at alleviating human suffering and economic destitution converted a former frontier community into a modern, progressive-minded state. As the CWA, PWA, and WPA focused their collective energy on public buildings, recreational parks, municipal airports, and educational institutions in impoverished cities and towns, the CCC and NYA imposed roads, dams, bridges, and utilitarian facilities on the once seemingly indomitable landscape.

Despite all the good it accomplished, the New Deal did not end the Great Depression. Rather, the riotous clamor for war among the highly militarized and politicized societies of Europe and Asia dramatically transformed a financially stagnant global economy into one of unparalleled wartime prosperity. One early indication of the imminent threat to peace was the mobilization of the New Mexico National Guard and the subsequent posting of the predominantly Spanish-speaking 200th Coast Artillery to the Philippines in September 1941. Neither New Mexico nor the wider world would emerge unchanged in the aftermath of war.

CHAPTER 10

The Age of Vigilance
World War II and the Cold War, 1940–1965

> The 1,000,000 expected deaths represented a million reasons to drop
> the atomic bomb on Japan, in order to force the Japanese surren-
> der. Dropping the bomb would also send a strong message to the
> Russians; top American leaders expected that the Soviet Union
> would be their enemy in the post–World War II Cold War.
>
> ROGERS AND BARTLIT, *SILENT VOICES OF WORLD WAR II*

BARELY SIXTEEN HOURS AFTER the detonation of the world's
first atomic weapon, President Harry S. Truman broadcast to the
American people the news that the city of Hiroshima, the main embarkation point for Japanese military deployment to the Pacific Islands,
had been obliterated. "The force from which the sun draws its power,"
the nation's chief executive said solemnly, "has been loosed against
those who brought war to the Far East." The cataclysmic events of
Monday, August 6, 1945, followed three days later by a second nuclear
attack on Nagasaki, a vital shipbuilding and repair center located on
Japan's southernmost island of Kyushu, concluded nearly five years of
warfare against the Axis powers. The two devices, christened "Little
Boy" and "Fat Man" respectively, instantly destroyed 140,000 people in
Hiroshima and an estimated 80,000 more in Nagasaki. Six days later,
Japan announced its intent to surrender, which officially ended World
War II on September 2, 1945.

Unbeknownst at the time to Major Charles W. Sweeney and the
crew of *Bock's Car,* the B-29 aircraft that delivered the second lethal device
to Nagasaki, native-born New Mexican Manuel Armijo, a Japanese-held
prisoner of war and survivor of the infamous Bataan Death March,
watched the rising radioactive plume from the solitude of his tiny

cubicle in Kokura, not too many miles distant from ground zero. First Sergeant Armijo, for his part, could not have known that the devastating weapon which hastened the capitulation of America's most resolute enemy was first assembled and tested within earshot of his birthplace in Hot Springs (present Truth or Consequences), New Mexico.

America's successful deployment of the atomic bomb just months after the surrender of Nazi Germany was one of the most life-changing events of the twentieth century. The war taxed the human and natural resources of the entire world beyond imagination. An estimated sixteen million American men and women served in the armed forces during World War II. Of that number, approximately 2.5 million were still living as of 2007. While the exact number of combatants from New Mexico is not certain, the Veterans Administration listed somewhere around 20,000 known veterans in residence across the state. According to one estimate, "New Mexico had the highest per capita casualty rate of any U.S. state during World War II." Indeed, during his eyewitness report "Letter from America," BBC correspondent Alistair Cook observed that Deming, New Mexico, a community with a total population of 2,000 in 1942, already had lost 150 men to overseas combat.

The unprecedented pace with which the United States mobilized its industry and resources in response to conflicts on two continents set the standard for national and regional expansionism in subsequent decades. New Mexico, according to the 1940 U.S. census, held a total population of 531,815 inhabitants occupying a landmass ranked fourth largest among the states. Along with other states located west of the Mississippi River, New Mexico benefited measurably from the wartime and postwar economic booms. World War II and the decades of the 1950s and 1960s (the first half of the Cold War) left an indelible imprint on New Mexico's contemporary development. "For most of its modern history, the state of New Mexico languished in the shadow of more populous and wealthy regions," noted western historian Michael Welsh. "Unable to finance its own public works projects, New Mexico survived by means of tourism, federal social programs, and small amounts of agriculture." The unanticipated Japanese attack on Pearl Harbor in December 1941 triggered an "economic and social revolution of staggering proportions" throughout the West and the Southwest.

"The period from 1940 to 1990 was clearly the most dynamic era in the state's long history," wrote University of New Mexico professor emeritus Gerald D. Nash. "No other period witnessed such dramatic changes and such dramatic growth—for good or ill." Without question, the arrival of the first Europeans in the sixteenth century, the American conquest and the attendant industrialization in the nineteenth century, and the territory's elevation to statehood in the early twentieth century wrought profound changes among the preexisting societies of New Mexico. Still, on the eve of World War II, 41 percent of the state's population lived without indoor plumbing or running water, 30 percent of all New Mexican families earned less than $100 a year (one-twelfth of the U.S. family average), and the state's most populated municipality numbered fewer than 50,000 citizens; only two other localities claimed more than 10,000. One urban scholar summarized his impression of the "Duke City" before the war: "Albuquerque was little more than a small town that attracted tourists and health seekers and served as a trading and distribution center for a limited heartland."

Both that city and the state experienced rampant growth during and immediately after the war. In less than a decade, the state's per capita income quadrupled as Albuquerque's population consistently doubled every five years from 1940 until the mid-1960s. Several key factors contributed to the state's phenomenal postwar growth. First, was the pervasive influence of the federal government in general and the military in particular—especially the Army Air Corps and its heir apparent, the U.S. Air Force. Virtually unlimited government spending in the name of national security and global freedom from tyranny contributed mightily to the once-marginal New Mexico economy.

The war changed population trends among the traditional Hispanic and Indian communities as thousands of men and women left the state either to serve in the armed forces or to take the myriad defense-related jobs suddenly made available in the Pacific states. Science and technology went hand in hand with the defense industry and the ubiquitous military presence. Not only did science contribute directly to the successful outcome of the war, it hastened the modernization of a heretofore unyielding provincial community. The enduring presence of Los Alamos National Laboratory (LANL) and the subsequent attraction of Sandia National Laboratories (SNL), the Intel Corporation, Philips Electronics, and other research giants enabled New Mexico to challenge the primacy of California's Silicon Valley in the 1970s.

Finally, during the war thousands of Hispanic and American Indian men and women were exposed to a world community beyond New Mexico, with profound effects on the traditional villages they left behind. Most minority servicemen returned with a new political and racial consciousness, bolstered in part by the somewhat more egalitarian treatment they experienced in the military—especially on the battlefield. Ethnic New Mexicans, many of whom served with the utmost distinction in defense of their country, returned home determined to eradicate the racial inequities that had traditionally limited their social mobility. Their collective thirst for social, economic, and political equality was emphatically demonstrated in the artistic, literary, musical, and political activism that fostered the civil rights movement of the 1960s.

For all of its significance and contribution to the illustrious history of New Mexico, statehood in 1912 did not usher in transformative modernization. Rather, it was the urgency of world war and America's relentless appetite for the abundant human and natural resources of the West. The inescapable response from this once-remote, Spanish/Mexican frontier colony was adaptation to progress and resignation to rampant social and economic change. New Mexico, albeit unknowingly, stood poised to make extraordinary contributions to the war effort. Yet, in the fall of 1940, world events were not particularly important to the state's general population. Local energy focused on the Coronado Cuarto Centennial commemoration, the four hundredth anniversary of European arrival in the middle Rio Grande Valley.

The yearlong celebration included pageants, Indian ceremonial dances, mariachi music, and rodeos. Nearly a thousand re-enactors, dressed in assorted costumes of the period, participated in a serpentine procession through the streets of Santa Fe. The so-called Land of Enchantment had cause to celebrate. Virtually from the moment the last contingent of mounted U.S. cavalry had abandoned their lonely outposts in the 1890s, the state's multiethnic community had embraced a half-century of peace and cultural coexistence. Rumblings of an impending conflict in Europe abruptly changed all of that.

Germany's triumphant march into Paris in June 1940, on the heels of the Wehrmacht's well-executed invasions of Czechoslovakia, Poland, Denmark, Norway, and the Netherlands, left Great Britain the sole defender of the European continent. Meanwhile in the Far East, Japanese belligerence in Manchuria and China in the late 1930s, fueled by their nonaggression pact with Germany and Italy, inspired the war-bent leaders of the Empire of the Rising Sun to assert their military hegemony over the resource-abundant British Malaya and the Dutch East Indies as well as the American-occupied Philippine Islands. It was Japan's strategic designs on the latter, more specifically the well-positioned Clark Army Air Field located sixty miles north of Manila, that would in time disrupt the mood of New Mexico's celebratory and unsuspecting Anglo, Hispanic, and American Indian communities a half-world away.

Military historian James Hyink points to some early indications that U.S. neutrality might inevitably succumb to global aggression. In the summer of 1940, for instance, the nation's "regular army staged mock combat exercises along the Rio Grande that involved troops, tanks and artillery from various military bases located in Texas and Colorado." Concurrently, the July 2, 1940, edition of the *Albuquerque Journal* discussed the government's plans to "co-locate an army air corps base with the city's municipal airport."

Earlier that year, the Roosevelt administration had shifted national emphasis away from federal relief to military preparedness. Accordingly, the role of the U.S. Army Corps of Engineers in New Mexico—and the remainder of the Southwest—evolved from dam building and flood control to the construction of municipal air fields suitable for rapid conversion to military use. This task required a specialized knowledge of concrete and asphalt construction designed to support heavy payloads such as bomb-laden aircraft. The primary responsibility for building these facilities fell to Lieutenant Colonel James H. Stratton, who not only had published a scholarly paper on the subject, but acquired hands-on experience during the construction of Conchas Dam. "The Chief of Engineers ordered Stratton to Washington to perfect his methods as quickly as possible as over 100 airstrips awaited results," Welsh noted. The American Southwest offered the most consistently favorable weather for flight training. Accordingly, the majority of air fields were targeted for California, Texas, Arizona, Oklahoma, and New Mexico.

Within months of Stratton's transfer to Washington, residents on Albuquerque's East Mesa witnessed activity that presaged America's imminent entry into the European conflict. In anticipation of the Army Corps of Engineers' monumental undertaking, the U.S. Army Air Corps leased 2,000 acres of land four miles west of Oxnard Field (formerly Albuquerque Airport). Sometime in early 1940, the federal government condemned the commercial field and the army assumed control for military use.

On January 7, 1941, construction began on what was originally designated Albuquerque Army Air Field, which became operational in April 1941 and was the precursor to today's Kirtland Air Force Base. With the transfer of five army B-18 bomber aircraft to the windswept terminus early that spring, Albuquerque's sixty-plus-year association with the War Department (later redesignated the Department of Defense) officially began. Within two years of Japan's disastrous attack on Hawaii, New Mexico hosted eight military-related air fields to form a strategic web extending north-south from Albuquerque to Carlsbad and east-west from Hobbs to Deming.

Carlsbad Army Air Field represented a classic example of a municipal airport readily converted into a functioning military training facility. Long associated with the world-class underground caverns located twenty-five miles south of town, the city of Carlsbad proved a worthy candidate for a WPA-funded municipal airport during the waning years of the Great Depression. In 1938, approximately 50,000 personnel and slightly more than 6,000 aircraft comprised the U.S. Army Air Force (USAAF). With the ever-increasing threat of war in 1940, the War Department authorized "the training of 7,000 pilots and 3,600 bombardiers and navigators yearly." The municipal airport at Carlsbad, completed in August 1941, proved an excellent candidate for conversion to a USAAF training base.

In March 1942, according to one informative archaeological report, "the War Department chose the Carlsbad Municipal Airport as the site of an army air corps training center at a cost of $5,000,000." The report continued, "The site was chosen because of 345 flying days a year and flat terrain." As was typical of emergency war planning, the army filed condemnation suits against thirty-two local landowners to acquire the additional 1,600 acres needed to complete the facility. From its first day of training on September 9, 1942, until the base ceased to become operational on September 30, 1945, Carlsbad Army Air Field prepared more than four thousand pilots, navigators, bombardiers, and expert aerial gunners for combat in North Africa and Europe.

A more ominous indication that war was imminent was the sudden federalization of the New Mexico National Guard on January 6, 1941. The tradition of a citizen's militia in New Mexico (precursor to today's National Guard) dated to the Spanish colonial period. For centuries, nuevomexicanos were expected to defend their homes and adjacent lands from all manner of external threats—foreign and domestic. The New Mexican sense of obligation to military service did not abate with the American takeover in 1848. As previous chapters make clear, New Mexicans were no strangers to war or the defense of their homeland. The men who joined their local National Guard units in December 1940, however, may have done so more out of economic necessity than overt patriotism. In less than two years, the loyalty of some 1,800 New Mexico national guardsmen would be tested beyond all human endurance. Sometime during 1939, the long-established cavalry unit was converted into the 200th Coast Artillery, a new anti-aircraft component of the U.S. Army. The "Old Two Hundred" recruited statewide for young men eager to earn "$18 per month plus one dollar for each weekly training meeting attended."

According to World War II specialists Everett M. Rogers and Nancy R. Bartlit, the National Guard had a broad appeal to New Mexico's youth for a number of reasons. Aurelio Quintana, barely fifteen years old at the time, joined the army to prove the marksmanship skills he had acquired as a hunter; Vicente Ojinaga, a native of Santa Rita, wanted desperately to enlist, but instead waited to be drafted because his mother would not allow him to leave home; Nick Chintis, a local football hero in Silver City, joined to impress the "prettiest girl I had ever seen" with his new uniform; in fact, the rest of his teammates followed the young tailback into the Guard; First

Sergeant Manuel Armijo of Santa Fe, the unit's elder statesman at age twenty-eight, and compadre Evans Garcia enlisted because they "wanted to be with their *amigos.*" No doubt Tommy Foy from Bayard; Ruben Flores of Las Cruces; Albuquerque's Joe Bergstein; recently honored Death March survivors Tony Reyna of Taos Pueblo and Albuquerqueans Ralph Rodríquez and Nano Lucero; and others from all across the state each had his own personal reasons to seek employment in the Guard.

Within weeks of the unit's federalization, the army transported all the enlistees to Fort Bliss in El Paso, Texas. During months of "specialized training" in the relentless West Texas heat, during which time the unit was not allowed to fire live ammunition because it was in short supply, army officials determined the New Mexico recruits well suited for deployment to the Philippines because "the majority of its members spoke Spanish." Army strategists were confident the New Mexicans would readily identify with their Filipino allies because of "cultural and linguistic similarities." (Filipinos are Asian, not European, and their native language is Tagalog, not Spanish). Despite these glaring misconceptions, the 1,800 national guardsmen assigned to the 200th Coast Artillery regiment, "the New Mexico Brigade," were deployed to the Philippine Islands in September 1941 and charged with protecting the B-17 bomber aircraft recently arrived at Clark Army Air Field.

For most Americans, World War II did not begin until a few months later with the Japanese surprise attack on Pearl Harbor. But on the morning of December 8, 1941 (Sunday, December 7, Hawaii time), fifty-four Mitsubishi bombers left Formosa (today's Taiwan) to initiate World War II in the Pacific. Meantime, under the protection of a vicious aerial assault on Clark Army Air Field, a quarter-million combat-seasoned Japanese infantry made coordinated amphibious landings on Luzon and Mindanao. Armed only with "antiquated World War I equipment and ammunition," American and Filipino defenders were "overwhelmed by thousands of battle-hardened Japanese veterans, fresh from the conquest of parts of China." In the wake of the near-fatal surprise attack on the American Pacific Fleet anchored in Pearl Harbor, there was little hope the 25,000 besieged

American troops in the Philippines would be rescued. Effectively, the U.S. government abandoned these poorly armed, inadequately supplied, and hopelessly outnumbered forces to fend for themselves.

Although New Mexicans could rightfully claim to have fired the opening salvos of the war in the Pacific—downing five enemy aircraft in the process—the 170 Mitsubishi Zero fighters blanketing the sky after the lethal bombing raids hardly took note. Sometime during the night of December 8, the two-thousand-man 200th was split into two units; the second unit, composed of five hundred New Mexican troops and renamed the 515th Regiment, proceeded south to establish a defensive perimeter around Manila. Rogers and Bartlit argue the division was pointless inasmuch as the unit "constituted the largest single military organization in the Philippines and was unnecessarily weakened."

Realizing the defense of Luzon was futile, Douglas MacArthur, commander of U.S. forces in the Far East, ordered the evacuation of all remaining troops to nearby Bataan Peninsula. One Japanese observer who witnessed the retreat likened the withdrawal to "a cat going into a bag." There was no escape from Bataan except by sea. Thus, the only options left to the battle-weary American and Filipino troops on Bataan were surrender or total annihilation. It did not take long for the unsavory prediction to bear fruit. On the eve of the Japanese attack, however, President Roosevelt ordered General MacArthur— whom his troops had disdainfully nicknamed "Dugout" Doug—to relinquish his command and escape to Australia (where, ironically, he was named supreme commander of all the Pacific forces).

MacArthur left behind Generals Edward King and Jonathan Wainwright and an army half-starved (because the bulk of its food rations and medical provisions were left behind during the retreat), disease-ridden, and physically exhausted, though willing to fight on rather than face the prospect of Japanese capture. Their fate was sealed as the beleaguered American commanders saw no recourse but to surrender the 75,000 combined American—including 1,800 New Mexican—and Filipino combatants. The mass surrender on April 8, 1942, according to historian Ferenc Szasz, was "the largest capitulation in the history of the American military."

On the occasion of the seventieth anniversary of the Bataan Death March, the last known survivors of the New Mexico 200th Coast Artillery salute fallen companions to the sound of taps. *From left to right:* Nano Lucero, Ralph Rodríquez, John Love, William Overmire, Ernest Montoya, and Tony Reyna (Courtesy of the *Albuquerque Journal*)

For the soldiers, unimaginable atrocities began when their Japanese captors force-marched groups of about five hundred prisoners seventy-five miles in seven days, bayoneting or shooting stragglers along the way. According to one source, "5,000 of the 12,000 Americans on the tortuous Bataan Death March died. That works out to an average of one corpse every 20 yards of the 75-mile journey." Miraculously, the New Mexicans suffered only twenty killed during the siege on Bataan. However, estimates of those among the 1,800 members of the original 200th who died en route to Cabanatuan and other prison camps run as high as 20 percent.

More than half of the 1,800 enlistees who sailed to the Far East in the fall of 1941 never came home. Adding to the cumulative death toll were casualties directly attributed to the Death March, subsequent detention under barbaric conditions, inhumane treatment, transport to Japan on the infamous "death ships," and forced labor in various camps scattered throughout the Japanese mainland. Personal interviews with former captives years after the unforgettable nightmare revealed a common theme. Every survivor to the man adamantly declared that he and his Filipino comrades "were surrendered" to the Japanese by fainthearted commanding officers. Otherwise, they insist, they would never have been captured.

A truly extraordinary contribution to the war effort came from a most unlikely source—the vast, sparsely populated Navajo reservation. Early in the war, Philip Johnson, a son of Presbyterian missionaries who had spent much of his youth in the Southwest, proposed to the army that the Navajo language be used in military communications. At the time, fewer than thirty known individuals not born into the tribe spoke Navajo, in part because it remained an unwritten language in 1941; and the odds were good that none of the speakers were Japanese. In an impressive demonstration on the utility of the language for military purposes, Johnson, one of the handful of nonnative speakers, convinced the U.S. Marine Corps to adopt the language as a device for coded telecommunications.

The idea of the strategic use of American Indian languages was not new. During World War I, the U.S. Army used Comanche during field operations in France to confuse the enemy. What made this idea unique was the incorporation of a secondary layer of encoded terminology embedded within each transmission. The code itself could never be written down; therefore, it was known only to a select few Navajo combatants and military strategists. In fact, the very existence of the now-celebrated Navajo Code Talkers was kept a high-priority secret until 1968. During the course of the war, some 420 Navajos received training as Code Talkers under the aegis of the U.S. Marine Corps.

Carl Gorman, father of famed southwestern artist R. C. Gorman and a successful commercial painter himself, was thirty-four years old—well beyond the standard enlistment age—when he was recruited into the newly formed unit. "I went to fight for Indian lands," Gorman later informed a deeply appreciative audience attending an awards ceremony honoring the Code Talkers in 1982. "The Navajos have always thought of this as our land, and we have all the rights to fight for it." Inasmuch as the BIA-operated boarding schools imposed a rigorous—usually harsh—discipline on their young, American

Indian residents, Marine Corps recruiters targeted schools located at Fort Defiance and Chinle in Arizona in addition to Fort Wingate and Shiprock, New Mexico.

Soon thereafter, Gorman and John Benally bid goodbye to Kaibito, Arizona, to join "Cozy" Brown and Dean Wilson of Shiprock and twenty-five others at the Fort Defiance recruitment center. The Marine Corps bused the young Navajo enlistees 1,200 miles to Camp Pendleton, California, for basic training. According to the military way of thinking, the future radio operators had to become good marines first. Thus, the Navajo recruits became well versed in jungle warfare and other combat skills in addition to being communications experts.

For the remainder of the war in the Pacific, the Code Talkers time and again proved themselves vital to America's "island-hopping" campaign against a formidable enemy. Always part of the first assault wave, Navajo radiomen, such as Private First Class Frank Toledo and his teen-aged nephews Preston and Bill Toledo from Torreon, New Mexico, were present at every major amphibious landing from Guadalcanal to Okinawa. Shortly before his death from a sniper's bullet on Okinawa in April 1945, newspaper correspondent Ernie Pyle interviewed Code Talker Alex Williams who hailed from Albuquerque, where Pyle lived at the time. No doubt neither man expected to encounter a fellow New Mexican eleven thousand miles from home.

The night before Pyle's death, Williams and some of his fellow American Indian marines allowed the famed newspaperman to witness a "war dance" performed to give them strength in battle. Sometime after the war, a tribal spokesman said of the Code Talkers' contribution to World War II, "the power of the Navajo language became a weapon that helped win the most destructive war in history." Of the estimated 50,000 Navajos living on the reservation in 1941, some 3,600 served in the armed forces during the conflict. On returning home, some became prominent political figures among their people. Peter MacDonald, a member of the elite group (although never deployed to the Pacific), was elected Navajo Nation tribal chairman four times during the 1970s and 1980s. Although his tenure was marred by political corruption, MacDonald's wartime association with bona fide tribal war heroes no doubt garnered him a number of votes.

New Mexicans fought with distinction on every foreign battlefield. Five native sons were listed among the dead at Pearl Harbor. Leopoldo Gonzales of Santa Fe served in North Africa and Italy before returning home to recuperate from severe burns sustained in a tank battle with German panzers. In his many essays on American GIs, Ernie Pyle profiled Martin Quintana of Albuquerque and John Trujillo of Socorro, two frontline sergeants he met while in Sicily. "It was good to get back to those slow-talking, wise and easy people of the desert," Pyle wrote nostalgically, "and good to speak of places like Las Cruces, Socorro and Santa Rosa." Meanwhile in southern France, nineteen-year-old Jose F. Valdez of Gobernador was at the time the youngest American to earn the Congressional Medal of Honor (awarded posthumously), recognized for extraordinary heroism in a fight with two German SS infantry companies.

Combatants in other branches of service were also recipients of battlefield commendations. Sergeant Paul Leonard of Artesia was one of three New Mexicans said to have participated in Jimmy Doolittle's daring raid over Tokyo in 1942. Leonard "earned a Distinguished Flying Cross for his role as a gunner in the attack." African American James Buchanan Williams flew a P-52 Mustang fighter with the famed Tuskegee Airmen in the skies over Italy. "It was unusual for us [African Americans] to be involved in combat," stressed the Las Cruces native when interviewed years later.

Staff Sergeant Everardo R. Gómez, born in the small farming community of Plazas Largas west of modern Española, also earned the Distinguished Flying Cross. Gómez, known to his fellow crew members as "Chico" because of his diminutive stature, reported for duty at Chipping Ongor, England, two months before the Allied invasion of Normandy. From April 1944 until May 1945, he participated in sixty-three aerial combat missions as a radio-waist gunner on a B-26 medium-range bomber. While Gómez was eligible to rotate home after thirty-five missions, he opted to continue flying.

Toward the end of the war, Hitler, left with a nearly defeated Luftwaffe, introduced the world's first jet fighter as a last-ditch defense against Allied air attacks. On April 18, 1945, two weeks before Gómez was scheduled to leave Europe, an ME-262 jet attacked his plane, ripping open a hole in the fuselage next to his position big enough for two men to stand in (shown in an official military photo). According to the award citation, rather than call for the crew to bail out, the seasoned veteran kept firing, drove off the jet fighter and splashed down two conventional, prop-driven aircraft to enable his crew a safe return to their home base in the Netherlands. When asked why he chose to hold his position rather than call in the full extent of the damage, Gómez replied, "I was scheduled to go home [to the United States] soon and didn't much relish the idea of ditching into the Channel." Gómez was safely back in the United States with his wife, Verna, when Germany surrendered in May 1945. Four months later, Japan capitulated. The great conflagration that had engulfed planet Earth was over at last.

New Mexico: A Guide to the Colorful State, a work compiled by the WPA Federal Writers Project, was perhaps the most widely read publication of its day across the state—perhaps second only to Life magazine. Although the original focus of the book was to have been the 1930s, it did not appear in print until August 1940, thus providing historians with a vivid snapshot of New Mexico on the eve of World War II.

The section titled "The State Today" was particularly revealing with regard to demographics, economic development, and recreational amenities. As noted earlier, New Mexico's culturally diverse population in 1940 stood right at a half million people distributed across roughly 121,000 square miles. This translated to a population density ratio of six people per square mile, thus making open space the state's most abundant commodity. These physical characteristics would prove significant in attracting both military and scientific interests to New Mexico during and after the war.

Prior to World War II, the state capital claimed a mere 20,000 residents, bested only by Albuquerque's 35,000 inhabitants. Author/journalist V. B. Price captured the essence of the bustling railroad town. "By 1940, Albuquerque was a confusing, if heart-warming, jumble of incongruities," he opined. "It was a rough and tumble cow town and regional shopping center that served ranchers, farmers, miners and reservation Indians." Price added, "The city was the commercial capital of one of North America's few centers of Hispanic culture in a state governed largely by bilingual Hispanic politicians."

State census figures showed just three other communities with populations exceeding 10,000—Las Vegas, Roswell, and Hobbs—and eight others—Raton, Las Cruces, Tucumcari, Gallup, Clovis, Carlsbad, Portales, and Silver City—with between 5,000 and 10,000 people. State officials claimed 62,000 miles of highways, two-thirds of which were unpaved and designated as rural. Transportation service in and out of the state was limited to three railroads (the Santa Fe, the renamed Denver & Rio Grande Western, and the Southern Pacific), numerous intrastate and interstate bus lines, and one major air service (TWA). Standard entry into New Mexico was via automobile on either of two crisscrossing thoroughfares—U.S. 85, running south-north from Texas to Colorado and beyond, and U.S. 66, running east-west from Chicago to the Pacific coast.

The state's economy in 1940 was diversifying yet still overwhelmingly traditional. Professor Szasz's provocative essay "New Mexico during the Second World War," offers the following succinct summary:

> Straddling the northern and middle Rio Grande Valley and stretching west to Zuni, Pueblo Indians tilled the land as their ancestors had done for centuries. In the northwest, Navajo herdsmen pastured their sheep and goats throughout their sprawling reservation in New Mexico, Arizona and Utah. Scores of compact Hispanic farm villages dotted the central Rio Grande Valley as well as the northern counties, where people spoke a Spanish dialect that Coronado's soldiers would easily have recognized. In the far northwest Latter-Day Saints had created a thriving agricultural community along the San Juan River, whereas Anglo American cattle and sheep ranches, usually hailing from states of the former Confederacy, dominated the southern plains and fertile Mesilla Valley.

The advent of the petroleum industry offered another economic boon. As the WPA guide proudly heralded, there were more than twenty-one hundred producing oil wells in Lea County alone, no doubt contributing to the oil boom in the state's southeast corner and the attendant 244 percent population increase, said to be "the highest population growth rate for a New Mexico county during any decade of the twentieth century." The quest for "black gold" in the northwest sector of the state accounted for a modest population increase (16.4 percent) there as well, spread among traditionally agricultural communities like Farmington, Aztec, and Bloomfield.

Despite these impressive statistics, ranching and agriculture prevailed as the state's chief economic endeavors in 1940. According to the guide's index, New Mexico's gross income from "all classes of livestock and livestock products" totaled $40 million that year, compared with $36 million derived from petroleum revenues. As U.S. entry into the European conflict appeared inevitable, New Mexicans prepared to satiate the appetite of a nation at war.

The eventual military mobilization provided a ready market for New Mexico's foundering lumber industry. Most sawmills in operation before the Great Depression had fallen silent by 1940. As was also true of the mining industry, global conflict instantly rejuvenated what had been considered to be a fading economic venture. The cordon of Army Air Corps training bases that appeared virtually overnight near Albuquerque, Alamogordo, Clovis, Roswell, Carlsbad, Ft. Sumner, Deming, and Hobbs clamored for unprecedented quantities of manufactured wood products to construct barracks, hangars, administrative buildings, hospitals, and officers' quarters.

The prolific stands of harvestable timber—in the Sangre de Cristo Mountains near the mill towns of Chama, Lumberton, and El Vado; the Nacimiento near Cuba and Jemez Springs; the Zuni west of McGaffey; and the Mogollon southeast of Reserve, Luna, and the village of Mogollon—were prime sources for much-needed spruce, pine, and oak construction materials. Ready access to rail lines, combined with an embryonic trucking industry, enabled the transport of fresh-cut lumber from remote mill sites to destinations across the state.

The war also resuscitated the nearly defunct mining industry. Increasing nationwide demand for manufactured steel and the industry's decision to decentralize by building modern steel plants in the West, created a thriving regional market for locally mined coal. Federally-subsidized steel mills in Pueblo, Colorado, Provo, Utah, and Fontana, California, consumed all of the bituminous coal (used as coking material) they could get their hands on. Although Colorado Fuel & Iron (CF&I) located its new plant near Pueblo in southern Colorado, the company held leases in northern and central New Mexico. America's newest steel producers quickly demonstrated their craving for the abundant coal-enriched veins buried underneath Los Cerrillos, Madrid, and Dawson, along with the seemingly inexhaustible supply near Gallup. In 1940, Gallup and Raton accounted for 90 percent of the state's total output. At its peak the industry reported two hundred mines operating in New Mexico, employing upwards of five thousand people, most of them Hispanic.

Copper, zinc, and other nonferrous metals were of such importance to the war effort that they could not be produced fast enough or in sufficient quantity. Copper, long valued for its electrical conductivity, had the capacity to alloy with tin to form bronze and with zinc to form brass. These characteristics made copper especially critical to the manufacture of planes, tanks, warships, and munitions. The historic mines in Grant County—Fierro, Santa Rita, and Tyrone—remained the premier copper producers in the state's southern sector, converting to open-pit mining methods to satisfy wartime demands. Up north, near the old colonial town of San Antonio del Río Colorado (today's Questa), lay the only known molybdenum and manganese mines in New Mexico. These metals proved vital to the war industry for their steel-hardening attributes.

Meantime, traditional ranching and agricultural communities—like Artesia and Hobbs in the south, as well as Aztec, Bloomfield, and Farmington in the San Juan Basin—were undergoing painful metamorphoses into petroleum boomtowns. Blue-collar roughnecks and field hands, many of them African Americans from the former cotton-producing states of Texas and Oklahoma, converged upon Lea, Eddy, and to a lesser extent Chaves, Roosevelt, and San Juan counties. While never in the production category of its neighbor states, New Mexico contributed its share of oil to the Atlantic coast via a network of transcontinental pipelines—dubbed "Big Inch and Little Inch"—for shipment to military operations overseas.

Toward the end of the war, a curious, accidental discovery occurred in central New Mexico near Grants that would prove to have a

The Rattlesnake oilfield, looking toward Shiprock in northwestern New Mexico, was the state's earliest oil discovery (1924). This photograph, taken in May 1941, shows the well still in production during World War II. (Photograph by the Department of Tourism. Courtesy of New Mexico State Records and Archives, negative no. 7747.)

significance long after Germany and Japan both capitulated. Sometime during the early 1920s, Hollywood mogul Stella Dysart invested in property at Ambrosia Lake near Grants with the intent to drill for oil. After twenty-five years of dry holes and near bankruptcy, Dysart's foundering enterprise uncovered a seventeen-foot seam of pure uranium. In previous decades private industry had mined deposits of vanadium near the town for commercial use, mainly as a bonding agent in house paint. During the war vanadium's capacity to temper steel significantly increased its value.

Inasmuch as the military and scientific development of an atomic weapon remained top secret until the events at Hiroshima and Nagasaki, uranium, a derivative of vanadium, as yet had no commercial value. Production of the atomic bomb nearly halted entirely in the face of limited supplies of fissionable U-235, derived exclusively from mines located deep in the Belgian Congo. In the aftermath of World War II and with the onset of the Cold War, New Mexico once again figured prominently as a national source for nuclear material.

The state's ranching and agriculture commitments during the war inspired "revolutionary" changes in the industry after the war. The New Mexico directory estimated 41,369 ranches and farms dotted the local landscape. Most of these were small, irrigated subsistence farms owned by or leased to Hispanic and American Indian families. In the northern counties, victims of severe drought and an ever-shrinking land base, the tenuous nature of agricultural production was such that local observers wrote, "Individual holdings, divided as families increased in size, have become so small that now often half of the adult male population of the rural farming communities is obliged to leave their homes for as much as half of the year to seek work and wages in the industrial area."

If New Mexico hoped to have any agricultural impact on the national wartime economy, it would have to come from the larger, commercial enterprises that, with a few exceptions (the Bell Ranch in Harding County), were located on the southern periphery of the state. For the most part the days of extensive cattle (30,000 head) and sheep (500,000 head) operations had long since passed. Most cattle herds in 1940 hardly exceeded 3,000 head, whereas sheep men generally maintained flocks of 10,000 to 20,000 animals. Meanwhile, the federal Food for Victory campaign during the war encouraged local farmers and ranchers to increase productivity, a feat that appeared unattainable for most local agriculturalists. The military's demand for fresh fruits and vegetables and quality-grade beef, pork, and poultry could not be ignored, however. Less obvious but certainly just as critical was the need to supply blankets, flight jackets, and other winter apparel fashioned almost exclusively from the products of sheep ranchers. "Wool and beef will win this war," was the mantra of the day on the western home front.

Although wanting to satisfy their patriotic duty, New Mexico ranchers and farmers well understood that theirs was a fragile land made even more vulnerable by the rigors of the Great Depression. Most agreed that "it [New Mexico] could never absorb a dramatic expansion of pasture for cattle or sheep." "Thus, industry spokesmen viewed their wartime assignment as less a call to produce 'more' than to produce a 'better' product." The decision to shift emphasis from quantity to quality proved enormously successful. With the help of research specialists assigned to various state agricultural institutions in Las Cruces and Portales, local ranchers and farmers raised the state standard for commercial stock breeding and cultivation practices.

Heretofore-marginal agricultural communities like Portales and Tucumcari in eastern New Mexico, along with Hatch and Las Cruces in the south, emerged as economic giants after the war. Farmers in Portales, for example, experimented with exotic "specialty" crops such as peanuts. In Las Cruces, it was pecans and pistachios. Near Socorro they cultivated grapes. These crops replaced more traditional products such as pinto beans and green chile, for which New Mexico was the leading producer in 1940. Local farmers' and ranchers' willingness to veer away from standard practices and become more innovative in the cause of national patriotism transformed an unstable agrarian economy before World War II into a consistent pacesetter during peacetime. One scholar summarized, "New Mexico had been scorned by the East for producing poor cotton, low-grade wool, and inferior cattle. By mid-century the state's agricultural production ranked favorably with that of any other state in the nation."

In the absence of experienced local farm labor, lost either to the draft or West Coast defense plants, New Mexicans turned to an unexpected source. Beginning in 1943, farmers from communities surrounding Lordsburg and Roswell relied on an estimated eight to ten thousand detainees in nearby POW camps as a prime source of labor. Before the war, a number of these German and Italian prisoners had grown up in the rural farmlands of Europe. Their familiarity with planting and harvesting methods, farm machinery, and animal husbandry made them a valued resource for New Mexico farm owners. This symbiotic exchange between prisoner and farmer lured many ex-POWs back to the state after the war.

For all of the manpower and resources New Mexico pledged to America's war machine, nothing compared with the enormous, life-altering contributions resulting from scientific research and development. The two focal points for all of this scientific activity were Los Alamos, located in the Jemez Mountains northwest of Santa Fe, and a barren strip of desert near Alamogordo known as the Tularosa Basin. In the fall of 1942 the outlook for a swift conclusion to war on three continents was grim. The U.S. Navy had not fully recovered from Pearl Harbor; Japanese naval power seemed invincible. The Japanese Imperial Army's lightning-swift sweep across the Philippines, British Malaya, Indonesia, and French Indochina was testimony to its might and efficiency as well. Meantime, the United States was heavily engaged in North Africa against the German and Italians.

More ominous still, reputable eastern and western European scientists, barely escaped from Hitler's tyrannical regime, brought rumors of German progress—although its success was uncertain—in developing a fissionable weapon. In response, the Roosevelt administration authorized the Manhattan Project under the auspices of the U.S. Army Corps of Engineers. In September 1942, the army promoted Leslie R. Groves, former project construction supervisor for the Pentagon, to the rank of temporary brigadier general and appointed him to oversee the top-secret undertaking as overall military commander. Groves's academic counterpart was University of California, Berkeley, physics superstar J. Robert Oppenheimer. Three separate components, each assigned specific tasks, constituted the Manhattan Engineering District: Site W, located in Hanford, Washington, was assigned to produce enriched, weapons-grade uranium; Site X in Oakridge, Tennessee, was to attain the same objective, but using plutonium; and Site Y, yet to be determined, would design and test the nuclear device designed using the two radioactive elements.

After months of intensive reconnaissance for a suitable Site Y location that considered but rejected sites in Nevada, California, and Utah, Groves and Oppenheimer determined the isolated, cliff-bound surroundings of the Pajarito Plateau, north of Santa Fe and west of Española, to be ideally suited for the project's primary research facility. Oppenheimer, a victim of tuberculosis at an early age, was familiar with the arid atmosphere and juniper-studded ambiance of the Jemez Mountains. He praised the selection for its "openness and invigorating mountain air." More important, the broad plateau, which appeared on older maps under the collective Spanish name Los Valles del Monte, offered plenty of room for expansion.

Centuries before the appearance of any Europeans, Puebloan people occupied the land and utilized its resources. Antonio Sánchez, the first known Hispanic homesteader in the area, did some dry-farming on the plateau from 1885 to 1911, after which Harold Hemingway Brook built the more permanent settlement he called Los Alamos Ranch. In 1917, Brook's property passed to a retired Detroit auto manufacturer—rumored to have ridden with Teddy Roosevelt's Rough Riders during the Spanish-American War—who converted the old homestead into a boy's ranch. A devotee of outdoor recreation like his former commanding officer, Ashley Pond believed boys should become men through hard work and a strenuous lifestyle. The Los Alamos Ranch School enjoyed short-lived success in the face of nagging financial difficulties, despite generous annual donations from benefactor Edward J. Fuller, for whom Pond named the school's principal building.

When General Groves and Oppenheimer expressed an interest in purchasing the school, Pond eagerly responded. The government appraised the land and its ancillary buildings at $224,000. To the owner's dismay, the army "used condemnation proceedings to take over the school and decreed all records for the transaction immediately sealed." Next, the army ordered classes to terminate at the end of the semester in December, when it assumed ownership of the rustic campus.

Notably, the War Department completed its task on December 7, 1942, exactly one year after the Pearl Harbor debacle.

From January through May 1943, the corrugated canyons of the plateau echoed with construction activity that bordered on total chaos. As many as 1,500 army construction workers and private builders hurriedly fabricated the unsightly compound that would soon house the first wave of an anticipated three hundred scientists and technicians. (Oppenheimer originally planned for no more than one hundred occupants). Historians estimate that during the peak of activity in mid-1945 "the total population of the 'secret city' numbered 6,000 scientists, technicians, dependents, and military personnel." First to arrive was a cadre of elite—in some instances Nobel Prize–winning—scientists from the German-occupied territories of Europe. General Groves referred to the unprecedented assemblage of world-class notables—Edward Teller, Enrico Fermi, Richard Feynman, Hans Bethe, Niels Bohr, George Kistiakowsky, Ernest O. Lawrence, and John von Neumann among others—as "the largest gathering of crackpots ever assembled."

Despite the often acrimonious relationship between the civilian scientists and military administrators, the alleged "crackpots" accomplished their seemingly impossible task in just two years' time. "Working fifteen-hour days, six days a week," Szasz noted, "the scientists produced two types of nuclear weapons: a uranium bomb, Little Boy, which destroyed Hiroshima, and a plutonium weapon, Fat Man, which destroyed Nagasaki."

Once the bombs were assembled, determining the best location to test these devices of unknown destructive potential was even more problematic. During the intervening years between 1943 and 1945, the army considered several different localities as possible nuclear test areas. Those sites included Colorado's San Luis Valley, the Barrier Sand Reef in South Texas, the army's training area in California's Mojave Desert, an island off the coast of southern California and three potential sites in New Mexico—the El Malpais area near Grants, the area southwest of Cuba, and the Tularosa Basin.

According to military historian Tom Starkweather, the military established a stringent set of physical criteria with which to evaluate a site: (1) the location had to be relatively flat to minimize the blast effects; (2) weather patterns had to be favorable; (3) the site had to be isolated from centers of population, yet be close enough to Los Alamos for easy transport of men and materials; and (4) no Indian occupants were to be uprooted in the process. The requirement of proximity to Los Alamos eliminated Texas and California, thus leaving New Mexico as the army's only viable option.

Concurrently, both the USAAF and the U.S. Navy were in search of a suitable location as a firing range to test guided missiles and long-range artillery. Their search led them to the notoriously barren Jornada del Muerto (Journey of the Dead Man), situated near the Texas–New Mexico border. At the time, two military installations—Alamogordo Army Air Field (renamed Holloman Air Force Base in 1948) and the massive army training center at Fort Bliss in El Paso—had laid claim to the vast, meagerly populated wasteland. In an act that must have seemed providential to leaders of the Manhattan Project, the War Department, after an exhaustive search of sites in Nevada, Utah, and California, selected the Tularosa Basin as the joint military long-range missile and rocket proving grounds. In his fascinating history of what became White Sands Proving Grounds (WSPG) Starkweather reports, "The first documentation I have been able to find . . . is a Memorandum for the Under Secretary of War from the Office of the Chief of Engineers, dated 2 February 1945, subject: Acquisition of Proposed Rocket Range in New Mexico for Ordnance Department."

The newly christened military facility satisfied all of the criteria as a Manhattan Project test site as well. Located in a basin at an elevation of 4,000 feet, the stark strip of Chihuahuan Desert, approximately 125 miles in length by 41 miles at its widest point, appeared virtually uninhabited except for a few scattered ranches and one pitiful mining operation. Best of all, "ninety-five percent of the 877,000 acres was under federal ownership or state contract." Finally, the selected location was accessible to rail transportation in nearby Alamogordo and showed great potential for vehicular accessibility to Las Cruces via a pass between the San Andres and Organ mountains (modern-day U.S. 70).

On July 9, 1945, the War Department publicly announced the establishment of White Sands Proving Grounds in Doña Ana and Otero counties. One week later, Los Alamos scientists designated their test area the Trinity Site. After constructing a hundred-foot steel tower to elevate the so-called Gadget, the Trinity team detonated the world's first atomic explosion, said to have contained such force that "the sound waves broke windowpanes as far away as Gallup." The day the weapon's destructive power was demonstrated at Hiroshima, it was rumored to be the equivalent of two hundred tons of TNT. A young war correspondent named Walter Cronkite, unable to fathom an explosion of such magnitude, corrected the figure to read "20 tons" before sending the report to United Press offices stateside. World War II ended one month later.

When news reached America on October 4, 1957, that the Soviet Union had beaten the United States into space with the successful launching of *Sputnik 1,* comedian Bob Hope was said to have quipped, "Apparently, their German scientists are better than our German scientists." While the revered Hollywood personality tried to minimize the dramatic impact the landmark achievement had on most Americans, no one was laughing. The scientific triumph underscored the seriousness with which both the Americans and the Soviets viewed what news correspondents nicknamed the Cold War.

During a news conference held in Minsk immediately after the momentous event, a boastful Nikita Khrushchev taunted the American scientific community, saying, "If Germans helped Russians, why don't Germans help the United States?" He added, "After all, the American troops seized the chief designer of the V-2, took him to America, and now he builds rockets there." Unbeknownst to most Americans at the time, the Soviet chairman had referenced two top-secret programs that began as Operation Overcast and gradually evolved into one called Operation Paperclip. Under the latter program, the army interrogated captured German scientists with the aim to deploy them to America.

After Hitler's defeat in May 1945, it became abundantly clear to military and civilian officials in the United States, France, and the United Kingdom that the Soviet Union stood poised to fill the political vacuum left after the German surrender. In all likelihood, conjectured members of the Joint Chiefs of Staff, the Soviets would emerge from World War II as the foremost military rival of the United States.

For these reasons, as the American and the Red armies converged on Berlin in early 1945, the capture of personnel and material associated with Germany's vaunted rocketry and missile programs was of paramount importance.

As the fall of Berlin became inevitable, Dr. Wernher von Braun, technical director for the experimental V-1 and V-2 rocket station in Peenemünde, Germany, assembled his most experienced scientists and technicians. "Let us not forget that it was our team that first succeeded in reaching outer space," von Braun began. "Each of the conquering powers will want our knowledge; to what country shall we entrust our heritage?" By unanimous decision, his scientific team voluntarily surrendered to the Americans not only themselves but also an estimated fourteen tons of plans, designs, and detailed notes accumulated from years of experimentation with rocket propulsion. After preliminary interrogations, during which time the army conducted exhaustive background investigations on each of their captives, 126 German scientists and technicians, along with one hundred dismantled V-2 rockets, were transferred to the rocketry testing facility still under construction at WSPG in southern New Mexico.

While the scientists' stay at WSPG and Fort Bliss was of relatively short duration, each former Nazi scientist was offered a five-year contract to work for the U.S. Army. In return, the army promised housing for them and their families, who remained in Germany until their immigration to America could be arranged. While at WSPG, the Germans proved invaluable in translating technical documents and instructing American scientists on the nuances of the V-2 rocket.

Although the German assistance proved enormously helpful in developing the U.S. missile and space programs, the presence of former Nazi Party members in this country was a direct violation of President Truman's dictum that explicitly prohibited anyone associated with the Nazi Party or Hitler's military regime from entering the country. The justification for the egregious breach of postwar policy was, not surprisingly, the Cold War. Former Eighth Air Force commander Lieutenant General Carl "Tooey" Spaatz summarized the military thinking at the time: "Occupation of German scientific and industrial establishments has revealed the fact that we [the United States] have been alarmingly backward in many fields of research. If we do not take this opportunity to seize the apparatus and the brains that developed it and put the combination back to work promptly, we will remain several years behind while we attempt to cover a field already exploited."

The willingness of top German scientists to share in-depth knowledge with their American cohorts enabled the United States to accelerate its rocketry and space programs without "having to start from scratch." It remains an indisputable fact that Neil Armstrong's landing on the moon in 1969 was in large measure courtesy of von Braun's rocket team. The German involvement was not without controversy, however. America's adopted hero von Braun was a good case in point. An admitted member of the Nazi Party—though he made the disclaimer that he was forced to join or be banned from all future scientific activity—von Braun held the prestigious position as technical director at Peenemünde. That facility was notorious for its use of forced labor brought in from nearby concentration camps. As director of a highly successful armaments program, von Braun could not escape the fact that his rockets were built on the graves of more than twenty thousand Polish and Russian prisoners.

In his haste to exploit the services of von Braun and his team of scientists, Allen Dulles, director of the Central Intelligence Agency (CIA), "ordered the scientists' dossiers sanitized before they departed Germany." No doubt von Braun and his fellow ex-Nazis welcomed their new identities and the promise of a prosperous new life in postwar America. In 1949, the secretary of the army transferred the Ordnance and Research Division at Fort Bliss to the Redstone Arsenal near Huntsville, Alabama. Among those transferred were von Braun and his elite entourage. In 1970 von Braun was appointed director of the National Aeronautics and Space Administration (NASA) facility in Huntsville.

In contrast to the German program, America's rocket science program had its incubation period on the sands of southern New Mexico. When asked during their intensive interrogations where German scientists had learned the fundamentals of rocket propulsion, they chorused in unison, "from your American scientist, Dr. Robert Goddard." The suggestion that the U.S. rocketry program had to "start from scratch" following World War II ignored the fact that since the summer of 1930, Goddard had supervised fifty-six test flights near Roswell, seventeen of which exceeded altitudes of one thousand feet.

Although Robert Hutchings Goddard was a native of Worcester, Massachusetts, the wide open spaces of the West beckoned to him early in life. Infatuated with the science fiction tales of Jules Verne and H. G. Wells, the naturally inquisitive young Goddard once described his personal dream: "How wonderful it would be to make some device which had even the possibility of ascending to Mars." For most of his adulthood Goddard relentlessly pursued that goal. With financial assistance from the Smithsonian Institution, he designed and tested the world's first known liquid fuel rocket on March 16, 1926. Goddard's genius quickly caught the attention of national icon Charles Lindbergh and renowned philanthropists Daniel and Florence Guggenheim, whose financial backing enabled the tireless scientist to work full time on his rocket designs. Desiring to properly test the rockets in flight, Goddard coveted the arid spaces of southern New Mexico near Roswell. Why Roswell? What eventually became Goddard's test area had flat terrain, a favorable altitude, consistent climate, and most important, a community of fewer than ten thousand inhabitants. In 1934, to the townspeople's utter amazement, Lindbergh and his wife visited Goddard's laboratory at Mescalero Ranch, in the Eden Valley just outside Roswell.

Despite acquiring 214 personal patents, Goddard proved unable to convince the navy or army of the long-term viability of his inventions. Ironically, it was left to German scientists—von Braun and his chief propulsion engineer, Konrad Dannenberg—to apply Goddard's knowledge of solid fuel rocketry to create the most destructive weapon loosed upon Europe during World War II, the dreaded V-2 "vengeance weapon" rocket that assailed London, Paris, and Antwerp virtually at will.

German-born civilians residing in the United States became unsuspected threats to America's war effort. For all of the security measures General Groves applied to keep the atomic bomb a secret, he had no way of knowing the project's innermost details had already been passed on to the Russians. Klaus Fuchs, a German-born, British-educated member of the Communist Party who joined the Manhattan

Project in 1943 with other British scientists, was the instrument of stealth and treason. A brilliant physicist, Fuchs immediately impressed the American team, especially mathematician Hans Bethe, supervisor of the project's theoretical division. One military scholar observed that as a trusted member of Bethe's team, Fuchs "couldn't have been better placed to provide the Soviets information about the U.S. atomic bomb program." At one meeting with Harry Gold, his Soviet courier, Fuchs handed over, "a precise drawing with measurements of the Fat Man bomb that was eventually dropped on Nagasaki."

After the war, Fuchs returned to England, where he continued his work at the Harwell Atomic Research Establishment. On December 21, 1949, four months after the Soviet Union successfully detonated its first nuclear device, British intelligence officers arrested Fuchs on suspicion that he had passed on classified material to the Russians. During his subsequent trial, which lasted only two hours, Fuchs admitted his guilt. Not only had he provided the Soviet Union with detailed information on the atomic bomb, he also passed on in-depth details regarding the so-called Super Bomb (hydrogen bomb), which reportedly had one hundred times the destructive force of its predecessor. Fuchs, it was later revealed, was not the only Soviet spy embedded at Los Alamos. However, his treacherous activities from 1943 to 1950 caused the most long-term damage to U.S. national security. The outcome served to heighten Cold War tension between the United States and the Soviet Union by placing the two global superpowers on a collision course.

The immediate negative reaction within the scientific community to the success of Little Boy and Fat Man was wholly unanticipated. Nuclear physicists across the country, most of whom had been involved in some capacity in the bomb's creation, publicly protested the military's continued research on atomic weapons. As far as they were concerned, America's goals had been satisfied with Japan's surrender; their task was finished. Project director Robert Oppenheimer, reputed to have uttered a phrase from Hindu scripture, "I am become death, the destroyer of worlds," as he witnessed the ominous mushroom cloud at the Trinity Site, concurred. In 1949 he recommended the U.S. "not embark on a crash program to build the H-bomb."

Inevitably, the national uncertainty about ongoing atomic research threatened the future of scientific activity in Los Alamos. From the onset, planners of the Manhattan Project never intended that Site Y be a permanent research facility, as evidenced by the haphazard manner in which it was built. More menacing were the congressional debates centered on the question of whether future nuclear development should remain strictly in the hands of the military or be transferred to civilian authority. The outcome would affect the military-directed activities in northern New Mexico.

There appeared to be no pressing need for Los Alamos after Hiroshima and Nagasaki. Oppenheimer resigned as director in October 1945, only to have the federal government revoke his "Q" security clearance nine years later because of his early leftist leanings. Most of his scientific team found jobs as faculty members at the country's most prestigious universities. Finally, the indefatigable General Groves announced he would relinquish his duties at Los Alamos to the Atomic Energy Commission (AEC), established on January 1, 1947. The acerbic commander, however, did not plan to leave without assuring Los Alamos's continued presence in New Mexico.

In the words of Professor Szasz, "the question, then, was not should the government desert the field of atomic research, but should the field of atomic research desert the mesas of northern New Mexico?" At first, the ever-skeptical Groves favored transferring ongoing work in Los Alamos either to a more populous urban locality or to one of several major West Coast universities. The qualities that made Los Alamos an ideal site for the America's most secret undertaking during the war had become a deterrent to the military imperatives of the Cold War.

Oppenheimer's hand-picked successor to supervise the once-vibrant scientific community did not agree. Norris Bradbury, the former naval commander whom Oppenheimer had recruited from the Physics Department at Stanford University, harbored loftier plans for LASL. Because of its near-iconic reputation, Bradbury envisioned the laboratory as a place with the potential to become a national—if not world—pacesetter in scientific research. Furthermore, the lab's isolation and mountainous setting might prove beneficial in recruiting a new generation of instructors, scientists, and technicians to Los Alamos. In response to his professional colleagues' backlash against future nuclear applications, Bradbury proposed Los Alamos become the center of research on the peaceful uses of atomic power.

Groves was on board with Bradbury's ideas. Before leaving the West, he presented a convincing argument to the AEC in favor of keeping LASL in place, at least for the time being. Groves pursued a more practical approach than Bradbury. First, he argued it would take the government no less than two years to find a suitable site to relocate the lab. In an appeal to Republican fiscal conservatism, he reminded the AEC that $75 million had already been expended to establish the laboratory in New Mexico. In summary, Groves concluded, "The only solution, therefore, is to stay at Los Alamos for at least the next few years, and to improve the existing facilities to such a degree as is necessary."

It seems that even Groves greatly underestimated LASL's growth potential initiated under Bradbury's direction. What was intended to be a six-month, interim position evolved into a twenty-five-year directorship from which Bradbury retired in 1970. The facility's workforce grew from the approximately one thousand remaining employees in 1946 to an estimated thirteen thousand workers employed by the laboratory in 2010. Near the end of World War II, Oppenheimer and Groves decided to transfer the lab's engineering department, or Z-Division to Kirtland Army Air Field in Albuquerque. The division renamed itself Sandia National Laboratories in honor of the reddish-hued mountains visible east of the city. Combined, the scientific facilities in Los Alamos and in Albuquerque enabled New Mexico's unprecedented postwar expansion in the coming decades.

The Cold War pallor that shrouded the world community in fear from 1945 to 1965 centered upon two mutually expressed commitments by two superpowers: (1) the buildup of nuclear weapons arsenals, driven in large measure, by an all-consuming fear of mutual self-destruction; and (2) a national obsession to launch a man into space. The significance of the Soviets' successful launch of the world's first satellite was not the 184-pound object itself. Rather, it was the awesome power it took to hurdle *Sputnik 1* beyond the Earth's gravitational pull. Just four years earlier, the USSR had exploded its first hydrogen bomb;

Sputnik demonstrated to the outside world the Russian capability to deliver a payload—likely a nuclear weapon—thousands of miles away. The implications were especially unnerving to the United States. Within six months, Congress increased the national budget for space research and development from a half-billion dollars annually to an impressive $10.5 billion. One year after *Sputnik's* ascent, President Eisenhower authorized the creation of NASA, and by executive order, transferred all Department of Defense (formerly the War Department) responsibilities for satellite and space projects to the civilian agency. With respect to what became popularly known as the "space race," New Mexico played a low-profile but nonetheless significant role in preparing future American astronauts to land on the moon.

As mentioned earlier, the army transferred all missile research activities from the Southwest to the Southeast in October 1949. Von Braun and his team of specialists did not depart WSPG before supervising the successful launch of a modified V-2 rocket designed under a military program called Project Bumper. The event marked the first time a U.S. missile left Earth's atmosphere. After their move to the Redstone Arsenal in Huntsville, Alabama, the German scientists proceeded with a vengeance. Competing with the navy (which had been directed by President Eisenhower to build the Vanguard rocket, essentially from scratch), von Braun's team members worked to modify and improve their Redstone model for the army. In less than a decade they designed and tested the technology for the Redstone, Jupiter, and Jupiter-C intermediate range ballistic missiles, each model more sophisticated than the previous version.

The Vanguard rocket, contracted to the Glenn L. Martin Company, showed great potential to become the first American vehicle to reach orbital altitude. However, during its nationally televised launch, the rocket lifted off a few feet, sputtered, and exploded into a gaseous inferno. Concurrently, the Jupiter-C missile, "Flew 3,355 miles; attained an altitude of 682 miles, achieved a velocity of Mach 18 (eighteen times the speed of sound) and carried a retrievable nose cone large enough to hold a passenger." To no one's amazement, the German-designed Jupiter-C carried America's first orbital satellite, *Explorer* 1, into space in early 1958.

These early achievements led to larger and more powerful multi-stage rockets—the Atlas and the Titan—that enabled the nation's first manned spaceflight on May 5, 1961. On that cloudless, humid morning at Cape Canaveral, Florida, Naval Commander and Mercury Program astronaut Alan B. Shepard, Jr., piloted the country's first successful suborbital flight. As a reward for their numerous contributions to the American space program, thirty-nine of Redstone's German-born scientists, including von Braun, and the wives of two other Operation Paperclip immigrants were awarded U.S. citizenship

As German scientists in Huntsville worked feverishly to design the vehicle that would eventually carry a man to the moon, American medical specialists in New Mexico analyzed the adverse aspects of prolonged space travel on the human body. Once again, Holloman Air Force Base outside Alamogordo and nearby WSPG provided the settings for these extraordinary events. The army called the program Project Manhigh. Its objective was to use manned, high-altitude balloons to measure the debilitating effects of sustained exposure to the sub-stratosphere. Historians have referred to the volunteers for these life-threatening experiments as "pre-astronauts." Craig Ryan, the foremost authority on the subject, described them as "a small fraternity of daring, brilliant men [who] made the first exploratory trips into the upper stratosphere to the edge of outer space in tiny capsules suspended beneath plastic balloons."

Army Colonel John Paul Stapp, a graduate of the Baylor University Medical School and the "world's fastest human," the first person known to exceed six hundred miles per hour strapped to a rocket sled, led the team of daredevils. Included among the handful of team members were German-born aeronautical engineer Otto C. Winzen, who designed the lightweight, aluminum-enclosed gondola that would in years to come serve as the prototype for the Mercury space capsule.

On August 16, 1960, an air force test pilot named Captain Joseph "Little Joe" Kittinger voluntarily bailed out of a high-altitude balloon at an astounding 102,800 feet—19.5 miles—to determine the impact on the human body. During his free-fall, Kittinger became the first man to approach the speed of sound (741 mph) without the benefit of an enclosed vehicle. His jump exceeded six hundred miles per hour (Mach 0.9) and lasted thirteen minutes. The *Albuquerque Journal* reported on July 26, 2012, that Austrian extreme athlete "Fearless Felix" Baumgartner had completed a second stratospheric leap of 96,640 feet—18 miles—in his ongoing attempt to break Kittinger's fifty-two-year-old record. After a successful landing on the desert floor near Roswell, Baumgartner promised to return to southern New Mexico to attempt a jump from 125,000 feet—23 miles—to claim Kittinger's seemingly invincible record. Kittinger, who turned eighty-four during that week, was on hand to cheer the Austrian parachutist on. Three months later, Baumgartner returned to southern New Mexico, landing successfully after jumping from 128,097 feet (25 miles) from above the earth's surface. During his free-fall, Baumgartner traveled at Mach 1.24 (833.9 mph), making him the first human to break the sound barrier without benefit of an enclosed vehicle or spacecraft.

The fearless space warriors of the early 1960s contributed mightily to the success of the Mercury and Gemini space programs. In the ensuing decades pioneer astronauts relied on the 9.6-mile-long "supersonic" sled at Holloman Air Force Base to measure the effects of extreme gravitational force. Such innovations made the southern New Mexico facility an icon in early aerospace experimentation.

Albuquerque-born William Randolph "Randy" Lovelace II was among the many medical doctors of his generation fascinated with the emerging field of space medicine. A second-generation physician, Lovelace earned his medical degree from Harvard University in 1934, after residencies at Bellevue Hospital in New York and the famous Mayo Clinic in Rochester, Minnesota. Prior to America's entry into World War II, Lovelace volunteered as a flight surgeon with the Army Medical Corps Reserve. His primary focus was to research the detrimental effects of high-altitude flights on pilots and crew members.

To this end, Lovelace designed and patented a high-altitude, removable oxygen mask that proved to be a valued contribution to aerial combat personnel in both combat theaters. Many American lives had been lost when pilots and crew members exited their aircraft at high altitude without the benefit of oxygen. Lovelace was not above using himself to test his theories and inventions. In June 1943, Colonel

Lovelace volunteered to conduct an experiment in emergency egress from a bomber flying at forty thousand feet, well above the altitude limit of humans' ability to breathe normally. Although he had never parachuted before, Lovelace unhesitatingly donned his oxygen mask, attached to a small oxygen canister taped to his leg, and exited the plane. The force of the parachute's deployment at high altitude knocked him unconscious. He nearly suffocated and experienced frostbite from the frigid temperature at that height, but survived the jump, proving that high-altitude egress was dangerous but possible.

Lovelace's exploits made him a local hero. He returned to Albuquerque after the war and with his uncle, a victim of as well as medical expert on pulmonary disorders, founded the nonprofit Lovelace Foundation for Medical Education and Research in 1947. Three years later, the Lovelace Foundation built a modern, state-of-the-art clinic on the corner of Gibson and Ridgecrest, today's Lovelace Hospital. The new clinic quickly became a mecca for young physicians interested in the treatment of tuberculosis and other pulmonary ailments. By building Lovelace Clinic, the Lovelaces preserved Albuquerque's reputation as a premier recuperative destination for tubercular patients since the early 1900s. In addition, the modern facility established a new legacy as a pioneer in advanced medicine. One source observed, "The clinic opened the state's first intensive care unit, first virus laboratory and first nuclear medicine laboratory."

In the late 1950s Lovelace Clinic gained national recognition as a leader in aviation and space medicine research. In 1959, perhaps because of the younger Lovelace's previous connection with the aviation community, NASA awarded the New Mexico facility a contract to perform a battery of strenuous physical and psychological tests on thirty-two candidates competing to become Mercury astronauts. Although *The Right Stuff*, the popular epic of the Mercury space program by novelist Tom Wolfe, cast Albuquerque in an unfavorable light, the city earned national respect for its part in the ultimate selection of the famous "Mercury Seven" astronauts. To his credit, Lovelace proposed a similar battery of tests for women, whom he believed should be qualified for space travel, just as the female Soviet cosmonauts were. In 1964 President Lyndon B. Johnson, who was instrumental in moving the NASA Space Center to Houston, appointed Lovelace NASA's director of space medicine.

Tragically, the innovative New Mexico physician did not have the opportunity to witness Neil Armstrong and "Buzz" Aldrin's momentous "giant leap for mankind" in July 1969 as millions of other Americans did. In 1965 a small private aircraft carrying Lovelace and his wife on holiday to Aspen, Colorado, struck a mountain, killing all passengers on board. It seems a strange irony that the man who survived a harrowing parachute jump from forty thousand feet would some twenty-two years later die in a plane crash.

The continuous stream of people from all corners the United States during the postwar years fostered a cultural renaissance in New Mexico during which regional art, literature, and music flourished. Albuquerque became a haven for ethnic and feminist activists during the 1960s and 1970s, replacing Santa Fe and Taos as the epicenter for postwar modernist activity. The ethnic expressions of artists such as Luis A. Jiménez, Luis Tapia, Diego Romero, Emmi Whitehorse, and Maurice Dixon are excellent visual examples of this particular period. Similarly, the works of Judy Hahn, Jane Abrams, Harmony Hammond, Anne Noggle, and Judy Chicago represented the emergence of the statewide feminist art community. Finally, sculptors Tony Price and Roger Sweet, painter Eugene Newmann, and photographers Beatrice Mandelman and Patrick Nagatani poignantly addressed the antiwar and antinuclear protests that dominated the 1960s and 1970s.

A pervading ethnicity—both American Indian and Hispanic— energized New Mexico's art scene and presaged the highly politicized ethnic consciousness that reached its zenith in the 1960s. The civil rights movement, the Chicano movement, and the American Indian Movement (AIM) were all by-products of postwar urbanization. An entire generation of people of color abandoned their rural identities, lured to the frenetic urban centers of the American West, such as Albuquerque, Denver, Phoenix, Seattle, and Los Angeles. Subtle protests against the impact of postwar modernization on the land, as detected in the paintings of Roswell-born Peter Hurd or the stark realism associated with the black-and-white images of Albuquerque photographer Eliot Porter, are reminders of the unyielding attributes of the southwestern landscape.

The postwar twentieth century stimulated the emergence of cultural tourism as both Indian and Hispanic artists indulged in a creative renaissance. The widespread success in the 1930s of San Ildefonso potters María and Julian Martínez and other indigenous artists, such as Crescencio Martínez, Awa Tsireh, and Tonita Peña, set the standard for energetic new artists and artisans to carry on the tradition. Since the resurrection of Santa Fe's Spanish Market in 1965, an entire generation of Hispanic artists and artisans has ascended to national prominence. Charles Carrillo, Gloria López Córdova, Félix López, and Arlene Cisneros Sena are but a few of the rising stars who have endeavored to revitalize the Hispanic arts tradition.

In similar fashion, the literary standouts of the period highlighted the difficult postwar transition from a rural, traditional lifestyle to an urban, modernized society. Rudolfo Anaya, Edward Abbey, and Tony Hillerman, all three giants in their genres, best exemplify this generation of writers. Rudolfo Alonso Anaya was born during the nadir of the Great Depression in the tiny village of Los Pasturas, not far from Santa Rosa, where he spent his childhood. After graduating from Albuquerque High School in 1956 he enrolled in a local business school. At the urging of his wife, Patricia, Anaya left his business training to major in English at the University of New Mexico with the aim of becoming a fiction writer.

Ironically, Anaya's first prize-winning publication, *Bless Me, Ultima,* was in many respects an autobiography of his early years in rural New Mexico. In this provocative work, Anaya tells the story of a young, impressionistic boy who befriends a local *curandera,* a spiritual healer with knowledge of herbal remedies. Through her Antonio learns to deal with the typical confusion of adolescence by embracing the profound influences of his Hispanic culture and Catholic faith. In Anaya's sequel, titled *Heart of Aztlán,* Antonio's father moves the family to Barelas, a long-established barrio in Albuquerque near the railroad yards. During his painful transition to city life, Antonio learns to survive in a harsh, fast-paced world in which the values he most cherishes are threatened by his need to assimilate in a bicultural society. Thousands of ex-GIs who returned to their rural villages in New Mexico only to emigrate to major urban centers in search of work and a more vibrant life identified with Anaya's work in the 1960s.

Ed Abbey, from the coal country of Pennsylvania, used the GI Bill to attend the University of New Mexico, where he earned degrees in English and philosophy, while becoming a defender of the desert landscape. *Desert Solitaire* (1968), his deeply personal and poetic nonfiction critique of overdevelopment and the positives of desert wilderness and isolated slickrock canyons, captured the attention of the new conservation movement. His most famous novel, *The Monkey Wrench Gang* (1975), set in New Mexico and the Four Corners region, spurred the radical arm of the environmental movement along with the creation of such fringe groups as Earth First! His protagonists—including an Albuquerque surgeon and his assistant, a Jack Mormon river guide, and Vietnam vet and munitions expert George Washington Hayduke—engage in recreational activities of burning or chainsawing roadside billboards, which expand to sabotaging environmentally threatening development projects, such as Glen Canyon Dam. During the 1970s, the fictional "Hayduke" and his eco-warriors became cult heroes. Although he distanced himself from radical environmental organizations, Abbey used his acerbic wit and acidic pen to harshly criticize industrial tourism, welfare ranchers, land developers, and chambers of commerce. Texas writer Larry McMurtry called Abbey the "Thoreau of the American West."

Oklahoma-born Anthony Grove "Tony" Hillerman, like many of his neighbors, left the farm to join the army during World War II. He returned to New Mexico a highly decorated combat veteran and found work as a newspaper journalist. His fledgling success as an author earned him a teaching post in the Journalism Department at the University of New Mexico. From 1970 to the early 2000s, Hillerman produced a compendium of best-selling novels that all took place on the Navajo reservation. Using "Navajo building blocks" to produce first-rate mysteries, Hillerman underscored the clash between traditional Navajo culture and religion, represented by Tribal Police officer Jim Chee, and the modern technological world. His countercultural opposite is Joe Leaphorn, a streetwise metropolitan detective who over the years has become far removed from his American Indian upbringing. Like Anaya, Hillerman emphasized the issues of postwar change in traditional reservation life and the challenges of negotiating between two cultures.

If Memphis and Nashville spawned legendary performers like Elvis Presley, Jerry Lee Lewis, and Johnny Cash, Norman Petty Studios in Clovis introduced Buddy Holly, Roy Orbison, and the Fireballs to radio audiences across America. Petty converted a local grocery store into a first-rate recording facility that became the Southwest equivalent of Sam Phillips's nationally renowned Sun Records. A native of Clovis and a professional musician in his own right, Petty was just twenty-seven years old when he launched Charles Hardin "Buddy" Holley to stardom (when the media repeatedly misspelled his last name, Buddy adopted "Holly" as his professional name). Holly, who had just failed miserably in his attempt to record his compositions in Nashville, blossomed in the more relaxed and creative atmosphere just ninety miles up the road from his hometown of Lubbock, Texas.

Together, Petty and Holly created the "Clovis Sound," a country-rock style that permeated the airwaves from 1957 until Holly's tragic plane crash two years later. Other celebrities contributed to Petty's musical success. Roy Orbison, the operatic-voiced soloist from nearby Wink, Texas, recorded his first of many stellar hits in Petty's studio. George Tomasco, lead guitar virtuoso for the Fireballs, hailed from Raton. Petty's recording and engineering genius enabled Tomasco's band (which recorded under the name the String-Alongs as well as the Fireballs) to rival California-based surf bands—the Ventures (actually from Tacoma, Washington) and the Chantays—for a spot on the national charts.

Other New Mexico imports who left their stamp on the national music scene included Rosalie Hamlin, composer and lead singer for Rosie and the Originals; Glen Campbell, who as a talented teenage guitarist left Delight, Arkansas, to join his uncle's band, Bill Williams and the Sandia Mountain Boys; and a recent transplant to Santa Fe from Nashville named Randy Travis. Hispanic standouts in the regional and national music field include Roberto Griego, Al Hurricane and his son Al Jr., Darren Cordova and his band Calor, Española's Los Blue Ventures de Louis Sánchez, four sisters from Albuquerque known throughout the Latino music world as Sparx, and Tobías René, whom former Governor Bill Richardson designated the "King of New Mexico Music."

The quarter-century following World War II was a period of persistent change. During those years the state population not only increased but diversified. Prior to Pearl Harbor, New Mexico counted slightly more than a half-million inhabitants, the majority of whom were of Hispanic descent. By 1960 that figure had doubled to more than 950,000, and in the following forty years it doubled again, reaching 1.8 million in 2000. In the second half of the twentieth century Hispanics, for the first time in the state's history, were no longer in the majority. Not only did the European American and American Indian populations increase during this time, but an influx of African Americans, Asians, Pacific Islanders, and other peoples augmented the once–predominantly Spanish-speaking population.

With the advent of the twenty-first century, the recreation and tourism industry challenged—if not eclipsed—all other forms of economic endeavor in the state. New Mexico's scenic and recreational amenities, anchored by a system of state and national parks and the Albuquerque International Balloon Fiesta, have become must-see global attractions. Recent progress on a proposed Spaceport in south-central New Mexico, and the controversial, though comedic, depiction of alien beings in a media campaign that advertised the "universal" appeal of the state, speak to the optimistic, if not futuristic, self-image of a state irrevocably altered by the forces of wartime technology and postwar geopolitics.

CHAPTER 11

Reach for the Sky
Balloons, Space Science, and Civic Boosterism, 1965–2012

> One of the results of Sputnik was that instead of having a war, we
> had a race. The prize was the moon and the repercussions were far-
> reaching. . . . There was an unprecedented infusion of technology
> to both cultures. Sputnik is in the laptop. It's in the cell phone. It's in
> almost everything we see in modern life. The space race forced us to
> create new technology. I think it compelled us to better ourselves.
>
> PAUL DICKSON, *SPUTNIK: THE SHOCK OF THE CENTURY*

ON THURSDAY, SEPTEMBER 18, 2008, nearly ten thousand exuberant spectators packed themselves into the city of Española's central
plaza to hear presidential candidate Barack Obama speak. The municipality, which according to the U.S. Census of 2000 claimed 9,688 residents, nearly doubled in size the day of the event. "The line waiting
to get in stretched about two miles," reported one local columnist.
"When the plaza was full, more people crammed into the spaces outside the barriers." The crowd was justifiably euphoric. Not since John
F. Kennedy's brief stop in the remote, mostly Hispanic community in
1960 had a nationally viable presidential candidate visited northern New
Mexico. In his address, Obama challenged New Mexico voters, especially those of Hispanic origin, who until the surprising outcome in the
election of 2004, had consistently voted Democrat, to "step up"; that is,
let their numbers influence the outcome of the forthcoming election.
In singling out the Hispanic electorate in New Mexico, Obama was in
fact addressing the national Spanish-speaking community, especially the
escalating population living in the West. Since 2000, as recently affirmed
in the 2010 U.S. Census, Hispanics have represented the largest single

minority in the United States. Recent demographic surveys, moreover, have predicted that three out of every five births in the United States during the next quarter-century will be to parents of Hispanic origin.

Obama's visit to Española, which some journalists identify as the "gateway to the Hispanic north," was one of several scheduled stops in different sectors of the state during the campaign. Television political analysts interpreted the gesture as the candidate "paying his respects to the voters who just might put him over the top in the presidential election." Rival candidate John McCain also held political rallies in New Mexico with the hope of luring the Hispanic vote based on his military service record and his unwavering stance against abortion. From all appearances, New Mexico, the much-maligned backwater, the non-English-speaking territory once deemed unworthy of statehood, had politically come of age. In previous elections, no state had proved itself to be more unpredictable. In 2000 Al Gore carried the state by a few hundred votes; four years later, Republican candidate George W. Bush shocked the nation by narrowly winning the state. Local news correspondents reasoned that the 2008 "shootout" in the West conceivably could come down to one state. "If that state turns out to be New Mexico, Hispanic voters could make the difference," said one. "Forty percent of adults there [New Mexico] are Hispanic." Although the one-state prediction did not prove true, President Obama did carry New Mexico by a significant margin. He won the popular vote in the state again in 2012, but with a slightly smaller majority than in 2008.

While the 40 percent figure appears quite accurate for the percentage of Hispanics across the state as a whole, the ratio is substantially higher in Rio Arriba County at almost 72 percent. As the Hispanic population in other sectors of the state eroded in the wake of massive Anglo immigration in 1879, the northern counties remained decidedly ethnic, in part because of their geographic isolation and limited availability of marketable land, with tracts belonging to eight of the state's nineteen pueblos. As noted earlier, the state lost its Hispanic majority to Anglo numerical increases for the first time in the 1960s. At the same time, however, New Mexico mirrored the demographic trends of the remaining Southwest and Pacific coast states, which saw influxes of recent immigrants from Mexico and Central America.

New Mexico's transformation from a sparsely populated, agrarian based, Spanish-speaking territory into an expanding industrial and technological community with a racial mixture of inhabitants began in earnest after World War II. Add to this the unsettled atmosphere of the Cold War years, which not only ensured the ongoing presence of the military and scientific communities in New Mexico, but facilitated their expansion far beyond their wartime capabilities. At every turn, a cadre of astute, well-seasoned congressional leaders positioned themselves to enable the state's economic and political metamorphosis. As the traditional postwar economy strengthened, New Mexico's indulgence in more volatile sources of revenue—heritage tourism, outdoor recreation, civic boosterism, and the film industry—increased with measured confidence during each coming decade.

Sustainable change has not taken place without pain, however. Cultural coexistence has not always been easy. Legal haggling over civil rights, water rights, and property rights has tempered the collective hope of a utopian lifestyle in the romantic—if not mythical— Southwest. Also at risk is humans' ability to "live in harmony" with nature. Like other western states, New Mexico's hydrologic resources are finite. The great reclamation projects of the late 1950s and early 1960s have failed to alter the fact that New Mexicans reside in a desert—a "high" desert, but nonetheless fragile. If New Mexico ever experiences another range war such as the famous Lincoln County debacle of the 1870s, the battle will be over water, not cattle.

Equally vulnerable is the landscape itself. Natural calamities such as wildfires and floods have become a routine consequence of living in the West. History has shown that federal and state bureaucracies have not always chosen the path most beneficial to the state in the long term. Los Alamos National Laboratory, the heroes of World War II scientific development, also left an ominous legacy in the form of subsurface toxic waste. The controversial Waste Isolation Pilot Plant (WIPP) site in southern New Mexico is a short-term remediation—though not necessarily the ideal solution—to a long-term problem. Despite these issues, New Mexico welcomes its second century as an administrative entity with unfaltering confidence. The blueprint for a successful future was carefully drafted during the last five decades of the twentieth century.

Much of New Mexico's postwar modernization can be attributed to three basic elements: a pervasive military presence, persistent scientific advancement, and a persuasive congressional delegation. One issue that surfaced at war's end concerned the status of the military air fields in New Mexico. The army had abandoned half of them by the fall of 1947, the year the National Security Act designated the U.S. Air Force an independent branch of the military. The outbreak of the Korean War in 1950 and the specter of U.S. involvement in a major land confrontation on the Asian continent provided ample justification for the reactivation of military bases throughout the West. New Mexico found itself in an especially favorable position to retain a high-profile, military presence as the Korean stalemate hopelessly dragged on.

By this time a senior member of Congress, Senator Dennis Chavez had ascended to the chairmanship of the prestigious Senate Subcommittee on Defense Appropriations. With his introduction of the Defense Department Appropriation Bill (H.R. 12378) to the Senate floor in July 1958, El Senador almost single-handedly underwrote an unparalleled peacetime expansion of the nation's armed forces. He endorsed funding for America's first nuclear submarine, the B-52 bomber (the workhorse of the Vietnam War), the Polaris missile system, and the first atomic-powered aircraft carrier, and he supported awarding millions of dollars to scientific research and development.

Concurrent with Chavez' appointment, his senatorial colleague, Clinton P. Anderson, became a member of the congressional Joint Committee on Atomic Energy (JCAE). This appointment in 1951 virtually assured New Mexicans that scientific research at Los Alamos and Sandia Labs would continue unabated. Like hundreds of newcomers before him, Anderson, a South Dakota farm boy matriculated to Dakota Wesleyan University and the University of Wisconsin School of Journalism, before relocating to New Mexico to seek a cure for tuberculosis. In a few short years, he became one of Albuquerque's most respected insurance businessmen and a rising star in the Democratic Party.

Anderson's baptism into national politics came during the Great Depression when he accepted an appointment as the second director of the New Mexico Emergency Relief Authority. From 1941 to 1945 he served in the U.S. House of Representatives, but resigned to accept a cabinet post as secretary of agriculture in the Truman administration. Four years later Anderson successfully ran for the U.S. Senate and took his seat beside senior incumbent, Dennis Chavez, in January 1949. From that time until the latter's death in 1962, the two veteran bureaucrats, with help from longtime House Democrats John J. Dempsey, Antonio M. Fernández, and his successor, Joseph M. Montoya, secured a revitalized military presence in New Mexico.

To that end, Chavez oversaw the appropriation $51 million to expand and improve existing military installations and scientific research facilities in the state. Alamogordo Army Air Field, renamed Holloman Air Force Base in 1948, was now home to the Air Force Materiel Command and became a major test site location for pilotless aircraft, guided missiles, and aerospace research. Under its new designation, Cannon Air Force Base (1957), located just west of Clovis, became a training center for F-86 Sabre fighter pilots bound for Korea. Roswell Army Air Field, renamed Walker Air Force Base, hosted the 509th Bombardment Group, comprising the B-50A Super Fortress (precursor to the B-52), the B-36 Peacemaker, and the KC-97 aerial refueling tanker. In 1960, one month before the Cuban Missile Crisis, Atlas missile silos dotted the Roswell landscape, giving the air force its first offensive nuclear strike capability from the interior West. At the time of its closure in 1967, Walker had become the largest Strategic Air Command (SAC) facility in the country.

The lion's share of the Department of Defense allocations were directed to Albuquerque's Kirtland Air Force Base (1948). In a unique civilian-military partnership, Kirtland AFB became headquarters for the Air Force Special Weapons Center, while Sandia National Laboratories (SNL) assumed responsibility for all scientific research and development. The merger set the stage for a new era of base expansion. In 2000, Kirtland AFB reported 23,000 employees, including 4,200 active members of the 188th Fighter-Bomber Squadron of the New Mexico Air National Guard, and an estimated annual economic contribution to the state of $2.7 billion. Correspondingly, the city's population grew from 35,000 in 1940 to an astounding 201,189 by 1960, with a modest increase to 244,501 during the 1970s.

As chairman of the Senate Public Works Committee, Senator Chavez wielded enormous influence in the civilian sector as well, especially in the areas of transportation improvements and highway construction. Returning from Europe profoundly impressed with Germany's *Autobahn*, President Eisenhower announced his "Grand Plan" to place 50 billion dollars' worth of highways under immediate construction. Ever mindful of the miserable condition of primary and secondary roads in his home state, Senator Chavez voiced early support for Eisenhower's proposal. "Hitler's staff laid out across Germany a system of magnificent four-lane highways," Chavez reminded his congressional colleagues, while "America is slogging along in 1952 on roads inadequate for even 1935's traffic." One government survey reported automobile production had increased from 65,000 cars in 1945 to 3.9 million at the end of the decade. During that time national roads became functionally obsolete as narrow paving standards and antiquated engineering severely retarded their carrying capacity.

U.S. Highway 66 historically traversed New Mexico en route to Los Angeles from Chicago. Route 66 attained mythic status in 1946 in part because of Bobby Troup's lyrical road map, popularized in song by Nat "King" Cole, and Albuquerque publisher Jack Rittenhouse's entertaining *Guide Book to Highway 66*, which described in vivid detail the entire 2,295-mile stretch of highway. The "Mother Road" did not fare well during the war years, however, and by all accounts fewer travelers by 1942 were "getting their kicks." While America's railroads transported soldiers and sailors to various duty stations and points of embarkation, lumbering eighteen-wheel trucks transferred war materiel from coast to coast. Not a well-built highway to begin with, Route 66 proved to be especially vulnerable to the excesses of wartime trucking.

While the roadway enjoyed a near miraculous revival after the war, civic leaders identified the deterioration of Route 66 as one of the New Mexico's major postwar issues. Under the guiding hand of Senator Chavez, Congress authorized an unprecedented $845 million for the National System of Interstate and Defense Highways. Accordingly, the Federal Highway Act of 1956 allocated $14 million to New Mexico on a 50-50 matching basis for proposed roads construction during the first of a projected ten-year program.

The threat of another protracted war in the Pacific fed what President Eisenhower later criticized as the "military-industrial complex." Two examples of the postwar phenomenon in New Mexico centered on the wholesale exploitation of the state's enormous natural gas deposits. The high cost of oil, kerosene, and gasoline resulting from wartime shortages created a new market among national consumers. Considered a waste by-product within the oil industry, natural gas was generally "flared" rather than captured. The postwar demand for natural gas as an alternative heat source coincided with the discovery of San Juan County's Barker Dome gas field in 1945 on the Colorado–New Mexico border. Petroleum engineers calculated the new recovery (thought to be in the trillions of cubic feet) would yield 127 million cubic feet (MCF) daily for the next twenty years.

In the planning of the major petroleum companies, the immediate problem was how to supply consumers, especially the incipient West Coast metropolitan areas—San Diego, Los Angeles, San Francisco, Seattle, and Portland. The solution was an interstate transmission pipeline similar to those used to transport oil and aviation fuel during the war. Senators Anderson and Chavez emphasized the strategic value of such a pipeline in their effort to secure congressional funding. By 1955 more than 6,400 gas wells were in production in Blanco, Bloomfield, Kutz Canyon, and Fulcher Basin (all in San Juan County). The mass influx of geologists, petroleum engineers, and fieldworkers to Farmington between 1950 and 1965 nearly tripled the town's population, making it the region's only municipality to exceed 50,000 people.

In 1953 the Federal Power Commission authorized the El Paso Natural Gas Company to build an interstate pipeline and to increase the proposed delivery of natural gas to the Pacific coast to 800 MCF daily. The company's merger with the Pacific Northwest Pipeline Company a year later enabled the West Texas–based firm to employ hundreds of Anglo, Hispanic, and Navajo construction workers and complete the 1,400-mile pipeline in April 1955. As demands for natural gas exceeded the industry's ability to keep pace, El Paso Natural Gas proposed the use of an underground nuclear device to "fracture" deeper, gas-bearing rock formations in an effort to create more recoverable gas. (Today this process, called fracking, often involves high-pressure hydraulic applications.)

The idea of using a nuclear device for commercial purposes was rooted in President Eisenhower's "Atoms for Peace" proposal before the United Nations in December 1953. After his presentation eighty nations pledged to encourage research on the peaceful uses of nuclear energy. The U.S. commitment, endorsed by New Mexico's Senator Anderson, now chairman of the JCAE, fell under an umbrella program known as Project Plowshare, inspired by the Old Testament.

One of the two inaugural atomic blasts under the new federal program took place near Carlsbad. Despite objections from the National Park Service and several local potash mine owners that the ten-kiloton nuclear blast might collapse the world-famous caverns, Project Gnome took place on December 10, 1961. Senator Anderson commissioned a National Academy of Science study in advance of the experiment to assure local residents of the project's safety. The JCAE wasted little time in touting the dramatic event as "the world's first atomic blast for wholly peaceful purposes." Six years later, the JCAE returned to New Mexico, this time in partnership with El Paso Natural Gas. Code-named Project Gasbuggy, the subsurface detonation took place near Gobernador on December 10, 1967. The event promised to be the first cooperative effort between the federal government and the private sector to use atomic power for commercial purposes. Although the twenty-five-kiloton blast—larger than the devices dropped on Hiroshima and Nagasaki—caused much anxiety among two nearby communities (Farmington, New Mexico, and Durango, Colorado) the outcome of the blast was disappointing. The nuclear experiment failed to release significant amounts of fractured gas.

The petroleum industry's recent application of highly pressurized water in lieu of nuclear fission to enable captured oil and gas deposits to move more freely has proven more successful in the recovery of new sources of oil and gas from shale deposits dominant in several western states. The industry's latest technological achievement has inspired a petroleum renaissance across the West that promises to eclipse most of the known global sources of petroleum.

Dallas Federal Reserve Bank observers have described renewed oil and gas activity across the Permian Basin (encompassing West Texas, southern and northern New Mexico, and southwest Colorado) as "frenetic." In the hundred-year-old oil patch once believed exhausted, science-driven techniques of hydraulic fracturing have rendered heretofore-impervious deposits of oil and natural gas recoverable in inestimable quantities. The oil-laden communities in Eddy, Lea, and Chaves counties in the south and San Juan County in the north are booming as never before. A combined 6.2 percent jump in employment in these various boomtowns did much in 2012 to improve the state's otherwise dismal employment record as workers scramble to fill petroleum-related jobs. One source reported "numerous rail terminals and several pipelines under construction all through the southwest in an effort to move their [petroleum] products to major oil and gas refineries in the West."

Not all results of the latest oil and gas activity have proven completely satisfactory. As a leading producer of natural gas in the country, New Mexico faces a unique dilemma. Gas deposits are being produced in such staggering quantities that the supply far exceeds the demand, especially in light of recent global warming, which has minimized the impact of winter weather nationwide. During the past drought-ridden decade, the market for natural gas to be used strictly as a heating source has dramatically declined, causing serious concerns within the petroleum industry. Conversely, environmentalists see natural gas production as "a means to transition away from coal and oil to renewable sources of energy such as wind and solar." Toward this end, Public Service of New Mexico (PNM) has emerged as a leader among western states in its expansion of wind farms and solar plants. In 2011, wind and solar power provided the energy needs of more than 8,000 homes in southern New Mexico. In its 2014 Renewable Energy Plan the company anticipated a significant increase in those numbers.

The state welcomed its returning servicemen and -women with guarded exuberance. World War II veterans—hoping to begin life anew with a good job, affordable housing, and opportunities to further their education—were profoundly disappointed, perhaps even shocked. New housing starts in Santa Fe virtually ceased during the war. Building materials—lumber, plywood, and electrical and plumbing supplies—were redirected toward the war effort. Private contractors were either drafted into military service or were under contract to work for the government. Thus, when hundreds of thousands of veterans returned from overseas duty, there were no new housing developments or apartment complexes to accommodate them. In desperation, the Santa Fe chamber of commerce proposed housing veterans in the recently abandoned barracks at the Japanese internment camp located on the edge of town. Moving their families into lodging that had once been occupied by ethnic Japanese detainees—albeit American citizens, not Japanese-born POWs—would have proven problematic for veterans just returned from the Pacific theater. Another option was to relocate original CCC housing for use in Santa Fe. By the fall of 1946 city officials estimated five hundred new housing units were needed to satisfactorily accommodate returning veterans.

Fortunately for Santa Fe, Allen Stamm, recently discharged from the U.S. Navy, determined to fill the void by designing modest, adobe-style homes priced at between $10,000 and $15,000 each. He purchased lots on the nearly desolate west side of town, and within a decade built a thousand homes to accommodate 15 percent of the city's population. Equally attractive to the returning service men, Stamm's construction firm employed 168 mostly Hispanic carpenters, electricians, and other construction laborers. As a result of Stamm's effort—and later Albuquerque's Dale Bellamah—the postwar construction industry ranked third behind government and tourism as Santa Fe's leading business venture. New neighborhoods such as Casa Linda and Casa Alegre required schools and shopping centers within a short driving distance, and the effect was to shift the city's population distribution along present-day Cerrillos Road.

Stamm had a reputation as a man of integrity, and his firm may have been more the exception than the rule: veterans throughout the United States complained that good-paying jobs were so scarce and the competition for them so fierce that employers profited by paying less than a livable wage. Furthermore, women, who had filled a critical vacuum in the nation's defense industry left by thousands of men pressed into military service, were now asked to relinquish their jobs to returning male veterans. Unfair employment practices were common in the United States immediately after the war. The growing number of underemployed veterans and women in New Mexico, however, found a champion in Senator Chavez.

One of the fundamental planks of Chavez's 1946 reelection campaign was an appeal for fairness and equal treatment among all Americans, and he did not limit his concern to employment practices. The senator's commitment to civil and human rights apparently stemmed from his personal experience with discrimination growing up Hispanic in an underdeveloped region dominated by corrupt territorial officials. Chavez also became a voice for women during and after the war, arguing for wage parity between male and female officers who served in the medical corps. Gender discrimination within the army had become so notorious that women refused to enlist as nurses. Fearing the long-term impact on America's war effort, Chavez persuaded the War Department to reverse its policy and grant equal pay to female officers.

On being reelected and returning to Congress in March 1947, Senator Chavez promptly cosponsored a bill to revitalize the wartime Fair Employment Practices Commission (FEPC), established to minimize if not eliminate discriminatory practices among defense contractors. The bill failed to reach the Senate floor, however, after meeting formidable opposition from Southern Democrats. Undaunted, Chavez introduced the bill three more times but to no avail. Despite his failure to win approval for the FEPC, Chavez had introduced an idea that was clearly ahead of its time. Not until the passage of the Civil Rights Act in 1964, two years after the senator's death, were all citizens of this country guaranteed equal treatment under the law.

Some returning servicemen and servicewomen of color experienced overt racism. Sadly, these veterans were reminded that their service to their country had not changed the situation at home. In one of his many firebrand speeches to Congress, Senator Chavez attacked these inequities. He referenced an incident in South Texas in which a non-Hispanic funeral home owner denied Private Félix Longoria, killed in the line of duty while serving in the Philippines, the right to be buried in his hometown cemetery. Chavez reminded his fellow senators that if a person of ethnic origin was expected to die for his country, he or she was entitled to the same rights and privileges as all other American citizens.

In the less populated reaches of New Mexico, American Indian veterans were vying for the same treatment afforded their non-Indian counterparts. Nearly 25,000 American Indians from various tribes served in the armed forces during World War II. Their cumulative decorations—fifty-one Silver Stars, forty-seven Bronze Stars, and thirty-four Distinguished Flying Crosses—constituted an impressive record of service. Yet more than thirty-six hundred Navajo, Pueblo, and Apache veterans returned to New Mexico only to learn they still were barred from voting in the upcoming 1946 general election.

The Indian Citizenship Act of 1924 (also known as the Snyder Act) granted full U.S. citizenship to America's indigenous people. By 1947 states with large Indian populations, except Arizona and New Mexico, had extended voting rights to the nation's newest citizens. New Mexico based its denial on Article VII, Section 1, of the 1912 state constitution, which denied suffrage to "Indians not taxed." While the tribes as a whole were reluctant to challenge the provision for fear they might jeopardize their status as sovereign nations, Michael H. Trujillo, a schoolteacher from Laguna Pueblo and former staff sergeant in the U.S. Marine Corps, refused to be denied his right to vote. Trujillo, at the time an employee of the Bureau of Indian Affairs, became a dissident voice representing twenty thousand Indian people in New Mexico.

Trujillo had the support of the federal government. In 1947 the Truman-appointed President's Committee on Civil Rights published a report condemning the disenfranchisement of Indians in New Mexico and Arizona. The report argued that as U.S. citizens American Indians were subject to all manner of state and federal taxation with the exception of assessments against lands held in trust. In the committee's opinion, to deny Indians the vote stood in violation of rights guaranteed to all citizens under the Fifteenth Amendment of the U.S. Constitution. Based on this fundamental premise, Trujillo challenged the state constitution in federal court and won. In a stunning reversal on August 3, 1948, a federal triumvirate ruled that the New Mexico statute violated the Fifteenth Amendment and was, therefore, null and void. Thirty-six years after gaining statehood, New Mexico finally granted the right to vote to its American Indian citizens.

Nevertheless, it took the New Mexico legislature five more years to amend the constitution of 1912. Some scholars argue that the political climate of the late 1940s enabled Trujillo to challenge the longstanding issue. It was, after all, the beginning of the Cold War; it would have seemed hypocritical for the United States to condemn Soviet tyranny while denying its own citizens suffrage. It is more likely that Trujillo and his legal advisers seized the opportunity to press the point that thousands of New Mexico's Indian people had answered their country's call to duty so should not be denied one of the "inalienable" rights for which they fought and died.

As the battle for individual rights morphed into a full-fledged civil rights movement by the mid-1960s, the voice that resonated loudest in New Mexico was not that of politically disaffected college students or riot-bent urban mobs gathered in Roosevelt Park. Rather, it was the voice of a fiery, Texas-born Pentecostal minister named Reies López Tijerina. While student protests against the Vietnam War at all the major state universities were in step with campus behavior on the national level, Tijerina's rural-based movement brought a unique twist to the civil rights movement.

A longtime political dissident and fugitive from the law in Texas and Arizona, Tijerina found a cause in New Mexico that catapulted him to national prominence as a civil rights leader. While hiding in Gobernador during the late 1950s, Tijerina befriended a local rancher named Don Manuel Trujillo, who educated the innately curious Texan about the history and the tragedy of Spanish/Mexican land grants. During a brief hiatus in Mexico, Tijerina became familiar with archival material detailing the legitimacy of original grants of land to New Mexican colonists before 1848. He also familiarized himself with the Treaty of Guadalupe Hidalgo, the document that ended the war with Mexico, especially the original draft that guaranteed the property rights of all former Mexican citizens now living under American jurisdiction.

In 1958 Tijerina returned to New Mexico and invited eighty northern New Mexico families to sign a petition requesting the Eisenhower administration to investigate land claims they believed were illegally wrested from them through the American judicial system. After a curt, negative response from Washington, Tijerina returned to Mexico with the aim to appeal directly to President Adolfo López Mateos. After a second rejection, the Texas firebrand organized the Alianza Federal de Mercedes, which he incorporated in Albuquerque on February 2, 1962. The grassroots organization, headquartered in the northern New Mexico village of Tierra Amarilla, pledged to "organize and acquaint the heirs of all Spanish land grants with their rights under the Treaty of Guadalupe-Hidalgo." The enormous popularity of the Alianza, especially in the northern, mostly Hispanic sector of the state, resulted in a membership exceeding 20,000. At the time of the organization's first state convention in 1966, it was rumored the wife of incoming Republican Governor David Cargo was a dues-paying member.

The Alianza's political activism—and in time, flagrant civil disobedience—lost it the support of middle-class urban Hispanics. Most viewed Tijerina at best as an outsider and at worst as a dangerous agitator. U.S. Senator Joseph Montoya, who won Senator Chavez's seat in 1964 shortly after the latter's death, publicly denounced Tijerina and his organization, saying, "The last thing Spanish-speaking New Mexicans need is agitation, rabble-rousing and the creation of false hopes." Montoya further cautioned, "Tijerina is an outsider who sparked violence, set back racial relations, and [is] an enemy of the United States."

Many resident Santa Feans agreed. During a public presentation at St. John's College in October 1967, Tijerina offended the audience when he "decried older European and Jewish races for despoiling the heritage of what he called a new breed of Hispanos." At one point the local chapter of B'nai B'rith labeled him an anti-Semite. The gradual dissipation of the land grant movement and the inevitable demise of the Alianza resulted in part from a fundamental lack of support among the state's urban population. The grassroots organization was a collection of rurally based, disenfranchised farmers and ranchers who pinned their hopes on an oratorical demagogue. By the summer of 1967, all of the Alianza's aspirations were shattered.

In October 1966, about three hundred Alianza members, a handful of them armed, occupied Echo Amphitheater Park near Tierra Amarilla, proclaiming it the "Republic of San Joaquín de Chama," after the name of a major colonial land grant. In the process, the claimants issued visas to tourists and made a citizens' arrest of two U.S. Forest Service rangers who had been sent to investigate the situation. The crowd tried and convicted the rangers of trespassing, then released them. Five days later federal and state law enforcement officers arrested eleven Aliancistas, charging them with destruction of government property and assault on two federal employees. Reies Tijerina evaded capture and was kept in hiding by local villagers. On the morning (June 5, 1967) of the defendants' hearing in the Rio Arriba County Courthouse, Tijerina led an armed raid in a bold attempt to free his compatriots, among them his younger brother Cristóbal. While Tijerina's violent antics may have earned him the admiration of local villagers—journalists referred to him as "King Tiger"—his disregard for the law brought the power of the state's law enforcement agencies and the local National Guard to bear on the unsuspecting rural New Mexico population.

The sight of combat-ready troops riding armored vehicles, escorted overhead by jet fighters deployed from Kirtland Air Force Base, must have shocked farmers and sheep ranchers armed only with hunting rifles. In effect, Governor Cargo declared martial law in northern New Mexico. All suspected Alianza members were rounded up and placed in outdoor holding pens. The massive search for Tijerina, the escaped prisoners, and two captives was reported to be "the largest manhunt in New Mexico history." Tijerina eventually surrendered to legal authorities in Albuquerque and was charged with fifty-four criminal counts, including kidnapping and armed assault. He was ultimately convicted of destroying federal property and assaulting a federal officer, for which he served two years in prison. In 1970, the state extradited Tijerina to a federal prison in Texas, where he remained for a time. President Gerald Ford pardoned Tijerina in 1978.

Although the villagers of northern New Mexico harbor little hope of ever reclaiming their lands, the issue is still under legal deliberation. Since the Tijerina debacle, the state has endeavored to ameliorate the political disaffection that permeates northern New Mexico

Alianza members in northern New Mexico were confronted by armed National Guardsmen, armored vehicles, and even air support in the search for Reies López Tijerina in the fall of 1967, which was the state's greatest manhunt. (Photograph by Ray Cary. Courtesy of *Albuquerque Journal*)

to the present day. One positive outcome was the construction of a fully equipped, permanently staffed medical facility in Tierra Amarilla. Managed through a local cooperative headed by Anselmo Tijerina (Reies's older brother) and his wife, Valentina, La Clínica provides badly needed services to remote northern villages. For years Española, located one hundred miles distant, had the nearest medical facility, presenting an especially problematic situation in cases of dire emergency.

Despite the tragic circumstances that shrouded the infamous courthouse raid, land grant diehards invited the aging rebel back to northern New Mexico in recognition of the event's forty-fourth anniversary in June 2011. Introduced to a handful of loyalists in Alcalde, New Mexico, as "the most influential Hispanic ever to have lived in New Mexico," Tijerina, now eighty-four years old, displayed some of the fiery oratory that made him a local icon in the mid-1960s. True to form, one newspaper reported, Tijerina spun "conspiratorial theories about the history of land grants in Spanish and Mexican New Mexico," as well as about world politics in general, that in his view is driven by "Israel and Palestine, Jewish money, and Israeli intelligence."

The years 1965 to 1975 proved momentous for New Mexico. According to the 1970 U.S. Census, the state's population exceeded one million for the first time. While Albuquerque remained the state's largest metro complex with 244,501 people, New Mexico claimed at least nine communities—Santa Fe, Las Cruces, Rio Rancho, Roswell, Farmington, Alamogordo, Clovis, Hobbs, and Carlsbad with populations between 25,000 and 50,000 people. Although the Hispanic population remained in the minority (36 percent of the state's population), the ethnic awareness aroused in the 1960s carried into subsequent decades. In 1974 voters elected Las Cruces–born Democrat and former college athletic standout, Raymond S. "Jerry" Apodaca, the state's first Hispanic governor since Octaviano Larrazolo in 1919. Also in 1974 the Roman Catholic Church consecrated Robert F. Sanchez as the first native-born New Mexican archbishop of Santa Fe. Apodaca and Arizona's Raúl Castro, elected the same year, were the nation's only Hispanic governors in the United States at the time.

New Mexico also emerged as a major tourist destination, making tourism and outdoor recreation the state's most lucrative industries. Completion of New Mexico's portion of the interstate highway system in 1966 accounted in part for the success, along with the Albuquerque International Balloon Fiesta. These combined with such long-standing attractions as the Opera, Spanish Colonial and Indian Markets, and Fiesta (especially the burning of Zozobra, "Old Man Gloom") in Santa Fe; the Inter-Tribal Indian Ceremonial in Gallup; the New Mexico State Fair in Albuquerque; All American Futurity quarter horse races in Ruidoso; world-class skiing in Taos as well as numerous other resorts across the state; and a superb network of national and state parks and monuments.

The junction of Interstates 25 and 40 in Albuquerque was the only freeway interchange in the state when completed in 1966. Designed to accommodate 40,000 vehicles per day, the so-called "Big I" (for interchange) not only connected New Mexico with the remainder of the nation but directed the flow of interstate traffic from each cardinal direction into the general downtown vicinity. If the railroad divided Albuquerque into two distinct communities east and west of the tracks, the interstate freeway completed the division into four well-defined quadrants. As a result, older Hispanic communities—Old Town, Los Griegos, Atrisco, Barelas, Martineztown, and the entire South Valley—became cultural and geographic islands within the greater metropolitan area. In time, the city's population and commercial vendors inched outward from downtown into the Northeast Heights and the Sandia foothills, facilitating modernized shopping venues such as Nob Hill (1947) at Central and Carlisle, the city's first shopping center; and Hoffmantown (1951) at Montgomery and Wyoming, the first shopping complex, built in the Northeast Heights. During the following decade Winrock Center (1961), named after Winthrop Rockefeller, its chief benefactor, and Coronado Center (1964) followed. Both were located just off I-40 and represented the city's first fully enclosed shopping malls.

While Albuquerque sought to establish its identity as an emerging Sunbelt city during the 1960s, it remained for the most part a stopover point rather than a final destination for automobile travelers. It was just one of several fascinating curiosities along the mythologized Route 66 (I-40) journey through the American Southwest. With the city's introduction of the first International Balloon Fiesta in the spring of 1972, however, Albuquerque became an international "hotspot" for hundreds of balloon pilots and like-minded enthusiasts. The nine-day fiesta, held each year in October, hosts upwards of 750 balloonists, making it the "largest hot air balloon festival in the world."

The brainchild of KOB radio station manager Dick McKee and Sid Cutter (reputed to be the first person in New Mexico to own a hot air balloon), the first event attracted only thirteen balloonists from across the country. To the sponsors' surprise, twenty thousand people turned out to watch the first group ascension from the Winrock Center parking lot on April 8, 1972. Two years later Albuquerque moved the event to October to host the World Hot Air Balloon Championships, and by 1975, the fiesta had become an international event as well as a permanent fixture on the northern New Mexico calendar.

In the summer of 1978, Albuquerque residents Max Leroy "Maxie" Anderson and Ben Abruzzo, along with Larry Newman, were the first pilots to successfully complete a transoceanic flight from the United States to continental Europe in a hot air balloon named the *Double Eagle II*. Their daring adventure that summer established an international record for distance (3,107 miles) and flight duration (137 hours). The two New Mexicans had conceived the idea as a way to commemorate Charles Lindbergh's heroic flight fifty years earlier. Anderson, a self-made mining industry tycoon, continued his adventurous lifestyle, making the first attempt to circumnavigate the world in his updated balloon, the *Jules Verne,* on January 11, 1981. Anderson died in a tragic ballooning accident on June 27, 1983. Abruzzo died on February 11, 1985, when his private plane crashed near Albuquerque.

The aviation exploits of these two audacious New Mexicans secured for Albuquerque its reputation as the hot air balloon capital of the world. The number of registered participants in the 2000 fiesta peaked at 1,019 balloons, prompting the Balloon Fiesta Board to limit entries to 750 balloons since 2001. On any given day the event draws upwards of a hundred thousand spectators to watch the much-publicized mass ascension. In recent years smaller balloon celebrations have become annual events at Alamogordo, Angel Fire, Artesia, Clovis, Deming, Elephant Butte, Farmington, Gallup, Raton, and Silver City. In a sporting tragedy in the fall of 2010, Ben Abruzzo's son, Richard, and his copilot, Dr. Carol Rymer Davis of Denver, were declared lost on October 3 after their balloon plunged into the Adriatic Sea. The announcement cast a somber mood on Albuquerque's otherwise festive International Balloon Fiesta kickoff that year. The 2012 Albuquerque gathering was dedicated to balloon enthusiasts Abruzzo and Rymer Davis as well as to cofounder Sid Cutter, who had died earlier that year.

With New Mexico's reputation as a tourist mecca secured, state officials turned to the ski industry in hopes of making outdoor recreation a year-round attraction. Skiing as a recreational hobby originated in northern New Mexico in 1936 when local attorney Robert Nordhaus organized the Albuquerque Ski Club, and with the help of the CCC, cleared the first known trails in the nearby Sandia Mountains. Nordhaus left New Mexico in 1942 to help organize the U.S Army's Tenth Mountain Division in Colorado. The division saw combat against the Germans in Italy's Po Valley. Nordhaus, who visited Switzerland before returning home from Europe, became intrigued with the Europeans' efficient use of cable trams as a way to transport skiers up mountains.

Returning to Albuquerque, Nordhaus introduced the idea of building a cable tram near Sandia Peak to local businessman Ben Abruzzo, himself an air force veteran recently discharged from Kirtland. In the early 1950s, the two ex-servicemen combined their talents and finances to build the tram that today ascends to Sandia Peak Ski Area (originally called La Madera), despite the fact they could not convince a local bank to finance the enterprise. Years later Abruzzo's son Louis, who manages the company today, remarked, "It amazes me how much my father and Nordhaus were able to accomplish at a time when Albuquerque boasted relatively little capital."

In 1955 Nordhaus helped Coloradan Joe T. Juhan with the development of the Santa Fe Ski Basin. "At age 90 Nordhaus made his final run down Sandia Peak," the younger Abruzzo reminisced. "He was a man who knew no limits and no boundaries." Nordhaus lived to be ninety-seven, and was inducted into the New Mexico Ski Hall of Fame on January 7, 2007.

Farther north in the pristine valley at the base of the Sangre de Cristo Mountains near Taos, a Swiss-German couple, Ernie and Rhoda Blake, built the foundation for what would become a world-class ski resort. In 1956, however, a J-bar lift and one ski trail were all that comprised Taos Ski Valley. The next year Blake added a Poma lift and with the assistance of Pete Totemoff, an Aleutian Indian from Alaska, added more trails. As the former manager of Santa Fe Ski Basin, Blake clearly understood the industry. Traditionally, skiing had prospered only in colder northern climates such as Sun Valley, Idaho; Alta, Utah; and Vail, Colorado. The notion to establish ski resorts in the Southwest—though these would be more readily accessible to patrons in Texas, Oklahoma, Georgia, and other southern U.S. markets—was risky, if not revolutionary. During the next several decades, reliable annual snowfall in the Sangre de Cristos (the southernmost extension of the Rocky Mountains), the addition of particularly challenging trails aimed at more accomplished skiers, and "the best ski school in North America" for beginners contributed to the resort's national and international acclaim. Its proximity to Taos Pueblo, one of the oldest continuously occupied Indian communities in North America, was an added attraction. In 2003–2004 the Blakes and Totemoff joined Nordhaus as inductees to the state's Ski Hall of Fame.

By the early 1990s New Mexico touted a half-dozen major ski areas—Angel Fire, Red River, Sandia Peak, Ski Apache, Ski Santa Fe, and Taos Ski Valley—and a handful of local facilities, such as Pajarito near Los Alamos and Sipapu between Peñasco and Mora. With two notable exceptions (Ski Apache and Cloudcroft), all were located in the northern sector of the state. Ski Apache, which originally opened as Sierra Blanca Ski Resort on Christmas Day 1961, is the only Indian–owned and operated ski facility in the state. Wealthy petroleum financier Robert O. Anderson located the facility in the Sacramento Mountains near Ruidoso. By its second season the resort proudly boasted "twenty-five thousand skiers who came to enjoy the very first mono-cable four passenger gondola in the region."

In 1963, Anderson sold the operation to the Mescalero Apache tribe, which renamed the facility Ski Apache and has successfully managed it ever since. The ski industry added the year-round economic dimension the state had desired for tourism. In December 2007, Ski New Mexico, the industry's trade organization, reported, "The ski industry generates about $290 million and attracts thousands of tourists to the state each year." What it failed to mention was the fact that New Mexico, along with a number of its southwestern neighbors, remains firmly in the grip of a severe drought. Since the mid-1990s, reduced annual snowpack and above-normal winter temperatures throughout the Mountain West have posed an ominous threat to the future of the ski industry. According to one *Albuquerque Journal* report, in late 2011, New Mexico enjoyed unusually heavy snowfall in advance of the Christmas holiday openings planned for most ski areas. The year 2012 promised to be a banner year for the southwestern ski industry. However, unlike long-established ski resorts in the central Rockies of Colorado and Utah, the southernmost ski facilities received only occasional flurries from January through March.

Since congressional passage of the Indian Gaming Regulatory Act in 1988, Indian tribes across the nation have enjoyed unprecedented economic self-sufficiency. The proliferation of gambling casinos, racetracks, Las Vegas–style resorts, and championship-caliber golf courses on New Mexico's Indian reservations since that time attract thousands more tourists per year to the state. While the profits from these enterprises have benefited the Pueblo, Apache, and to a lesser degree, Navajo tribes, the relationship between these sovereign entities and state government has been less than amicable. Contention centers upon the state's entitlement to tax revenue from gambling profits.

Until his death in 1998, Wendell Chino, the autocratic chairman of the Mescalero Apache Tribal Council, stood at the forefront of the Indians' bid for economic self-determination. First elected tribal chairman in 1955 at the age of twenty-eight, the acerbic Apache leader served in that capacity for thirty-three years. During his tenure as chairman, Chino guided his people away from the brink of economic disaster to become an industrious Indian nation that now proudly claims ownership of a profit-making, Apache-supervised sawmill, a fully operational ski facility, and a 250-room resort hotel and casino, complete with the nation's first tribally owned championship golf course. The tribe also has numerous financial investments in the mineral extraction industry.

Mindful of his personal stature among American Indian leaders, Chino refused to recognize state administrators as legitimate entities. Rather, he insisted on negotiating directly with the federal government as one sovereign nation to another. Chino, in effect, "sought to secure sole control of Mescalero Apache natural and economic resources. His grim determination earned him the epithet the "Martin Luther of Indian Country" among his people. His refusal to honor the revenue-sharing agreement with the state, however, would later cause a rift with other tribal leaders.

The population of New Mexico, according to geographer Jerry L. Williams, witnessed an impressive 37 percent increase during the years 1960 to 1980. The 1980 U.S. Census estimated 1.3 million residents, and noted that the state had become decidedly more urban since World War II. A robust military presence accounted for substantial increases in Bernalillo, Otero, and Curry counties. The one anomaly was Chaves County, which experienced a 28 percent decline in population when the Department of Defense suddenly ordered Walker Air Force Base closed in 1967. Roswell, home to 35,000 residents at the time, "lost an estimated 5,000 military personnel associated directly with the base plus an additional 5,000 support personal virtually overnight." It took the small, southern city most of the following decade to recover from the unexpected blow.

Other counties—Grant, Lea, McKinley, and San Juan—attributed their population growth to the extraction industry, especially to the production of oil, natural gas and low-sulfur coal. In San Juan County, for example, the metro complex of Farmington, Bloomfield, and Aztec experienced a combined population gain of more than 600 percent from 1950 to 1970. Finally, a consistent migratory stream of newcomers to New Mexico during these years bolstered urban centers in Bernalillo, Sandoval, and Doña Ana counties. A majority of these immigrants have settled within commuter range of Albuquerque. Rio Rancho, home to Intel and other notable high-tech firms, doubled in size during this period. Las Cruces, meanwhile, became a haven for retirees and ex-military personnel seeking a consistently dry climate and plenty of sunshine. Census data indicated another migratory trend, away from rural counties—Harding, Mora, and Colfax all lost population in the 1970s—to areas that offered better job opportunities.

In his thought-provoking but somewhat caustic comparison of Santa Fe and Albuquerque, author V. B. Price wrote:

> Santa Fe chose to be a specialty city, a distinctly New Mexican place, capitalizing on its exotic qualities and committing itself to the economics of tourism. Albuquerque chose to become the state's progressive city, an American place, modern and up-to-date, committing itself to an eclectic economy, keeping its options open for any kind of growth that came along. Santa Fe chose directions that guaranteed it would remain a small city. Albuquerque saw in its future the possibility of becoming a major metropolis in the West. Santa Fe made a decision to direct its growth. . . . Albuquerque grew in response to market forces, with a minimum of planning until after World War II.

He concluded, "Santa Fe became the victim of its own popularity, of its own extraordinary successful image-making efforts." The city council's adoption in 1957 of an ordinance "to preserve and maintain historic architecture and style within certain areas of town (the notorious

H-Zone Ordinance)" effectively marked the beginning of Santa Fe's image-making process.

The brainchild of renowned architect John Gaw Meem and like-minded conservationists, the ordinance was heralded in the *New York Times* as an unprecedented triumph in the cause of historic preservation. In March 1962 the city officially incorporated the ordinance into its first master plan. In doing so, Santa Fe made a conscious commitment to embrace tourism rather than manufacturing or industry as the foundation for its economic future. The area the city set aside in the 1960s for industrial zoning totaled a mere 103 acres near the railroad yards. By 1989, manufacturing still represented only 4.7 percent of an economy thoroughly dominated by the service industry (47 percent) and government employment (30 percent).

From this point forward, Santa Fe faced the difficult task of preserving its historic character in the face of rampant development and nationwide popularity. Critics of the city's decision to impose the restrictive policy argue the design code has turned a once-distinctive community into "an Adobeland of fake Pueblo architecture." They believe Santa Fe sacrificed too much of its authenticity to create a mythical, romanticized image designed to lure more tourists to the state. For example, longtime residents lament the transformation of the central plaza downtown. Before the 1970s, it was the hub of daily community activity where local residents gathered to patronize Kaune's Market, Zook's and Capital pharmacies, C. R. Anthony's department store, Plaza Cigar, Dunlap's, F. W. Woolworth's, and the Plaza Café. The latter, a downtown institution since 1938, suffered severe damage from a kitchen fire in 2010. On July 11, 2012, the *Santa Fe New Mexican* proudly announced the restaurant's restoration and reopening. With the exception of that inter-city landmark, the plaza has been transformed into a menagerie of brand-name curio shops, jewelry stores, art vendors, and high-end restaurants that mainly beckon transient visitors. The result has been the gradual displacement of local merchants out of the downtown area to join the sprawling strip of homogenized businesses along St. Francis Avenue (built in 1964) and Cerrillos Road.

Traditionally Hispanic neighborhoods such as Canyon Road also experienced irrevocable change as a relentless stream of Anglo newcomers pressured, perhaps unwittingly, older Hispanic families to move out because they could no longer afford to pay exorbitant rents or escalating property taxes. The abandoned homes were quickly converted into the unbroken chain of art galleries that perennially attract well-to-do collectors. Today the Canyon Road neighborhood typifies what one critic calls "the Anglo commercialization of Hispanic culture." By contrast, in the more recently platted housing developments on the west side of town, Hispanic and Anglo homeowners appear to have achieved parity. Meanwhile, the juniper-studded hillsides north of Santa Fe, heading in the direction of Tesuque Pueblo, have become favored sites for movie celebrities and other affluent homeowners.

The founding of the Santa Fe Opera (1957) north of town and St. John's College campus (1964) on the fashionable east side, combined with the construction of the Santa Fe Ski Basin in Hyde Park (1954), the Santa Fe Downs racetrack (1971) on the south side, and the behemoth El Dorado Hotel (1986) downtown, all contributed to Santa Fe's inflated reputation by the 1980s. Articles touting the southwestern community as one of America's "most livable cities" appeared regularly in *Time, Newsweek, Esquire, New Yorker, National Geographic,* and countless travel magazines with national circulation. Added to the above, the phenomenal success of annual events like the Indian Market, Spanish Market, and the city's four-hundred-year-old Fiesta made Santa Fe one of the America's "hotspot" travel destinations. These accomplishments, however, were not attained without a profound sense of loss among many of the community's older inhabitants. Santa Fe native A. B. Martínez, Jr., after an unsuccessful bid for mayor in the late 1970s, expressed his chagrin saying, "What is overwhelming our [Hispanic] culture now is the fantastic, seemingly uncontrolled influx of new residents who live here but are not really part of the community."

Contrasting Santa Fe with Albuquerque, Price writes that for thirty years following World War II, "Albuquerque never paid enough attention to the feelings evoked by its physical image." He adds, "The city's leadership was never interested in creating a unified urban image to rival Santa Fe. Albuquerque has had a perverse zest for demolition." It was no coincidence that the trend began in 1954. That year marked the demise of Boss Tingley's political machine and the city's electoral sweep of the commission he so thoroughly dominated.

Weary of Tingley's stranglehold on Albuquerque's downtown development since the heyday of the WPA, the new leadership saw an opportunity to introduce a progressive look downtown with the help of massive federal funding under the umbrella of urban renewal. For the next twenty years Albuquerque committed what one detractor callously labeled a "cultural lobotomy" by razing "hundreds of its historic properties." Architectural icons such as Hunning Castle, the Franciscan Hotel, the Masonic Temple, and the venerated Alvarado Hotel became unwelcome remnants of the past and thus, early casualties of postwar urban planning. Old Town evaded the wholesale destruction after city officials designated it as a historic district in 1957 to ensure its preservation.

Like other urban municipalities in the West, Albuquerque experienced the near abandonment of its downtown core area. Merchants moved department stores, auto dealerships, and service industries west of Carlisle, the new line of demarcation between downtown and uptown, closer to the "nearly two million square feet of retail space" at the intersection of Menaul and Louisiana boulevards. The auto dealers claimed the open space closer to I-40 at Lomas and Wyoming, near the main entry gate to Kirtland Air Force Base. The only structures remaining downtown in 1970 were a cluster of lifeless government buildings, the "futuristic" assemblage on the plaza, and the newly built Convention Center and Hyatt Hotel complex. After a decade of outward expansion, during which houses were built in clusters of three hundred to five hundred at a time to fill the open space in between, Albuquerque replicated the growth pattern of Phoenix and Dallas.

Still, Albuquerque's expansion had limits. Natural barriers like the Sandia Mountains and Cibola National Forest along with human-made obstacles (Kirtland) restrained the city's growth. The 1980s would see a demographic shift toward the Northeast Heights as well as the West Mesa across the Rio Grande. The WPA-built Albuquerque Sunport underwent a multimillion-dollar facelift and was renamed Albuquerque International Airport as the municipal population swelled to 332,920 people, three times that of 1950.

In 1975, Albuquerque adopted an environmentally sensitive comprehensive plan to address the city's ongoing battle with air pollution, introduced its first housing code, and officially adopted a program of historic preservation. Local developers viewed the plan as a threat to future growth, but Republican mayor and retired Sandia National Laboratories engineer Harry Kinney had no recourse but to endorse it in the face of a nationwide heightening of environmental awareness. Two years later, Kinney lost the mayoral election to California transplant David Rusk (son of former secretary of state Dean Rusk). The young Democrat not only saved the KiMo Theatre and other historic structures from destruction, but he sponsored their restoration to former glory.

Pro-growth advocate Kinney was reelected mayor in 1981, and the next year, his administration introduced one of the city's most progressive pieces of environmental legislation. From then on Albuquerque acknowledged the historic and environmental significance of the Rio Grande. Kinney authorized the creation of Rio Grande Valley State Park for the protection of "6,000 acres of river environment from Corrales to Isleta Pueblo." Under a modified version of the comprehensive plan adopted in 1987, the city assigned a higher premium to open space, a policy shift prompted by encroachment on the West Mesa from multiple housing developments.

In 1990, city officials endorsed the designation of Petroglyph National Monument, a 7,500-acre urban archaeological park—the only unit in the country managed by the National Park Service in cooperation with a municipal Open Space Division—in the hope of establishing some mechanism of protection on the West Mesa. As of 2010, the Albuquerque suburb of Rio Rancho (population, 87,521) became the state's third-largest urban entity, surpassing Santa Fe (population, 67,947).

The military-industrial complex, which by 1980 had enjoyed an uninterrupted seventy-year presence in Albuquerque, remained the single largest factor in the municipal—if not the state's—economy. During the Cold War, the Department of Defense channeled millions to Sandia National Laboratories to develop and test nuclear warheads, and millions more to Kirtland Air Force Base to house the deadly arsenal in a nearby underground storage facility known as Manzano Base. One local journalist speculated, "There are more nuclear weapons in that mountain than anywhere in the country, probably more than anywhere in the world." In 1971, Sandia Base (including Sandia National Laboratories) and Manzano Base were merged into a single entity under the supervisory authority of Kirtland Air Force Base, which underwent a second major expansion in response to the added responsibilities in Kirtland's operational plan.

Municipalities in the southern sector of the state also benefited from their economic codependency with the military. While still a major agricultural producer and railroad distribution center, Alamogordo attributes much of its postwar prosperity to its sixty-eight-year association with Holloman Air Force Base and White Sands Missile Range. Moreover, NASA's establishment of an experimental facility between Las Cruces and Alamogordo in the mid-1960s substantially augmented the economies of both communities. Comprising almost 60,000 acres (set aside at the expense of some one hundred local cattle ranches), Holloman has functioned throughout its history as a fighter training base. During the 1960s, Holloman was home to the F-4 Phantom, which saw combat in Vietnam, and more recently the F-117A Nighthawk "stealth fighter," combat-tested in Iraq during Operation Desert Storm.

The relationship between Cannon Air Force Base and the city of Clovis has been historically similar, but with an added measure of uncertainty. Curry County has long been the nucleus of prosperous agriculture and ranching activity. Clovis is located just seventeen miles northeast of Portales; the two communities combined produce the state's largest harvest of cotton and peanuts. In addition, Clovis values its longstanding reputation as a major producer of beef and dairy cattle. In 2005 the Southwest Cheese Company, reputed to be "one of the largest plants of its type in the world, processing in excess of 2.3 billion pounds of cheese yearly," located its regional headquarters between the two towns. The cumulative worth of ranching and agriculture to the local economy is approximately $220 million a year. Because of Clovis's preeminent standing, it has become a regional financial center. Since 2000, Clovis has enjoyed a population spurt to an estimated 37,775 people.

In early 2005, however, the Pentagon's Base Realignment and Closure Commission (BRAC) announced its decision to deactivate Cannon Air Force Base, which at the time employed four thousand military personnel and about six hundred civilian employees. Upon receiving the shocking news, Clovis and Portales organized a grassroots movement to save the base from closure. In June 2006, Cannon was given a new lease on life when the Department of Defense announced the base would continue operations but with an entirely new mission. In October 2006, the air force announced the 16th Special Operations Wing at Eglin Air Force Base in Florida would transfer five thousand active-duty personnel and more than one hundred aircraft to south-central New Mexico by October 2010.

As in earlier years, the military installations in New Mexico owe their longevity to an aggressive New Mexico political delegation. Former senior U.S. Senate members Pete Domenici and Jeff Bingaman (both retired as of 2012), U.S. Air Force Academy graduate and ex–U.S. representative Heather Wilson (who sought Domenici's Senate seat in 2012, but lost), and Governor Bill Richardson (who left office under the cloud of a grand jury investigation in 2010) combined their talents to influence BRAC's stunning reversal. Republican Senator Domenici, then chair of the Senate Budget Committee and long-standing member of the Senate Appropriations Committee, proved especially effective in persuading the Department of Defense to change its mind.

Pietro Vichi "Pete" Domenici grew up in the Italian section of Albuquerque and became a hometown sports hero after he pitched one season with the Albuquerque Dukes, a one-time Brooklyn Dodgers farm club. After graduating from the University of New Mexico with an education degree and spending several years teaching high school, Domenici earned a law degree from the University of Denver Law School. In 1966, he ran successfully or his first political post on the Albuquerque City Commission. Two years later he was selected as chairman of the commission, in those days the equivalent of being mayor. Domenici lost his bid for governor to Democrat Bruce King in 1970, but two years later won election to the U.S. Senate seat vacated by the legendary Clinton P. Anderson. In doing so, Domenici became the first Republican to represent New Mexico in the U.S. Senate since

1925. He served from 1973 to 2009, the longest consecutive term in office by any New Mexico politician. Like Dennis Chavez before him, Senator Domenici did his utmost to protect the status of the military in his home state until his retirement from office.

Unlike Clovis, the city of Roswell had to reinvent itself economically after the Walker Air Force Base deactivation in 1967. In response, civic leaders pinned their economic future on a bizarre event that allegedly took place in 1947. The so-called Roswell Incident stems from rumors that members of the 509th Bomb Group stationed at Roswell Army Air Force Base recovered a crashed extraterrestrial vehicle— including corpses—after a severe thunderstorm on the evening of July 8. The following day, the army retracted its initial press release, altering it to read that the debris found at the crash site had been identified as a high-altitude weather balloon associated with a secret military operation known as Project Mogul.

For three decades newspaper reporters reluctantly accepted the army's version of the recovery until an interview with Major Jesse Marcel. Marcel divulged that he had "accompanied the debris after it was recovered to Fort Worth." During the interview the retired officer insisted there was a deliberate military cover-up. Subsequent investigations from 1978 to 1995 presented plausible arguments that an alien craft may have crashed that summer's evening, but all failed to produce any substantive evidence.

The mere suggestion of an actual UFO penetrating the earth's atmosphere attracted national and international attention. Despite the contentious wrangling the incident has generated for more than fifty years, the prospect of tiny alien space travelers touching down somewhere in the southern New Mexico desert has proven too intriguing to ignore. Each year around July 4, the city hosts its UFO Festival, which lures thousands of believers to Roswell. The gathering has generated a subculture all its own. The city's eagerness to exploit the incident—be it myth or reality—is just one of the innovations Roswell used to overcome the loss of the Walker base.

The festival's enormous popularity is testimony to the resilience of Roswell's civic leaders and its residents. Soon after the military's departure, local boosters converted the abandoned site into an industrial park focused for the most part on the aeronautics industry. The community's historical affiliation with the New Mexico Military Institute since 1891, coupled with the successful adaptation of the now-defunct air base, retains for Roswell some vestige of more prosperous times. The community's population has increased from 33,908 in 1970, three years after the air force's departure, to 48,366 in 2010.

In May 2012 the *Albuquerque Journal* reported that the city of Hobbs in the southern New Mexico, long recognized as a petroleum industry leader, would soon be involved in future scientific planning in the high-tech industry. The city was chosen to host a fifteen-acre, $1 billion–dollar suburb where "no one will live." Pegasus Global Holdings, LLC, revealed Hobbs as the company's chosen site to build a modernized ghost town, resembling a typical, midsized American community, that will serve as a facility for testing "driverless cars and intelligent washing machines" in a controlled environment. The proposed project would require 1,500 laborers to construct the so-called Center for Innovation. An estimated 359 test engineers, design experts, and attendant technical assistants will then work at the futuristic city but will reside in Hobbs. City officials anticipated a renewed housing development boom, as well as the expansion of ancillary businesses, to follow from the facility's completion in either late 2012 or early 2013.

Sometime in the 1990s, Las Cruces achieved the status of the state's second most populous municipality. The city owes its recent growth to a massive influx of new residents determined to survive on fixed incomes. Persistent sunshine, affordable housing, inexpensive domestic and landscape services, and until the recent drug wars, the community's proximity to the international border—making low-cost prescriptions and health-care professionals readily available—attract thousands of immigrants annually from the Frostbelt communities of the Midwest. The presence of New Mexico State University since 1881 substantially augments a high-functioning agrarian-based economy.

Near the New Mexico–Colorado state line, where the waters of the La Plata and Las Animas rivers flow into the San Juan, the city of Farmington (with 45,877 residents in 2010) has reigned supreme as the citadel of New Mexico's northwest since the 1960s. For centuries the Navajo called the area Totah, "the place where the waters meet." More recent occupants call it the Four Corners, a unique geographic spot where the borders of four U.S. states intersect. Farmington takes immeasurable pride in its reputation as a blue-collar, industrial boomtown.

Beyond that, it is also the commercial epicenter for the sprawling Navajo Reservation as well as the former mining communities of southwestern Colorado. With the exception of Navajo Lake State Park, established after Navajo Dam was dedicated in 1963, Farmington offers few scenic or recreational amenities. For this reason, perhaps, the local chamber of commerce has adopted a marketing approach that highlights amenities located closer to Durango, Colorado, many of which are a two-hour drive from the New Mexico state line. Correspondingly, Durango publicizes the schedule of cultural events sponsored by the Farmington Civic Center in its local newspaper and tourism magazine.

San Juan County has a capricious economy that is inextricably linked to three American Indian communities (the Navajo, the Southern Ute, and the Jicarilla Apache). For the past three decades coal, not oil, has emerged as the subregion's most marketable commodity. The struggle between the city of Farmington and the Navajo Nation to monopolize power generated from a federally sponsored hydroelectric facility on the San Juan River best illustrates the city's determination to resurrect its commercial-industrial preeminence.

Proposed in 1962 as a means of assuring Navajo tribal economic self-sufficiency, the $20 million, coal-fired power plant has been fraught with political tension—sometimes erupting in outbreaks of racial violence between Indians and non-Indians—over ultimate management authority. In 1986 the two litigants reached a compromise whereby the city agreed to deposit $2 million in escrow to enable the Navajo Nation to draw electricity for reservation use from their Farmington-owned utility distribution system. In 2000, however, the Navajo Nation Tribal Council complained that it had yet to derive any money from the 1986 accord. In 2012 syndicated columnist George Will lamented the Environmental Protection Agency's decision to assess millions of dollars worth of anti-pollution improvements against the Navajo-owned plants in northwestern New Mexico and northeastern Arizona. What Will perceived as "bureaucratic overkill" would, in his judgment, result in the inevitable closure of these valuable sources of energy in the American Southwest.

Despite these and other economic setbacks, resulting in a steady population decline from the city's one-time high of more than fifty thousand inhabitants, Farmington grimly clings to its reputation as the Four Corners' most prominent urban complex. The resurgence of petroleum activity in 2010 promised to make a reality the hope of Farmington's civic revitalization as the region's preeminent industrial center.

New Mexico's unfettered growth and unwavering commitment to technological advancement since 1945 have exacted a toll on both the landscape and its people. The most immediate issue is water, or more specifically, the lack of it. A decade-long drought throughout the American Southwest literally has altered the state's environment. The once ubiquitous piñon tree, so plentiful that it was officially declared the state tree, faces total eradication from the lack of rainfall and the ravages of bark beetle infestation. Biology experts predict an 80 to 85 percent reduction of the species by the end of the coming decade. Moreover, the critical depletion of natural groundwater, compounded by the visible dissipation of vast stores of surface water impounded behind state-owned dams, imposes intrinsic restrictions on New Mexico's immediate and future growth.

One ominous side effect of prolonged drought is the frequency of uncontrolled wildfires, such as those that have devoured millions of acres of forested lands in Montana, Wyoming, California, Utah, Colorado, Arizona, and New Mexico. The calamitous 45,000-acre Cerro Grande fire near Los Alamos in May 2000, the result of an NPS-supervised "controlled burn" that went awry, consumed 255 homes and threatened to destroy the national laboratory, in the process exposing hundreds of people to toxic, radioactive waste that the military had carelessly disposed of decades ago. The conflagration forced the evacuation of eighteen thousand residents from Los Alamos and nearby Santa Clara Pueblo. In retrospect, the Cerro Grande fire was a prelude to a chain of incendiary events that the West had not witnessed since 1910.

The years 2011 and 2012 proved to be the worst fire seasons in New Mexico state history. The 156,593-acre Las Conchas fire burned virtually nonstop for most of the month of June 2011 and forced evacuations of Los Alamos, White Rock, parts of Española, and Santa Clara Pueblo. The blaze eclipsed the 2000 Cerro Grande fire as the state's fiercest historic wildfire. An assessment ten months later determined that the fire burned with such fury that most of the acreage affected has sustained irreparable damage and is not likely to ever recover. Rather than what foresters consider a healthy burn, most of the damage inflicted upon the west Jemez Mountains landscape—including a large portion of the famous volcanic Valles Caldera—has, according to State Biologist Craig Allen, "been virtually decimated." Local communities suffered total devastation as well. Santa Clara Pueblo's once-pristine backcountry wilderness sustained immeasurable damage from both the conflagration and the flooding that followed. In July 2012 Governor Susanna Martinez declared the razed pueblo lands to be in a state of emergency.

Another permanent casualty, in the nearby Rio Grande Valley, was the legendary family-owned Dixon Apple Orchards north of Española. The fire destroyed more than a third of the farm's mature trees. Nonetheless, the Mullane family at first pledged to take out the huge loan necessary to fully revitalize their apple-producing enterprise. But then, the unabated flooding, the result of the woefully eroded, fire-damaged landscape, broke the Mullane family's spirit and sent them packing to Wisconsin to start all over again. The Mullanes left New Mexico fully expecting to lease the destroyed 8,500-acre orchard to neighboring San Felipe Pueblo, whose many residents were employed by the farm. As of May 2012, however, the state Land Office had declined to honor any past or present agreements to lease between the Mullane family and San Felipe Pueblo.

The lead headline in local newspapers in January 2012 read, "1,000 Fires Burned across the State." While that number included fires in the past several years, 2012 witnessed the worst fires ever in the state's one-hundred-year history. In June, several fires raged simultaneously across the state, causing damage to the Gila Wilderness Area and the tourism-dependent communities of Ruidoso and Santa Fe. The so-called

Whitewater-Baldy Complex fire began in the Gila Wilderness on May 9 and burned with such ferocity that NASA took satellite pictures of its smoke plume from outer space. The blaze required more than twelve hundred firefighters from several states to achieve only 15 percent containment before it destroyed 354 square miles in southwestern New Mexico. As of this writing, the fire (actually a two separate fires that merged on May 24 to form a more "complex" burn) was a little more than 50 percent contained and had burned 279,378 acres—more than four hundred square miles of land surface—thus eclipsing both the Cerro Grande and Las Conchas as the state's single largest historic wildfires.

Concurrently, the Little Bear fire, sparked by lightning on June 4, 2012, scorched 44,330 acres and consumed 254 structures—a number equivalent to the 250-plus homes lost in the Cerro Grande fire. Despite the obvious threat to the community of Ruidoso, the town remained intact and, as local residents were relieved to proclaim, "open for business." Business, however, is very slow to return as newscasters' premature forecast of the once-famous quarter-horse racing town's demise have made tourists—who flock there annually from Texas to beat the heat—wary of making Ruidoso their annual destination.

Meanwhile, sparks emitted from an electric grinder caused ignited dry grass to cause a mid-level fire near the Santa Fe Airport. Although the blaze immediately threatened several small housing communities along Airport Road, local firefighters minimized the damage with no loss of personal property. The recent rash of seemingly unpreventable wildfires through the state prompted Governor Martinez to issue an official drought declaration for all of New Mexico. "I am hopeful this declaration," she said, "will enable ranchers, farmers, and small businesses adversely affected by these on-going drought conditions [to] qualify . . . for any available federal monetary assistance." For the cattle industry, particularly the dairy cattle industry, years of prolonged drought have caused a serious decline in the production of hay and alfalfa. This shortage, compounded with a 51 percent decline in corn production throughout the West and Midwest, has greatly minimized the ranchers' ability to maintain their herds. The once-prosperous ranchers in the southern part of the state are drastically reducing their stock, resulting in subsequent declines in the supply of meat, milk, and dairy products at local grocery stores.

Water rights issues have historically bred contention in New Mexico. Confrontation over water use in turn has fueled seemingly endless litigation. Municipal water users in the northern communities of Albuquerque, Bernalillo, Rio Rancho, Santa Fe, and Los Alamos, for example, are in heated competition with southern and eastern agriculturalists in Las Cruces, Roswell, Artesia, Portales, and Clovis for the limited hydraulic resources of the middle Rio Grande and the Pecos River. In the Chama River valley the proprietary rights of the Pueblo Indian communities further complicate the situation. In the early 1900s, the federal government determined there was insufficient water in the West to supply the growing multitude of immigrants from the water-abundant regions of the East and the Midwest. Congress passed the Newlands Reclamation Act in 1902, authorizing government sponsorship of massive irrigation projects, which eventually led to damming every major river in the West. As legislated, the act addressed the water concerns of the region's Anglo-dominated cities and towns with little regard for the agricultural needs of the rural ethnic communities.

As redistribution of the waters from these reclamation and irrigation projects in New Mexico occurred in the 1930s and 1940s, the proprietary rights of Indian and Hispanic users, which predated the American takeover in 1848, were casually ignored.

During the Great Depression one of the projects proposed by the National Resources Planning Board was the transmountain diversion of water from the San Juan River in southwestern Colorado into northern New Mexico's Chama River Basin. The intent was to use the Chama to substantially augment the waters of the middle Rio Grande for future consumption. In exchange, a portion of the flow from the headwaters of the Rio Grande in southern Colorado would be diverted to the prolific farmlands of the San Luis Valley.

Although planning for the massive project continued for nearly thirty years, the San Juan–Chama Transmountain Diversion Project did not achieve fruition until the Bureau of Reclamation completed the Upper Colorado River Storage Project in the early 1960s. Cognizant of Cold War priorities, the bureau assigned the largest apportionment of upstream Rio Grande water for municipal and industrial use to Los Alamos, Albuquerque, and Santa Fe. At no time, however, did the federal government consult with the pueblos nearest to those communities about their irrigation needs. Ever mindful of their science and technology mission, Albuquerque and Los Alamos claimed their full share of reallocated water. Meanwhile, Santa Fe, at the time a small city with a population well under fifty thousand, claimed only half of its apportionment.

In 1966 the State of New Mexico filed a lawsuit to adjudicate all of the tributaries of the Rio Grande, resulting in a forty-four-year litigation, the *State of New Mexico v. Aamodt*. The case involves four Indian pueblos located on the Pojoaque River, a tributary of the Rio Grande historically used by Indian and Hispanic farmers for agricultural purposes centuries before Anglo-Americans arrived. Critical to the indigenous communities of the West was the ruling that their rights to water are protected before all other users' rights regardless of whether the water is in use or not. The decision in the *Aamodt* case has broad implications for Hispanic farmers and municipal users in the state. Santa Fe, for instance, which today harbors somewhere between 65,000 and 70,000 inhabitants, will most likely not be allocated the second half of its initial apportionment of water from the San Juan River before the upstream pueblos receive their entitlement. Recent commercial development on Pueblo lands—gambling casinos, resort hotels, golf courses, and other attractions—make Santa Fe's prospects for additional water doubtful. In December 2010, President Obama signed the Claims Resolution Act, which codified the rights of Pueblo and non-Pueblo water users in the Pojoaque River Basin and thus ending the case.

Other squabbles over the use of water from the Rio Grande are the by-product of "urban imperialism." During the decades of remarkable postwar growth and expansion, municipal leaders hoped to attract "clean" industry to New Mexico by offering inexpensive land and favorable tax incentives. Albuquerque's attraction of computer industry giants Intel Corporation and Hewlett-Packard to the Rio Rancho area was hailed as a major coup at the time. In 1994, despite scientific reports that the West Mesa did not possess sufficient water resources to sustain both industrial and municipal growth, the New Mexico state engineer approved Intel's application to drill additional wells in Rio Rancho, to the detriment of the neighboring communities of Albuquerque, Bernalillo, and Corrales.

Another threat to the environment is a direct consequence of unregulated disposal of nuclear waste produced during and after World War II. Recent concerns stem from a 2005 negligence and wrongful death lawsuit filed against the University of California, the principal civilian administrator for Los Alamos National Laboratory during the 1940s and 1950s. Lawyers for the plaintiff filed what they hope will become a "medical-monitoring class action suit" on behalf of the surviving families of children who grew up in Los Alamos during those frenetic years. A startling number have died of cancer-related illnesses, which litigators attribute to their prolonged exposure to radiation as children. Since 1991 the Department of Energy has been under a consent order with the State of New Mexico to clean up subsurface toxic and radioactive waste in Los Alamos and at the Trinity Site. Subsequent debates over the imposed cleanup have focused on the method and the location of disposal.

In March 1998, after more than twenty years of scientific study and public consultation, the Environmental Protection Agency sanctioned the Waste Isolation Pilot Plant (WIPP), a facility "licensed to permanently dispose of radioactive waste for the next 10,000 years." Located twenty-six miles east of Carlsbad in Eddy County, the site is said to be only the third subsurface geological repository in the world. Hazardous material is trucked from its point of origin to the WIPP site in specially designed metal containers, which are then deposited to isolated rooms buried 2,100 feet underground. By 2006, the facility had processed an estimated five thousand containers filled with radioactive waste.

In 1991, hazardous waste disposal became a hotly contested issue on the Mescalero Apache Reservation. The reservation's tribal council, at the time under the heavy hand of the enterprising Wendell Chino, applied for and received a total of $300,000 in Department of Defense (DOD) grants to study the feasibility of building a Monitored Retrievable Storage site on the reservation to house spent nuclear fuel rods. Seizing the opportunity to exercise what he labeled as his policy of "red capitalism," Chino estimated potential earnings for the tribe to be around $250 million during the forty-year partnership with the federal government. The proposal, however, caused a rift not only among Apache tribal leaders but also between the Mescalero and other New Mexico tribes. After considerable pressure from Senator Bingaman, the DOD terminated the controversial grant program in 1993.

New Mexicans take pride in the fact that three distinct cultures have, for the most part, "harmoniously" coexisted for much of the state's modern history. Nevertheless, racial and social tensions persist to this day. Few nuevomexicanos care to admit that Santa Fe was host to one of several Japanese American internment camps scattered across the West during World War II. During the period of mass hysteria following the attack on Pearl Harbor, the U.S. Immigration and Naturalization Service transferred some forty-five hundred Japanese American citizens from Hawaii and the Pacific Northwest to the outskirts of Santa Fe to endure four years of internment. After the camp's abandonment in March 1946, the location was absorbed into the Casa Solana housing subdivision.

In 1990 the Santa Fe City Council voted to erect a monument near the obscured camp site. The proposal drew angry responses from a large sector of the Santa Fe population—the most vociferous protests coming from surviving Bataan Death March veterans and their families. Although the controversy raged on for more than a decade, the city council enacted a proposal in March 2002 to place a small plaque honoring the former internees. Recalling the emotion-filled event that she attended, Gail Okawa, the maternal granddaughter of Tamasaku Watanabe, wrote to her grandfather, who had died in 1968. "We must understand that though you were silent, like so many others, about this difficult time in your life, you were no less affected by the degradation, no less courageous for bearing it." In April 2012, Okawa returned to the state capital to cohost a symposium to honor the memory of her grandfather and the thousands of other Asian American citizens who spent the remainder of World War II in questionable confinement.

Other indications of lingering racial attitudes appeared in an article published in the *Santa Fe New Mexican* on October 26, 2009. The story told of a local motel owner in Taos who would not allow his

Hispanic employees to use their given Spanish names. If the employee's given name was Martín (Mar-teen), for example, it was to be pronounced "Martin" with no accent; the Spanish name Marcos became Mark. Moreover, the motel owner, recently arrived to northern New Mexico from Abilene, Texas, forbade his employees to speak Spanish in his presence. When several employees, including former manager Kathy Archuleta, protested the humiliating treatment, they were fired without notice. The owner's behavior fueled public outrage from several of the community's predominantly ethnic residents and evoked a formal letter of protest from the New Mexico chapter of the League of United Latin American Citizens (LULAC), a national civil rights organization.

A more insidious form of discrimination in northern New Mexico appears to have surfaced within the last ten to fifteen years. Many native-born New Mexico Hispanics harbor antipathy toward migrant Mexican and Central American construction workers and service industry employees, fueled more by economic and class distinctions than racial differences. Immigrant labor, whether legal or illegal, poses an immediate threat to the economic livelihood of the local population, especially in today's troubled economy when jobs are scarce.

Migrant workers, particularly those arrived from Mexico, have frequented southern New Mexico since the late nineteenth century. Traditionally, local businessmen have employed them as seasonal farm laborers or ranch hands. Compared with other southwestern states, New Mexico has exhibited much greater tolerance for migrant labor and, according to one author, has "passed some of the most progressive legislation dealing with the human rights of immigrants." Recent arrivals to Albuquerque, Bernalillo, Rio Rancho, Santa Fe, Las Vegas, Las Cruces, and other urban areas, however, bring marketable skills and job experience to construction sites and service establishments. Seasoned stonemasons, bricklayers, and plaster specialists from Mexico and Central America are fiercely competitive in today's local job market and, U.S. workers assert, are willing to work longer hours for lower wages.

The beginning of 2009 marked a turning point in New Mexico politics as the cumulative influence of a once-powerful state delegation waned, either by natural attrition or self-induced political controversy. Republican Senator Pete Domenici announced his retirement from the

Senate in 2009 for health reasons. To public dismay, Domenici ended his brilliant senatorial career in the shadow of a Senate Ethics Committee investigation and admonishment for his alleged attempt to influence the outcome of a Justice Department investigation. U.S. Congresswoman Heather Wilson, Domenici's heir apparent in the Senate, was also implicated, which may have accounted for her stunning upset by Steve Pearce in the hard-fought Republican congressional primary in 2010. New Mexico Democrats were not immune to accusations of political indiscretion. Governor Bill Richardson, the charismatic, Mexican-born state chief executive also came under public scrutiny during a federal grand jury investigation that alleged he had awarded lucrative state contracts in exchange for hefty contributions to his unsuccessful presidential bid in 2008. In January 2009, the Justice Department exonerated Richardson of any political wrongdoing, but not before he had removed his name from nomination as secretary of commerce in the Obama administration. At this writing, the investigation of Richardson's activities as former governor continue but with no apparent change in the outcome.

These public servants were merely suspected of unethical behavior; none was brought under formal indictment. Such was not the case, however, for former state congressional titan and longtime Democratic Party boss Manny Aragon. In October 2008, the one-time Highlands University president was investigated, indicted, tried, and convicted of federal corruption charges. While still an active member of the New Mexico Senate, Aragon became embroiled in a conspiracy to "skim $4.4 million dollars during the construction of the Bernalillo County Metropolitan Courthouse in downtown Albuquerque." Aragon pled guilty after bargaining for court leniency. In 2010 Aragon, also ordered to pay restitution in the amount of $1.5 million, was serving a five-and-one-half-year imprisonment.

The passing of former governor Bruce King on November 13, 2009, signaled the end of an era for New Mexico politics. The congenial cowboy-executive served an unprecedented three nonconsecutive terms as state governor between 1971 and 1994. Known for his folksy political style, the former cattle rancher from Moriarty (east of Albuquerque) once rode his horse to the steps of the state capitol to make the point that New Mexicans should be mindful of excessive gasoline consumption. In the tradition of Clyde Tingley, King endeared himself to his constituents with colorful—sometimes outrageous— comments, such as "I'm afraid that issue might open a whole box of Pandoras." Fabián Chávez, Jr., King's indomitable Republican opponent, admiringly commented, "He was genuinely loved and respected, which in the New Mexico political field is really saying something."

With the midterm elections of 2010, the state political face changed once again. Republican Susana Martinez of Las Cruces edged out a strong field of candidates to win election as the nation's first female Hispanic governor. Not surprisingly, former governor Bruce King's son, New Mexico attorney general Gary King, recently announced his intent to challenge incumbent Martinez in 2014. The 2010 census also indicated that New Mexico's population once again has a Hispanic plurality, accounting for some 46 percent of the state's residents, followed by Anglos at 41 percent. This nationwide trend toward a larger population of relatively young Hispanics not only boded well for the impending presidential election but also portended a continued reconfiguration of the state and national political landscape.

Despite recent political and economic setbacks, New Mexico residents celebrated their centennial celebration in 2012 with unfettered optimism. In common with the majority of the nation's voters in the 2008 general election, New Mexicans who journeyed to Española expressed genuine enthusiasm and a renewed sense of hope for Democratic candidate Barack Obama. The exuberant and articulate African American from Chicago carried New Mexico by 57 percent compared to 42 percent for Arizona's longtime senator John McCain. The election also marked an era of Democratic ascendancy as party members occupied four of New Mexico's five congressional seats in the U.S. House and Senate until the mid-term elections of 2010. The political outlook promised to change again in 2012, however, with the announcement that Senator Jeff Bingaman would retire from office and Republican Heather Wilson's subsequent loss to Democrat Martin Heinrich in the race to fill Bingaman's seat.

New Mexico continues to seek ways to grow and diversify its economy. The Obama administration's focus on renewable energy—

a perspective mirrored in Santa Fe—bodes well financially for New Mexico, especially in the fields of wind and solar energy. Revenues derived from the construction and operation of these relatively clean sources of energy, coupled with a revitalized petroleum industry, may offset a $500 million budget deficit for fiscal year 2010. The state's recent history of financial setbacks correlate directly with a near-decade of plummeting oil and gas revenues, which historically had provided a healthy surplus to the state budget. Both the Richardson and Martinez administrations supported seeking renewable energy sources, but only in conjunction with increased exploration for new sources of recoverable oil and gas.

The film industry offers another option for bolstering the state's sagging economy. According to one UNM professor, "Motion pictures have been filmed in New Mexico essentially since the beginning of the industry." Since Mary Pickford and cowboy legend Tom Mix starred in *Pueblo Legend* and *The Rancher's Daughter*, respectively, in the early 1900s, New Mexico's multihued sunsets have served as a colorful backdrop for more than one hundred Hollywood productions. In 1975 the state reportedly earned $70 million in movie revenue, making a handsome payoff for New Mexico's effort to compete with Arizona, Utah, Nevada, Colorado, and California as a prime location for the film industry. In 2008 state officials announced earnings in excess of $200 million. The Richardson administration predicted the industry would more than compensate for the recent decline in winter sports revenues resulting from a twenty-five-year sustained drought throughout the West.

Governor Martinez, however, entered the state capitol with considerably less enthusiasm about filmmakers' economic contributions. The governor worried most that the generous tax incentives granted to the film industry by her predecessor would result in an overall net loss in the state's annual revenue. For this reason, Martinez placed a moratorium on film starts in New Mexico until a reasonable compromise with the Hollywood film companies could be reached. Her detractors, however, argued that the industry would only turn to rival states still willing to provide handsome tax breaks. Despite the uncertainty of the film industry's long-term future, producers and directors are apparently still enamored with the stunning natural settings offered by New Mexico's scenic amenities. Among the most recent films produced within the state are Rudolfo Anaya's classic novel *Bless Me, Ultima* (2013) and a remake of the legendary western epic *The Lone Ranger* (2013), featuring box-office megastar Johnny Depp as Tonto. Still, Governor Martinez remained less bullish about the industry, waiting to see whether film-makers are willing to support the state's ongoing economic recovery.

Threats to the environment have been significantly minimized since President Obama visited Española in September 2008. Most nota-ble has been a massive nuclear waste cleanup of the original World War II–era laboratory site in Los Alamos. Mandated by the state in 1991, the cleanup project languished in the planning stages for years with little prospect for implementation. In 2008 the daunting task received finan-cial support from the Obama administration's much-maligned eco-nomic stimulus package. In June 2009, LANL announced the first ship-ment of "remote-handled transuranic waste," which had been readied since 2007, to the WIPP site near Carlsbad. The inaugural cargo of plu-tonium and other radioactive elements is the first of an estimated five hundred 55-gallon drums of material scheduled for transport south during the forthcoming year.

During the past decade the U.S. Forest Service has made great strides to mediate age-old enmity between local environmentalists and resi-dent Hispanics in northern New Mexico. Centuries before the arrival of American governance, nuevomexicanos held sacred the Spanish admin-istrative concept of the *ejido,* that is, lands set aside for common use by each community. In the traditional Spanish view of land tenure, all citi-zens were entitled to an equal share of water, timber, and forage, three natural resources vital to sustained community livelihood.

In the early twentieth century, Theodore Roosevelt's authorization of forest preserves under the supervision of the U.S. Department of Agriculture initiated an era of government interference and regulated use of the forest, which proved to be a flashpoint of contention with the former Spanish and Mexican villagers of northern New Mexico. Since it took over forest management in 1907, the U.S. Forest Service has been a symbol of oppression to traditional Spanish-speaking resi-dents who earned their living by the production and manufacture of forest products. During the 1940s and 1950s there were an estimated seventy-two sawmills operating in northern New Mexico. By century's end, U.S. Forest Service constraints, increasingly demanding safety regulations, and strident environmentalists intent on rescuing the Mexican spotted owl had brought New Mexico's timber industry to a screeching halt.

Since 2001 residents of Vallecitos, a mountain village nestled deep within Carson National Forest, have participated in an innovative federal program known as the Collaborative Forest Restoration Program. The venture bonds Hispanic loggers with regional environmentalists in a common goal. One result has been the dramatic reduction of accumulated brush and downed timber, the residue of nearly a half-century of misguided fire suppression in lieu of controlled, periodic burning. The unattended buildup from early logging activity has contributed to the rash of unrelenting wildfires throughout the West since early 2000. A second benefit has been the thinning, under USFS supervision, of thousands of beetle-infested piñon trees and small conifers, resulting in a healthier forest environment. In the words of one observer: "Diehard logging opponents propose tree-cutting, while loggers scramble to align with environmental groups. Peace has broken out where violence once threatened . . . a few loggers are once again working in the woods."

Perhaps the state's most intriguing commitment to the future, though highly controversial, has been the decision to enter into a joint venture with British entrepreneur Richard Branson to design, construct, and operate a "spaceport" in south-central New Mexico just west of White Sands Missile Range. In December 2008 Governor Richardson entered into a twenty-year formal agreement with Virgin Galactic, a futuristic derivative of Branson's financially successful Virgin Atlantic Airways, to formally adopt the initiative as a state-supported program. The agreement "proposes the creation of an 18,000-acre recovery facility for commercial and government orbital re-entry capsules." In lay terms, the so-called Spaceport America will enable passengers to book a suborbital flight into space for a frequent-flyer rate of $200,000 per person. Branson's company announced in March 2012 that actor Ashton Kutcher became the five hundredth person to reserve a flight on the vaunted spacecraft.

The space-age terminal, located thirty miles north of Las Cruces and thirty miles east of Truth or Consequences, extends into Sierra and Doña Ana counties, promising both a long-needed economic shot in the arm. Adjacent to White Sands Missile Range, the site was carefully chosen because the famous Cold War landmark enjoys protected airspace from the Federal Aviation Agency. Scheduled for completion in 2013, Spaceport America will stand as the "first built-from-scratch commercial spaceport in the world." This latest $225 million commitment to the state's tourism economy—and perhaps the future of commercial travel—typifies the state's determination to keep pace with the wider world in coming decades. Carefully planned to coincide with the state centennial celebration, construction of the facility neared completion except for one salient oversight. After an expenditure of some $209 million dollars to ready Spaceport America for its maiden commercial flight—perhaps by late 2012—engineers have determined that the nearly two-mile-long runway is two thousand feet too short to guarantee Virgin Galactic a safe landing. Accordingly, New Mexico Spaceport Authority board members voted in March 2012 to expend $7 million in state taxpayer money to remedy the miscalculation. It appears the much-publicized "fantasy" of British tycoon Sir Richard "Knight of the Realm" Branson's space-bound company remains true to its tongue-in-cheek mantra, *"Carpe mañana,"* proudly displayed on T-shirts and bumper stickers all across the state.

As New Mexico continued to celebrate its one-hundredth year in 2012, state politicians, government administrators, and local citizens pledged to capitalize on the promise of prosperity that enticed America's first European visitors to this once-remote desert frontier more than four centuries ago.

Suggested Readings

The history of New Mexico has a rich literary tradition. The following list of suggested readings provides a sampling of books, articles, and unpublished (including online) materials that will serve the reader well who wishes to dig deeper into New Mexico's past. Titles that cover more than one period or chapter are listed only once.

Chapter 1

Cordell, Linda S. *Prehistory of the Southwest*. San Diego: Academic Press, 1984.

Dixon, E. James. *Bones, Boats, and Bison: Archaeology and the First Colonization of Western North America*. Albuquerque: University of New Mexico Press, 1999.

Kohler, Timothy A., Mark D. Vrien, and Aaron M. Wright, ed. *Leaving Mesa Verde: Peril and Change in the Thirteenth-Century Southwest*. Tucson: University of Arizona Press, 2010.

Lippard, Lucy R. *Down Country: The Tano of the Galisteo Basin, 1250–1782*. Santa Fe: Museum of New Mexico Press, 2010.

Lister, Robert H., and Florence C. Lister. *Chaco Canyon, Archeology and Archeologists*. Albuquerque: University of New Mexico Press, 1981.

Noble, David Grant, ed. *In Search of Chaco: New Approaches to an Archeological Enigma*. Santa Fe: School of American Research, 2004.

Ortiz, Alfonso, ed. *Southwest*. Vol. 9 of *Handbook of North American Indians*. Washington, D.C.: Smithsonian Institution, 1979.

Powers, Robert P. *The Peopling of Bandelier: New Insights from the Archaeology of the Pajarito Plateau*. Santa Fe: School of American Research Press, 2005.

Sebastian, Lynn. *The Chaco Anasazi, Sociopolitical Evolution in the Prehistoric Southwest*. Cambridge, U.K.: Cambridge University Press, 1992.

Stuart, David E. *Anasazi America*. Albuquerque: University of New Mexico, 2000.

Chapter 2

Bolton, Herbert E. *Coronado: Knight of Pueblos and Plains.* Albuquerque: University of New Mexico Press, 1949.

Covey, Cyclone, trans. and ed. *Cabeza de Vaca's Adventures in an Unknown Interior of America.* Albuquerque: University of New Mexico Press, 1961.

Flint, Richard, and Shirley Cushing Flint. *The Coronado Expedition to Tierra Nueva: The 1540–1542 Route across the Southwest.* With historiographical chapters by Joseph P. Sánchez. Niwot: University Press of Colorado, 1997.

Hammond, George P., and Agapito Rey. *The Rediscovery of New Mexico 1580–1594: The Explorations of Chamuscado, Espejo, Castaño de Sosa, Morlete, and Leyva de Bonilla and Humaña.* Albuquerque: University of New Mexico Press,1966.

Sánchez, Joseph P. *The Río Abajo Frontier, 1540–1692: A History of Early Colonial New Mexico.* 2nd ed. Albuquerque: Albuquerque Museum, 1996.

Villagrá, Gaspar Pérez de. *Historia de la Nueva México, 1610: A Critical and Annotated Spanish-English Edition.* Edited and translated by Miguel Encinias, Alfredo Rodríguez, and Joseph P. Sánchez. Albuquerque: University of New Mexico Press, 1992.

Weber, David J. *The Spanish Frontier in North America.* New Haven: Yale University Press, 1992.

Chapter 3

Bancroft, Hubert Howe. *History of Arizona and New Mexico, 1530–1888,* vol. 17. San Francisco: History Co., 1889.

Kessell, John L. *Pueblos, Spaniards, and the Kingdom of New Mexico.* Norman: University of Oklahoma Press, 2008.

Noble, David Grant, ed. *Santa Fe: History of an Ancient City.* Rev. ed. Santa Fe: School for Advanced Research Press, 2008.

Pino, Pedro Baptista. *The Exposition on the Province of New Mexico, 1812.* Edited and translated by Adrian Bustamante and Marc Simmons. Albuquerque: University of New Mexico Press, 1995.

Sánchez, Joseph P. *Explorers, Traders, and Slavers: Forging the Old Spanish Trail, 1678–1859.* Salt Lake City: University of Utah Press, 1997.

Simmons, Marc. *The Last Conquistador: Juan de Oñate and the Settling of the Far Southwest*. Norman: University of Oklahoma Press, 1991.

———. *Spanish Government in New Mexico*. Albuquerque: University of New Mexico Press, 1968.

Warner, Ted J., ed., and Fray Angélico Chávez, trans. *The Domínguez-Escalante Journal: Their Expedition through Colorado, Utah, Arizona, and New Mexico, 1776*. Salt Lake City: University of Utah Press, 1995.

Chapter 4

Gregg, Josiah. *Commerce of the Prairies*. Edited by Max L. Morehead. Norman: University of Oklahoma Press, 1990.

Sánchez, Joseph P. "Nuevo México Infeliz: New Mexico under the Mexican Eagle, 1821–1848." In *Between Two Rivers: The Atrisco Land Grant in Albuquerque History, 1692–1968*. Norman: University of Oklahoma Press, 2008.

Simmons, Marc. *Murder on the Santa Fe Trail: An International Incident, 1843*. El Paso: Texas Western Press, 1987.

Tyler, Daniel. "New Mexico in the 1820s: The First Administration of Manuel Armijo." Ph.D. diss. University of New Mexico, 1970.

Weber, David J. *The Mexican Frontier, 1821–1846: The American Southwest under Mexico*. Albuquerque: University of New Mexico Press, 1982.

Chapter 5

Comer, Douglas C. *Ritual Ground: Bent's Old Fort, World Formation, and the Annexation of the Southwest*. Berkeley: University of California Press, 1996.

Cook, Mary J. Straw. *Doña Tules: Santa Fe's Courtesan and Gambler*. Albuquerque: University of New Mexico Press, 2007.

Gómez, Laura E. *Manifest Destinies: The Making of the Mexican American Race*. New York: New York University Press, 2007.

González, Nancie. *The Spanish-Americans of New Mexico: A Heritage of Pride*. Albuquerque: University of New Mexico Press, 1969.

Griswold del Castillo, Richard. *The Treaty of Guadalupe Hidalgo: A Legacy of Conflict*. Norman: University of Oklahoma Press, 1990.

Hyslop, Stephen G. *Bound for Santa Fe: The Road to New Mexico and the American Conquest, 1806–1848*. Norman: University of Oklahoma Press, 2002.

Limerick, Patricia Nelson. *The Legacy of Conquest: The Unbroken Past of the American West*. New York: W. W. Norton, 1987.

McWilliams, Carey. *North from Mexico: The Spanish-Speaking People of the United States*. Philadelphia: J. B. Lippincott, 1949.

Remley, David. *Kit Carson: The Life of an American Border Man*. Norman: University of Oklahoma Press, 2011.

Reséndez, Andrés. *Changing National Identities at the Frontier: Texas and New Mexico, 1800–1850*. Cambridge: Cambridge University Press, 2005.

Ricketts, Norma Baldwin. *The Mormon Battalion: U.S. Army of the West, 1846–1848*. Logan: Utah State University Press, 1996.

Sánchez, Joseph P. *Between Two Rivers: The Atrisco Land Grant in Albuquerque History, 1692–1968*. Norman: University of Oklahoma Press, 2008.

Simmons, Marc. *The Little Lion of the Southwest: A Life of Manuel Antonio Chaves*. Chicago: Swallow Press, 1973.

Sisneros, Samuel E. "'She Was Our Mother': New Mexico's Change of National Sovereignty and Juan Bautista y Alarid, The Last Mexican Governor of New Mexico." In *All Trails Lead to Santa Fe: An Anthology Commemorating the 400th Anniversary of the Founding of Santa Fe, New Mexico, in 1610*. Santa Fe: Sunstone Press, 2010.

Smith, Henry Nash. *Virgin Land: The American West as Symbol and Myth*. Cambridge, Mass.: Harvard University Press, 1950.

Torrez, Robert. "The Taos Revolt." Office of the New Mexico State Historian. http://newmexicohistory.org/.

Chapter 6

Alberts, Don. *The Battle of Glorieta: Union Victory in the West*. College Station: Texas A&M University Press, 2000.

Boyle, Susan Calafate. *Los Capitalistas: Hispano Merchants and the Santa Fe Trade*. Albuquerque: University of New Mexico Press, 1997.

Brooks, James F. *Captives and Cousins: Slavery, Kinship, and Community in the Southwest Borderlands*. Chapel Hill: University of North Carolina Press, 2002.

Chávez, Fray Angélico, and Thomas E. Chávez. *Wake for a Fat Vicar: Father Juan Felipe Ortiz, Archbishop Lamy, and the New Mexican Catholic Church in the Middle of the Nineteenth Century.* Albuquerque: LPD Press, 2004.

Ebright, Malcolm. *Land Grants and Lawsuits in Northern New Mexico.* Santa Fe: Center for Land Grand Studies Press, 2008.

González, Deena J. *Refusing the Favor: the Spanish-Mexican Women of Santa Fe, 1820–1880.* New York: Oxford University Press, 1999.

Hämäläinen, Pekka. *Comanche Empire.* New Haven: Yale University Press, 2008.

Horgan, Paul. *Lamy of Santa Fe.* Middletown, Conn.: Wesleyan University Press, 2003.

Iverson, Peter. *Diné: A History of the Navajos.* Albuquerque: University of New Mexico Press, 2002.

Kiser, William S. *Turmoil on the Rio Grande: The Territorial History of the Mesilla Valley, 1846–1865.* College Station: Texas A&M University Press, 2011.

Meinig, D. W. *The Shaping of America: A Geographical Perspective on 500 Years of History.* Vol. 3: *Transcontinental America, 1850–1915.* New Haven: Yale University Press, 1998.

Montoya, María E. *Translating Property: The Maxwell Land Grant and the Conflict over Land in the American West, 1840–1900.* Lawrence: University Press of Kansas, 2002.

Nolan, Frederick. *The West of Billy the Kid.* Norman: University of Oklahoma Press, 1998.

Nostrand, Richard L. *The Hispano Homeland.* Norman: University of Oklahoma Press, 1992.

Sides, Hampton. *Blood and Thunder: An Epic of the American West.* New York: Doubleday, 2006.

Spude, Robert L. "Santa Rita del Cobre, New Mexico: The Early American Period, 1846–1886." *Mining History Journal* 6 (1999): 8–38.

Steele, Thomas J., S.J., ed. and trans. *Archbishop Lamy: In His Own Words.* Albuquerque: LPD Press, 2000.

Utley, Robert M. *Billy the Kid: A Short and Violent Life.* Lincoln: University of Nebraska Press, 1991.

Chapter 7

Ball, Larry. *Elfego Baca in Life and Legend*. El Paso: Texas Western Press, 1992.

Caffey, David L. *Frank Springer and New Mexico: From the Colfax County War to the Emergence of Modern Santa Fe*. College Station: Texas A&M University Press, 2006.

Gonzales-Berry, Erlinda, and David R. Maciel, eds. *The Contested Homeland: A Chicano History of New Mexico*. Albuquerque: University of New Mexico Press, 2000.

Greever, William S. *Arid Domain: The Santa Fe Railway and Its Western Land Grant*. Stanford, Calif.: Stanford University Press, 1954.

Lamar, Howard R. *Charlie Siringo's West: An Interpretive Biography*. Albuquerque: University of New Mexico Press, 2005.

———. *The Far Southwest, 1846–1912: A Territorial History*. Rev. ed. Albuquerque: University of New Mexico Press, 2000.

Myrick, David F. *New Mexico Railroads*. Rev. ed. Albuquerque: University of New Mexico Press, 1990.

Nostrand, Richard L. *El Cerrito, New Mexico*. Norman: University of Oklahoma Press, 2003.

Parish, William J. *The Charles Ilfeld Company: A Study of the Rise and Decline of Mercantile Capitalism in New Mexico*. Cambridge, Mass.: Harvard University Press, 1961.

Remley, David. *Bell Ranch: Cattle Ranching in the Southwest, 1824–1947*. Albuquerque: University of New Mexico Press, 1993.

Rosenbaum, Robert J. *Mexicano Resistance in the Southwest*. Dallas: Southern Methodist University Press, 1981.

Servin, Manuel P., and Robert L. Spude. "Historical Conditions of Early Mexican Labor in the United States: A Neglected Story." *Journal of Mexican American History* 5 (1977): 43–56.

Spude, Robert L. "Mineral Frontier in Transition: Copper Mining in Arizona, 1880–1885." *New Mexico Historical Review* 51, no. 1 (1976): 30–34.

Chapter 8

Baxter, John O. *Dividing New Mexico Waters, 1700–1912*. Albuquerque: University of New Mexico Press, 1997.

Bogener, Stephen. *Ditches across the Desert: Irrigation in the Lower Pecos Valley.* Lubbock: Texas Tech University Press, 2003.

Dye, Victoria E. *All Aboard for Santa Fe: Railway Promotion of the Southwest, 1890s to 1930s.* Albuquerque: University of New Mexico Press, 2005.

Gibson, Arrell Morgan. *The Santa Fe and Taos Colonies: Age of the Muses, 1900–1942.* Norman: University of Oklahoma Press, 1983.

Holmes, Jack E. *Politics in New Mexico.* Albuquerque: University of New Mexico Press, 1967.

Holtby, David V. *Forty-Seventh Star: New Mexico's Struggle for Statehood.* Norman: University of Oklahoma Press, 2012.

Huggard, Christopher J., and Terrance M. Hubble. *Santa Rita del Cobre: A Copper Mining Community in New Mexico.* Boulder: University Press of Colorado, 2012.

Jaehn, Tomas. *Germans in the Southwest, 1850–1920.* Albuquerque: University of New Mexico Press, 2005.

Jones, Billy M. *Health-Seekers in the Southwest, 1817–1900.* Norman: University of Oklahoma Press, 1967.

Kern, Robert. *Labor in New Mexico: Unions, Strikes, and Social History since 1881.* Albuquerque: University of New Mexico Press, 1983.

Larson, Robert W. *New Mexico's Quest for Statehood, 1846–1912.* Albuquerque: University of New Mexico Press, 1968.

Meléndez, A. Gabriel. *Spanish-Language Newspapers in New Mexico, 1834–1958.* Tucson: University of Arizona Press, 2005.

Mitchell, Pablo. *Coyote Nation: Sexuality, Race, and Conquest in Modernizing New Mexico, 1880–1920.* Chicago: University of Chicago Press, 2005.

Rivera, José A. *Acequia Culture: Water, Land, and Community in the Southwest.* Albuquerque: University of New Mexico Press, 1998.

Schackel, Sandra. *Social Housekeepers: Women Shaping Public Policy in New Mexico, 1920–1940.* Albuquerque: University of New Mexico Press, 1992.

Stratton, David H. *Tempest over Teapot Dome: The Story of Albert Fall.* Norman: University of Oklahoma Press, 1998.

Whaley, Charlotte. *Nina Otero-Warren of Santa Fe.* Albuquerque: University of New Mexico Press, 1994.

Chapter 9

Biebel, Charles D. *Making the Most of It: Public Works in Albuquerque during the Great Depression, 1929–1942.* Albuquerque: Albuquerque Museum, 1986.

Cohen, Stan. *The Tree Army: A Pictorial History of the Civilian Conservation Corps, 1933–1942.* Missoula, Mont.: Pictorial Histories, 1980.

Cutter, Charles R. "The WPA Federal Music Project in New Mexico." *New Mexico Historical Review* (July 1986): 203–16.

Deutsch, Sarah. *No Separate Refuge: Culture, Class, and Gender on an Anglo-Hispanic Frontier in the American Southwest, 1890–1940.* New York: Oxford University Press, 1987.

Fergusson, Erna. "The Tingley's of Albuquerque." Unpublished manuscript. University of New Mexico. Zimmerman Library. Center for Southwest Research, Collection, MSS 45. Box 13, Folder 3.

Fergusson, Erna, Papers. University of New Mexico. Zimmerman Library. Center for Southwest Research. Collection MSS 45.

Flynn, Katheryn A., ed. and comp. *Treasures on New Mexico Trails: Discover New Deal Art and Architecture.* Santa Fe: Sunstone Press, 1995.

Flynn, Katheryn A., with Richard Polese. *The New Deal: A 75th Anniversary Celebration.* Salt Lake City: Gibbs Smith, 2008.

Gómez, Arthur R. "Farther on Down the Road: An Auto Tour of New Mexico's New Deal Legacy." Unpublished manuscript. Santa Fe: National Park Service, Intermountain Region, 2008.

———. "New Mexico Mining in the Twentieth Century: A Photographic Essay." *New Mexico Historical Review* 69 (October 1994): 357–68.

———. "Profile in Commitment: U.S. Senator Dennis Chavez." Unpublished manuscript. Santa Fe: Dennis Chavez Foundation. 1996.

Kammer, David. "The Historic and Architectural Resources of the New Deal in New Mexico." Santa Fe: New Mexico Historic Preservation Division Report, 1994.

Melzer, Richard. *The Coming of Age in the Great Depression: The Civilian Conservation Corps Experience in New Mexico, 1933–1942.* Las Cruces: Yucca Tree Press, 2000.

Montoya, Maria E. "Dennis Chavez and the Making of Modern New Mexico." In *New Mexican Live: Profiles and Historical Stories.* Edited

by Richard W. Etulain. Albuquerque: University of New Mexico
Press, 2002: 242–64.
———. "The Roots of Economic and Ethnic Divisions in Northern
New Mexico: The Case of the Civilian Conservation Corps."
Western Historical Quarterly 26 (Spring 1995): 15–34.
New Mexico Emergency Relief Administration. "The Bulletin."
Washington D.C: GPO, 1935–1936. University of New Mexico,
Zimmerman Library, Center for Southwest Research.
New Mexico Office of the State Historian. http://www.newmexico
history.org.
Noe, Sally. *Greetings from Gallup: Six Decades of Route 66*. Gallup:
Gallup Downtown Development Group, n.d.
Pickens, William H. "Cutting vs. Chavez: Battle of the Patrones." *New
Mexico Historical Review* 46 (January 1971): 5–36.
Seligman, G. L., Jr. "The Purge that Failed: The 1934 Senatorial
Election in New Mexico: Yet Another View." *New Mexico Historical
Review* 47 (October 1972): 361–81.
Traugott, Joe. *How the West Is One: The Art of New Mexico*. Santa Fe:
Museum of New Mexico Press, 2007.
U.S. National Park Service. *"Old Santa Fe Trail Building."* Tucson:
Western National Parks Association, 2004.
Weigle, Marta, and Kyle Fiore. *Santa Fe and Taos: The Writer's Era,
1916–1941*. Santa Fe: Ancient City Press, 1982.
Welsh, Michael E. *U.S. Army Corps of Engineers: Albuquerque District,
1935–1985*. Albuquerque: University of New Mexico Press, 1987.
Williams, Jerry L., ed. *New Mexico in Maps*. 2nd ed. Albuquerque:
University of New Mexico Press, 1985.
Wilson, Chris, Stanley Hordes, and Henry Walt. "The South Central
New Mexico Regional Overview." Santa Fe: State of New Mexico,
Historic Preservation Division, Office of Cultural Affairs Report,
1989.

Chapter 10

Chenoweth, William L. "Raw Materials Activities of the Manhattan
Project on the Colorado Plateau." *Nonrenewable Resources* (1997):
33–41.

Clifton, Don. "The Carlsbad Army Air Field." Report No. 509. Santa
Fe: Bureau of Land Management, 2004.

Conant, Jennet. *109 East Palace: Robert Oppenheimer and the Secret City
of Los Alamos.* New York: Simon & Schuster, 2005.

Gómez, Arthur R. *Quest for the Golden Circle: The Four Corners and
the Metropolitan West, 1945–1970.* 1990. Reprinted, Lawrence:
University Press of Kansas, 2002.

Hunner, Jon. *J. Robert Oppenheimer, the Cold War, and the Atomic West.*
Norman: University of Oklahoma Press, 2009.

———. *Inventing Los Alamos: The Growth of an Atomic Community.*
Norman: University of Oklahoma Press, 2004.

Hyink, James. "The Second Coming: The Military in New Mexico,
1945–1949." Paper presented to Annual Conference of Historical
Society of New Mexico, 1985.

Kammer, David. *The Historic and Architectural Resources of Route 66
through New Mexico.* Santa Fe: New Mexico Historic Preservation
Division, 1992.

Lasby, Clarence G. *Project Paperclip: German Scientists and the Cold War.*
New York: Atheneum Press, 1971.

Lewis, Tom. *Divided Highways: Building the Interstate Highways,
Transforming American Life.* New York: Penguin Books, 1997.

Los Alamos National Laboratory. *Los Alamos: Beginning of an Era,
1943–1945.* Los Alamos: Los Alamos Historical Society, 1997.

Morín, Raul. *Among the Valiant: Mexican Americans in WWII and Korea.*
Alhambra, Calif.: Borden Publishing Co., 1966.

Nash, Gerald D. *The American West Transformed: The Impact of the
Second World War.* Bloomington: Indiana University Press, 1985.

Niemeyer, Lucian, and Art Gómez. *New Mexico: Images of a Land and
Its People.* Albuquerque: University of New Mexico, 2004.

Rogers, Everett M., and Nancy R. Bartlit. *Silent Voices of World War II:
When Sons of the Land of Enchantment Met Sons of the Land of the
Rising Sun.* Santa Fe: Sunstone Press, 2005.

Ryan, Craig. *The Pre-astronauts: Manned Ballooning on the Threshold of
Space.* Annapolis, Md.: Naval Institute Press, 1995.

Spidle, Jake W. "Axis Invasion of the American West: POWs in New
Mexico,1942–1946." *New Mexico Historical Review* 49 (April 1974):
93–122.

Starkweather, Tom. "WSMR Roots." Unpublished paper, 1989.
Szasz, Ferenc M. *Larger Than Life: New Mexico in the Twentieth Century.* Albuquerque: University of New Mexico Press, 2006.
Weigle, Marta, ed. *Telling New Mexico: A New History.* Santa Fe: Museum of New Mexico Press, 2009.
Writer's Program of the Works Progress Administration, comp. *The WPA Guide to 1930s New Mexico.* 1940. Reprinted, Tucson, University of Arizona Press, 1989.

Chapter 11

De Buys, William. *Enchantment and Exploitation: The Life and Hard Times of a New Mexico Mountain Range.* Albuquerque: University of New Mexico Press, 1985.
Hammet, Jerilou, et al. *The Essence of Santa Fe: From a Way of Life to a Style.* Santa Fe: Ancient City Press, 2006.
Herrera, Mary. *New Mexico Blue Book, 2007–2008.* Albuquerque: LithExcel, 2007.
The New Mexican. Santa Fe, New Mexico. Various issues, 1965–2010.
Norton, Hana Samek. "'Fantastical Assumptions': A Centennial Overview of Water Use in New Mexico." *New Mexico Historical Review* 73 (October 1998): 371–87.
Price, V. B. *A City at the End of the World.* Albuquerque: University of New Mexico Press, 1992.
Simmons, Marc. *Albuquerque: A Narrative History.* Albuquerque: University of New Mexico Press, 1982.
Szasz, Ferenc M. "New Mexico's Forgotten Nuclear Tests: Projects Gnome (1961) and Gasbuggy (1967). *New Mexico Historical Review* 73 (October 1998): 347–70.
Tobias, Henry J., and Charles E. Woodhouse. *Santa Fe: A Modern History, 1880–1990.* Albuquerque: University of New Mexico Press, 2001.
Wilson, Chris. *The Myth of Santa Fe: Creating a Modern Regional Tradition.* Albuquerque: University of New Mexico Press, 1997.

Index

References to illustrations appear in italic type.

Abbey, Edward, 292–93
Abiquiú, N.Mex., 72, 107, 126
Abó Pass, 35
Abó Pueblo, 50
Abrams, Jane, 291
Abreu, Ramón, 89
Abreu, Santiago, 75
Abruzzo, Ben, 313–15
Abruzzo, Richard, 314
Acoma Pueblo, 36–41; attack on Spanish at, 34–37, 41; on early maps, 13; mission established at, 54; revolt against Spanish, 58; Spanish attack on, 38–40; Spanish expeditions at 18, 25, 29
Adams-Onís Treaty (1819), 71–72
African Americans, 157; as coal miners in New Mexico, 163; cultural activities of, 220; discrimination against in New Mexico, 192–93, 195, 306; population of in New Mexico, 123, 189, 192, 295; role in World War II, 268; and slavery in New Mexico, 116; as soldiers during Apache wars, 167; with Vázquez de Coronado's expedition, 20; as workers in petroleum industry, 272
Agriculture, 95; African Americans in, 192; among ancient cultures, 4–8; and commercial centers, 190, 272; crops grown, 184; in Curry County, 323; demonstration trains, 185, 187; as economic force in New Mexico, 72–73, 177, 257, 271; growth of, 180, 206, 274–75; impact of drought, 8, 330; impact of Great Depression on, 225–27; irrigation, 181–83; and land grants, 97; methods of, 123, 142, 184, 187–88; during Mexican War, 106–107;

and 1920s depression, 212–13; in Pecos River Valley, 191; among Pueblo Indians, 9, 11, 24–25; and Soil Erosion Service, 233; use of migrant workers in, 229, 335; use of prisoners of war in, 276; and water issues, 331–32
Alameda Land Grant, 59
Alamogordo, N.Mex.: Federal Art Project in, 254; founding of, 188; military as economic force in, 323; New Deal projects at, 245; population of, 312; railroad in, 185, 188; role of in space program, 288; and World War II scientific research, 276
Alamogordo Army Air Field, 279. *See also* Holloman Air Force Base
Alarid, Jesús María ("El Chico"), 90
Alarid, Jesús María Hilario, 170–71
Albuquerque, N.Mex., 9, 24, 60, 74, 83, 90, 94, 154, 170, 177, 189, 194, 205, 263, 301, 310, 314, 336; African American community of, 192; Barelas barrio in, 236, 292, 313; as center of postwar activists, 291; Civilian Conservation Corps camps near, 239; Confederate occupation of, 131; description of in 1940, 269–70; ethnic groups in, 291; festivals in, 312; flood control project in, 246; founding of, 59; during Great Depression, 225, 227; growth of, 258, 313, 318, 320–23; Harvey House in, 217; hot air balloon festival in, 313–14; housing developers of, 305; hunting clubs of, 214; Indian boarding school at, 169; industry in, 332; in literature, 293; Mexican Americans deported from, 251; migrant workers in, 335; military air base at, 261, 271, 286,

327; as part of New Mexico Territory, 122, 144; joint statehood with New Mexico proposed, 193; railroad land grants in, 153; statehood for, 196; U.S. annexation of, 112; voting rights of Indians in, 307

Arkansas River, 21, 42, 103; as boundary of New Spain, 69–71; Comanche raids along, 62; map of, 72; Spanish Indian campaign on, 60, 64

Armijo, Antonio, 66, 76

Armijo, 1st Sgt. Manuel, 263

Armijo, Manuel, 88, 256–57; and American occupation of New Mexico, 98, 103–104; flees, 111; land grants conferred by, 96–98, 148; as New Mexico governor, 91–92, 98, 105; and New Mexico rebellion, 88–91; and Texas invasion of New Mexico, 94–96

Armijo, N.Mex., 95

Armstrong, Neil, 282, 291

Army Medical Corps Reserve, 289

Art: colonies of, 222–23; and Federal Art Project, 252, 254; by Hispanic artists, 221; and Indian crafts, 221; postwar revival of, 291–92; use of at Hyde Park, 241

Artesia, N.Mex., 220, 268, 314; discrimination against African Americans in, 192; founding of, 188; and petroleum industry, 272; and water issues, 331

ASARCO (American Smelting & Refining Company), 205

Atchison, Topeka & Santa Fe Railroad, 163, 187, 223, 270; advertisement for, 154; building of, 151–52; coal properties of, 205; completion of, 150, 163–64; hotels and health resorts along, 228; impact of Great Depression on, 226; impact on New Mexico, 154, 191; impact on Pueblo settlements, 168; land grants to, 172; lawyers for, 199; marketing of tourism by, 185, 187, 217–18, 221; spur lines of, 155, 164, 185

Atlantic & Pacific Railroad, 152–53, 172; impact of on New Mexico, 152

Atomic bomb: development of, 274, 276–80, 283; for hydraulic fracturing, 303; Soviet acquisition of, 284; use of in Japan, 256–57

Atomic Energy Commission, 285–86

Atrisco, N.Mex., 58, 95

Aubrey, Felix, 129

Austin, Mary, 223, 254

Austrians, 203; as coal miners, 208; population of, 163, 189

Automobiles, 215–16, 301; growth of tourism of, 216–17, 228; and New Mexico highways, 270; women as drivers, 218

Averill, Charles, 142

Aztec, N.Mex., 271–72, 318

Baca, Elfego, 160

Baja California, 16, 78–79, 111

Baker City, N.Mex., 143

Bandelier, Adolph, 214

Bandelier National Monument, 8

Barboncito (Navajo chief), 136, 138

Barceló, María Gertrudis, 107

Barela, Patrocino, 254

Barelas barrio (Albuquerque), 236, 246, 292, 313

Barnes, Will, 213

Bartlett, John, 127

Bartlit, Nancy R., 256, 262, 264

Basketmakers, 4–5

Bataan Death March, 256, 265, 334; survivors of, 263

Battle of Acoma, 37–41

Battle of Brazito, 108

Battle of Glorieta, 133

Battle of La Cañada (1838), 91

Battle of Peralta, 134

Battle of Sacramento (Mexico), 108

Battle of Valverde, 131–32, 134

Battle of Washita (Oklahoma), 139

Bauman, Gustav, 222

Baumgartner, Felix ("Fearless Felix"), 289

Bayard, N.Mex., 206, 263

Caballero, Señora Lope de, 17
Cabeza de Baca, Ezequiel, 197–98
Cabeza de Baca, Fabiola, 158
Cabeza de Vaca, Álvar Nuñez, 12, 14–15, 22
Cabrillo, Juan Rodríguez, 21
Calhoun, James, 119, 122
California, Confederates plans for, 131; Hispanic citizenship rights in, 113; miners in New Mexico from, 144; New Mexico trade with, 76; population of, 125; statehood for, 116–17; U.S. annexation of, 100–101, 103, 112
California Volunteers, 143, 146
Camino Real de Tierra Adentro, 33, 151; communication along, 74; development of, 32, 43, 73; immigrants travel along, 49–50; Indian threat to travelers on, 59, 62; modern highway following, 215; Texas prisoners escorted along, 94–95; as trade route, 76, 129
Camino Real de Tierra Adentro National Historic Trail, 73
Camp 833 (Civilian Conservation Corps), 241
Campbell, Glen, 294
Canadian River, 66; cattle operations along, 156; Mexican land grants along, 97; settlements along, 126; Spanish expeditions along, 21, 34. See also South Canadian River
Cana Pueblo, 29
Canby, Edward R. S., 130–31, 134
Cannon Air Force Base, 300, 323–24
Canyon de Chelly, 137
Capitan, N.Mex., 204–205
Carbajal, Luis de, 30
Cárdenas, Garcia López de. See López de Cárdenas, Garcia
Cargo, David, 309–10
Carleton, James H., 134; Indian campaigns of, 135–37, 142; mining claim of, 143; and removal of Navajos to Bosque Redondo, 138

Carlisle Indian School (Penn.), 169
Carlsbad, N.Mex., 200; atomic tests near, 303; cattle ranches near, 204; founding of, 188; irrigation project at, 181–83; military air base at, 261–62, 271; nuclear waste dump in, 333, 339; population of, 270, 312. See Eddy, N.Mex.
Carlsbad Army Air Field, 261–62
Carlsbad Caverns, 215, 241, 303
Carnuel Land Grant, 59
Carranza, Venustiano, 201–202
Carrie Tingley Hospital, 249–50
Carrillo, Charles, 292
Carrizozo, N.Mex., 188
Carson, Christopher "Kit": commands New Mexico Volunteers, 130; as guide to California, 129; image of in literature, 142; Indian campaigns by, 134, 136–39
Carson National Forest, 214, 340
Carter, George, 115
Carthage, N.Mex., 163, 205
Cassidy, Gerald, 222, 252
Castañeda, Pedro de, 19–20, 42
Castaño de Sosa, Gaspar, 30–31, 33–34
Castro, Raúl, 312
Cather, Willa, 140, 223
Catholic Church, 121, 198; archbishop of, 312; at center of Hispanic cultural activities, 221; and clashes with Protestants, 166; heritage of, 177; Inquisition office of, 50–51; reform of in New Mexico, 140–41; role of in New Mexico statehood movements, 117; role in politics, 119, 198. See also Franciscans; Missions
Catron, Thomas: challenge to land grant of, 172–73; as lawyer for cattle companies, 160; as lawyer for Hispanics, 149; and Maxwell land grant, 148–49; as member of constitutional convention, 194; opposition to women's suffrage by, 200; political career of, 178; power of in New Mexico, 147; as promoter of railroads, 155; as U.S. senator, 197, 199

Cattle industry, 156–58, 252; cattle
growers' association, 158, 162;
expansion, 155–56, 167; impact of
drought on, 330; ; need for during
World War II, 274; and railroads, 152;
and range wars, 159; and rustling, 161–
62, 210; in southern New Mexico, 270.
See also Livestock industry; Ranching
Caypa Pueblo. *See* San Juan de los
Caballeros Pueblo
Central, N.Mex., 206
Cerrillos, N.Mex., 58
Cerro Grande Fire, 328, 330
Cervántez, Pedro López, 254
Chaco Canyon, 3, 6–8
Chaco Canyon (Lister and Lister), 3
Chaco culture: agriculture methods of, 9;
and ancestral Apaches and Navajos,
10; description of, 5–7; legacy of in
Ancestral Puebloan lifestyle, 8
Chaco Culture National Historical Site,
6, 215
Chacón, Fernando, 69
Chacón, Rafael, 104
Chacón, Soledad, as New Mexico
secretary of state, 200
Chama, N.Mex., 72, 152, 271
Chama River, 9, 331
Chamuscado. *See* Sánchez Chamuscado,
Francisco
Chamuscado-Rodríguez expedition, 22, 25
Chapuis, Jean, 62
Charles, Tom, 240
Chaves, J. Francisco, 120, 125, 130, 178
Chaves, José, 97
Chaves, Manuel, 125, 130, 133; as member
of New Mexico Volunteers, 131–32
Chaves, Mariano, 90
Chaves County, N.Mex., 169; during Great
Depression, 243; petroleum industry
in, 272, 304; population, 190–91, 317;
WPA project in, 248
Chaves family, 124–25, 129–30, 160
Chavez, David, 235–36
Chavez, Dionisio ("Dennis"), 324; death
of, 309; discrimination against in U.S.

Senate, 251; and fair employment,
306; and funds for road improvement,
300–301; and natural gas pipeline,
302; political career of, 236–37; as
supporter of Tingley, 235; as U.S.
senator, 299–300
Chavez, Fabian, 337
Chávez, Felipe, 125
Chia Pueblo. *See* Zia Pueblo
Chicago, Ill., 155, 182, 185, 244, 270;
railroad lines from, 150–51, 185; Route
66 from, 216, 301
Chicago, Judy, 291
Chicago, Rock Island & Pacific Railroad,
185, 187–88
Chihuahua, Mexico, 9, 12, 63, 69, 73,
77, 87, 103, 113, 167, 187, 199, 220;
capture of during Mexican War, 111;
cattle herds from, 156; immigrant
labor from, 188; and international
boundary dispute, 127; Manuel
Armijo flees to, 104; Mesilla Valley
settlers from, 128; miners from, 129,
143, 206; New Mexico citizens relocate
to, 113; New Mexico trade routes to,
92, 129; Pershing's punitive expedition
into, 201; Spanish expeditions from,
22, 30–31; Spanish troops from, 91;
threat of Texas invasion of, 96
Chihuahua City, Mexico. *See* Ciudad
Chihuahua, Mexico
Chihuahua Trail. *See* Camino Real de
Tierra Adentro; Santa Fe–Chihuahua
Trail
Chililí Pueblo, 49–50
Chinle, Ariz., 267
Chino, N.Mex., 208
Chino, Wendell, 317, 333–34
Chino Copper Company, 199, 205–206,
207, 208
Chintis, Nick, 262
Chiricahua Apaches, 136, 166–67
Chisum, John, 144–45; cattle operations
of, 156; role of in Lincoln County
War, 146; against Thomas Catron, 147
Chloride, N.Mex., 164

Church of Jesus Christ of Latter-day
Saints. *See* Mormons
Cíbola, 12–13, 16–18, 22
Cibola National Forest, 321
Cicuye Pueblo. *See* Pecos Pueblo
Cimarron Cattle Company, 158
Cimarron River, 97–98
Ciudad Chihuahua, Mexico, 63, 70, 77,
95, 108
Ciudad Juárez, Mexico, 127. *See also* El
Paso del Norte, Mexico
Civilian Conservation Corps, 232–33, 242;
camps of, 305; New Mexico projects
of, 238–41, 255; and Conchas Dam,
244; ski trails cleared by, 314
Civilian Conservation Corps
Reforestation Relief Act, 239
Civil Rights Act (1964), 306
Civil War, 117, 121, 138, 145, 147, 157,
172, 174; battlefields of, 240; impact
on New Mexico, 119, 129–31, 134–35,
143; impact of railroad development,
151
Civil Works Administration, 232, 247; in
New Mexico, 241; projects of, 245–
46, 255
Claims Resolution Act (2010), 332
Clark, William, 68
Clayton, N.Mex., 152, 157, 185, 223
Cleaveland, Agnes Morley, 158
Cleveland, Grover, 149, 168, 170, 172
Cloudcroft, N.Mex., 204, 316
Clovis, N.Mex., 324; Civilian
Conservation Corps camp near, 239;
economy of, 323; evidence of Archaic
hunters at, 4; founding of, 188; Harvey
House of, 217; hot air balloon festival
at, 314; military airbase at, 271, 300,
324; population of, 190, 270, 312; race
riot in, 192; railroad line to, 172, 185,
188; recording studio at, 294; water
issues in, 331; WPA project in, 247
Coahuila, Mexico, 60, 63, 69, 73
Coal industry, 212, 304; growth of, 177,
204, 271–72, 318; immigrant miners
in, 220; miners strike in, 208; opening

of coalfields, 163, 204–205; political
power of, 199; in San Juan County,
327; towns of, 190–92; and workers'
compensation, 210
Cochiti Pueblo, 59, 79; revolt against
Spanish by, 58; settlements near, 90,
123; Spanish expeditions to, 28, 34, 56
Code Talkers, 266–67
Cold War, 280, 284, 308, 322, 331, 341;
need for nuclear material during, 274;
Los Alamos and, 285; New Mexico's
role, 257, 298; space race during, 281,
286–87
Coleman, Robert, 249
Colfax County, N.Mex.: coal industry in,
191, 199; creation of, 144; population
of, 169, 189, 191, 318; ranching in, 158;
warring factions in, 148; WPA projects
in, 248
Colfax County War, 148, 159
Collaborative Forest Restoration
Program, 340
Colonization Law of 1824 (Mexico), 78,
96
Colorado, ancient cliff dwellings in, 8; and
Confederates plans for, 131; diversion
of water from, 331; land grants in, 97,
148; New Mexico laborers migrate
to, 229; New Mexico land transferred,
144; U.S. annexation of, 112
Colorado Fuel & Iron Company, 205,
208–209, 272
Colorado River, 42, 66, 122, 152, 331
Colorado Volunteers, 131, 134
Columbus, N.Mex., 201, 203, 210
Comanche Indians, 112; collapse of
empire of, 138–39; language used in
World War I, 266; raids on Indian
settlements by, 11, 138; raids on
Spanish settlements by, 54, 60, 62;
Spanish campaigns against, 63–64;
trade with, 62, 85, 139
Comancheros, 139
Comentarios, by Álvar Nuñez Cabeza de
Vaca, 42
Compañía Mexicana de Carbón, 163

relocate near, 113; Oñate expedition at, 32; Pueblo Revolt refugees travel to, 56–57; Spanish military at, 59

El Paso & Northeastern Railroad, 204

El Paso & Southwestern Railroad, 185, 188, 199

El Paso Natural Gas Company, 302–303

El Portuelo. *See* Abó Pass

El Turco (Indian guide), 21

El Vado, N.Mex., 271

El Voz del Pueblo (Las Vegas), 175

Embudo, N.Mex., 109

Empire Zinc Company, 208

Environmental Protection Agency, 327, 333

Escalante, Silvestre Vélez, 66

Española, N.Mex., 123, 153, 268, 294, 311; atomic bomb developed near, 277; merchants of, 161; Obama's visit to, 296–97, 337; railroad to, 152, 155; wildfire near, 329. *See also* Santa Cruz de la Cañada, Villa de

Española Valley, 60, 72

Espejo, Antonio de, 26–30, 42

Espejo, Pedro de, 26

Esquivel, Juan José, 89

Estancia, N.Mex., 162

Estancia Valley, 172

Esteban the Moor, 12, 14–18

Exposition on the Province of New Mexico, 1812, The (Pino), 70

Fair Employment Practices Commission (1946), 306

Fall, Albert, 210; and Teapot Dome Scandal, 211–12; as U.S. senator, 197, 199

Farfán, Marcos de, 32

Farmington, N.Mex., 303; economy of, 326–28; hot air balloon festival at, 314; petroleum industry at, 272, 302; population of, 271, 312, 318

Farm-Labor Party, 198

"Fat Man" (atomic bomb), 256, 278, 284

Federal Aid Road Act (1916), 215

Federal Art Project, 252, 254

Federal Emergency Relief Administration, 232–33, 238, 245

Federal Highway Act (1956), 301

Federal Power Commission, 302

Federal Writers Project, 269

Fergusson, Erna, 218, 234

Fergusson, Harvey B., 166, 170, 187, 218; as member of constitutional convention, 194–95

Fergusson Act (1896), 166

Fermi, Enrico, 278

Fermín de Mendinueto, Pedro, 83

Fernández, Antonio M., 300

Feynman, Richard, 278

Fierro, N.Mex., 208

Fierro Copper Mine, 272

Fiesta de Santa Fe, 218, 223, 320

Film industry, 338–39

First National Bank of Santa Fe, 149, 230

Fish and Wildlife Service, U.S., 240

509th Bombardment Group, 300, 324

Flores, Ruben, 263

Flynn, Kathryn, 240

Folsom, N.Mex, 4

Food for Victory campaign, 274–75

Ford, Gerald, 310

Ford, Henry, 215

Forest Reserve Act (1891), 213

Forest Service, U.S., 214, 254, 310; and Civilian Conservation Corps, 240; and timber industry, 339–40

Fort Bayard, during Victorio War, 167

Fort Bliss (El Paso, Texas), 263, 279, 281–82

Fort Craig, 131–32, 134

Fort Defiance, 267

Fort Fillmore, 127, 130

Fort Marcy, 107, 249

Fort Selden, 167

Fort Stanton, 146, 167

Fort Sumner, 136, 220, 271

Fort Union, 131, 143

Fort Wingate, 267

Fort Worth, Tex., 152, 155

Fountain, Albert Jennings, 162, 210

Foy, Tommy, 263

Fragoso, Francisco, 66
France, 62, 67, 140, 268, 280; influence on
  Great Plains, 69; occupation of Spain
  by, 70–71; threat to Spanish territory,
  60–61; trade with New Mexico by,
  66, 68
Franciscans, 33, 66; conflict with
  Spanish government by, 48–49, 54,
  58; and conversion of Indians, 22,
  25–26; expansion of mission system
  by, 50, 54; as members of Spanish
  expeditions, 15–16, 22–23, 27; during
  Pueblo Revolt, 56, 58
Fraternal lodges, 219
Fred Harvey Company, 223. See also
  Harvey, Fred
French, William, 158, 166
Frost, Max, 166, 180, 184
Fuchs, Klaus, 283–84
Fuller, Edward J., 277

Gadsden, James, 127–28
Gadsden Purchase (1854), 122, 127–28
Galisteo Basin, 9, 18, 24–25, 31, 34–35
Galisteo Pueblo, 50, 55, 60
Gallagher, Peter, 93
Gallegos, Hernán, 23–24, 26
Gallegos, José Manuel, 115, 119–20
Gallup, N.Mex., 203, 247, 280; Civilian
  Conservation Corps camp near, 239;
  coal fields at, 163, 205, 272; festivals
  in, 312, 314; founding of, 152; mining
  strikes in, 208–209; population of, 270;
  racial discrimination in, 192
Gallup America Coal Company, 199, 205,
  208
García, Alonso, 55
Garcia, Evans, 263
García, Fabián, 187, 221
Garfield, James G., 157
Garland, John, 127
Garrett, Pat, 147, 181, 204
Gaspar of Mexico (Mexican Indian), 29
Georgia, 21, 244, 315
Germans, 203; cultural activities of in
  New Mexico, 220; as New Mexico

residents, 123; as Operation Paperclip
  scientists, 278, 280, 282–83; as
  prisoners of war in New Mexico, 276;
  role of in space race, 287–88
Germany, 202, 201, 314; acquisition of
  atomic bomb by, 283–84; surrender of,
  269, 274; in World War II, 257, 260
Geronimo, 167
Gibson, Arrell, 222
Gila Cliff Dwellings, 8
Gila Cliffs National Monument, 215
Gila National Forest, 214
Gila River, 5, 122, 126, 128
Gila Trail, 128
Gila Wilderness Area, 329–30
Gilpin, William, 131
Glen Canyon Dam (Ariz.), 293
Glenn L. Martin Company, 287
Glorieta Pass, 129, 132
Gobernador, N.Mex., 268, 303, 308
Goddard, Robert H., 282–83
Gold, 168; mining of, 163–65
Gold, Harry, 284
Gomez, Everardo R., 268–69
Gómez, Laura, 110
Gomez, Verna, 269
Gómez Montesinos, Alonso, 40
Gonzales, José, 90–91
Gonzales, Leopoldo, 268
González, Deana, 126
Goodnight-Loving Trail, 144
Good Roads Association, 215
Gore, Al, 297
Gorman, Carl, 266–67
Gould, Jay, 151–52
Governor's Palace. See Palace of the
  Governors (Santa Fe)
Grand Canyon (Ariz.), 18, 66
Gran Quivira, 14, 21–22, 52
Grant, Ulysses S., 148, 172
Grant County, N.Mex., 144; during Great
  Depression, 243; mining industry in,
  165, 206, 272; population, 169, 189, 318;
  Victorio raids in, 167
Grants, N.Mex., 152, 274, 278
Great Britain, 62, 73, 183, 202, 268, 280, 284;

role in cattle industry, 155–56; as threat to Spanish Empire, 66, 68; U.S. border dispute with, 100–101; in World War II, 260

Great Depression, 226, 292; and Hispanic artists, 254; impact on agriculture, 212, 275; impact on New Mexico, 225, 227; and Indian New Deal, 252; labor migration from New Mexico during, 229; New Deal programs of, 233, 250, 255, 261, 299; recreation during, 246; relief programs for, 238, 242; timber industry during, 271; unemployment during, 227; water diversion projects of, 331

Great Plains, 13, 18, 25, 69, 174, 184, 188; collapse of Comanche empire on, 138; growing French influence on, 60–61, 68; Indians of, 40, 53; New Mexico trade routes across, 66; Spanish explorations of, 19, 21, 25, 31, 34, 42, 48, 73

Great Salt Lake (Utah), 44, 64, 66, 73, 107

Greever, William, 172

Gregg, Josiah, 85, 89–90

Griego, Roberto, 294

Grolet, Jacques, 60

Groves, Leslie R., 276–78, 283, 285–86

Guadalupe County, N.Mex., 169, 198, 243

Guadalupe Mountains, 215

Guggenheim, Daniel, 283

Guggenheim, Florence, 283

Guggenheim family, 205–206

Guide Book to Highway 66 (Rittenhouse), 301

Gutiérrez de Humaña, Antonio, 31–32, 34

Hagerman, Herbert, 182

Hagerman, James J., 181–82, 185, 204

Hahn, Judy, 291

Hall, Willard, 105

Hamlin, Rosalie, 294

Hammond, Harmony, 291

Hannett, Arthur, 209–10, 215

Hanover, N.Mex., 208

Harding, Warren G., 210

Harding County, N.Mex., 243, 274, 318

Harrell brothers, 146

Harvey, Fred, 188, 217–18, 223

Harwell Atomic Research Establishment, 284

Hatch, Carl, 237

Hatch, N.Mex., 126–27, 275

Hawikuh, N.Mex., 16–19

Hawikuh Pueblo, 29

Hearst, George, 157, 183

Heart of Aztlan (Anaya), 292

Heinrich, Martin, 337

Hernández, Benigno Cárdenas, 211

Herrera, Juan José, 174–75

Herrera, Nicanor, 174–75

Herrera, Pablo, 174–75

Hewett, Edgar Lee, 214, 252

Hewlett-Packard, 332

Hidalgo, Father Miguel, 71

Highway Journal, 217

Hillerman, Anthony Grove ("Tony"), 292–94

Hillsboro, N.Mex., 164–65

Hilton, August, 205

Hilton, Conrad, 205

Hiroshima, Japan, 256, 274, 278, 280, 285, 303

Hispanics: and Alianza Federal de Mercedes, 309; as artists, 254, 292; and attempts to "Americanize," 193; and Billy the Kid, 147; Dennis Chavez as leader of, 236–37; and Chicano movement, 291; citizenship for, 112–13, 116; in Civilian Conservation Corps, 241; civil rights for, 195, 306; as coal miners, 163, 272; communities of, 198, 221; Democratic Party faction of, 235; discrimination against, 334–35; encroachment on lands of, 173–77; farms of, 184, 227, 274; in housing construction, 305; impact of Great Depression on, 230, 243; impact of World War II on, 258–59; as members of the constitutional convention, 194; after Mexican War, 114–15; mix of cultures among, 220; as musical artists,

of languages in war, 266; voting rights of, 307–308; water rights of, 331–32; U.S. policy for, 138–39, witch purges in communities of, 141. *See also names of individual tribes*

Indians, superintendent of, 118

Indian Territory, 138–39

Inscription Rock. *See* El Morro

Intel Corporation, 259, 318, 332–33

Interior Department, U.S., 211

Inter-Tribal Indian Ceremonial, 312

Irrigation, 188; and Elephant Butte Dam, 183–84; and Office of the State Engineer, 197; in Pecos River Valley, 181; projects of, 204, 331; by Pueblo Indians, 8–9; use of acequias for, 46–47, 107, 123, 146; use of public domain for, 211; and water rights, 182, 332

Isleta Pueblo, 19, 35, 56, 95, 322; boundaries of, 168; Jumano Indians visit at, 52–53; mission established at, 49; railroad built from, 152, 172

Italians: cultural activities of in New Mexico, 220; as miners, 163, 208; population of, 163, 189, 191; as prisoners of war in New Mexico, 276

Iturbide, Agustín de, 75

Jackling, Daniel, 206

Jackson, Andrew, 71, 100

Japan, 257, 260, 276; atomic bomb dropped on, 256; attack on Pearl Harbor by, 261; New Mexico troops as prisoners of war of, 265–66; surrender of, 269, 274, 284; taking of Philippines by, 263–64

Japanese, 305, 334

Jaramillo, Cleofas, 221

Jefferson, Thomas, 68, 70, 100

Jemez Mountains, 206, 276–77, 329

Jemez Pueblo, 59; mission established at, 50, 54; revolt against Spanish by, 58; Spanish explorations to, 21, 29

Jemez Springs, N.Mex., 229, 271

Jensen, Joan, 190

Jews, 24, 51, 129

Jicarilla Apaches, 134, 327; removal of to Mescalero reservation, 167–68

Jiménez, Luis A., 291

Johnson, Andrew, 170

Johnson, Lyndon B., 290

Johnson, Philip, 266

Joint Committee on Atomic Energy, 299, 303

Jones, Andrieus A., 183, 199–200, 236

Jornada del Muerto, 33, 95, 279

Journal of the Santa Fe Expedition (Gallagher), 93

Juhan, Joe T., 315

Julian, George, 171–73

Jumano Indians, 52–53

Jurisdicción de las Salinas, 47

Jusepe (Indian guide), 31, 34

Justiniani, Colonel, 91

Kabotie, Fred, 254

Kaibito, Ariz., 267

Kammer, David, 227, 238

Kanab, Utah, 66

Karankawa Indians, 60

Kearny, Stephen Watts, 111, 116–17; establishes civil government, 105–106, 110; and occupation of New Mexico, 98, 103–105, 107–108

Kearny Code, 105, 110, 181

Kelly, N.Mex., 164–65, 208

Kendall, George W., 94–96

Kere Indians, 7, 33

Kern, Robert, 209

Kewa Pueblo. *See* Santo Domingo Pueblo

Khrushchev, Nikita, 280

King, Bruce, 324, 336–37

King, Edward, 264

King, Gary, 337

Kingston, N.Mex., 164–65

Kinney, Harry, 322

Kinney, John, 162

Kirtland Air Force Base, 261, 300, 310, 315, 321–23; Sandia National Laboratories at, 286

Kirtland Army Air Field, 249

waste facility, 334; removal to Bosque Redondo, 137–38

Mescalero Ranch, 283

Mesilla, N.Mex., 177; as Confederate Arizona capital, 130–31, 134; federal wagon road through, 128; railroad in, 151, 153

Mesilla Valley, 126, 130, 270; and dispute over international boundary, 126–27; irrigation projects in, 183; mercantile trade route through, 129; as part of Gadsden Purchase, 128

Mexica Indians, 14

Mexican-American Boundary Commission, 126

Mexican-American War. *See* Mexican War

Mexican Independence Day, 75, 98–99

Mexican Indians, 33, 37, 39

Mexican National Congress, 77–78, 80, 82, 84–85

Mexican Revolution (1910), 192, 201–202, 210

Mexican War, 76, 102, 114, 141, 150; impact of on New Mexico, 46, 103; public opinion about, 106

Mexico, 4, 13–14, 17, 20, 24, 30, 52, 63, 82, 157, 199, 202, 308–309; American investors in, 210; Chaco trade with, 5–7; discrimination against immigrants from, 251, 335; and international boundary dispute, 126–27; and Gadsden Purchase, 128; governance of New Mexico by, 76–81, 83, 85, 87, 91; immigrants from, 49, 188, 189, 192, 220, 206, 208, 297; independence of, 71, 73–76; land grants issued by, 96, 114; and Mexican War, 100–106, 110–11, 115, 141; New Mexico trade with, 9, 68, 129; oil fields of, 211; Pershing's punitive expedition into, 201–202; rebellion against, 84–85; Spanish northern frontier in, 22, 98; stolen cattle sold in, 162; and Texas invasion of New Mexico, 96; Texas rebellion against, 95, 100; and Treaty of Guadalupe Hidalgo, 112–14; U.S.

acquisition of territory of, 100–101; United States as threat to, 68; Victorio killed in, 167; water treaties with, 183. *See also* New Spain

Mexico City, 12, 15–17, 26, 32, 42, 48, 56, 62, 72, 74, 108, 127; Camino Real de Tierra Adentro from, 43, 76; government in, 47, 50, 76–77, 79, 84, 87, 96, 101, 105; railroads to, 151; and rebellion in New Mexico, 91; Texan prisoners sent to, 94–95; U.S. occupation of, 103, 111

Middle Rio Grande Conservancy, 246

Middle Rio Grande Irrigation Project, 211

Miera y Pacheco, Bernardo, 67

Miles, Nelson A., 167

Military, 107; during Civil War, 130; as economic force, 299, 300, 322–24; Indian campaigns by, 134–36, 167; installations in New Mexico, 300

Mills, William J., 173, 175, 194–95

Mimbres Apaches, 166–67

Mimbres Culture, 5

Mimbres Valley, 184

Mining industry, 129, 136, 143–44, 148; and Bisbee deportation, 203; boom camps of, 164–65; expansion of, 167, 177–78, 204, 208, 271; impact of Great Depression on, 225–26; Indians in, 25; laws for, 120, 210; need for timber by, 206; political power of, 199; railroads' impact on, 152, 163; and strike in McKinley County, 200; taxes on, 170, 197; and unions for miners, 209; use of foreign labor by, 188–90, 229. *See also* Copper industry; Gold; Silver mining

Miranda, Guadalupe, 96

Missions: after Acoma battle, 37, 40; in California, 48, 51, 64; and conflict over control of Indians, 54–55; destruction of during revolts, 56–57; establishment of, 43–44; expansion of system of, 48–51, 54; reestablishment after Pueblo Revolt, 58

Mississippi River, 14, 44, 68, 72, 103, 152, 257; Spanish claims to, 21, 62, 733

expedition of, 32–33, 42–43, 55, 156; and establishment of Santa Fe, 47; explorations of, 34–35, 42; as governor of New Mexico, 41, 46, 48; relations with Indians by, 35, 63, 49

Onorato, Fray, 16

Operation Paperclip, 280, 288

Oppenheimer, J. Robert, 276–78, 284–85

Oraibi Pueblo, 66

Orbison, Roy, 294

Organ Mountains, 33, 56, 143, 279

Ortelius, Abraham, 13

Ortiz, Max, 254

Ortiz, Tomás, 98, 103, 108, 119

Ortiz Land Grant, 143

Ortiz y Pino, Concha, 254

Otermín, Antonio de, 55–56

Otero, Antonio José, 106

Otero, Manuel, 120, 172

Otero, Miguel, 115, 119, 153, 178, 180, 184, 193

Otero County, N.Mex., 199, 279–80, 317

Otero family, 129, 160

Otero-Warren, Adelina ("Nina"), 200

Oviedo y Valdés, Gonzalo de Fernández, 42

Oxnard Field, 261. See also Kirtland Army Air Field

Pacific Northwest Pipeline Company, 302

Pajarito, N.Mex., 95, 316

Pajarito Creek, 94

Pajarito Land Grant, 59

Pajarito Plateau, 277–78

Palace of the Governors (Santa Fe), 74–75, 107, 119, 131, 218, 249

Paradinos, Juan de, 17

Paradinos, María Maldonado. See Maldonado, María

Paredes y Arrillaga, Mariano, 102

Parke, John G., 151

Parman, Donald, 252

Partido del Pueblo Unido. See Populist Party

Pasó por aquí (Rhodes), 162

Pawnee Indians, 60–61, 69

Paxton, Bertha, 201

Pearce, Steve, 336

Pearl Harbor, Hawaii, 257, 263, 268, 276, 278, 295, 334

Pecos, N.Mex., 62, 64, 104

Pecos Pueblo, 9, 13, 21, 25, 55, 121; Indian raids on, 10, 60; Spanish expeditions to, 18–19, 30–31, 34–35

Pecos River, 11, 18, 121, 123, 181, 198, 213, 331; Bosque Redondo Reservation on, 136–37; cattle on, 144, 156, 204; literature about life on, 220; settlements along, 9–10, 15, 18, 21, 30, 122, 125

Pecos River Valley, 134, 185, 201, 220; African American in, 192; agriculture in, 184, 191; cattle operations in, 145, 156; irrigation projects in, 181–82

Peenemünde, Germany, 281–82

Pegasus Global Holdings, LLC, 326

Peinado, Fray Alonso, 48–49

Pelham, William, 131

Peña, Tonita, 292

Peñasco, N.Mex., 72, 316

Penitente Brotherhood, 140–41, 177

Peonage, 124–25, 159, 178; banning of, 139–40; New Mexico laws for, 117, 120

Peralta, Francisco, 21–22

Peralta, N.Mex., 134

Peralta, Pedro de, 44, 48

Peralta-Reavis Land Grant, 175–76

Perea, Doña, 125

Perea, Francisco, 120

Perea, Friar Estevan, 50

Perea, Juan, 119–20

Perea, Pedro, 178

Pérez, Albino, 84–86; monument to, 91–92; opposition to as New Mexico governor, 84–90

Pérez, Demetrio, 92

Pérez de Luján, Diego, 27–29

Permian Basin, 304

Pershing, John J. ("Black Jack"), 201–202

Peters, De Witt, 142

Petroglyph National Monument, 322

Petroleum industry: as economic force in

327; petroleum industry in, 272, 302, 304

San Juan de los Caballeros Pueblo, 34–37, 41, 43, 48

San Juan Mountains (Colo.), 143–44

San Juan Pueblo, 34, 55

San Juan River, 7, 168, 270, 326–27, 331–32

San Luis Valley, 92, 97, 126, 144, 278, 331

San Marcial, N.Mex., 23, 27, 33

San Mateo Pueblo, 24–25

San Miguel County, N.Mex., 108, 121, 169, 175, 198, 243; coal industry in, 199; population of, 190

San Miguel del Vado, N.Mex., 94, 104, 123, 126

San Miguel Pueblo, 23, 62, 94. *See also* Taos Pueblo

Santa Anna, Antonio López, 84, 91–92, 95, 101–102, 128

Santa Bárbara, Chihuahua, Mexico, 22–23, 25–27, 32

Santa Clara Pueblo, 59, 328–29

Santa Cruz de la Cañada, Villa de, 58, 109, 123. *See also* Española, N.Mex.

Santa Fe (magazine), 221

Santa Fe, N.Mex., 24, 58, 66, 70, 72, 106, 109, 116, 119, 121–22, *124*, 125–26, 140, 143–44, 147, 162, 177, 215, 219, 225, 227–28, 240–41, 268, 276–77, 309, 329, 335; as art colony, 222–23; as capital, 43, 62, 64, 77, 79, 83–84, 86, 94, 155, 165, 193–94; celebrations at, 74–75, 98, 259, 312; Civilian Conservation Corps camps near, 239; commercial business of, 129, 153, 292; Confederate occupation of, 131; founding of, 41, 44, 48, 176; description of, 107; French traders in, 60–62; image making of, 217–18, 318–20; as literary community, 223; military garrison at, 59, 61; monument to Gov. Pérez in, 91–92; New Deal projects in, 246–49, 254; occupation of by Americans, 101, 103–105, 107–109; population, 51, 123, 190, 269, 312, 322; postwar housing in, 305; public health and sanitation in, 166; and Pueblo Revolt, 55–57; railroads to,

150, 155; and rebellion against Mexico, 90; schools in, 87, 169, 214; Seligman, Arthur, from, 229–30; and Spanish-American War, 179–80; trade with, 85; trade routes to 66, 85, 76, 92; United States threat to, 68–69; water issues in, 331–32; WPA project in, 247–49

Santa Fe–Chihuahua Trail, 76, 92–94, 122, 129. *See also* Camino Real de Tierra Adentro

Santa Fe County, N.Mex., 108, 140

Santa Fe Downs racetrack, 320

Santa Fe Indian Market, 222

Santa Fe Indian School, 254

Santa Fe National Forest, 213

Santa Fe New Mexican, 150, 166, 180, 235, 319, 334

Santa Fe Opera, 320

Santa Fe Republican (newspaper), 113

Santa Fe Ring, 146, 148–49, 154, 170

Santa Fe River, 48, 249

Santa Fe Ski Basin, 315, 320

Santa Fe Trail, 66; crossing of Pecos River, 123; establishment of, 44; merchants use of, 95, 229; military use of during Civil War, 132; modern highway following of, 215; and New Mexico commerce, 76, 128–29; replaced by railroad, 150–51; Texan raids on, 142; trade along, 102

Santa María, Fray Juan de, 23, 25–26, 28

Santa Rita, N.Mex., 164, 206, 262

Santa Rita del Cobre Mine, 129, 143, 164, 206, *207*, 272

Santa Rosa, N.Mex., 185, 247, 268, 292

Santo Domingo Pueblo, 31, 35, 51, 58, 90; Oñate at, 33–34; trial of Acoma warriors at, 40–41

Sarracino, Francisco, 87–88, 90

Satren, Pierre, 61–62

Scholly, John, 97

School for Advanced Research, 214

School of American Anthropology, 214

Schools. *See* Education

Scurry, William, 132

Seligman, Arthur, 229–32

Seligman, Bernard, 229

Tiguex War, 20
Tijerina, Anselmo, 311
Tijerina, Cristóbal, 310
Tijerina, Reies López, 308–11
Tijerina, Valentina, 311
Timber industry, 86, 188, 190, 192, 197,
    225; and conflicts with Forest Service,
    339–40; growth of, 206, 271; in
    Sacramento Mountains, 204
Timpanogo Indians, 66
Tingley, Carrie (Wooster), 234, 250
Tingley, Clyde, 227–28, 236, 250, 321, 337;
    career of, 234–35; and Conchas Dam,
    243–44; and New Deal programs, 233–
    34, 246–49; as New Mexico governor,
    235–36
Tiwa Indians, 19–20, 24–26, 28, 39, 49
Tiwa Pueblo, 53
Toledo, Bill, 267
Toledo, Frank, 267
Toledo, Preston, 267
Tomás (Mexican Indian), 33, 37
Tomasco, George, 294
Tomé, N.Mex., 90
Tompiro Pueblo, 54
Torreon, N.Mex., 267
Totemoff, Pete, 315
Tourism, 215, 330; cultural form of,
    223, 292; as economic force in New
    Mexico, 216–17, 228, 240, 257, 295,
    298, 305; and hot air balloon festivals,
    313–14; impact of automobiles
    on, 229; and Indian gaming
    establishments, 316–17; promotion of,
    217–19, 217, 224, 235, 312; in White
    Sands National Monument, 240–41; in
    Santa Fe, 318–20; and skiing, 314–16;
    and Spaceport America, 341
Trade, 62–63, 123; by Americans in Santa
    Fe, 104; among ancient cultures,
    5–7; along Camino Real, 73; by
    Comancheros, 139; by France, 61–62;
    on Indian reservations, 168; Mexican
    regulation of, 85–86; by Pueblo
    Indians, 9–11, 18; along Santa Fe Trail,
    128–29

Treaty of Guadalupe Hidalgo (1848),
    111, 115, 143, 308–309; and dispute
    over international boundary, 126–27;
    Hispanic rights under, 112–14, 182,
    195
Treaty of San Ildefonso (1800), 67
Trías, Ángel, 127
Trinity Site, 280, 284, 333
Troup, Bobby, 301
Truchas, N.Mex., 72
Trujillo, Antonio María, 109–10, 308
Trujillo, Manuel, 308
Trujillo, Michael H., 307
Truman, Harry S., 256, 281, 300, 307
Truth or Consequences, N.Mex., 183,
    341. See also Hot Springs, N.Mex.; Las
    Palomas, N.Mex.
Tsireh, Awa, 292
Tucson, Ariz., 128, 251
Tucumcari, N.Mex., 185, 188, 200, 243–
    44, 270, 275
Tucumcari Water District, 243
Tularosa, N.Mex., 145
Tularosa Basin, 126, 145, 162, 276, 278–79
Tules, Doña, 107, 125
Tunstall, John, 146–47
Tusayán Pueblo, 36
Tutahaco Pueblo, 19–20
Twitchell, Ralph Emerson, 221
Tyrone, N.Mex., 208
Tyrone Copper Mine, 272

Ulibarri, Juan de, 60
Uña de Gato Land Grant, 157, 172
Union County, N.Mex, 169, 213, 243
United Mine Workers, 208–209
United National Educational, Scientific,
    and Cultural Organization, 73, 215
United States, 76–77, 81, 112, 128, 202,
    204; annexation of New Mexico by,
    46, 96, 98, 100, 102–103, 105, 112; and
    boundaries of New Spain, 69–72; and
    international boundary dispute, 126–
    27; and Mexican War, 102, 106, 115;
    New Mexico trade with, 94; Soviet
    Union as military rival of, 280–81;

space program of, 282–83, 287; as
threat to Spanish Empire, 66–68, 73
University of New Mexico, 166, 228, 245,
258, 292–93, 324, 338
U.S. Air Force, 258, 279, 299
U.S. Army, 130, 239, 279, 287, 306, 314;
Indian campaigns of, 137, 139, 167;
and New Mexico National Guard,
262–63, 268; railroad surveys by, 128
U.S. Army Air Corps, 258, 260–61; air
fields of in New Mexico, 261–62, 271,
299
U.S. Army Corps of Engineers, 243, 260–
61, 276, 278
U.S. Boundary Commission, 127
U.S. General Land Office, 157, 171–72, 213
U.S. Marine Corps, 266–67, 307
U.S.-Mexican War. *See* Mexican War
U.S. Navy, 276, 287, 305
U.S. secretary of war, 103, 110, 131, 150
U.S. 66 (highway). *See* Route 66
U.S. surveyor general, 172–74
Utah, as U.S. territory, 112, 117
Ute Indians, 63, 72, 85, 128, 137;
campaigns against, 134; raids by, 11,
54, 60; as Spanish allies, 62

Vado, N.Mex., 192
Vail, Colo., 315
Valdez, Jose F., 268
Valencia, N.Mex., 95, 125
Valencia County, N.Mex., 106, 159–60
Valenciano, Juan, 27
Valenciano, Lázaro, 27
Valenciano, Pedro, 27
Valle, Alexandre "Pigeon," 132–33
Vallecitos, N.Mex., 340
Valles Caldera, 329
Valverde, Antonio, 60–61
Van Dyke, Willard, 254
Vargas, Diego de, 60, 156; fiesta in honor
of, 218; as New Mexico governor,
58–59; and reconquest of New
Mexico, 57, 60
Vázquez de Coronado, Francisco, 270;
anniversary celebration of, 259; attack

on pueblos by, 28; expedition of,
17–23, 29, 156; exploration of New
Mexico by, 12, 14, 20; literary heritage
of, 42; and Marcos de Niza expedition,
16–17; and Tiguex War, 19–20
Velarde, Pablita, 254
Veterans Administration, 227, 257
Vial, Pierre, 66, 69
Victor American Fuel Company, 205
Victorio (Mimbres leader), 166–67
Vietnam War, 299, 308
Vigil, Cornelio, 97
Vigil, Donaciano, 98, 105; and land grants,
114, 145; as New Mexico governor,
110–11, 113, 122; political career, 106,
121
Vigil y Alarid, Juan Bautista, 75, 88, 98,
105
Villa, Pancho, 201–202
Villagrá, Gaspar Pérez de, 42
Villanueva, N.Mex, 62
Villasur, Pedro, 61
Villegas, Juan de, 19–20
Virgin Atlantic Airways, 340
Virgin Galactic, 340–41
Von Braun, Wernher, 281–83, 287–88
Von Neumann, John, 278

Waddingham, Wilson, 173
Wagon Mound, N.Mex., 190, 200, 220
Wainwright, Jonathan, 264
Waldo, Henry, 152
Walker Air Force Base, 300, 317, 324, 326
Wallace, Lew, 147
War Department, U.S., 243, 278, 306; air
fields in New Mexico, 261–62; and
development of atomic bomb, 279. *See
also* Department of Defense, U.S.
Warren-Otero, Nina, 221
Washington, John M., 113–15
Waste Isolation Pilot Plant (WIPP), 298,
333, 339
Watanabe, Tamasaku, 334
Water issues, 298; flood control projects
for, 246; and water rights, 120, 160,
181–82, 331–32. *See also* Irrigation